The Master Ghost Hunter

A Life of Elliott O'Donnell

Richard Whittington-Egan

First edition published 2016 (Hardcover)
This edition 2019 (Softcover)

Copyright © Richard Whittington-Egan, 2016/2019

The right of Richard Whittington-Egan to be identified as
the author of this work has been asserted in accordance
with the Copyright, Designs & Patents Act 1988.

All rights reserved. No part of this book may be reprinted or reproduced
or utilised in any form or by any electronic, mechanical or other
means, now known or hereafter invented, including photocopying
and recording, or in any information storage or retrieval system,
without the prior permission in writing of the publishers.

ISBN: 978-1-911273-17-2 (softcover)
ISBN: 978-1-911273-01-1 (ebook)

Published by Mango Books
www.MangoBooks.co.uk
18 Soho Square
London W1D 3QL

For Mimi

A very much beloved
Chihuahuan companion

Contents

Acknowledgements i

To Meet Mr. Elliott O'Donnell 1

1. The Making of a Ghost Hunter 3
2. The Apprentice Ghost Hunter 20
3. Hibernian Hauntings 36
4. New World Ghosts 55
5. Hitting the Ghost Trail Home 73
6. A Ghostly Farewell to New York 89
7. Spectral London in the Nineties 101
8. Ghost Writer 121
9. The Cornish Ghost Coast 131
10. Spooks in the Smoke 145
11. Spirited Times 161
12. The Ghostly Dogs of War 177
13. Ghosts and Ghouls 193
14. Phantasmal Gore 207
15. Dreads and Drolls 225
16. Lonely Road 241
17. The Twilight Zone 255
18. Passing the Gate 269

Appendix: List of Stories by Elliott O'Donnell 273

Bibliography 297

Index 299

Best wishes
from
Elliott O'Donnell

Acknowledgements

This book has only been made possible in the authenticity of the entirety of its biographical details by the gracious permission of the Director, Mr. Rob Rogers, and the Special Collections Librarian, Jennifer Namsiriwan, of the Maryland Historical Society, to quote from the manuscript of Elliott O'Donnell's unpublished autobiography, which is preserved, in the Elliott O'Donnell Papers, MS 727, the H. Furlong Baldwin Library, Library of the Maryland Historical Society.

Although O'Donnell put a considerable amount of autobiographical data into the public arena in his autobiographical volumes – *Twenty Years' Experiences as a Ghost Hunter* and *Confessions of a Ghost Hunter* – and scattered personal material liberally throughout his fifty-odd books and 800 or so stories, it would have been extremely difficult to reconstruct the complete picture of his life without the Maryland Historical Society's material, and I want to acknowledge with the deepest gratitude my debt to the Society.

As a corollary, a prelude really, I acknowledge the brilliant tracking down by Stephanie Bilton of the autobiographical manuscript to Maryland; and this was just one of the literally dozens of ways in which she has contributed invaluable help, including the discovery and provision of illustrations.

The seeming inexhaustibility of Stewart Evans' remarkable library and goodwill have played a most significant part in the gathering of unique O'Donnell data. He has never failed me, and I thank him very sincerely.

To Nicholas Connell I am deeply indebted for the copious, careful, and vital research which he carried out on my behalf.

Nicholas Smith, of the Rare Books Department, of the University of Cambridge Library, rendered very much appreciated bibliographical help, for which I most gratefully thank him.

Anne Buchanan, Local Studies Librarian, of Bath Central Library, provided valiant aid, and I am most grateful to her.

The late Peter Underwood also contributed interesting sidelights on O'Donnell, and my friend Dr. Jan Bondeson has been of enormous help both as to factual matters and in the provision of a number of illustrations.

My wife, Molly Whittington-Egan, herself a biographer, has, as usual, played a vital rôle, personal, practical, and professional, throughout the gestatory period of this book. To her, my infinite gratitude.

Richard Whittington-Egan.

*

RICHARD WHITTINGTON-EGAN was born in Liverpool in 1924. His paternal great-grandfather was the Irish Crown Pathologist; his maternal great-grandfather was Jakob Zeugheer Herrmann, the first conductor of the Liverpool Philharmonic orchestra.

Whittington-Egan was reading Medicine, but went into the Army in the Second World War, serving in France, Italy, Austria, and Switzerland. After his discharge, he went to Fleet Street, where he spent thirty years as a journalist with Lord Northcliffe's Associated Newspapers.

He is the author of many books of literary biography, on Liverpool, and on criminals cases, including a mammoth volume on Jack the Ripper.

He died in 2016; *The Master Ghost Hunter* was his final book.

To Meet Mr. Elliott O'Donnell

Whatever you may think of Elliott O'Donnell, whether you regard his tales as true records of the workings of some mysterious power of the Unknown, or as the mere fables of a Baron Munchausen of the psychic world, one thing is indisputable: over the span of nine decades he was the universally accepted crown prince of ghost hunters – *the* Ghost Man of the West, master teller of tales of the haunted and the haunter. He had the true Irishman's gift of the written gab. And he has left behind a wonderful catalogue of creepy books from the pen of one who, as a boy, was afraid of being alone in the dark.

His family was a haunted one, boasting, if that is the right word, its own death-and-disaster-warning banshee. Eerie tales told to him by his sister and his mother's sewing-maid gave him a fear of, and taste for, the world of the weird and wonderful.

He was neither spiritualist nor psychic scientist. He was an unashamed entertainer. He would allow his tongue to stray mischievously from time to time into his cheek, but he would never foster untruths. There is, I think, absolutely no doubt that he believed in ghosts, in spirits, good and bad, and in the after-life. But he distinguished between legend and genuine, spontaneous manifestations of unreality.

He was convinced that there was no substitute for personal experience, and sat many a night keeping lonely vigil in some haunted country mansion, waiting alone in hope of bearing personal witness to the flittings of some tortured, earthbound wraith in the moonlight. And he was rewarded here and there, now and then, with what he deemed to be glimpses and echoes of the shades and shadows of old mortality.

Did he really believe all he wrote?

Should we?

That is a question which every reader must decide for his or her self.

There can be no denying that he does occasionally stretch credulity – but, come to that, so does life sometimes. And coincidence can really prove a puzzlement, a nurturer of disbelief.

The great fictional ghost story writer, M. R. James, author of *Ghost Stories of an Antiquary*, once expressed the hope that O'Donnell's writings were entirely fictitious, fearing that, if true, life would be "a risky business."

Elliott O'Donnell spread the net of his interest wide. As well as investigator of haunted houses, he was actor, playwright, schoolmaster, lecturer, broadcaster, novelist, and criminologist. He wrote more than fifty books, dealing not only with the supernatural, but also with such topics as the Irish abroad, famous curses, rooms of mystery, strange disappearances, strange sea mysteries, strange cults and secret societies, fatal kisses, and women bluebeards. A fine gallimaufry.

Read on...

1

The Making of a Ghost Hunter

A tall, thin, white-haired figure with gold-rimmed pince-nez, given to the wearing of cloaks and the carrying of a silver-topped cane, Elliott O'Donnell exuded an ectoplasmic air of occult mystery, which was indeed appropriate for the man universally regarded as the world's most celebrated ghost hunter.

As some collecting men are philatelists, phillumenists, numismatists, lepidopterists, and coleopterists, so was he a conservator of ghost stories, preserving not only other men's psychic flowers, but also those meticulously recorded blossoms of his own, first-hand, eerie, other-worldly experiencings.

Through the pages of the books – some fifty of them – which he had written over the span of sixty industrious years, range phantoms and grotesques of every kind – historic, contemporary, helpful, harmful, pathetic, and downright dangerous; timeless denizens of the realm of time. The box-headed Elemental, its eyes glowing like yellow moons, is the most enduring spirit to stalk the printed acres of his supernatural chronicles.

But he made his stance in psychic matters clear: "Let me state plainly that I lay no claim to being what is termed a scientific psychical researcher. I am not a member of any august society that conducts its investigations of the other world, or worlds, with test tube and weighing apparatus; neither do I pretend to be a medium or consistent clairvoyant – I have never undertaken to 'raise' ghosts at will for the sensation-seeker or the tourist. I am merely a ghost-hunter. One who lays stake by his own eyes and senses; one who honestly believes that he inherits in some degree the faculty of psychic perceptiveness from a long line of Celtic ancestry; and who is, and always has been, deeply and genuinely interested in all questions relative to phantasms and a continuance of individual life after physical dissolution."

"I am," Elliott O'Donnell himself declared, "of mixed extraction – Celtic, Irish, Maryland, Leicestershire, and very remotely French." His Irish ancestors of the seventeenth century were all, he believed, staunch Jacobites. Himself, dominatedly Irish, in thought, word and deed, proud claimant of grand old chieftain lineage, looked affectionately back along his putative bloodline to Naighiallach, otherwise known as Niall of the Nine Hostages, the King Arthur of Irish folklore, and to Shane Luirg, elder brother of Niall Garbh, forebear of Red Hugh. This was safe enough voyaging, for all the records were, in predictably characteristic Erse turmoil; which is not to say, however, that his genealogical pretensions were anything other than totally *bona fide*. Especially interesting is the suggestion, not put forward by him, that through his great-grandmother, who was one of the Elliotts of Boston, he was, appropriately, related to Edgar Allan Poe. Sadly, this does not seem to be so.[1]

To descend from the rarefied heights and clouding mysteries of antiquity to the realms of down-to-earth fact: the location of his nativity, which he would seem to have been inclined to shroud with talk of his birth in "the old house in Ireland", was, more mundanely, and alas accurately – for the entries of the National Register of Births are seldom, if ever, detected in error – Bristol, where, although the blood that coursed his veins was indubitably Irish, the first light of day that he saw was English, filtering into No. 16 Wellington Park, in the suburb of Clifton. It was there, on Tuesday, February 27th, a Tuesday's grace full child, that, in the leap year, 1872, he was born.

His father, the Reverend Henry O'Donnell, M.A., late scholar of Trinity College, Dublin, hailing from Limerick, where he was born in Thomas Street, was Irish through and through. He had wanted to embark on a career in the army, but in deference to his mother's wishes took Holy Orders. He came to England, was chaplain to Lord Kingsdown. He was thirty-three, serving as a Church of England curate at Cold Ashby, in

---

[1] The sole source for this information is *The Ghost Hunters*. Peter Underwood. Robert Hale, London, 1985. pp.33-34.

Northamptonshire, when, in 1861, he married, at Warwick, Elizabeth Sarah, widow, since 1856, of the Reverend William Morris Mousley, who was the son of the Reverend William Mousley of Cold Ashby Hall. She, too, was thirty-three, and mother of a four-year-old daughter, Elizabeth Sarah M. Mousley. Henry O'Donnell was, according to his son, "very fond of his wife and children, but very strict with the latter." In character he was "very hasty, impetuous and restless, quick-tempered and venturesome, fundamentally religious, extremely self-willed, generous and scrupulously honest with regard to money." He was of an independent cast of mind, as is illustrated by the fact that on July 28th, 1870, he sailed merrily off on his own, aboard the Cunarder, *Cuba*, from Liverpool to New York, with the object, one gathers, of going bear shooting in the States. He made the lone voyage from Liverpool to New York again on June 14th, 1871, on board the S.S. *Russia*.

Elliott O'Donnell's mother, the daughter of George Harrison, of Oxendon Magna, in Northamptonshire, came from an old Leicestershire family, a long line of exceedingly prosperous agriculturists and landowners dating back to the sixteenth century, but she, her sister, Hannah, and brothers, William Henry, John, and Harris, were all born at Oxendon.

The Reverend Henry and Elizabeth O'Donnell had four children – Henry, born at Ashby, in 1863; Petronella, born at Lymington, Hampshire, in 1864; Helena, born at Whittington, Worcestershire, where the Reverend Henry was Vicar of Upton Snodsbury, in 1869; Elliott, named after his grandfather, Dr. Elliott O'Donnell, M.D., of Trough Castle, County Limerick, was born at Clifton, Gloucestershire, in 1872.

The Reverend Henry's life span turned out disconcertingly short. He died, aged forty-five, when his son, Elliott, was just 13 months old. Three lines, bland and innocent-seeming enough, in the Deaths column of the *Bristol Mercury* of May 17th 1873, announced:

> O'Donnell – April 2, at Arkiko, near Massoas, Red Sea, of
> Sunstroke, the Rev. H. O'Donnell, M.A., of 1, Sherborne Villas,
> Clifton.[2]

But the circumstances of that premature demise were cocooned in disquieting mystery.

---

2   The family had recently moved to No.1 Sherborne Villas, later numbered No. 24 Alma Road, Clifton.

In the spring of 1873, at a loose end between ecclesiastic preferments, Henry O'Donnell had announced to his wife that, while awaiting the bestowal of a living, he was, in fulfilment of a long cherished ambition to see Jerusalem, off on a visit to Palestine, in company with a friend and fellow Anglican cleric, the Reverend Richard Allwood Henry Stroud, of Clifton. It transpired that things had not gone precisely to plan. On their outward bound vessel the Reverend Henry had encountered, and apparently fallen well under the enchantment of, a shipboard acquaintance; one who represented himself as a colonel, late of "the Anglo-Indian army, who had been engaged by the King of Abyssinia to help in the work of remodelling the Abyssinian army", and who claimed to be, and in fact was, a member of a well-respected London banking family. Accepting him at his own face value, O'Donnell, who, according to his son, was a lover of big-game hunting, and who "had hunted bears and other wild animals in the mountain fastnesses of the United States," had yielded to the temptation held out to him by the Colonel of hunting lions and leopards in the wilds of Abyssinia. He had accordingly severed himself at Alexandria from the company of his parsonic colleague, who had travelled on alone to Palestine.

Some sort of extrasensory perception must have been triggered into play, for O'Donnell did not, it would appear, altogether like, or entirely trust, the Colonel. Indeed, the two had frequent disagreements and, on one occasion, an actual stand-up fight, blood flowing freely from both combatants.

A diary, subsequently found in the pocket of an old coat and sent back to his family in England, together with one or two other of his effects, by a servant of one of the Consuls at Massowah, came later into Elliott's hands, and he quotes extracts.

17th March.	A very dull evening. I have my grave doubts of Colonel K. He is so impudent.
18th March.	*En route* for Jeddo in company with Maghera Tub, K. and Mr. B.
25th March.	K. and B. go to Assouakim. I wish I had never come with K.
26th March.	Had a sharp dispute with Col. K. In the end the Col. promises to give me security before we leave the ship. Start for Massowah. Anchor off a reef twenty miles from Suakim. Have a quarrel on board.

| 28th March. | In quarantine. Write to Munsinger Bey. [This Munsinger Bey was a very sinister character.] |
| 29th March. | We are to live in a house promised by Hassan. (This Hassan turned out to be a man of a most disreputable past. More than one crime was attributed to him.) Another row. |

Elliott O'Donnell, in a letter addressed to the Society for Psychical Research on January 13th, 1899, wrote of Colonel K. – here designating him Colonel Y. – as having "afterwards proved to be a member of the Weymouth Swindling Gang". He continues: "My father went hunting, leaving the little village of Arkiko in the company of several natives and, so we believe, his white comrade, Colonel Y. The exact manner of his death has never been ascertained, but it was suggested by various inhabitants of Massowah that he was murdered."

In his book, *The Oriental Zigzag*, (Chapman & Hall, London, 1875), Charles Hamilton relates how, after several attempts, he eventually succeeded in seeing Munzinger, the Governor of Massowah,[3] who, upon hearing that he was about to travel inland from Massowah, had offered to find a guide for him. Hamilton's view of the Governor is very favourable: "One of the best Pashas in the Egyptian service."

"I could not help connecting his offer with the untimely fate of the Rev. Henry O'Donnell, who had died there (Arkiko), a few days before my arrival at Massowah of alleged sunstroke. Various sinister reports had got into circulation regarding his death, which was looked upon as most mysterious; and Munziger (*sic*) obviously desired to supply no further occasion for malicious gossip."

Elliott informs us that his mother received a letter from the French Vice-Consul at Massowah informing her that her husband had died at Arkiko, on the Red Sea coast, under circumstances strongly suggestive of foul play. There was no doubt at all that he had been murdered by a gang of European adventurers, who, making a certain hotel in Massowah their headquarters, robbed and murdered any stranger with money who fell into their clutches. It is asserted that the Colonel induced the Reverend Henry to put up at this hotel. It was kept by two Europeans, both of whom were individuals of ill-repute.

---

3   An ex-member of the Turkish Secret Police.

Writing to the English Consul at Suez, the aforesaid French Vice-Consul at Massowah referred to reports which he had heard regarding the disappearance of boxes and other things, such as his sun helmet, gun and money, belonging to O'Donnell, and the hotel proprietors affirmed that they had found nothing of any value belonging to the Reverend Henry in his room. Which was, to say the least, odd, since O'Donnell was known to have had three hundred pounds with him when he left Alexandria. Albeit the bogus colonel had practically lived on O'Donnell, continually borrowing money from him during the journey to Massowah. The Vice-Consul also commented on the exceedingly bad character of one of the hotel proprietors, who had been dismissed from the Secret Police in Constantinople, and was suspected of being the instigator of two unsuccessful attempts which had been made to assassinate the French Vice-Consul.

Further suspicions of foul play were penned in a letter addressed to the Reverend Henry's widow. Writing from the Langham Hotel, in July, 1874, the Baron de Cosson, a French gentleman who said that he was staying in Massowah at the time, confirmed what the French Vice-Consul had said about the former agent of the Turkish Secret Police and the absence of the Reverend Henry's belongings, and said that very ugly rumours were afloat regarding what had really happened to him, and that it had been expressed in several quarters that the Reverend Henry had not, perhaps, died a natural death.

A careful combing through of the newspapers of the period has failed to disclose any reference whatsoever to this, therefore dubious, affair. Some credence is lent to the notion of death by sunstroke, in that *The Columbia Lippincott Gazetteer of the World* reports the city of Massawa (sic) as "one of the world's hottest places". It is worth remembering, too, that in those days "sunstroke" was a widely employed euphemism for madness; one has only to think of the case of Richard Dadd, the artist who developed paranoid schizophrenia in Egypt.

Colonel K., who, by the way, never at any time served in the British Army, left Massowah hurriedly after the Reverend Henry O'Donnell's death, and what became of him subsequently was never known. Neither has the Weymouth Swindling Gang proved amenable to latter-day detection.

Elliott O'Donnell recounts how his father, before setting off on his, aborted as it proved, Jerusalem pilgrimage, told his wife, half jestingly, "If anything happens to me while I am away, you will know."

"Oh, don't appear in spirit form, Hal," she said. "You know I have such a horror of ghosts." She was a great believer in the supernatural and had spent her childhood in a well-known haunted house in Northamptonshire.

"Very well then," he said, "should the unexpected happen, I won't let you see me, but you will hear."

And hear, the family most certainly did.

In the late evening of April 1st, 1873, Mrs. Elizabeth O'Donnell was sitting reading in the dining-room, overlooking the back garden at Sherborne Villas. The house was semi-detached, actually the first in a row which, at that time, was not completed, and was situated in a rather lonely spot, rarely visited after nightfall. On one side of it, and to the rear, there were good stretches of garden, bounded by fields.

Suddenly, she, her children, and the servants were harrowed by a terrifying sound burst. Their ears rang with the echoes of series of the most appalling agonised cries, as of a woman being murdered. The noises seemed, at first, to be coming from outside, under one of the windows. Then, to everyone's horror, they moved to within the house. So far as Mrs. O'Donnell was concerned, the subsequent searchings inside and out were really no more than a matter of form, for she had realised only too well that what they had all been hearing were the death-warning keenings of the O'Donnell Banshee.

Earlier that same evening, the Banshee herself had, in fact, been glimpsed. Just about twilight, one of the O'Donnell girls, nine-year-old Petronella, had been on her way upstairs to fetch something from her bedroom. She had reached the landing outside her room, when she felt a sudden urge to look over towards the staircase leading on up to the top storey, and saw what looked like a spherical light resting on the balustrade of the top landing. As she watched, she saw the light metamorphose into the clearly defined shape of a head, a head which bore upon it a tangled mass of tow-coloured hair. Then, like a developing photograph, features began to build up. A fleshless face, skin drawn taut across the bones, pale, obliquely set eyes that glittered with what she would afterwards describe as "a sort of diabolical glee." As the thing's expression slid over into a kind of acutely menacing leer, the child took fright, turned in terror, and fled back downstairs to the illusive safety of the drawing-room, her mission aloft left unaccomplished.[4]

The following night, Wednesday, April 2nd, and every single night for the next six weeks, a voice, identified by those who heard it as that of the Reverend Henry O'Donnell, and footsteps were heard about the house. The disturbances always began at about midnight and lasted until around 1 a.m.

Elliott reports: "At the time they first occurred my mother had no other intimation, saving the cry of the Banshee, that any harm had befallen my father, but, after they [the disturbances] had been going on for a week or more, she received tidings from someone at Massowah, saying that he had been robbed and murdered on 2nd April, close to the village of Arkiko." The death took place at noon on the day after the Banshee had been heard in the O'Donnells' home.

The records conflict. So what is evidenced, sunstroke or murder? Clearly, the encrusting patina of time has rendered the whole affair inscrutable. Only an open verdict seems now possible.

The Reverend Henry O'Donnell's will was proved on July 3rd, 1873. The total value of his effects was under £3,000.

Long after her husband's death, Elizabeth O'Donnell would cry out in the night, and tell next morning of how she had heard pistol shots in her bedroom, accompanied by the Reverend Henry's voice. Although she was not Irish, she was very likely of Welsh extraction, and had the Celtic tinge of mysticism running through her veins. In any event, she seems to have been possessed of 'the gift'. She was actually a member of an old Midland family, the Fowkes of Leicestershire. Elizabeth Fowke was, through the Cottons and the Halfords, descended from Richard, the second son of William De Cotton, who was killed at St. Albans in the War of the Roses.

---

[4] In a letter written to the Society for Psychical Research, Petronella O'Donnell supplies a somewhat different account. She says: "It was in the morning of a day in the spring of 1875 (she subsequently corrected the year to 1873) that I saw the head which was afterwards seen by another member of our family. I had been sent out of the room for someone, and as I looked up to call them, I saw the most terrible head looking over the banisters at me. It was the face of a man, but the hair was long like a woman's. The parchment-like skin was drawn closely over the face and gave a skull-like look to it. The mouth, full of great teeth, was twisted in a horrid leer; but what frightened me most was the expression of the eyes. They were so very light and full of the most wicked cruelty, as if they existed for the sole purpose of terrifying a little child like I was then."

The De Cotton family were, because of their descent from Robert Bruce through Mary de Wesenham, of the Blood Royal. Elliott O'Donnell's mother could therefore boast a tincture of royal blood,

"From the time of his death to the end of the following May," writes Elliott O'Donnell, "every night at twelve o'clock, a terrible disturbance took place in the hall, sounds as if the furniture was being thrown about being distinctly heard, together with a tramping upstairs. Moreover, the reflection of a lighted candle was seen under the crack of the nursery door, which, although bolted, was thrown violently open, and to the horrified inmates some one (whose voice they recognised as that of my father) was heard jabbering incoherently."

It was in 1877, when he was just five years old, that Master Elliott had his first conscious encounter with a ghost. Although he had been put to bed at the customary time of seven o'clock, it had seemed to him unusually early, because, on this long summer's evening the sun was still shining brightly outside, and its light was coming into the room through the drawn blinds. Lying on his side, intent on relieving the boredom of the situation by counting the spots on the counterpane of the bed which lay parallel with his own, he heard the handle of the bedroom door give a little click, and, looking in its direction, saw that it was being very slowly turned. As he watched, gradually, very gradually and silently, the door inched open, and he was amazed to see a strange figure shoot suddenly into view. He judged it to stand some six feet in height, reckoning it to be about as tall as a certain tradesman who called each morning and whom he had heard being referred to as "a good six feet." It had extremely long arms and a disproportionately massive head, was nude and, the final grotesquery, covered in places with large yellow spots. The figure stood there, against the wall, just inside the door, still as a statue, regarding him sphinx-like with bright yellowish-green eyes. There was intensity, but no hostility in its wall-eyed gaze. Then, after lolling there fixedly staring at him for some minutes, it turned about and swiftly and silently walked out, closing the door stealthily and noiselessly behind it.

When, next morning, he told his mother about his visitant, predictably she said he must have been dreaming. What, in after years, O'Donnell himself thought was that his ghostly caller had been one of those phantasmagoria that have never known human form, denizens of the nether world, named by him 'Elementals'. We shall be coming upon them again.⁵

Looking back in old age, O'Donnell remembered with pangs of nostalgia the Clifton of his childhood. Archery, previously the fashionable and favourite sport of the Clifton ladies, was dying out and was being largely replaced by roller skating at the Victoria Rooms, and he recollected being taken to the rink to see his step-sister, Elizabeth Mousley, skating, and how afraid he had been that she might fall and hurt herself.

Another memorial picture from the past was of the year 1878, and how excited his mother, a worshipper of the royal family, had been at the prospect of the visit by the Prince of Wales to Bristol. She had hired a room in Whiteladies Road, which thoroughfare was for the occasion dressed on either side by lines of soldiers in red uniforms and shakos. The O'Donnell family all sat in waiting at the window for the Prince to pass by. Great amusement, and embarrassment, was caused by a man bowling along in a two-wheeler open carriage being mistaken for His Royal Highness. When, after what seemed an unconscionably long wait, the Prince did eventually flash past their window, the O'Donnell family were perfectly certain that the smile and nod he gave was intended for them.

That same year, the Bristol Volunteers spent a week encamped on Durdham Downs, and the O'Donnells enjoyed a red-letter day expedition to see their manœuvres.

What lingered in his mind from the following year, 1879, was the scare created throughout the country by the terrifying image of the murderous burglar, Charlie Peace, with his dyed face, false arm, and lethal life preserver; the dreadful murder with a cleaver, dismemberment and parboiling of her mistress, Mrs Thomas, by her servant, Kate Webster, at Richmond; and the creepy Great Euston Square Mystery. Filed away in his memory, too, were the alarming tales of other vintage – those of Henry Wainwright, who, in 1874, had murdered, and subsequently butchered, Harriet Lane in a Whitechapel warehouse, and the ferocious John Owen who murdered with an axe the entire Marshall family of the sweet, old-

---

5   One is inclined to wonder whether it is perhaps not unusual for young children to experience 'visions' of what O'Donnell called Elementals. The author had a similar experience at an early age, when, looking out of a high window over a well and saw, rearing itself against the background of a facing blank wall, a long-necked, sort of mustardy-yellow-coloured creature which carried with it the air of Ancient Egypt, and looked not unlike one of those strange golden animal figures from the tomb of Tutankhamen.

world village of Denham, in the merry month of May, 1870.[6] The fear which, from his childhood, he had harboured, of being alone – or, rather, of not being alone – in the dark, he was afterwards to ascribe to those terrifying tales of ghosts that he had heard for the main part from the lips of Miss Milward, a dressmaker employed by his mother. She and her sister were natives of Worcestershire, a county in which Mrs. O'Donnell had spent what she looked back upon as some of the happiest days of her life. Miss Milward's preoccupation with ghosts was to be expected, for she had, so she said, lived in a haunted house in Worcester, where a phantom with a white, evil face used to peer in at windows, open doors at night, and crawl under the beds. It was her habit to vary her spookish repertoire by giving the young O'Donnell the creeps with goose-flesh-raising accounts of the most ghastly murders.

The two O'Donnell household servants, Fanny Coldwell, the cook, and her elder sister, Sarah Coldwell, the housemaid, were also very superstitious, and Elliott well remembered Fanny telling him that she was sure her elder brother, Tom, would die because the previous evening there had been a winding sheet in their candle, and it had pointed to her. Then she had dreamt that one of her teeth had fallen out, and on it was Tom's face. Her fears were realised. The very day that she told O'Donnell about the omens, she received a telegram saying that her brother had died suddenly.

Other anxieties at the time were the Zulu and Afghan Wars, which his mother took very much to heart. She numbered among her Cliftonian friends relatives of Lieutenant Bromhead, one of the gallant defenders of Rorke's Drift, a first hand account of which action O'Donnell heard delivered at Poole's Panorama, at the Colston Hall, Bristol, by a non-commissioned officer of the 24th Regiment.

The family spent their August, 1879, holiday at Ramsgate, where the great excitements were caused by the stranding of two whales on the beach and a ship on fire on the Goodwin sands.

But the O'Donnell children's greatest treat was the annual Christmas tree party – the blaze of candles, the cornucopian harvest of presents suspended from its green-needled branches. And there was, of course, the

---

6   For the details of the murder of Harriet Lane see *Trial of the Wainwrights*. H.B. Irving. Notable British Trials Series. William Hodge, Edinburgh, 1920. For the details of John Owen and the murder of the Marshall family see *Murderers' England*. Ivan Butler. Robert Hale, London, 1973. pp.129-130.

pantomime.

How well I remember my first pantomime, *Sinbad the Sailor*, at the Prince's Theatre, in Park Row, Bristol. Prior to going to it, my mother read to me the story in *The Arabian Nights*. Great, therefore, was my disappointment and indignation when the pantomime hardly resembled the *Arabian Nights*' story. Sinbad was actually a girl, and, to my astonishment and disgust, there was a Tinbad the Tailor and Jinbad the Jailer – characters that were most certainly not in the tale my mother had read to me. It was nothing to me that very pretty, blue-eyed Grace Huntley was principal girl, the only time she played that rôle in a Bristol pantomime. In subsequent years she was several times principal boy. Nelly Bouverie was Sinbad, a part she played with wonderful spirit and vivacity. Her song, "Crutch and Toothpick", was very popular. Julia Bullen, who was Zorilda, scored a tremendous hit two years later in *Aladdin*, at the Prince's, with her song "Tiddy-fol-lol". In that pantomime pretty Sarah Beryl was Aladdin, and Kate Ryan was Princess Badroulbadour. Both of them were prime favourites.

No pantomime was complete in those days without the local comedian, Fosbrook (Fossy), who was a great favourite with Bristol audiences, and the transformation scene, harlequinade, Joey the clown, and the pantaloon. While the transformation scene was still on, the harlequin, in his tight spangled dress, visor and magic wand, and Columbine, his sweetheart, appeared and danced. Before they had ended, clown and pantaloon popped out from somewhere; Joey never omitting to announce his advent with a "Here we are again."

The transformation scenes were often very lovely, really works of art; the dancing of the harlequin and dainty Columbine delightfully quaint and attractive, and the doings of Joey and his pantaloon pal, who were never without the sausage shop, always very amusing and not infrequently very clever. One of the reasons for abolishing the transformation scene and harlequinade was probably because the children became apparently too blasé to enjoy them. In addition to the pantomime in the Prince's Theatre, in Park Row, and the Royal Theatre, in King Street, there was Hengler's Circus every autumn at the Drill Hall, about where the Bristol University is now, and Poole's Panorama at the Colston Hall. Hengler's performers included Whimsical Walker, one of the best known clowns in England, Bimbo and Handy Andy, whose droll face and antics convulsed everyone with laughter. I sometimes saw Hengler's men playing polo on the Durdham Downs, where their horses were taken for exercise.

I always went to the Panorama at least twice. To most people nowadays the painted scenery of those panoramas would doubtless seem laughably crude, but in those far away times our tastes were much simpler. There were no cinemas or wireless; we were not satiated with amusements. Mr. A. Poole acted as guide and explained each of the scenes as they followed one another. We were taken by rail and sea more or less round the world, starting as a rule from Charing Cross. You saw a little train leave the station and move jerkily across the stage. There was generally a battle scene. You saw an army preparing to attack a strongly fortified position, and then, with startling suddenness, there was a crash, the picture at which you were gazing illuminated, and, lo and behold! the troops were engaged in a desperate hand to hand fight with the enemy. Sometimes it was a band of Red Indians attacking a train or caravan; or a naval battle. At one moment two hostile vessels would be facing one another, and then suddenly one of them would be torpedoed. A deafening bang and a lurid glow always gave the culminating thrill. It was at the Colston Hall during a pantomime that I saw the double-headed nightingale, a ghastly freak of nature, resembling the Siamese Twins.

There was only one music-hall in Bristol in my childhood; a very primitive affair, in which a man sat at a table in front of a diminutive stage and rang a bell or banged a gong immediately before announcing a turn. The orchestra consisted of a piano.

There was no lack of minor amusements. There was often a Punch and Judy Show in the road, and a man with a barrel-organ and monkey, and very occasionally a man with a little performing bear. On May Days there was always a flower-bedecked queen, and at Christmas, when we were staying in the country, the accustomary waits.

German bands livened the streets with their music; at the ever popular Zoological gardens in the summer there were fireworks shows of various kinds, lawn-tennis and sports; and in a frosty winter, skating on the lake.

Also, in those days, there were crossing-sweepers, boys and men. Some of them did well. One old man, whose crossing was at the foot of Clifton Park, always wore a top-hat and frock-coat, both rather the worse for long service. He sold little wooden whistles which he made. He told my mother that he had made two fortunes as a crossing-sweeper, and had squandered both. Some of the sweepers were bare-footed, no uncommon sight then. There were muffin boys, who had bells, which they rang loudly to announce their advent; boys who sold hot cross buns on Good Friday and cried in shrill voices, "Hot cross buns! One a penny, two a penny; Hot cross buns!"

The streets were much safer then than now. There were no motors; nearly all vehicles were horse-drawn. For the public there were four-wheel cabs (flies), their drivers called jarvies; hansoms, omnibuses, trams, wagonettes holding six or eight persons; for business – vans, carts, etc.; for private use – barouches, phaetons, traps, pony-carriages, etc.; and for settling down roads that had been re-layed, steam-rollers, popularly known as "Bellowing Sampsons". Travelling by road was very slow compared with now, and in open vehicles – many of them were open – uncomfortable in wet weather. But we were a hardy lot in those days and no one seemed to mind the inconveniences and discomfort which we had to endure.

Where the place in Bristol called the Centre is now, there used to be a drawbridge over the river, and when it was drawn up, to enable ships to pass, traffic was at a standstill; and the delay was often very annoying, especially to business people and those hurrying to catch a train at Bristol Station. I recollect very distinctly the old drawbridge.

Glancing ruminatively back to the seemingly perpetually sunlit plains of childhood, O'Donnell remembered with pangs of nostalgia long-ago family holidays. He recalled affectionately Weston-super-Mare, a seaside resort never in those distant days crowded, except on bank holidays and in the month of August. It boasted no big hotels, no theatre, just a pier, but his mother harboured immense faith in the tonic effects of its sea air.

Another never to be forgotten holiday venue was Ifracombe. It was then very small, and, like Weston-super-Mare, totally lacking in any places of entertainment. Even in August, the Capstan Hill, its chief promenade for visitors, was comparatively deserted. The O'Donnells travelled there by boat, and Elliott suffered a memorable bout of seasickness – "I wished myself at the bottom of the sea, I felt so ill, without relief of being sick."

Among the passengers on the Ilfracombe-bound boat was a lady, a member of a very old French family, who kept a small, extremely select school for young ladies in Clifton. She was accompanied by her daughter. O'Donnell saw a good deal of her while in Ilfracombe, and thought her very jolly, attractive without being really pretty. In later years, this young woman was to figure as the central character in a sensational murder case in Melbourne. She had married an Irishman, with whom she was emigrating to Australia. On the voyage out, she became friendly with a handsome young Frenchman, and her husband, observing the overripening of the friendship, forbade his wife to have anything more to do with her Gallic admirer. But to this spousal edict she stubbornly refused assent. Learning one night that she had gone off to the theatre with the Frenchman, her frustrated husband followed them there in a green haze of jealous rage, found them together in a box, and turned a gun on the Frenchman, his wife, and then himself. She was the only one of the tragic trio to survive.

But what lodged in O'Donnell's memory of that holiday was hearing someone who called on his mother tell her that a mill stream near Ilfracombe was said to be haunted. A murder had once taken place close to the mill, and the ghost of the murdered girl, dressed in a winding-sheet, had so badly frightened people who had seen it that no one would ever venture near the place after dark. His mind set was, already this early, directed towards the realm of ghosts.

When he was six years old, Elliott shared a governess, Miss Maybury, with his youngest sister, Helena. She was the daughter of a Staffordshire editor and lived with her invalid mother in Richmond Terrace, Clifton. Resident in the same house as Mrs. and Miss Maybury was a Mr. Matthews. Short, stout, elderly and eccentric, he always wore out-of-doors a round sealskin hat and black cloak. He became very enamoured of Miss Maybury, and would wait outside the O'Donnells' gate in the afternoon to escort her home. His affection for Miss Maybury was counterbalanced by his extreme aversion to small boys, who returned the compliment in the form of persistent mockery, teasing, and the bestowal upon him of the street-shouted soubriquet of "Maddy Matthews". Whenever a boy came within the orbit of his reach, Maddy Matthews would lash out at him with his stick. We shall hear more of him later.

O'Donnell could recall a quite extraordinary link with the historic past. Living in The Avenue, Clifton, was his godfather, the Reverend T.G. Luckock, son of the aged Reverend Luckock, who lived in a house opposite him. One day when his mother took young Elliott to see him, the old man told the boy how he was at breakfast one morning when the great British victory at Waterloo was reported in the press. Also living in The Avenue then was Mr. Frank Townsend, a well-known Gloucestershire cricketer, father of the famous C.L. Townsend.

At the end of January, 1881, O'Donnell's mother died. She had caught a violent chill watching Elliott's brother and sister skating, and succumbed after a very short illness. She had survived her husband by eight years.

On the evening before her mother's death, Elliott's younger sister, Helena, saw a head similar in every detail to that which her elder sister, Petronella, had seen prior to the Reverend Henry's death, staring down at her from the balustrade of the top landing.

Days later, Elliott's old nurse, Sarah Coldwell, on going upstairs, saw in the waning daylight a white face looking down over the first floor landing banisters. She recognised it at once as that of Mrs. O'Donnell, whose funeral had only just taken place.

At about twelve o'clock on the actual night of the day of her burial, the servants at Sherborne Villas distinctly heard someone, whose footsteps they recognised as those of their dead mistress, walking round and round the middle landing, pausing outside each door, especially that on the room in which the nine-year-old Elliott lay, coughing. They heard, too, the door of the locked room in which her body had lain open, and then close with a loud bang.

And later that week, Fanny Coldwell, saw Mrs. O'Donnell looking down at her from an upper landing. In some consternation, she hurried back, thoroughly scared, to the kitchen.

Orphaned, Elliott became the ward of his step-sister, Elizabeth Mousley, "to whom I can never be sufficiently grateful, for no one could have been kinder. I was extremely fortunate in having sisters who were fond of me, and servants who were devoted to us all and more like members of the family than dependents." Elizabeth made herself also responsible for Helena and Petronella, and kept on the house and the two Coldwells.

A few months after their mother's death, Elizabeth, thinking it high time that Elliott and Helena should go to school, arranged for 12-year-old Helena to enter Miss Mary Ann Stewart Rowbotham's establishment in The Avenue, Clifton, and 9-year-old Elliott was packed off to a tutor, Albert Cole, of 9 Buckingham Vale, Clifton. He was, actually, chiefly concerned with preparing lads for examinations for the army, and finding himself attending class in the same room as youths of eighteen and nineteen, Elliott, believing that he was expected to be as advanced in work as they were, panicked and was discovered in tears. His state of dejection being observed, he was, after a few days, sent home with a letter to his guardian, saying that he was too young to be at Mr. Cole's and suggesting that it would be better to send him to a school for boys of his own age. At Mr. Cole's recommendation, Elliott was despatched, first as a day boy and afterwards as a boarder, to a dame school in Clifton, kept by two middle-aged sisters.[7] The younger of the two sisters was of a decidedly fearsome

---

7   Although it is now impossible to be certain, it seems likely to have been that kept by Catherine and Mary Adams, at 48 & 49 Canynge Square. O'Donnell refers to his having been a pupil at Clifton's then celebrated dame school, "Leeshome".

disposition. She always kept a cane on her lap and was wont to wield it mightily. Its swishings, alternating with loud thumps and slappings, could be heard whenever she was taking a lesson, and for any demeanour which she regarded as serious the miscreant would be handed over to the drill-sergeant, a rugged Highland soldier who had seen service in the battles of Alma, Inkerman, and Balaclava, whose brawny right arm would vigorously administer due punishment with a thick stick.

Schools, even dame schools, were much tougher in the time of Queen Victoria's golden reign. On his very first day there, Elliott had, in the dinner hour, to run the gauntlet of boys lashing at him with knotted handkerchiefs. There was one big lad who always made a point of ill-treating him whenever he got the chance, but, considering what a shy, delicate little fellow he was, generally speaking Elliott came off fairly well. He was told that a hole in one of the floorboards of the class-room was the abode of a bogey who would be very angry unless he gave him something, and to appease him Elliott dropped a halfpenny down into the bogey's lair. A halfpenny does not seem like a fortune, but to a boy whose pocket-money was only twopence a week it was a lot.

There were several other dame schools in Clifton, and one of them, whose boys were bigger and more numerous than those at O'Donnell's, were their bitter foes, and used to waylay them on their way to and from school, dishing out cuts, bruises, and very nasty blows to some of the smaller boys. Other omnipresent enemies were the town's errand-boys. They used to pelt them with snowballs into which they had put stones and horse dung.

Not long before O'Donnell left, a boy of about seven arrived at the school. His name was Tom Inskip. He was very sharp and tall for his age. He was the smart boy of the school, the one whom, when any visitors came that she wanted to impress, the headmistress would produce to recite a poem or something in French. One afternoon, Tom and several other boys went round to O'Donnell's house. Tired of playing cricket, they were debating what to do. Someone suggested an execution. Tom volunteered to be the victim. A cord was duly looped around his neck and the other end tied to a walnut tree. They were just about to hoist the future Lord Chancellor of England up, when Fanny Coldwell chanced to appear and put a prompt halt to the proceedings.

2

The Apprentice Ghost Hunter

Having in due season passed the entrance examination, O'Donnell entered the bottom form of the Junior School of Clifton College. The day boys were divided into houses according to an imaginary boundary line drawn through Clifton. Those on one side were North Town boys, those on the other, South Town boys. O'Donnell was at first in the South Town, but later on in the North Town House.

There was a certain amount of bullying, but, except for a kick and a blow on the face from two boys much older than himself, O'Donnell experienced none. Periodically, the school was swept by harmless crazes – for silkworms, horse chestnuts, Jews' harps, and so on.

One of his schoolfellows was D.G. Deane-Tanner. He was the brother of William Cunningham Deane-Tanner, better known as William Desmond Taylor, the film director at the centre of the Great Hollywood Mystery of 1922. He was found one February morning lying dead on the floor of the sitting-room of his bungalow, on Avarado Street, Los Angeles. He had been shot in the back. Born in Ireland in 1877, (some say 1872), the son of a wealthy British army officer, he had served with a Canadian regiment during the First World War. There was strong suspicion as to the identity of his killer, but insufficient firm evidence to make any arrest.[1]

O'Donnell was much addicted to fooling. One of his hilarious pranks was to mix bay salt with the coal in the class-room scuttle. The resultant cracks and bangs, when, in all innocence, the unsuspecting form-master put the coal on the fire, had those in the know positively choking and paralytic

---

[1] The best account of the case is to be found in *A Cast of Killers*. Sidney D. Kirkpatrick. Dutton, New York, 1986.

with suppressed laughter. This quirky sense of humour of O'Donnell's betrayed him into the use of strange devices to scare people.

Nor were his jollifications necessarily confined to his school and schoolfellows. He had always been rather fond of the theatre, of producing plays at home, and loved dressing-up. Upon learning from a friend that his grandmother was looking for a new maid the ideal jape crystallised in his head. Borrowing one of Sarah Coldwell's skirts, bodice, and bonnets, he presented himself thus attired to apply for the situation. His friend's grandmother was living with her spinster daughter, a lady of indeterminate age, ranging in the fifty to sixty zone. Mother and daughter both wore spectacles, and both were somewhat deaf. They came to the front-door to interview the disguised O'Donnell.

"What's your name?" demanded the daughter.

"Mary Smith."

"Your age?"

"Coming fourteen."

"What do you mean by that?" And, said in very severe tones, "always say 'Mam' when you address a lady."

"I mean I shall be fourteen very soon, Mam."

"What can you do?" asked the older lady, thrusting her head forward, casting a beady eye to get a closer look at the applicant.

Elliott noted that she looked in need of a shave.

"Most anything, Mam," replied Elliott. "I can cook, clean, sew and darn."

The ladies exchanged rapid satisfied-looking glances.

"Are you steady?"

"Yes, Mam. I haven't started courting yet."

More significant glances were exchanged.

The daughter named the very miniscule wage they were prepared to offer. O'Donnell accepted it. The daughter then asked if he could come that evening, and when he said that was impossible, she asked:

"When can you come?"

"Never," replied Elliott – and bolted.

They were very angry at being hoaxed, and when they realised who the hoaxer had been, they threatened to tell the headmaster. But they never did.

Although himself afraid of the dark, and a believer in, and wary of, ghosts, he on several occasions put up a turnip-lantern in a dark lane at the back of his house in order to frighten people. The joke was, however, turned upon himself, for one night he was scared nearly out of his wits when someone, getting wise to the nature of his turnip ghost, jumped out on him from a dark doorway, wearing a skeleton mask and garbed from head to foot in a spooky white robe.

Summer holidays held an important place in the calendar of Elliott's school years. They were spent in such places as Dublin, Aberystwyth, Penmaenmawr, Bridlington Quay, and Newquay, in Cornwall.

Although it has not proved possible to be precise in the temporal assignment of the succeeding cluster of O'Donnell's early psychic experiences, they unquestionably belong to his boyhood days. That said, the indications are that it is likely to have been in the August of 1881, when O'Donnell was nine, and on holiday at Aberystwyth, that his fingers touched again the hem of the world of phantasmata.

Aberystwyth conjured up for him memories of people on the beach searching among the pebbles for amethysts, topaz, cornelians, and other semi-precious stones. When any stone thought to be of value was discovered, it would be taken to a little building by the beach where a Miss Meredith would examine the find and quickly identify it. If it turned out to be a stone of value, it could be there and then cut and made into a locket or some other chosen ornament.

But the abiding memory of his Aberystwyth holiday was of the day when he was descending a steep path near the Devil's Bridge, leading to the hollow known locally as the Devil's Punch Bowl, when, glancing involuntarily back over his shoulder, he saw a tall, shadowy figure suddenly bound across the track behind him and vanish, flash-like, into the dense foliage. The description of that figure tallies with that of an Elemental – "It resembled one of those old-fashioned Dutch dolls that were in vogue many years before. It had the same sort of thin, long arms and legs, that seem to move all in a piece, and a perfectly rounded head, rather too smooth for its body. The speed with which it moved made it impossible to see its features with any distinctness, but the impression conveyed was that of a frank grotesqueness, a caricature of a human face." It did not strike O'Donnell as being evil or antagonistic.

The second and third psychic episodes were also set in Wales. It would appear to have been in the summer of 1882, when ten-year-old Elliott was staying in holiday lodgings at Penmaenmawr. One night he was awoken by a loud flapping noise, as of gigantic wings, accompanied by a curious croaking and groaning. His bedroom was at the front of the house and the sounds seemed to be coming from the street. At breakfast, he described his experience of the previous night to the landlady.

"Oh, that was the *Gwrach y Rhibyn*, the Hag of the Dribble," she said. "My husband and I both heard it, and Mrs. Thomas over the way saw it beating its wings against the window-frames of her room and looking in at her. One of her children is ill, and she says she's sure the *Gwrach y Rhibyn* came for the boy, and that he won't last through the day."

The *Gwrach* is a weird, shadowy form, half old hag, with a skull-like face, long massed hair, a hooked nose and gleaming eyes, and half a monstrous leathery-winged bat. It haunts only people of genuine old Welsh blood, and its appearance always portends a death. And, sure enough, later that day, the Thomas child, who had been ill for some time, suddenly took a turn for the worse, and by sundown was dead.

A few days later, young Elliott was involved in another psychic revelation. Walking with his old nurse, Sarah Coldwell, along a lane near Penmaenmawr, his eye was attracted to a solitary willow tree growing beside a pool on one side of the lane. The afternoon was sultry and breezeless, but the tree was swaying and shaking in a most peculiar way. He drew his nurse's attention to the odd behaviour of the willow. She made no reply, but turned pale and quickened her pace. When they got back to their lodgings and the landlady came in to lay tea, her tongue suddenly loosened, the nurse asked her if there was anything wrong with the willow by the pool in the lane.

"You mean the lane running in the direction of Llangevin? They do say it's haunted. One or two people have been found drowned in the pool, and there's a story about an old tramp hanging himself in the tree."

"Well," said Elliott's old nurse, "I don't need to be told that the tree's haunted, for as sure as I'm alive I saw a skeleton in a winding-sheet sitting on one of its branches, and it was he that made the tree shake. He was swaying to and fro and laughing at us as we went by."

O'Donnell records another adventure while out walking with his old nurse. This time the locus is a village in Northamptonshire. She took him to the cottage of a Mrs. Smith, a native of those parts who, all her life, up to the time she had grown too old to work, had been in the service of O'Donnell's cousin, with whom he was staying. The cottage, a tiny one, stood in a very isolated spot, and was entirely overshadowed by rows of gigantic elms that lined the road close to it. The three of them were having tea, when there came a loud knock at the door. Their hostess took no notice of it.

"There was someone a-rapping, Mrs. Smith", said Sarah Coldwell.

"Is there?" said Mrs. Smith, "I didn't hear no one." Then, raising her voice, she called out, "Come in."

There was no response.

A little later on, there was a second knock. Mrs. Smith munching away at her bread and butter, obviously had not heard it either.

Then there came a third knock. Sarah Coldwell went to the door, opened it a few inches, and peeped out.

"Did you hear another knock?" asked Mrs. Smith.

"I fancied I did, but it must have been only fancy, for there's no one there." Young O'Donnell noted the queer expression on Sarah's face as she spoke.

As they were making their way home, his old nurse confessed, "I'm terrible worritted about them knocks, I am."

"Why? Who was it?" asked O'Donnell.

"It wasn't nobody. That's where the trouble comes in. It was something supernatural and I'm terrible afeared something's going to happen to Mrs. Smith. You see, she didn't hear them knocks herself. But there, you don't understand. I oughtn't to have told you."

But O'Donnell did understand. His old nurse's dire prognostications proved true. The very next day poor Mrs. Smith had a stroke, and within a week she was Marley door nail dead.

Along with his sisters and his old nurse, Sarah Coldwell, he was to spend a couple of summer holidays staying at a small house on Mount Wise, Newquay, It was there, in August, 1885, that he saw his first phantasm of the living. It came about in this way. He was standing one afternoon on the staircase when he saw a friend of theirs, Miss Dutton, who was staying with them, coming down, followed by his two sisters and Sarah Coldwell. Her dress brushed over his feet as she went down the stairs, and was, testified O'Donnell, as material as any clothes of his own. She disappeared into the little front sitting-room at the foot of the stairs, shutting the door behind her with a bang. It seemed rather curious behaviour, but she had a cousin staying there with her, and the O'Donnells thought that perhaps he was in the room and that she might want a few minutes' private conversation with him. So … they waited politely outside. But, since they heard no sound of voices, one of them opened the door. The room was empty. About a quarter of an hour later, they bumped into Miss Dutton on the beach. It transpired that at the moment that four people had seen her in the house, she was actually walking about the town with a friend.

It was one night around the year 1886, that young Elliott went along with a party of people older than himself to a place on the Durdham Downs which was rumoured to be haunted at a certain season of the year by a phantom coach. The story went that there had once been a high road across the Downs, along which coaches used to travel from the Hotwells to and beyond Westbury-on-Trym. At that time, the Downs, like many other lonely localities, were infested with highwaymen, and on one occasion they held up a coach and robbed and murdered the travellers in it. Hence the haunting. The alleged site of the old coach road, which had long disappeared, was said to be the skeleton avenue of fine old trees which ran diagonally across the Downs. It was around that avenue that the party hovered that evening. It was nearly midnight. Nothing had happened and they were about to set off for home, when they were suddenly frozen in their tracks by the sound of a wild, unearthly scream that seemed to scimitar through the blackness of the night.

They did not stay to probe its origin, but ran, and never ceased running, till they were well clear of the Downs.

Those Downs are, incidentally, remarkable for the number of suicides which have taken place at one particular spot on the long line of cliffs towering over the River Avon. There are those who firmly believe that there is an evil spirit which lurks there, its influence tempting people to fling themselves to their death.

A phenomenon of a very different kind, the life force no less, beset O'Donnell during his 1886 summer holiday at Bridlington Quay.

> I fell desperately in love with a girl of about my own age, namely fourteen. Her name was Kitty Nelson and her home, if I remember rightly, was Kettleby Thorpe. She wore her dark hair in page-boy style, had neat features and very pretty dark blue eyes. I was far too shy to speak to her and confined myself to adoring gazes whenever I saw her out-of-doors. We were both staying in the Crescent, a few houses distant from one another, and when I sent her flowers she used to signify their

reception by waving them to me from one of the windows. On one occasion, with the idea of amusing her, I blacked my face. She did not see me, but a little boy in the next house did, and was so terrified that he nearly had a fit. His father, thinking I had blacked my face to frighten his silly little child, was infuriated and threatened to do all kinds of things to me. It was only after a considerable amount of explaining that he was ultimately pacified.

I shall never forget my surprise and joy soon after I had left Bridlington and returned to Clifton on receiving a delightfully friendly letter from Kitty. We corresponded for some time and then, alas, the letters that passed between us grew less and less till they finally ceased. I never forgot her, and have often wondered what became of my first love.

That year of 1886 seems to have been a romantic *annus mirabilis* for the maturing young O'Donnell, for, always very fond of the pantomime and a great admirer of actresses, he fell desperately in love again. This time the object of his devotion was Addie Blanche, the principal girl in *Sinbad the Sailor*. He saved up from his small allowance of pocket-money to buy flowers for her, and left them at the stage door of the Prince's Theatre, and hovered around for days hoping to see her. He never did – and she never got the flowers.

Cinderella was the pantomime at the Prince's in 1889-90, and the principal girl was Amy Murray, a very vivacious actress and an excellent dancer. His susceptible heart touched once again, O'Donnell, along with his school friend, Charlie Vivian, bent on paying her a tribute, went in search of her address. They found that a lady of that name was living in a road in Clifton. They bought a bouquet between them, attached to it a note expressing their admiration, and left it at the address they had found. Unfortunately, the recipient of their floral tribute turned out to be a prim elderly spinster, who never went to the theatre and was horrified at being mistaken for an actress.

A holiday in Dublin was not without its excitements, which included seeing an accident on the day of their arrival. A man was driving a cart and something frightened the horse to such an extent that it bolted. The driver was pitched on to the ground and was seriously injured. The weather was dry, and the O'Donnells were horrified to see, next day, some of the blood still on the spot where the man fell.

While they were in Dublin there was a pantomime, put on by the officers of the British garrison for charity, at the Gaiety Theatre, and Elliott's sister, Petronella, was in the chorus. His eye was taken by one of her fellow dancers, an exceedingly attractive blonde, the Hon. 'Cosie' Vereker. He was also greatly astonished and amused at seeing, early in the morning, old women sitting on doorsteps smoking pipes.

They were staying with relatives in a house in Ely Place.

> The staircases of the house were stone, and my sisters used to be awakened at night by the sounds of ghostly footsteps tramping up and down them. I never heard them, but then being very young and usually tired with much going about during the day, I slept very soundly. The house had a scaring effect on most of us, it was so gloomy and suggestive of ghosts.
>
> We had a number of relatives living in Dublin at that time, including my brother, who was stationed in the city with his regiment. We went about a lot with one or other of them. On one occasion we visited the Zoological Gardens and one of the monkeys, coveting Helena's hat, snatched it from her and, putting it on its own head, jumped about and made jeering faces at her in apparent great glee at her consternation. She never recovered her hat.
>
> There were, of course, no motor-cars in those days, only sidecars and four-wheelers, and one had to have a firm stomach to travel in the trams, for the jolting and bumping was terrible. One saw much poverty side by side with wealth; many carriages and pairs and very many children in ragged clothes and bare feet.
>
> After leaving Ely Place, we stayed for several weeks in Black Rock, and then returned to Clifton. The passage from Kingstown (Dun Laoghaire) to Holyhead was so abominably rough that we were all desperately sick.

There were also a couple of holidays at Newquay. They lodged there in a little house on Mount Wise. They played rounders on the beach and went for wagonette drives to places of interest in the neighbourhood. They were fascinated by the stories they heard about the nearby River Gannel. It had long borne an uncanny reputation, and its estuary was said to be haunted by the spirits of people who were drowned while attempting to cross its treacherous sands at low water. Many testified to having heard screams and cries coming from the river after dusk.

Before passing on to the time when O'Donnell was grown-up and actually hunting ghosts there are one or two more supernatural experiences which very much intrigued him as a boy.

Visiting a country house near Northampton in the holidays, as he lay in bed he saw a lady in a grey silk dress pass through his bedroom. Apart from the fact that her dress struck him as peculiarly old-fashioned, she looked completely natural. Seemingly compacted of flesh and blood, there was nothing phantasmic about her. Next morning, however, he learned that she had been a ghost, a harmless shade who was seen from time to time in that particular room which he had occupied.

Somewhat less tranquil was the spectre that he disturbed in the loft of an old disused barn in the grounds of the same Northamptonshire house. The gardener, who kept his tools in the barn, had warned the boy against the place, advised him not to go in there; but that, to an adventurous boy like O'Donnell, was tantamount to a challenge! Accordingly, one afternoon, after making sure that the gardener was nowhere about, he crept swiftly and surreptitiously into the building. Everything inside seemed perfectly normal, peaceful and still. He clambered up a ladder on to the floor of the loft. Up there, there was a curious feeling of gloominess, an air of forbidding. In one corner stood a huge chest. It appeared to have no lid to it. He was about to make his way over to it, intent upon exploring its contents, when a tall white form leapt out of the chest and stood facing him. The figure was indistinct, but seemed to be a naked human body, very thin, completely hairless, and with extremely large ears. Caught up in a wave of absolute terror, O'Donnell literally tumbled down the ladder and put as much distance, as fast as he could, between himself and the barn. Confessing to the gardener what he had done, and telling him what he had seen, he learned that he, too, had seen the spectre, as had several other people, and it was thought to be the ghost of a tramp who had hanged himself in the loft.

The supernatural continued to colour, to light and shade, his life as a schoolboy. Back in the mid-1880s, when he first remembered it, Durdham Downs, at Clifton, was quite a wild place, covered with gorse and yielding a splendid botanical variety of flowers. It was crossed by few roads, and there was no golf course. Various schools played their games on the daytime Downs, but it was otherwise pretty deserted; one met very few people there, late in the evening, except perhaps on Saturdays. Not far from the Sea Walls, was a narrow pathway, leading in gradual descent to the river Avon. In O'Donnell's schooldays, this path, which was known as the Gully bore a most sinister reputation. It harked back to the events of an evening in the 'fifties of the nineteenth century. That was when a little girl named Melinda Payne, who lived in a cottage at the foot of the Gully, was sent by her parents to Cook's Folly Tavern, about three-quarters of a mile away, to fetch some beer. She did not return. They scoured the Downs for her. They found her body pushed in beneath a heap of shells and stones lying to one side near the foot of the Gully. Her murder was never brought home to anyone.

Ever after, the Gully was said to be haunted. Viewed by after sunset dusk, ringed about by twilight, the Gully summons up no great stretch of imagination to see it as the realm and rendezvous of ghosts. The boys of O'Donnell's old school used regularly to dare each other to venture into the Gully, even in the day-lit hours of afternoon, on their own – and he was rash enough to take up the challenge.

"Never shall I forget my sensations, when, having left my companions seated comfortably on the Downs in full view of a school playing cricket, I commenced my descent of the narrow, tortuous path leading to the river. Braced up, however, by my love of adventure, I made up my mind to continue, and having at length gone as far as I said I would, I was about to retrace my steps when I suddenly saw through the foliage on one side of me... a man, a tall, wretchedly clad man with a bloodless face and a wild look in his eyes, stood there sharpening a knife. Even now, after all these years, I can hear the noise that knife made as it scraped the stone; I was convinced that it was being sharpened to plunge into me, and my terror was so great that I scarcely dared to breathe, whilst my knees shook to such an extent that I could hardly stand. I opened my mouth several times to shout to my companions, but my voice died away in my throat, and I could not articulate a sound. Neither could I stir, and this state of helplessness continued till a sudden movement on the part of the man broke the spell. With a wild yell of terror I fled up the path... my feet seemed weighed down with lead and my lungs bursting; but I managed somehow to struggle on, till I came within sight of my schoolfellows, when I tripped over a stone and fell.

Having struck my forehead with considerable force upon the ground, I was partially stunned, and in this state picked up by an old gentleman who happened to be passing at the time. He questioned me kindly as to why I had been in such haste, and when I told him my story, he advised me never to venture in the Gully again. 'I am not warning you against ghosts,' he said, 'because there are no such things, but there are evilly disposed men, and the Gully seems to attract them. You had better walk back to your school with me, and if we meet a policeman on the way, we will tell him.' My companions now joining us, we walked back to Clifton in a body; and upon meeting a policeman in Worcester Terrace, where my school was, the old gentleman, true to his word, stopped him and told him all about my adventure.

Chancing to meet this same policeman in the street two or three days later, I asked him if he had been to the Gully and seen the man with the knife, and he told me that he had not, because it was not on his beat, but that the policeman who patrolled the Downs had been there, and had seen no one. 'Perhaps,' he went on, jokingly, ' it was a ghost you saw. They do say as 'ow the Gully's 'aunted.'

'Do they?' I said. 'Why, that old gentleman who was so decent to me the other day says there are no such things as ghosts. Who was he?'

'What, didn't you know?' the policeman replied. 'He were old Mr. Matthews, all the boys in this 'ere neighbourhood calls 'im Maddy Matthews, because 'e gets annoyed if they h'only looks at 'im. 'e 'ates children, and I was not 'arf surprised, I can tell you, when I see'd 'im walking along with you.'"

Some time after the foregoing dialogue had taken place, O'Donnell met 'Maddy Matthews' in Clifton. Mr. Matthews had apparently completely forgotten him, for, as he approached, the old gentleman aimed a vicious blow at him with his stick, and, without evincing the slightest sign of recognition, passed on. Incidentally, Maddy's nephew was Henry Matthews, Q.C. Home Secretary, 1886-1892. Matthews was created Lord Llandaff in 1895.

As it did at most public schools, sport played a very important part in life at Clifton College, and O'Donnell religiously chronicled the sporting achievements of his contemporaries there.

> While I was there the school had many fine athletes. One term the XV included three future Internationals, namely L.J. Percival, probably the best forward in England, E. Bonham-Carter, and C.A. Hooper. E. Field, who was in the XV the following year, played full-back for England less than a year after he left the school. He was a cricket blue as well, and made several centuries for Middlesex. L.E. Pilkington represented Cambridge in the Hurdle Race v. Oxford, and also at Hockey. His brother, W.N. Pilkington, whose nickname at school was 'the rabbit', on account of his speed, not only represented Cambridge v. Oxford in the 100 yards, but got his rugger blue and International cap.

I must not end this category of Clifton athletes during the period I was in the school without mentioning the following outstanding cricketers: Ernest Smith, who was in the Oxford and Yorkshire Cricket XI, and played at least six times in the Gentleman v. Players match at Lords: H.S. Schwann, W.H. Brain, and W.G. Grace, son of the famous 'W.G.', all of whom won blues, Schwann and Brain at Oxford, and Grace at Cambridge.

J.R. Head played several seasons for Middlesex. And last, but by no means least, J.H. Curtis, whose batting average in 1894, when he skippered the XI was over 60.

A remarkable feat at cricket was performed by F.C.S. Norrington, who, when in the XI, hit a ball which broke the school clock, high up in the quadrangle. The distance was so great that doubt has been expressed as to whether the hit was made from the actual XI pitch, but I have ample testimony to prove it was a fact. F.C.S. captained the Sandhurst cricket XI, was in the Sandhurst XV, and played cricket for Gloucestershire.

While I was at the school the Shooting VIII won the much coveted Ashburton Shield three times, and the Spencer Cup once.

O'Donnell was no good at games – or work – which was partly due to ill-health. He had strained his heart at the annual athletic sports, and was for some weeks in a very critical condition. The doctor said that the illness would greatly affect his physical development, and it did. He did not continue growing for several years, and when he was seventeen did not appear to be more than thirteen. Twelve months after the onset of his first illness, he was diagnosed with rheumatic fever, was away from school for the best part of a term, and during the winter months generally suffered with severe bronchial colds. All this meant that he was unable to play games anything like as often as he would have wished.

It was indeed as a result of ill-health that, at the age of sixteen, in 1888, he left Clifton College, and was sent, most unwillingly, to the east coast of Scotland to recoup his health.

He went, ostensibly, as a pupil, to a farm near Montrose, where his host was a gentleman farmer with a large and somewhat boisterous family. He was to spend four months there, uneventful except for a visit to Ethie Castle and Lunan Bay. The castle was said to have been built by that Cardinal Beaton, who, having had George Wishart burned as a heretic, was in consequence assassinated by Wishart's friends. His Eminence had suffered from very severe gout, and could only walk on one foot with the aid of a stick, the other being protectively bandaged. Workmen who were carrying out repairs which the castle was undergoing swore that on several occasions they had heard the Cardinal's ghost's muffled one-footed movement up and down the staircases and passages, to the accompaniment of his tapping stick. Another wraith was said to flit about the castle; a lady in a green dress, whose appearance would portend a tragedy for the Northesk family, the owners of the castle.

Rather more material, literally, was the calamity that befell O'Donnell when he went rat hunting in a barn on his host's farm. A monster rat came racing towards him, and afraid that it would escape, he sat down on it, and it bit through his trousers.

Trying to make a bathing pool for themselves, O'Donnell, three of the farmer's sons and one of their cousins contrived to dam a mill-stream that flowed through their grounds. So effectively did they do so, that the miller could not get any water for his mill, and demonstrated his displeasure very palpably. Scarcely less irate was the farmer in whose cornfield they elected to cut down an old tree, which came down with a mighty crash, destroying a fair swath of his ripening corn.

Like many people, O'Donnell was subject to a repetitionary dream, and regularly, for five years, every first week in July, he would dream that he was cycling along a white dusty road, skirted on both sides by a low stone wall, giving on to a doleful landscape of long stretches of poor pasture, ending in distant barren, gloomy hills. He was riding down a rather steep incline, when, as he was nearing a turning, he heard the sound of wheels, and a pair of black horses drawing an open carriage dashed across the road in front of him. Forced to swerve, he crashed into the roadside wall. Stunned, he found himself lying on the ground, his bicycle, broken in half, by his side. At this point he invariably awoke.

Early one morning in the first week of July, he set out with the Montrose farmer and his family on an excursion to some picturesque ruins about a dozen miles away. They were in a wagonette. He was on a safety bicycle. They had proceeded some way when O'Donnell got a puncture, and he was left behind to repair it. The puncture mended, he was going full tilt down a steepish hill when he suddenly realised that he was totally familiar with his surroundings – it was the landscape of his recurrent dream. He was still experiencing the shock of recognition when an open carriage drawn by two black horses dashed across the road in front of him. Unable to stop, he swerved aside, crashed into the wall, and passed out. When he came to, he was lying in the road, his bicycle, broken in two, beside him.

"I have met people who believe that there exists a kind of dreamland where dreamers are in the habit of meeting one another and forming dream friendships and acquaintances," writes O'Donnell, and he recalls that, when a youth, he dreamt very vividly one night that he was walking along the promenade of some seaside resort. The place was absolutely deserted. A few lights were burning. He came to a shelter, saw something lying on the ground. Picking it up, he found that it was a red leather reticule with a brightly sparkling silver clasp. He was about to open it, seeking any clue as to the identity of its owner, when a young man approached him, and asked what was the matter. O'Donnell showed him the reticule and he said, "Well, that's strange, for I have just picked up a purse." They agreed to report their finds at a police station, and started off at once. They had got a mere matter of yards, when they heard a great tumult and found themselves enmeshed in a dense throng, one of whom told them that the Town Hall was on fire. That was in 1893.

In May, 1894, O'Donnell was sitting on the sea-front at Weston-super-Mare, watching the passers-by, when a young man whose face and general appearance seemed somehow familiar suddenly sat down beside him. They got into conversation. Then the young man blurted out: "I don't know why, but you remind me of a very peculiar dream I once had of this esplanade. One night last year I dreamed I picked up a purse somewhere near here, and I was walking along with it in my hand, when I came upon a young man very like you, who had just found a lady's reticule. We got quite friendly and were on our way to the police station with our findings, when we were suddenly overtaken by a crowd. I lost sight of my companion and was trying to wrest the purse from a rough who had snatched it from me, when I awake."

Since the date of their respective dreams coincided, O'Donnell felt that he could only conclude that by the strangest of coincidences they had projected themselves simultaneously to the same place. That that place was Weston-super-Mare, he tended to doubt, because no fire had occurred there on that particular date, when the young man had written it all down in his memorandum book.

Returned to Clifton, O'Donnell was to spend two years as a boarder with an army tutor, Charles Ford, whose premises were at 13 Miles Road, Clifton, being prepared to sit the Sandhurst entrance examination, with the intention of following his brother Henry's military steps into the army. Meanwhile, he had obtained permission to join the first Volunteer Battalion Gloucestershire Regiment. The C.O. was Colonel Methuen; the uniform was green; the helmets had spikes; and, when marching, the corps was preceded by pioneers, who carried axes. His experience as a member of the Cadet Corps at Clifton College stood him in good stead, having no difficulty with the drills or with qualifying at the butts. He was, however, occasionally troubled by the amorous attentions of a young woman who would persist in marching along beside him when he was parading from the Drill Hall at the top of Park Street, which was the battalion H.Q. He was also much bothered by a youth who, for some undivined reason, kept on pestering him to go with him to the theatre to see "Alone in London" and "The Colleen Bawn".

O'Donnell recalls of this period:

> A great sensation was caused in Bristol at that time by a schoolmistress who invented a sort of machine for birching refractory young ladies in her academy. Certain newspapers and, more particularly, a long defunct weekly journal, made much of the affair and published illustrations of the schoolmistress superintending the birching. Posing as a reporter, I went to her house and, on her answering the door in person, asked for an interview. If looks could kill I should have fallen instantly, dead as twenty muttons, so venomous was the expression in her beady eyes. Wrath prevented her speaking. She merely glared and shut the door furiously in my face. I immediately rapped and rang again, but there was no response. She was an ill-favoured dame, of a Victorian type mercifully seldom, if ever, to be encountered nowadays, and I was very glad I was not one of the girls committed to her charge. I could well imagine the sadistic pleasure she must have derived in applying her invention to the bare behinds of her pupils.

During his time at the army tutor's, O'Donnell had two fights. One was regularly conducted with boxing-gloves, the other, less usually, with thick sticks, his opponent, who had been to school in Germany, preferring the latter to fists. He was lucky to win the day on both occasions. Not so lucky, however, when he took on an N.C.O. in the Drill Hall Regimental Gymnasium. Just as he was pluming himself that he was getting along famously, a sudden punch sent him measuring his length on the floor. O'Donnell was only seventeen, his opponent was a man of twenty-four, who, it transpired, had boxed professionally.

Competition for admittance to the Royal Military College at Sandhurst was at that time very keen, there being only some 100 or 110 vacancies for every thousand candidates. Through an error, no fault of his own, O'Donnell turned out to be a subject short in his preparation for the Sandhurst examination when he went up to London to sit it in Burlington Gardens, and inevitably, he failed. As a matter of fact, it would not have made any difference had he passed, for he was rejected on medical grounds anyway, because of defective eyesight.

Back in Clifton, young Elliott O'Donnell faced a suddenly out-of-focus future with as stern a gaze as he could muster.

3

Hibernian Hauntings

Although Elliott O'Donnell liked to convey the impression that he had been born in Ireland, this was not, as we know, the case. He did, however, have relatives living in the old country, and when he was fourteen he had, in 1886, paid a first visit to Dublin, staying there with relations in a big old house in Ely Place, close to St. Stephen's Green, and had vivid recollections of the holes in its stone stairs, through which boiling oil had been poured on English soldiers at the time of the '98.

He recalled, too: "There were many large and stately rooms, oak-panelled and beautiful throughout, with much carving. I remember looking with awe and perplexity at the number of odd shadows that used to put in an appearance on the stairs and in the passages, just when it was my bedtime, but I did not then attribute them to ghosts. I simply did not know what they were. I heard sounds, too, clangs and clashes, and footsteps and tramping up and down the stairs."

A second boyhood reminiscence of Dublin was of another big, lone house in the city on the Liffey that had the reputation of being the worst haunted house in the whole of Ireland. The origin of the haunting went back to the eighteenth century, when, as rumour had it, a Spanish nobleman had rented the place from its owners, a well-known Kildare family.

Describing the house, he states: "It was imposing and gloomy enough in appearance, with its high, narrow windows and massive front-door, that looked as if it had been fashioned to withstand a siege. I can recall a picture of it as it stood facing me in the full glare of a fierce July sun. The grass and weeds grew in profusion on the stone steps leading up to the entrance, and the chimney pots were so cracked and slantwise that a big gust of wind, one imagined, must bring them crashing to the ground. I never crossed the threshold, and it was only in the broadest of daylight, when the sun was shining merrily and the noise of the traffic in the streets all around me rendered me momentarily bold, that I ever dared approach the cracked and broken windows near enough to peer through them into the awful gloom beyond. But what a magnificent house it was, with its wide flagged hall, broad staircase and oak-panelled rooms, rooms that had once no doubt echoed to the sound of many voices, but which now were absolutely still. According to rumour, the house had stood empty since the last tenants, a Colonel and his wife, had taken an abrupt departure, scared away by the ghosts. Wild screams and music were alleged to be heard proceeding from it on certain nights in the year, and the face of a dreadful looking hag was said to be sometimes seen peering out of one of the windows. Indeed, I heard many such tales when I was staying with my people in Ely Place."

One of O'Donnell's myriad Irish cousins, a boy named Maunsell, told him that, anxious to put what he had heard about the place to the test, he had gone along there one night, hoping that he would be able to get into the house by climbing through a window. This proved impossible, and he ended up mounted on one of the window-sills, cramped and uncomfortable, peering in through the broken glass. For some time nothing happened and he was beginning to get bored, when suddenly he was thrilled by the plaintive sounds of an old-world spinet, coming, he thought, from the upper part of the house. As suddenly as it had begun, the music abruptly stopped. He heard hurrying footsteps and beyond the wide-open door of the room that he was looking into, he saw a young and beautiful girl, clad in the finery of a bygone age, come racing down the broad oak stairs into the hall. Seconds later, a wild scream of fear and agony froze the blood in Maunsell's veins. To his absolute horror he saw a sinister-looking old woman come scuttling across the room, making for the window. She wore a skirt, something like a crinoline but not a crinoline, a multi-coloured shawl, and a white cap, the crimpled border of which fitted closely round her face. It was the face that transfixed him with horror – white as a corpse, hideously wrinkled, dark, evil eyes, and a wicked, leering expression. A gruesome light seemed to emanate from all over her as she raised a clenched fist and shook it menacingly at him. Unnerved, he fell from his precarious perch, picked himself up off the ground, and, more frightened than hurt, ran all the way home.

In 1891, O'Donnell arrived in Dublin once more. His relatives' old house in Ely Place was no longer in private occupation. It was now the Queen's Service Academy, an establishment run by Dr. Chetwode Crawley for the coaching of young men with ambitions to an active service career at Sandhurst, Woolwich, and the Royal Irish Constabulary. O'Donnell's failure had for a time flummoxed him, put him in the uncomfortable position of not knowing what to try for next. It was then that he had suddenly decided to try for an inspectorship in the Royal Irish Constabulary. The subjects in which he would be required to pass examinations did not strike him as particularly formidable, but it was necessary to obtain a nomination from the Lord Lieutenant before entering for the examination. Successful candidates, after doing a period of training, became inspectors in the force, which was of a semi-police and military character.

The R.I.C. students worked quite apart from those working for army commissions and they included English public schoolboys as well as several, slightly older, who had taken degrees at Oxford or Cambridge. O'Donnell found them a first rate lot, he had, he said, never met a nicer, more genial or livelier crowd. He particularly enjoyed the daily eleven o'clock break, when the class divided into two halves, two hostile parties, who waged a ten minutes' battle with any missiles that happened to be at hand. Books, screwed up balls of paper, sometimes even chairs, were thrown across the floor with potentially lethal effect. During one of these skirmishes O'Donnell accidentally hit a six-foot future cricket International in the face with an especially hard compressed paper ball. As he was, in fact, taking no part in the fray but was just sitting quietly reading a book, he was outraged by the unprovoked attack, and O'Donnell, observing the superior weight and strength of his unintended target made great show of an apology. It was not, however, received in the spirit offered, and O'Donnell was never quite forgiven.

O'Donnell liked, too, the men who were his teachers. To the end of his days he remembered with warmth Dr. Sparkhall Brown, Professor Dockerell and Mr. Giullgaut, all well known Dublin characters.

When, before his return to Ireland, O'Donnell had gone to the Montrose farm, in Forfarshire [now Angus], he had taken it into his head that he would like to learn French, and went for lessons to the house of a spinster who lived in the centre of the town. The room in which she taught was on the ground floor, and was separated from a room in the rear by folding doors. The morning of his first lesson he arrived about a quarter of an hour too early. Sitting alone in the front room awaiting the appearance of his teacher, he heard violent coughing coming from behind the folding doors. So violent and distressing did the coughing become, that, fearing the sufferer – a consumptive he thought – would either break a blood vessel or choke, he was about to run out into the hall and summon assistance, when the coughing abruptly ceased, and a moment or two later his teacher came into the room.

"Someone in your house has a very bad cough," he said. "Is it you?"

"No," she answered. "I have no cough. I hope you weren't alarmed?"

"I was a bit," said O'Donnell. "It sounded like someone in the last gasp of consumption."

The French teacher smiled. "Oh, no," she said, "it's not as bad as that. If you hear the same sounds again, take no notice."

The next morning he arrived about the same time and heard the same violent coughing. Again, he felt a sense of panic, and ran out into the hall, almost colliding with a young maid-servant. To his considerable surprise, she burst out crying. Thinking that he had somehow caused her distress, O'Donnell mumbled an apology.

"Oh, it isn't you, sir, it's the ghost."

"The ghost! What ghost?"

"Oh, what have I said?" she sobbed, "What have I said?"

"Is the house haunted then?"

"I daren't tell you, sir. The mistress would be ever so angry if I did. She won't have a word said about it."

"Then it is haunted. Is it the ghost that coughs?"

The girl nodded. "For mercy's sake, don't say I told you, sir, or I shall get into ever such trouble, and may lose my place."

Just then a latch-key was inserted in the front door. It was O'Donnell's French mistress returning. The little maid-servant scurried off and O'Donnell slipped back into the front room. He knew full well that it would be no good trying to get any information out of his instructress regarding the haunting. But he made enquiries elsewhere and learned that the house had long been reputed to be haunted. No one could tell him anything very definite about it, but it was generally believed to be the phantasm of an old man who had died there many years before under somewhat suspicious circumstances.

Some three years later, O'Donnell paid a second visit to Scotland. This time it was on holiday, to stay with an old school-fellow, Charlie Campbell, in Argyll. They were both keen anglers, and it was arranged that they should go on a night fishing expedition to Loch Fynne.[1] But Campbell was taken ill and could not go. He would not, however, hear of O'Donnell's being disappointed, and insisted in sending him off with one of his servants – a rugged, dour-looking Western islander, Neil MacPherson.

The night was fine and still, and very dark, and theirs, it seemed, was the only boat about. They were fishing at anchorage in absolute silence, when they heard the far-off plash of oars. O'Donnell was sitting facing the bows. The sound came from the rear. As it drew nearer, he turned round, peered through the Stygian darkness, but could see nothing.

"Oughtn't they to carry a light?" he asked MacPherson.

MacPherson did not reply.

On the boat came, so close that the blades of its oars seemed but a foot or two from their gunwales. As it passed, O'Donnell was impressed by the uncanny silence of the rowers. Such was the feeling of eeriness accompanying the passage of that silent vessel that O'Donnell was not surprised when a stricken MacPherson told him: "That was the death boat. It has haunted our family for hundreds of years, and is never seen or heard saving before the death of one of us. We all heard it the night before my father was drowned off Portree, in the Island of Skye, and again immediately before the death of my younger sister. I dread tomorrow, because I am sure I shall get a telegram saying that my brother Angus is dead. There were four rowers – there are always four – dressed in black, and Angus, my brother, dressed just like them, was sitting in the stern. It is he who is dead."

At noon the following day, MacPherson received a telegram from his mother saying that Angus had been caught in a sudden squall and drowned.

Arrived in Dublin in 1891, O'Donnell found it an enchanting place; veritably fairyland. But there was much of hell, too, in the Dublin of the 'nineties. Wealth cheek-by-jowl with terrible want. Fine ladies, clad in the height of fashion, and gentlemen strutting beside them, peacock proud, in superbly tailored and accoutred magnificence. On the other side of the

---

1   There is no such loch. The name has been made up by O'Donnell, as was his practice, to disguise the true locus.

road, threadbare men, women in virtual rags, barefoot children. Vice and immorality flourished. Gross poverty put plugs in the ears of the poor and a bridle on the tongues of the priests.

"We were warned by Dr. Chetwode not to go to Tyrone Street, which bore the worst of reputations. Needless to say, curiosity to see such an evil reputed street prompted us to go there. What we saw horrified and disgusted us. The street swarmed with the lowest class of prostitutes, O'Donnell reports. "Acts of flagrant indecency were committed before our eyes. We got out of the street very quickly. Never to visit it again. We were informed that venereal disease was rampant among the women. In short, the state of Dublin reflected little credit on the powers that governed it."

There were, though, happier sides to Dublin life. There were Saturday nights at Dan Lowry's music-hall; there were the Leopardstown and Punchestown races.; there was the Dublin Gymnasium, where an international competition in gymnastics was held, and Ireland, always well represented, was often successful; and for quieter moments there was the National Library of Ireland. More offbeat, O'Donnell went to "some hall, the name of it I have forgotten", to a concert at which Percy French, at that time a very popular entertainer in Ireland, performed, and to a dance in Fitzwilliam Square, where an old lady of ninety-six danced with an aged gentleman of ninety-nine, and a man six feet six inches tall spectacularly partnered a lady four feet high.

One of the events that he enjoyed most of all was the Centenary Celebration of the Masonic Female Orphanage of Ireland's Bazaar, which was held at Balls' Bridge – "I was so thrilled by the marvellous mediæval streets and houses, the picturesque costumes of the fair lady helpers, the gay airs of the military bands, and the enchanting atmosphere of the surroundings that I went there night after night. I had never seen anything so fascinating before, and I never have done since."

In the sports department, O'Donnell became a member of the celebrated Wanderers Football Club, on South Frederick Street, although he never played for it, and a highlight for him was seeing the Rugby International between Ireland and England.

He continued to enjoy fishing as one of his chief recreations, and would sometimes take his rod down to the canal. Owing to rumours of assaults and robberies having taken place on its banks, it had a bad reputation. O'Donnell was fishing there one evening when a woman approached him in a great state of agitation. She said that her sister was ill, and asked him if he would help carry her to the nearest house, where she could wait until the ambulance came for her. Suspecting nothing, he went with her to a spot about forty yards away, where a woman was lying on the ground. He was leaning over her and about to help to lift her, when a sixth sense warned him just in time to avoid a blow aimed at him by a burly ruffian who had emerged from behind a near-by peat stack. Dodging him and the two women who were his accomplices, he bolted, and got away, sound in limb and wallet... but he never fished in the canal again.

Dublin, was the scene in which, at the age of twenty, Elliott O'Donnell was to have his first serious encounter with a ghost. It was the summer of 1892. Searching for rooms, he was recommended to try a house in Upper Leeson Street, within an apport's throw of the Waterloo Road. It was kept by the Widow Davis (not her real name), with two "leviathan daughters", Mona and Bridget. He liked the apartment offered to him. It was spacious, well-ventilated, and, most importantly, exceedingly moderately priced. He settled in happily and uneventfully. Of ghosts he had not the shadow of a thought. His mind fully occupied with speculation as to how the extra attention he had recently bestowed on mathematics would serve him when it came to facing the next, and imminent, weekly exam. He remembered thinking, though, as he blew out the candle, that there was something about the room now that he had not noticed by daylight. To be fair, ever since childhood he had been afraid of the dark, of being alone in the dark.

It was not until he had been several nights in his new digs that the terrible thing happened. On the evening in question, Mona and Bridget were making such a racket in their room that he found it impossible to concentrate on his work, and, feeling pretty exhausted anyway, decided to have an early night. He locked his door, sat down on the edge of the bed, slipped out of his clothes, between the sheets, and extinguished the light.

"The room was not entirely dark; from between the folds of the thick plush curtains that enveloped the windows strong beams from the powerful moonlight filtered through and battled their way to the front of the bed. I was looking at them with some degree of curiosity, when I saw something move. I glanced at it in astonishment, and, to my unmitigated horror, the shape of something dark and sinister rose noiselessly from the floor and came swiftly towards me. I tried to shout, but could not make a sound. I was completely paralysed, and as I sat there, sick with fear and apprehension, the thing leapt on me, and, gripping me mercilessly by the throat, bore me backwards. I gasped and choked, and suffered the most excruciating pain. But there was no relaxation – the pressure of those bony fingers tightened and the torture went on. At last, after what seemed to me an eternity, there was a loud buzzing in my ears, my head seemed to spin round violently, and my brain to burst. I lost consciousness. On coming to, I found that my assailant had left me. I struck a light … the door was as I had left it, locked on the inside. I searched the room thoroughly; the window was bolted; there was nothing in the cupboard; nothing under the bed; nothing anywhere. I got into bed again, full of the worst anticipations, and, if sleep came to me, it was only in the briefest snatches. At dawn the room became suffused with a cold, grey glow, and the suggestion of something horribly evil standing close beside the bed and sardonically watching me impressed me so strongly that, yielding to a sudden impulse of terror, I hid my head under the bed-clothes, and remained there in that undignified position till the morning was well advanced and I was 'called'. I got up feeling downright ill, and although the sunlight metamorphosing everything now made the mere thought of a ghost simply ludicrous, I hurried out of the room as soon as possible. Nor did I venture to pass another night there.

My landlady did not demur when I asked her to transfer me to another apartment, and later, before I took my final departure from her house, she confessed to me that it was haunted. She believed that it had been used as a private home for mentally afflicted people, and that someone, either one of the patients or a nurse – she did not know which – had died under extremely painful circumstances, in the room I had first occupied. The Davises left the house soon after I did."

O'Donnell moved to new quarters in Lower Merrion Street. Some eleven or twelve years later, he made enquiries as to whether the Upper Leeson Street haunting still continued. He learned that the current occupants of the house had never admitted experiencing anything unusual, but they always kept the room in which he had undergone the sensations of strangulation carefully locked.

Looking back, O'Donnell recognised his experience with the Strangling Ghost of Dublin as not only having been the cause of his decision to adopt ghost hunting as a profession, but as having also played a primal part in the reorientation of his religious and philosophic beliefs. Having previously placidly accepted as irrefutable truth the religious dogmas hurled at him from the pulpit and drilled into him at school, he now began to rearrange his thinking. When he saw men, women, children, dogs, cats, horses, and other dumb creatures suffering terrible agonies from all manner of foul and malignant diseases; when he came upon the crippled, the maimed, the blind, and idiots and lunatics; when he read in the newspapers of man's inhumanity to man, of cruel swindles and murders and suicides; when he registered how, throughout nature, the strong prey upon the weak, with weapons for tearing, rending and sucking the flesh, inflicting the most excruciating tortures on the nerve centres; he was "given to understand that I must on no account comment upon it – to do so was impious and wicked – I must abide by the precept of my pastor and pedagogue, namely, that 'God is almighty and merciful, loving and wise.'"

But now it was different. He was no longer in the schoolroom, no longer under the immediate influence of the Church. He met people in Dublin imbued with the broader instincts of cosmopolitanism. He listened to their reasoning and arguments. Horribly shocked, scandalised at first, he came to embrace them as horribly sound and sane. Then it was, at this time of intellectual crisis, that there came the incident of the strangling. He tried to attribute it to a dream, but could not.

"I could only conclude that some spirit – the nature of my suffering and the horror it inspired leading me to suppose that it was particularly evil one – had been my aggressor. But why was it not in Hell? Had it escaped in spite of the strict supervision of the Almighty? Or, could it be possible that the orthodox Paradise and Purgatory did not exist, and that the spirits of the dead were allowed to wander about at will? I became interested – deeply so; all sorts of wild speculations floated through my mind; I resolved to enquire further. I would not be guided by any creed; I would set out on my work of investigation wholly unbiased; I would gain whatever knowledge there was to be gained of another world without the aid either of priest or occultist, medium or scientist."

Tidings came to him from friends of two houses in Dublin which had long borne the reputation of being haunted. He moved swiftly to put his investigative plan into practice.

The first house was within sight of the Queen's Service Academy. Strangely enough, O'Donnell had actually stayed there as a boy – in 1886, when he was fourteen.

He tried to get the owner's permission to spend a night in the premises. Innocent of the ways of landlords, he made what proved to be the mistake of telling him the truth about why he wanted to sleep there. The landlord, anxious no doubt to guard both the good name and leave unblemished the market value of his property, replied with a forceful rather than courteous negative. Thus collapsed O'Donnell's first attempt at ghost hunting.

O'Donnell's second venture succeeded no better. The house in question was a big, ugly, dirty grey coloured edifice at Blackrock, some five miles south east of Dublin. It turned out that the landlord had been bothered to death with requests from people to spend nights there, and he was trying to find out who it was who had been responsible for the original report that his place was haunted, with a view to bringing an action for Slander of Title. In the event, therefore, all that O'Donnell was able to do was to examine the house from outside.

More psychically substantial was the phenomenon that surfaced when O'Donnell set off to look for fairies in County Wicklow. Like many another of the fey Celtic blood, he harboured no doubts as to the existence of fairies – leprechauns, cluricauns, pookahs, and the rest. Indeed, he could recall with unimpaired, fixed-fast memory his first introduction to them.

"There was no one in the house, saving myself and our cook, who was downstairs in the basement, and I was sitting in one corner of my room reading, before getting into bed, when something caused me to look up, and I saw on the top of the wardrobe several queer shadowy forms moving noiselessly about. Thinking something must be wrong with my eyes, I closed them, but when I opened them again the figures were still there, and they now seemed to resemble human beings, except for the fact that their faces appeared to be singularly odd and grotesque. I had a dog by my side at the time, and when it suddenly began to bark, and evince signs of unrest, they all vanished. I ran downstairs at once and told the old cook of my strange experience, and, instead of laughing, as I more than half thought she would, she said: 'Shure, an' you've seen the fairies. I've seen them many times myself about the house and garden, and 'tis no harm they'll be doing you, unless you spake and interfere with them, and then they'll bring you bad luck, ochone.'

Now, for two consecutive nights, he had kept vigil at the junction of four cross roads on the southern slope of the Wicklow Hills, where, according to information laid, the fairies frolicked nightly. But he had failed to spot even as much as a single gauzy wing. Despite the onset of a bad cold, he had gone gallantly forth on his bicycle with every intention of undertaking a third night's watch. But within half a mile or so of the fairy site he began to feel very tired and decided, discretion burking valour, to stay the night at a cottage that he saw nearby. The tenants, named Mullins, were a drover and his wife. They gave him a good welcome and a pleasant little room to sleep in, facing the front and immediately over the tiny parlour. He soon dropped off, but awoke with violent palpitations of the heart to find the room bathed in silvery moonlight. As he lay there, the silence, which seemed so absolute as to produce actual pressure in his ears, was, at first very faintly, barely perceptibly, infiltrated by a sliver of sound; the muffled rhythm of footsteps in the distance, running at a well-regulated pace. Gradually, they came closer and closer, ringing out ever more sharply and clearly in the still air.

The Mullinses' dog in the back-yard began to bark and howl. O'Donnell heard Mrs. Mullins say: "The dog never barks like that unless there's a spirit about."

The steps were by now very near, each one accompanied by a peculiar, almost metallic, click.

"John," said Mrs. Mullins, "do you hear those steps? What are they? It's the first time in my life I've heard anyone running along the high road like that at this time of night. Hark! They've got to the turning. They're in the lane. They're coming here! Get up at once; go and bolt the front door. The thing's evil – evil, I'm sure, and its someone of us here it's after."

As the steps grew rapidly nearer, O'Donnell heard Mullins stumbling hastily down the stairs, bolting the door, and swinging the little wooden shutters into place. A moment later, the steps came right up to the cottage door. There was a brief pause, then a series of terrific knocks. Once the knocking had stopped, O'Donnell went over and peered out of the window. There was a good, wide view. He scanned right down the lane and for quite a long way along the high road. The landscape was brilliantly lit up, every stick and stone bathed in revelatory moonlight. There was no sign of anyone or anything that could have accounted for that thunderous knocking.

In the morning Mrs. Mullins greeted him: "You're not thinking of spending another night here, sir, are you?" He told her that he was not. "I'm glad of that, sir, because I couldn't let you stay. I suppose you heard the rapping, sir? Well, the knocking and the footsteps came after you. At least that was my impression, and my impressions are seldom wrong. I seemed to see some terrible form, half animal and half human; something indescribably grotesque and unnatural, something, my instinct tells me, was wanting to get at you."

Her description reminded O'Donnell so strongly of the awful thing that had tried to strangle him in the house in Upper Leeson Street, that he unburdened himself of the whole story. And when he had finished, she said: "You may depend on it, sir, that the ghost you've just told me about and the one that came knocking here last night are the same. I have heard that spirits will sometimes attach themselves to persons who've been staying in the house they haunt, and that they'll leave the house with them and follow them wherever they go. I only hope and trust that this one will never do you any harm, and that you'll succeed in ridding yourself of it, but my husband and I feel, asking your pardon, that we should not like to have you sleep here again."

The curtain came down on O'Donnell's Dublin idyll with the second great disappointment in his quest for a military style career; his failure to satisfy the medical examiner for the R.I.C. The doctor had been over him with a fine-toothed comb and, congratulating himself that all seemed to have gone well, he was just about to retire to the dressing-room to don his clothes, when the doctor called him back.

"I'm afraid I can't pass you," he said. "The varicose veins on your right leg might interfere too much with the work you'd be called upon to do, should you be successful in the literary examination."

O'Donnell suggested the possibility of an operation.

The doctor shook his head. "The veins would probably come back again."

It was a bitter blow, for he had already sat the literary examination, and been told that he stood a fair chance of having passed it.

So came to an end two years which, he said, were among the happiest he had ever known… "for my companions at that time were the nicest set of fellows I have ever met, and amongst them I formed many lifelong friendships. When I was not working, I usually spent my time playing football or cricket, to both of which sports I was devoted, and, when I was not thus engaged, I used to tramp across hill and dale continually exploring the country in search of adventure."

He also enjoyed fishing – although he was later to come to regard "that so-called sport as indefensibly cruel" – and used often to spend a Saturday fishing at Dalkey, or some equally pisciverously seductive locus. On one of these fishing excursions he hired a boatman to row him over to the small island known as Mugglestone Rocks, which lay a little beyond Dalkey. It was about eleven o'clock in the morning and he told the boatman before he rowed back to shore to come for him again at six o'clock that evening. As he was throwing in his first line, O'Donnell suddenly had an uneasy feeling that someone was standing by his elbow, watching him. He tried to shrug it off. But it persisted all day. The island was all bare rock and afforded no cover in which anyone could conceal themselves. The day went badly. He caught nothing and was pleasantly surprised when the boatman rowed into view at four o'clock.

He asked him why he had come two hours before the time arranged.

"Well, that's a queer question to be after asking," he said with a tinge of indignation." I came because you signalled to me to come."

O'Donnell protested: "But I did no such thing. Where were you?"

"I was rowing about some little distance off, and happening to look in the direction of the Island, I distinctly saw you wave your handkerchief at me, which meant that you wanted me to come. All I can say is that if you didn't stand up and wave a handkerchief, then the ghost did."

At the word "ghost", O'Donnell pricked up his ears.

"Ghost?"

It took a bit of persuasion, but in the end the boatman told him how some years previously the body of a drowned sailor had been washed up on the Island, and that a figure, believed to be his ghost, had, from time to time, been seen there ever since.

"Have you caught anything?" asked the boatman. And, on O'Donnell's replying in the negative, he said," I thought so! When the ghost's about, no one ever does."

On the night of his failure to pass the medical he had retired to bed early with a splitting headache. He had, by the way, left the house of the strangling ghost some time ago, and was now lodging in a psychically uninfested house in Lower Merrion Street. He had some little difficulty in getting off to sleep. He awoke to hear a clock strike two, and, practically immediately afterwards he heard a loud laugh. It seemed to come from just over his face, and so close that he felt the breath of the laughter fan his nostrils. Naturally, he associated this with the ghost that had tried to strangle him, and he was determined not to allow himself to fall into the kind of paralytic state which he had experienced in Upper Leeson Street. He sat up. The room was in pitch-blackness. Everything was breathlessly still. Heart beating like a sledge-hammer, he got out of bed and struck a light. He searched the room. The door was locked. He found no natural source to account for the noise. He moved over to the window, gently lifted the sash and peered out into the night. There was no moon but the street lamps and the stars wove a glittery net of light and by its radiance he looked down upon the empty streets. He leant far out, savouring the tranquillity until... suddenly... from immediately below there came the sound of running footsteps, ringing out loud and clear, and accompanied by an unwelcomely familiar almost metallic click.

What he was later on to describe as "perhaps the most fascinating and intensely interesting of the Irish hauntings" was that of the old churchyard of Eringle Truagh, in County Monaghan. The old church itself had been demolished around 1830, but the graveyard remained. Indeed, it was here that O'Donnell's grandmother and her cousin, David Roche, upon whom a baronetcy would later be conferred, used, as children, to come together in the hope of seeing the ghost; which, perhaps fortunately, they never did; for such an encounter was, as we shall presently discover, likely to prove fatal. The Eringle Truagh ghost materialised in two guises. To girls, it manifested as a very handsome young man. To youths, it appeared as an irresistibly beautiful young girl. Exclusive, it made itself visible only to those who were members of a family that had been resident in the neighbourhood of Truagh for many generations. Back in the days when the churchyard was in use as a burial place, the ghost would often present itself in seductive guise to the last person to linger near the newly-made grave, and would so bewitch him or her that they became instantly enamoured, and be persuaded to promise to meet their charmer again in the same spot exactly a month hence. The bargain would be sealed with a kiss – the Death Kiss of the Truagh. Instantly the kiss was given, the phantom would vanish. The unfortunate victim, realising then what folly he or she had committed, mad with fear and racked with despair, would flee to solicit salvation of the parish priest. But rescue there was none: and punctual to the very day and very hour of the tryst, the phantom's lover died.

Yet in his early teens, O'Donnell paid a fleeting visit to the old churchyard. Standing there, alone, "with the waning daylight imparting a ghostly glimmer to the mouldering tombstones," he thought he had "never seen a more eerie spot or breathed an atmosphere more strongly suggestive of the Unknown. The air was full of a concentrated sadness and despair that seemed to extend infinitely beyond life, for all time. I could feel eyes watching me and presences approaching me to peer into my face; and intuition told me that they had all, in their lifetime, fallen victims to the fatal kiss, and that what was left of their earthly bodies lay buried in the soil around me."

Thankfully, the fateful ghost did not appear to him, but he left the spot convinced that not only one, but many denizens from the Unknown had clustered round him there.

After the failure of his ambition to join the Royal Irish Constabulary, O'Donnell returned to England aboard what he described as "that tub-like old relic of mid-Victorian steamboats, the *Argo*," which had for many years sailed to and fro between Dublin and Bristol, "with as many passengers and cattle as could be crammed, with any degree of safety, into her dingy and clumsy-looking hulk." He had good reason to remember that passage home, for two of his fellow-students from the Queen's Service Academy were on board with him, and they spent practically the whole time on deck, telling ghost stories and earnestly discussing the possibility of a future life. They ended up making a solemn compact that the one of them who was the first to die would do everything in his power to give the two survivors some kind of demonstration of his continuing existence in the spirit world.

"Both my friends died within a few years of that date, and within three weeks of each other. The one who had a commission in a cavalry regiment was killed at the Battle of Omdurman, and the other, who, having followed in the footsteps of his distinguished father, had become a novelist of great promise, was kicked to death by a horse."

He arrived back in Clifton crestfallen and thoroughly dispirited. This was his second serious setback, hard on the heels of the failure of his previous attempt to follow in the tracks of his older brother, Henry, and pursue a military career at Sandhurst. Face to face now with the grim and urgent necessity of having to find a way of earning a living, he decided before tackling that problem to allow himself a brief respite.

Accordingly, he spent some weeks in the west of England, then journeyed north to Scotland, where he had been invited to stay with an old Clifton College friend of his whose father owned an estate near Inveraray, but on arriving at Glasgow he got wind of such a promising case of haunting in that city, that, like Oscar Wilde, able to resist everything except temptation, he yielded and postponed his journey west.

The haunted house was in Duke Street. It had been rented by James McKaye, a solicitor by profession. He had readily agreed to O'Donnell's investigating the place. Battling his way there one night through a veritable tornado of torrential rain and screaming wind, when he arrived at the house, drenched to the skin, frozen to the marrow from plunging ankle-deep in icy cold puddles, O'Donnell found McKaye standing on the doorstep, scarlet-faced and swearing furiously. He could not find the key. Eventually he did, and they were soon inside shaking the water off their clothes.

Those were the days before pocket torches, and lighting their way as best they could with flickering candles, off they went searching the premises to make sure that there was no one hiding in there. The house was four storeys high and had a basement. None of its rooms was very large, and their wall-papers were uniformly hideous. McKaye asked O'Donnell if he could detect anything peculiar in the atmosphere. He said that he could not; only the smell of extreme mustiness. The tour of the house uneventfully completed, they began their vigil sitting on the flight of stairs leading from the hall to the first-floor landing. O'Donnell suggested that they should extinguish their candles. McKaye refused point-blank. Just then there came a loud rat-tat at the front-door. It made them both jump.

"That's a policeman," said McKaye. "He must have seen our light."

It was. He had.

Suspicious at first, the policeman, a burly figure in helmet and cape, flashing his dripping bull's-eye in their faces, underwent an instant change of mien when he heard McKaye's name, and recognised him as an officer of the court. He relaxed and laughed loud and long at the mention of ghosts.

"Well, gentlemen," he remarked, waving his bull's-eye in the direction of the stairs, "you won't never be alarmed by an apparition so long as you have the dog with you. I bet he'd scare away any number of ghosts, and burglars, too. If I may be so bold as to ask, what breed do you call him?"

O'Donnell and McKaye both looked towards the stairs. There, half-way up, its face turned towards them, they saw the black shadowy outline of a big shaggy creature, looking not so much like a dog as a bear. It stood there stock-still for a matter of moments, then, retreating backwards, seemed to disappear into the wall.

Turning on his heel, the policeman was walking off.

"Wait a minute, constable," said McKaye, closing the door with a bang, "and we'll come with you."

"What about the dog?" said the policeman. "It ain't come out."

"And it never will," said McKaye. "You've seen the ghost, constable, or at least one of them."

From Glasgow O'Donnell carried on up north to Inveraray, where he thoroughly enjoyed himself, fishing and shooting.

His next port of call was Perth, and it was there that, quite by chance, he made the acquaintance of a Mr. and Mrs. Rowlandson, who told him that they were just about to leave a badly haunted house on the outskirts of the town. Its name was "Bocarthe", and it was a completely new property, only having been built within the last twelve months. They were its owners and its first occupants. There had, they told O'Donnell, been no murders, suicides, or any other tragedies that might have accounted for the haunting, and the Rowlandsons' neighbours declared that they must have brought the ghost with them. O'Donnell said that he would very much like to investigate, and the Rowlandsons were quite happy that he should do so.

He paid his first visit to "Bocarthe" at noon on the day after the Rowlandsons had left for Edinburgh, where they intended to live. His first impressions of the place were good – "When I entered the house, I thought I had seldom seen such a cheerful one. The rooms were light and lofty, and about them all there was an air of geniality, that hitherto, at all events, I had never dreamed of associating with ghosts."

Before their departure, the Rowlandsons had given O'Donnell an introduction to a young friend of theirs, Dr. Swinton, and he had been prevailed upon to accompany O'Donnell to "Bocarthe" for an all-night vigil. They had sat up until long after dawn, but neither saw nor heard anything that they were unable to account for by other than natural causes. Two further nights the pair kept watch, with no psychic happenings to report.

O'Donnell wrote to Mr. Rowlandson, returning the house keys to him and telling him of the negative result of the investigation.

On November 8th, 1893, Robert Rowlandson wrote from Edinburgh thanking him for the keys, and adding: "No wonder you did not see our ghost! It is here, and we are having just the same experiences in this house as we had in 'Bocarthe'." The note ended: "If you would care to stay a few nights with us, on the chance of seeing the ghost, we shall be delighted to put you up."

O'Donnell did not hesitate. He accepted the invitation.

When he arrived, he found the entire household in a state of panic. The ghost had appeared to them all the previous night. Tactful questioning elicited from the Rowlandsons the following story. Before they were married, Mrs. Rowlandson had known a man named Ernest Dekon, who was a very keen spiritualist. She had met him at a ball, and from that time until his death he had persecuted her with his unwanted attentions. He had deeply resented her marriage, and not long afterwards he had committed suicide... shot himself... and left a note pinned to the toilet-cover of his dressing-table, in which he wrote that his death was entirely due to the heartless conduct of Maud Rowlandson.

It was, O'Donnell thought, more than likely that it was the spirit of Ernest Dekon that was troubling them. Its activities were disconcerting. Said Maud Rowlandson: "The phenomena happen at all times and when we least expect it. For example, if I am going upstairs alone, it either springs out at me or peers down at me from over the banisters or, again it rouses us in the middle of the night by rocking our bed."

After dinner, the Rowlandsons, together with O'Donnell and their two other house guests, a Colonel and Mrs. Rushworth, retired to the drawing-room and planned their campaign for that night. Then, they all took their candlesticks and were following Mrs. Rowlandson upstairs, when, just as they had mounted the first flight, Mrs. Rowlandson suddenly halted, looked back at them over her shoulder, and said, "Hush! Do you hear anything?" They did. There was a thump. Then another. They seemed to come from a room just at the top of the stairs. There followed a very curious sound, as of something bounding backwards and forwards over bare boards with its feet tied together. At a signal from Mr. Rowlandson, they all immediately blew out their candles. A church clock struck twelve. The last reverberations of the final stroke had barely died away when a faint luminous glow dissipated the darkness ahead. As O'Donnell watched, it speedily intensified and shaped itself into a cylindrical column six or seven feet in height, and this developed – to his eyes, though not, it transpired, for any of the others – into a shockingly grotesque form. The head, ill-defined on the crown and at the sides, appeared to be abnormally high and long, and to be covered with a tangled mass of coarse, tow-coloured hair. The nose seemed hooked, the mouth cruel, the eyes leering. The body was grey and nude, very like the trunk of a silver birch, the arms long and knotted, the hands huge, the fingers red and club-shaped – exactly as Maud Rowlandson had described the hands of Ernest Dekon. That this hideous, baleful apparition was the symbolical representation of all carnal lusts, of Ernest Dekon, soulless, O'Donnell entertained no shadow of doubt. The figure seemed to move forward. Someone shrieked. Mr. Rowlandson struck a light, and simultaneously the apparition vanished. The most curious thing was that no two of the witnesses had perceived the ghost in the same form; and Mr. Rowlandson and Mrs. Rushworth had not seen it at all. Mrs. Rowlandson saw no face, only the hands, but she was sure that they were the hands of Ernest Dekon. She was very upset.

"Can't any of you think of a plan to get rid of him?" she asked.

Colonel Rushworth was the only one to offer advice. "Cremation is the one thing that I can think of," he said. "That is the means employed, I believe, by the hill tribes in Northern India. When a spirit they can identify begins to haunt a place, they dig up the body and burn it, and they say that as soon as the last bone is consumed the haunting ceases. Where did Ernest Dekon die?"

"In Africa."

"That's capital! If we can find the cemetery there ought to be no difficulty in getting at the body. The officials are, as a rule, open to bribery."

O'Donnell left Edinburgh the next day. Some months later, he heard from the Rowlandsons. The hauntings had ceased. They were moving back to "Bocarthe". From this he gathered that the attempt to exhume and cremate Ernest Dekon's body had succeeded.

A photograph claimed to depict a phantom monk haunting an old house near Bristol, from O'Donnell's Haunted Britain (1956)

A shaggy dog ghost makes an appearance in Glasgow, from O'Donnell's Twenty Years Experiences as a Ghost Hunter (1916).

4

New World Ghosts

Barely time for a breath-taking; at exactly the right psychological moment there plumped down on the Clifton doormat another invitation to Scotland. This time it was for a week's stay with a friend in Argyll.

En route, O'Donnell took a boat trip to the Isle of Arran. At Brodick, he encountered a craggy old Scot who insistently regaled him with the tale of the great Arran sensation of 1889, the murder on the island of a young English tourist, Edwin Rose.[1]

The body was found at a spot called Coire-na-fuhren, the gully of fire, on Goatfell, high above Glen Sannox, tucked in beneath a huge granite boulder, topping a sort of cairn, built up of 42 minor stones, and lined like a bird's nest with pieces of turf and heather. Another English tourist, 25-year-old John Watson Laurie, was ultimately found guilty of having bludgeoned Rose to death. Sentenced to hang, he was later reprieved and sent to penal servitude for life. What particularly interested O'Donnell was the fact that when, at Laurie's trial, his advocate, the Dean of Faculty, asked Police Sergeant Munro what had become of Rose's boots, which it was stated had not been on his feet when his otherwise fully clothed body was in the mortuary, the sergeant said that he believed that they had been buried on Arran beach below high-water mark. It was later admitted that this had been done in order to prevent Rose's ghost from haunting Glen Sannox.

Returned from his pleasant wanderings north of the border, O'Donnell was no longer able to postpone the moment of truth; the grim truth that

---

1 See: *Trial of John Watson Laurie*. William Roughead. Notable British Trials Series, William Hodge, Edinburgh, 1932.

the time was finally upon him when he must make a decision as to what he was to do with the remainder of his life. After much heart searching, he finally decided, as he was later to confess, rather on the spur of the moment, to turn his face to the New World and try his hand at ranching in Oregon, in the far west of America.

He set off from Liverpool to New York aboard the White Star liner *Majestic*, which was one of the largest, best equipped, and fastest vessels ploughing the Atlantic at that time. At 582 feet long and 10,000 tons, it seems pretty insignificant compared with the *Queen Elizabeth* and other later mighty twentieth-century liners. Price comparisons are also somewhat startling. In those days, saloon rates in the period from November 1st to July 15th, ranged between £12, £15, £18, £20, and £25 per berth; and all saloon passengers had equal privileges, mingling and dining together. The average passage between Liverpool and New York was just under six days.

O'Donnell thoroughly enjoyed the voyage.

> That particular journey was known as the millionaire voyage, on account of the number of reputed American millionaires on board. They all dined with their fellow saloon passengers. The food was excellent. Among the distinguished passengers were B.M. Croker, "Boss" Croker of Tammany fame, Lord and Lady Randolph Churchill, Mr. Julius Price, the black-and-white artist, famous for his illustrations in either the *Illustrated London News* or the *Weekly Graphic*, who was on a round the world trip for one of the papers, and the editor of one of the big New York papers.
>
> It was my custom in those days not to wear a hat, except, of course, in the very extremes of weather, and I was parading the deck one morning, bareheaded as usual, when Lord Randolph Churchill stopped me and very anxiously enquired if it was my intention to walk about hatless in New York. "At this time of year," he said, "it's sometimes terribly hot in New York, and if you land there with no hat, you run a very great risk of sunstroke." "Then I'll wear one," I replied, "for I've no desire to die just yet."
>
> I told him that I had often seen Frank Townsend, the father of the more illustrious Charles L. Townsend, play cricket on the Close at Clifton without a hat in the most scorching sun heat, and added that I supposed he felt no ill effect from the sun on account of his hair, which was very thick and curly. "What age man is he?" Lord Randolph asked. I told him I thought about forty, whereupon he said: "He evidently thinks going without a hat will preserve his hair, but it won't. There's no greater

fallacy, I've known scores of men who've done the same thing and eventually become absolutely bald. Baldness is in the blood, you inherit it just the same as you inherit gout and dipsomania, and nothing you take or do will prevent it. I asked Lord Randolph if he believed in ghosts, but before he could reply, someone (his secretary, I think) interrupted us, and I never had another opportunity of speaking to him. From the expression that came on his face, however, at my somewhat naïve question, I am inclined to think he was an out and out sceptic, but I may, of course have been mistaken.

During the trip there was a concert on board in aid of the Seamen's Orphanage, the American Seamen's Friend Society, and the Society for the Relief of the Destitute Children of Seamen. Among those who kindly assisted in the programme were Lady Randolph Churchill, who, in Part I and Part II, played a piano solo: and Mr. Horsley, who sang "Tommy Atkins", the song Hayden Coffin had made so popular in London and elsewhere, and "Di, Di, Di," a topical air.

Two incidents occurred during the voyage. One was an iceberg, which we sighted in the distance, and the other an escape from colliding with a small sailing ship, so narrow that special prayers were said by the Captain in gratitude for our salvation. The weather was very hot when we were near the American coast and, seeing me walking about the deck without a hat, Lord Randolph Churchill came up to me and, looking very concerned, warned me against going without a hat in New York. I thought it wonderfully kind of him.

Just before we landed, the editor of the New York paper likewise spoke to me. "You made a mistake in keeping so much aloof, young fellow," he said, "because several of us wanted to be friendly to you, but we were afraid you might resent it." It was just my bad luck. Had I not been so shy and diffident, I might have got to know people on board whose friendship might have proved beneficial and saved me from the further misfortunes that were looming ahead of me.

On his arrival in New York, O'Donnell was met by one of Gaze's agents, and directed to the Central Hotel on Broadway. It was not until he had been in New York some days before he met a man at the hotel who told him that he knew of a curious case of haunting in an office in Franklin Square. The ghost was described to him as a "regular 'tricky'" one. It hid pens and ink and sundry other articles, which would subsequently turn up in the most unexpected, unlikely and most inconvenient places. Water was constantly being thrown at people. Terrific crashes, as if a cartload of crockery had been thrown down from a considerable height, had on more than one occasion caused great alarm. Nothing, however, had ever been seen.

Having given his faithful promise that he would not divulge the precise location of the office, whose owner did not wish the affair to get into the newspapers, O'Donnell was escorted round there at nine o'clock one evening. With the exception of a porter, who was on duty at the main entrance to the building, they saw no one on the premises, and had the allegedly haunted office entirely to themselves. For an hour or so nothing happened, and O'Donnell was beginning to think that nothing was going to happen, when he heard a sound like the rush of water, and his companion leapt to his feet, spluttering and shaking his hair and coat collar, his head and coat literally soaked. They looked everywhere, but could see absolutely nothing that could account for the apparent phenomenon.

"That's the first time it's ever happened to me," said O'Donnell's companion, who did look very pale and scared, "and I'm not anxious to have another dose. Come along.", and, impervious to all O'Donnell's earnest entreaties to stay to see if anything else would happen, he doggedly refused to do so.

A couple of evenings after that adventure, O'Donnell crossed to Hoboken in search of an old Dublin friend who had written to him several times from a hotel there. With some difficulty he found the place, but his friend had departed thence some time before and left no forwarding address. It was not, however, a wasted excursion, for he met two men, like himself strangers to New York, and they invited him to go for a stroll with them. The evening proved most entertaining. After wandering through miles of streets and alleys, the trio found themselves outside a shoddy-looking music-hall. They paid a few cents and entered a big room full of small tables, seated at which was a cosmopolitan crowd of Germans, Poles, Italians, and Jews, some poorly, and others flashily, dressed. They were all orderly and out to enjoy anything put before them.

Let O'Donnell tell in his own words what he then experienced:

> I turned my attention to the stage just as an oddly assorted trio, consisting of a tall, lean man in short pantaloons and a Piedmontese, very short woman in a flaring red dress, and a pretty fair-haired girl of about twelve in a flimsy green costume came on to it. The woman made some remark in Italian and commenced beating a big drum, the tall man joined in on a long reed pipe, while the little girl, holding a tambourine in one hand and banging on it with the other, began to dance.
>
> The instant this occurred, I suddenly felt not merely an impression

but a conviction that I had witnessed the whole scene, in every detail, on some former occasion. I had seen the lean piper, the woman in red, the fluffy-haired little creature skipping about so nimbly with the tambourine, the throng of swarthy-faced spectators all around us, some leaning back in their seats, others leaning forward, their elbows on the tables and their chins in their hands; and over and above all, the great barn-like room itself, with its flickering, flaring gas-jets.

Not a single item in the scene was strange to me, and I was certain, positively certain, that I had been present at it and borne my part in it before. I also knew that it was the little speech made by the fat woman, combined with her loud and abrupt beating on her gaudily coloured drum, that had given me the clue and brought it all back to me.

O'Donnell's arrival in New York had coincided with a big railway strike which was affecting the whole country, and he was warned by the railway officials that there was small chance of his reaching his destination till it was over, that they would not guarantee that he would get even as far as Philadelphia, that if he decided to travel it would be at his own risk, and they would not be responsible for his baggage or his safety. But, fearing that his money would not eke out if he delayed, after remaining in New York for two days he decided to push on regardless, boarded a train at the B. & O. depôt, and headed West.

The train had reached Crown Point, about twenty miles from Chicago when the conductor announced that the passengers would all have to get out as the strikers had pulled up the rails, and the train could not go on. Two men of whom he did not at all like the look persuaded him to go shares with them in the hiring of a horse-drawn vehicle to the nearest town, Riverdale, from which there was an electric tram service to Chicago. On the way they kept stopping for drinks, and when they reached the town suggested he should stand them to a meal. The idea did not at all appeal to him, so he waited until they were seated at a table in a restaurant, then, on a pretext of going off to order food, managed to slip out and jump on a tram.

When he reached Chicago he found the city under martial law, blue-uniformed soldiers patrolling everywhere. With the exception of the small grip which he was holding, all his luggage was in the deserted tram, and when he felt in his pocket for his purse for the money to pay for a meal, to his intense dismay he found that it had gone. He had been robbed. Counting the loose coins in his pocket, he was horrified to discover that he had only two dollars left, and he was still wandering miserably around the streets at midnight, with nowhere to sleep. Providential salvation came in the shape of a man whom he encountered outside the New York and Chicago railway station. The man, observing the state he was obviously in, asked him what was the trouble, and, on learning his plight, identified himself as a passenger agent, led him to the Oxford Hotel, where he asked the landlord to put him up, and made himself answerable for O'Donnell's bill.

In the morning, O'Donnell cabled to England for money. Back came an answer from Elizabeth, telling him to call at a certain bank in Chicago, where he would find sufficient funds awaiting him to carry on his journey. There, he was asked to prove his identity before they would hand over any cash to him. This was awkward, a stumper in fact, for he had no means of establishing who he was. Once again, providence came to his rescue. When he told the cashier and manager that he came from Bristol, the former questioned him closely regarding the buildings and layout of Bristol. It transpired that he was a Bristolian, and quite prepared now to trust O'Donnell with the money. Rejoicing, a fistful of dollars in his pocket, he was able to pay, and proceed on, his way. Incidentally, during his enforced stay in the strike-bound city, he had served for a time as an auxiliary Chicago policeman.

One last curious Chicagoan happening. In his compartment on the train in which he travelled from New York he had had as a travelling companion a man of unmistakably foreign appearance – swarthy-skinned, dark, dreamy eyes, strong alien accent. They had fallen into conversation, and he identified himself as Sicilian. His name he gave as Count de Paoli. He had, he said, had to leave his country because his father had fallen foul of the Mafia, and been fatally stabbed one evening under the windows of his own house. The Society's vengeance did not end with the death of his father, it extended to the whole family. His mother had been shot dead, and, a few years later, his only brother was murdered, his body, stabbed in a dozen places, found floating in the harbour at Palermo. He had had no choice but to leave Sicily, as his life was no longer safe there. But no matter where he went he kept receiving threatening letters. The last had been delivered to him in New Orleans. It warned that he would be killed unless he left the United States in the next six months.

Then he confided to O'Donnell a dream that he had dreamt one night when he was staying in Paris. In it, he met a very beautiful woman in a park in Chicago, and she told him to meet her there again at a certain time. He had said that he would, and he had sealed the promise with a kiss. She had been so lovely and absolutely real that he simply could not believe that it was only a dream, and he was now on his way to Chicago to keep the appointment. O'Donnell was enchanted by his romantic story. He took a real liking to the Count and was truly sorry when he had to bid him goodbye, being unable to afford to accompany him to the expensive hotel at which he had chosen to stay.

Some time later, O'Donnell was standing in front of the mirror in his hotel bedroom, shaving, when he suddenly saw reflected in it the face of the Count de Paoli. He was peering over his left shoulder. He looked ghastly white and ill, and there was an expression of the deepest sorrow in his big, dark eyes.

A day or two after, he heard that the body of the Count had been found in Arlington Park, near Chicago, and that the police were on the trail of a man and woman, supposedly Italians, who had been seen with the Count in the park. Count de Paoli had kept his tryst. It was with Death. The Mafia had got their victim.

On the train taking him from Chicago to Omaha, O'Donnell got talking with one of the black conductors on, of course, the subject of ghosts.

"If you promise you not say a word about it to anyone, I tell you something about dis train dat will interest you," said the conductor.

O'Donnell duly promised.

"Very well, den. One of de berths is haunted. I have seen a ghost in it myself, and it gave me some fright, sure. It happened like dis. I was walking through de sleeping quarters one afternoon, looking everywhere for something I'd lost, when I suddenly see a head lying on de pillow of one of de berths, and when I look closer still I see de face too. It was de face of a man with very white cheeks, a black beard, and red mark just over one of his eyebrows. I sez to him: 'You've come to bed too early, sah; you must get up. It's against de regulations'. He made no reply, and on my repeating de remark with de same result, I put out my hand to shake him. To my horror and surprise I touched nothing, only de air; der was no one der. Den I got in a panic and ran, ran right out of de compartment into another. Two hours later a man came on board de train for de first time and I gave a mighty start. He was the living image of the face I'd seen in de berth. De same white cheeks, de same black beard, de same red scar. It was all exact. Well, dat evening dis stranger, he jumped out of de train, in a fit of madness it was reckoned, and so hurt himself dat he died. Now what was dat I saw? Sure it was his ghost, sah, wasn't it?"

"It certainly seems as if it was," agreed O'Donnell, "though why it should appear to you I don't know."

The conductor invited him along to see the berth where it had happened. He was about to say something, when his jaw dropped and his eyes looked as though they would bulge out on to his cheeks. "Do you see dat, sah? Dat black shadow on de pillow. It's in de shape of a coffin. Someone on dis train is going to die soon; I know dey are."

Several hours later, while they were stopping at a depôt, the conductor came to O'Donnell in a great state of excitement. "Der, didn't I tell you, sah," he said, "someone on de train was going to die? It was one of de passengers, an old gentleman from Baltimore, and he's just passed away in a fit. Dat shadow spoke de truth; I knew it did."

During his brief sojourn in Omaha, O'Donnell had another weird experience. It so happened that he arrived in that city on June 22nd, Midsummer Eve, one of the nights of the year when spirits, including those of the dead, are said to be in very close touch with the earth, and tradition has it that the performance of certain ceremonies and the recitation of certain words at about midnight will induce the spirits to reveal themselves.

Finding several people at the hotel where he put up interested in the supernatural, he proposed that they should experiment that night with a few old-world spells. They began at about half-past ten with the lead-boiling ritual. Some lead is melted in an iron spoon, then sprinkled over the surface of a tub of warm water. Any message from the other side is conveyed by the shape any of the lead assumes. O'Donnell reports that one of the party, a girl named Winnie Jones, was in equal measure surprised and alarmed when she came to examine her bits of lead lying at the bottom of the tub to discover one of them exactly resembling a death's head.

Next came the performance of the hempseed spell. You take as much hempseed as you can hold in one hand, and in the other hand an ordinary garden hoe. You go out of doors, preferably alone, and walk steadily ahead, scattering the hempseed before you, and at the same time covering it over with the hoe, and repeating the words:

Hempseed I sow, yes, hempseed I hoe.
Oh, thou who'st to wed me come after me and mow.

Then, if you look back over your left shoulder, you will see your future spouse. If you are not to marry, you will see no one. If you are to die within the coming twelve months, what you will behold will be something extremely unpleasant.

The group moved towards the passage leading to the hotel garden. It was nearing midnight when Winnie Jones' turn to go out came. She had hardly been gone a minute when the party heard a terrified scream. Rushing out, they found her lying on the garden path in a dead faint. Recovered, she told them that, looking over her shoulder she had seen a tall hooded figure, all in black, with a skeleton face, coming after her. O'Donnell never could glean any news of whether or not the ill omen had proved tragic for Winnie. It proved impossible to trace her after he left Omaha.

Stand alone in the dark front of a mirror combing your hair and at the same time eating an apple, and, on St. John's Eve – that is another name for Midsummer's Eve – the powers will reveal what Fate has in store for you. O'Donnell's turn came. He had scarcely bitten into his apple when the mirror went black and in it appeared the most vivid picture of a hand holding a black-edged envelope. This did prove prophetic, for he learned shortly afterwards that a great friend of his in Dublin had died.

The next of the party to stand in front of the mirror was a grey-haired veteran from St. Louis. His mirror image was of what looked like a lot of earth falling. "I reckon something unpleasant will happen to me before long," he said. He reckoned right. The very next week O'Donnell received a letter telling him that he had dropped dead with a heart attack in a friend's house in Omaha.

Next port of call, still heading west, was Denver. Travelling by train he found the heat overpowering, and by the time he reached Denver was feeling very ill. A kindly railway official took him to the Columbia Hotel. The second day of his stay, feeling no better, he went to a drug store where, hearing his symptoms, the proprietor informed him that he was suffering from a mild form of Asiatic cholera. He purchased some of the recommended appropriate medication, and in due course recovered.

A psychic adventure awaited him. The Reverend Dean Hart, of St. John's Cathedral, a well-known clergyman of that city, informed him that an old Bristolian named Robinson lived in the town. O'Donnell made it his business to pay him a visit, and it was from him that he learned of how one day on the road to Denver City, near the Zoological Gardens, a tramp had been found dead, and that ever since his headless ghost had been seen hovering about the spot where he had met his end.

Determined to find out what he could for himself, at eleven o'clock one night O'Donnell set out on foot for the unhallowed spot. It took him about an hour's walking before he recognised the place, close beside a pile of stones and out of sight of any human habitation. Perched atop a kind of cairn, he sat and sat and sat, patience on a monument, St. Simon Stylites on his pillar, waiting. Nothing happened. Hour after hour, breathing in the pure air from the distant desert and mountains, he remained, momentarily expectant.

At last he gave up, started for home. And that was when it did happen. He had not gone more than a dozen or so yards when he heard a loud cough. It came from just behind him. There was no one there. He let his eye rake the landscape. The night was lovely. Away on the horizon, snow-capped mountains, on either side flat, open land. A cloudless sky; set in its centre a great white moon, sprinkled around with a scintillating brilliance of a myriad stars. The long vista of roadway, gleaming whitely under the moonbeams. Not a living soul to be seen.

Walking on, he became conscious of the sound of his own footsteps breaking the stillness, and then, chillingly, of other footsteps, pattering in measured rhythm after him. Presently, their sound began to vary. They would slacken. They would come almost to a dead stop. They would quicken to a run. Then subside into an erratic walk. And every time he glanced back... nothing. A slow tide of fear began to rise within him. He made a conscious pretence of being braver than he really was. He halted, turned about, and, addressing the empty air, the whitest of moon-kissed roadways, flecked here and there with the blackest flickering shadows of trees and shrubs, behind him, in as composed a voice as he could summon up, called out sternly: "Be off, whoever you are; you won't scare me." But *it*, whoever or whatever it was, *did* scare him, and yielding to a submerging wave of panic, he took to his heels – and, to his unmitigated horror, the mysterious pursuivant footsteps ran too. After about half-a-mile the sound of the running steps suddenly ceased, and, to his immense relief, O'Donnell realised that the thing had left him.

When he arrived back at the hotel, he told the desk clerk all about his experience.

"That's what generally happens," said the clerk. "A cough first and then footsteps, just as you describe, though usually the headless figure is seen, too. Endless attempts have been made to lay the ghost, but they have ended always in failure."

The interrupted journey was resumed. Somewhere between Omaha and Sacramento, the train in which he was travelling to Sacramento was fired on by strikers. Several of the soldiers in it were wounded, but O'Donnell escaped unscathed. He spent the night at a quaint-looking inn, The Windsor, at Ogden, and was the only civilian in the train from Ogden to Sacramento. He was enormously thrilled when a ferry-boat carried him across from Oakland to San Francisco and he viewed for the first time that fascinating city.

As a result of all the various stoppages and manifold other difficulties which had beset his way, O'Donnell was once more running short of money. Awaiting the arrival of a cheque from home, he put up at the inexpensive International Hotel in Kearney Street.

> While there I was greatly interested in an argument between two men that took place in the lounge one afternoon about the Wandering Jew. One man declared his belief in such an individual. The other man ridiculed the idea. They were getting very heated when the landlord of the hotel appeared, and they appealed to him.
>
> "Well, all I can say, gentlemen," he remarked, "is that I have a reason for thinking such an individual actually exists. Thirty years ago I was living with my parents in New York, where they kept a small hotel. One day a man, whose features were unmistakably Jewish, came to the hotel and requested a bed for the night. On seeing my father, who eyed him very curiously, he exclaimed: "Don't you recognise me, sir? I came here exactly forty years ago. I'm Jacob Levi."
>
> "I thought I had seen you somewhere before," my father said, "but you don't look a day older than you did forty years ago. How old are you?"
>
> "You wouldn't believe me if I told you," Levi replied. "I well remember seeing your father when he was living in Boston, and had just recovered from being thrown from his horse." "Impossible!" my father cried. "Absurd! Why, that happened when my father was about twenty. Several years before I was born. He has been dead thirty years, and was eighty when he died. That would make you more, much more, than a hundred years old."
>
> "'So I am'," Levi sighed. And he told my father the most extraordinary tale; how he could distinctly recollect events that happened centuries ago. Only last week Jacob Levi came here, purposely to see me. He had

been told that I had moved from New York to San Francisco. He did not look a day older than he did when I last saw him, and that was twenty-five years ago. His hair was still black, with not a vestige of grey or white. He only stayed a short time, and said he was on his way to China. As he was leaving, he looked at me and said 'There will be a terrible disaster in this city within the next ten years.'² Can you wonder, gentlemen, after what I have told you that there is some justification for my belief in the famous Wandering Jew?"

The two arguers, who had listened with great interest to all he said, concurred.

San Francisco fascinated him.

I had expected to see everywhere the powerful evidences of Western modernity so characteristic of New Eastern towns. I was agreeably surprised. The business part of the city had a distinct look of age. It was paved with cobblestones, and had the greyness and gloom of the kind that envelopes ancient European cities. As I stood in the lower part of Market Street, and gazed at the dark begrimed stores and offices all around me, I might easily have imagined myself in some old English coastal town or continental city. The antiquity of the West with all the atmosphere of the East combined to produce a beguiling air of mysticism. It was the hidden and mysterious something in it that was so indescribably thrilling and alluring. I felt it at each step I took, impregnating the very air I breathed. At the same time, I felt more lonely than I had done either in Denver, New York, or even Chicago.

O'Donnell was thoroughly astonished by some of the things that he discovered about the American ways of life. For instance, one day when he was in a swimming-bath in San Francisco, he was surprised by a slap on the back, and, on looking round, saw standing there beside him an exceptionally pretty girl. He did not know her from Adam. She was a superb swimmer and diver, and had won many prizes. She was just of a friendly disposition. But it was her mere presence that really shook him: he had no idea that 'over there', there was mixed bathing in swimming-baths. Another shock was, on going to a barber's one morning, to find that it was a girl who cut his hair and shaved him.

At last, journey's end. The ranch he reached was small, no more than 400 acres, and its main produce was fruit, hogs, and some cattle. It faced

2   The Great Fire in San Francisco, due to an earthquake, occurred twelve years after O'Donnell's stay in that place.

a desert. To its rear was a forest, extending for many miles. For most of the time that he was there, there were only two hands, himself and Alfred Logan. Occasionally there was a third, a hired hand, Bill Kranz.[3]

He found the real Far West – Oregon and North California – very different from the Far West of film and story. The ranches were small. Few, if any, could boast more than 700 or 800 acres. The houses were plain modern structures; nothing picturesque about them. On quite a number of them there were no women, just two or three men, who did all the household chores as well as the outdoor work.

O'Donnell did a variety of jobs. Sometimes he would take fruit for sale. Sometimes he would be pitching hay. Other times he would be despatched on various missions, riding out on horseback. He was not a good rider. He had had very little practice in England. Fortunately, he was never faced with a frisky or bad-tempered horse at the ranch. His worst moments were having to dash after cattle on a mountainside. That could involve tearing through brushwood and heading down an almost sheer precipice, fearing the slip or stumble that could mean being hurled to a cruel death in the valley far, far below. Mercifully, the ranch horses did not slip or stumble, they were very sure-footed. They were also knowing and artful, and extremely resourceful in the avoidance of devices designed to get them to do what they did not want to do.

Often he would be the cook. He started off badly. At his first attempt he kept the potatoes hard on the boil for two hours, and ended up with a floury, watery mess. But he soon learnt, and it was not a very onerous job as the menus were somewhat limited. For breakfast, at 6 a.m., sometimes the local dish known as "mush", consisting of flour, bacon fat, and milk. Other times, eggs, bacon, bread and tea. For dinner, at about noon, either dried beef or bacon, with potatoes, and, beans or maize, and tea. For supper, at any time between six and seven-thirty, perhaps, eggs with beans or maize, and tinned fruit or apple pastry and jam. To drink, tea with every meal. The bread, also partaken of at every meal, came in man-sized chunks, and had been made by one or other of the hands. Sometimes they could break it with their teeth, other times it threatened to break their teeth.

The hands did not look at all like the cowboys of the cinema. They wore flannel shirts and blue canvas overalls. None of them wore the wide-brimmed hat or the elaborate sheep-skin trousers of the film cowboy.

---

[3] Not their real names.

Neither did they carry an array of revolvers and bowie knives.

The job which O'Donnell disliked most was feeding the hogs. In fact, he disliked the hogs. He could never bring himself to feel friendly towards them after he had witnessed them gobbling up a dead cow. "No tiger could have been more voracious than those ugly black hogs. They ate every particle with the greatest relish, burying their bloody jaws in the reeking entrails and leaving nothing of the cow save the bare bones."

His anti-hog prejudice was fanned by a, possibly apocryphal, story, which he chose to believe, of a woman who had a husband much older than she was, and, anxious to rid herself of him in order to marry someone else, she got him drunk, stripped him to the buff, and put his naked body in the hogs' pen, partly covered with maize. The hogs, living up to her hope and anticipation, duly ingested and digested maize and mate. Widely known for his fondness for drink, her tale that hubby, when drunk, had lain down in the hogs' pen, went undoubted and unquestioned. She had accomplished the perfect crime. When, however, flushed with success, she tried it a second time suspicion fell like a blanket upon her, but, shrewdly suspecting the suspicion, the wily widow absconded in time. She was never seen again.

It was riding alone in the forest one night that O'Donnell had a ghostly experience. His horse came to an abrupt full stop. Refused to move forward. They were facing a small clearing. Standing at its centre, moonlight falling on its whitened trunk, was a solitary tree. The effect was eerie, but over and above that, O'Donnell had the uncomfortable feeling that there was something else in the air, something much more uncanny than the mere weirdness of the moonbeams. Mentioning the incident and describing the location of the tree some days later to an old ranchman, he learned that it was known in the neighbourhood as the Suicide Tree. A number of people had been found either hanging from its branches or lying dead on the ground close beside it. It was a well known fact that no horse or dog would ever go near it after dark.

Bears, wolves, and pumas all made their homes in the forest, and, bearing this in mind, the majority of men carried a Winchester repeater, but, the occasional coyote apart, O'Donnell never came across any of them. He did see, and sometimes killed, rattlesnakes, and once sat down on what he thought was a log, and it turned out to be a large, but fortunately non-aggressive, snake.

Hearing that there were trout to be had in the Rogue River, O'Donnell set off in some excitement for a morning's fishing. The expedition was far from being an unqualified success. The bank of the river was swarming with rattlesnakes, and he fished hour after hour without as much as a nibble. At times, too, he had an unpleasant feeling that eyes, whether human or not he was unsure, were watching him covertly. When it began to get dusk, he packed up his tackle and started off homewards – and lost his way.

Wandering round, searching in vain for the track along which he had come to the river, he came to a log cab and rapped on the door. It was opened by the strangest and ugliest man he had ever seen. He said that as it was nearly dark O'Donnell should stay the night with him. He gave him supper and entertained him with a rich fund of stories. He was a strict vegetarian and thought the killing of any living creature, except in self-defence, wrong.

The man, Bert Lehman, was a freethinker, with little or no education, but a philosopher, possessed of sound reasoning and much commonsense. Although an atheist, he believed in the existence of phenomena for which he was unable to supply any rational explanation on natural grounds. He told how he had been watching from behind a tree the famous Ghost Dance of the Klamath Indians. They had been led to fight the white folk by the belief that their dead were about to be restored to life to lead them in a revolt against the oppressors and stealers of their land. At the command of the chief spirits, the lesser spirits assembled upon Mount Shasta, where they stayed until their living brethren started the Ghost Dance. The dancing began at noon, and old and young, men and women, kept on dancing hour after hour, singing, wailing, and howling like coyotes.

When the Redskins had been dancing for about an hour, Lehman had distinctly seen an outer circle of shadowy figures suddenly appear. They seemed to him to rise up out of the ground, each of them surrounded by a gruesome leadenish-blue light, and danced in tempo with the living Indians, and imitating all their fantastic antics. They all, living and dead, had their faces painted in a way that Lehman found grotesque and ghastly.

He told O'Donnell: "I got so scared – and it takes a lot to scare me – that I didn't stay watching them for more than a couple of hours. Afraid I might be discovered, I slunk quietly away and didn't feel safe until I got well on my way home. To have been found by the Indians would have meant sure death, preceded by torture and scalping."

O'Donnell had not since he left England been to any place of worship, yet he retained a profound belief in the Bible and the values which resulted from his having been brought up a vicar's son in a strict Church of England home. He was in consequence rather shocked by Lehman's dismissal of the Holy Scriptures and an Almighty and Merciful God. But the man had stated the reasons for his incredulity with such lucidity and rationality that he could not help thinking that he was probably right. And that thought greatly discomposed him, for so sudden a shaking of a lifelong faith was a considerable blow. He set out on his journey home in the morning dispirited and depressed. Something deep inside him, something that he had unconsciously valued very highly, was gone, and he felt that he could never be his old self again.

A picnic party was paying a visit to Crater Lake, one of the great national marvels of far western America, and O'Donnell went along with them. At that time there was no National Park near it, no way of getting to it except on foot, and few people apart from those who lived in the locality ever visited it. The way lay through a dense forest up a steep mountainside. They camped overnight in the forest, and were joined briefly by an old backwoodsman named Mat Keg, who had strange stories to tell... of how one night he had seen the headless Indian chief, who was said to haunt the forest, careering past on a phantom black horse, waving a tomahawk and uttering blood-curdling yells; of seeing unearthly lights flickering about Wizard Isle, in the centre of Crater Lake, the known haunt of wizards and demons. As Keg paused between tales, O'Donnell registered a chilling cacophony of appropriate sounds: the bodeful cry of the tree-toad, dismal hooting of the screech-owl, the sudden ghostly rustling in the trees of birds scared from their nests. The party were visited by several Indians, trading venison with them for clothes and ammunition. Ugly, ill-formed, they were very different in appearance from Fennimore Cooper's Indian braves.

O'Donnell was particularly struck by a log cabin that he saw with holes in its wooden walls, through which a white family had fired at a body of Indians who were attacking them. The Redskins won the skirmish and spared no one, inflicting frightful tortures on the vanquished before they killed them. After the massacre the cabin was rumoured to be haunted and no one ventured near it after sundown.

It did not take O'Donnell very long to discover that, except for the riding, life on a small ranch was too monotonous, wearisome, and lonely for him. He found few of the ranchers with whom his new life had thrown him into contact precisely companionable. Certain of their habits were not entirely to his taste – the squirting of tobacco juice out of their mouths, regardless of where it landed, and the picking of their teeth at meals with a pin, fork, or point of a knife, for instance. Moreover, they were in the main totally uneducated and despised people who were.

On the other hand, he could not complain of their being anything other than friendly disposed towards him; too friendly at times, when they slapped him on the back too heartily or suddenly fired at the ground within an inch or two of his feet just to see, in the most amiable way, how high he would jump.

The one exception was Gus Roker. Pitching hay one day in extreme heat, O'Donnell, unused to the work, was forced to break off for a rest. Roker, seeing him sitting whacked out on the ground, jeered at him and did his best to provoke him. O'Donnell was about to retaliate when the ranch boss, not wanting a row, and an Austrian named Schuler intervened.

Schuler afterwards told O'Donnell a very ugly story about Roker and his brother, Ern. Candy parties were a great feature of life in America, and the Roker brothers and a young Englishman, whom they disliked because he was a Britisher, were at a candy partying one night. The Englishman, talking to a girl, used, in all innocence, a word harmless enough in England, but banned in America in the presence of women. The girl, highly indignant, told Gus Roker. He was overheard asking brother Ern to meet him outside the house when the party was over, and lend him a hand in settling an account with the Britisher. The next day the dead body of the Englishman was found, head smashed in and throat cut. The Rokers were the immediate suspects, but they were influential in the community, the law in that part of the States was lax and bribery rampant, so nothing was done.

O'Donnell subsequently had ample confirmation of what Schuler, a native of Austria, utterly illiterate, and reputed to have a very bad temper, told him. For some reason Schuler took a liking to him and invited him to his cabin in the heart of the Rogue River forest. There was only one room, in which the family, consisting of his wife and 15-year-old daughter, Maggie, fed and slept, all three of them in one bed. O'Donnell slept on the ground. He passed a strange night. Outside the cabin, all was impenetrable darkness, because of the dense foliage. Sounds like death groans were made by the rubbing of one huge branch of a tree against another as they were swayed about by the night wind. Coyotes howled intermittently, and every now and then there was a cry of terror from some poor defenceless creature pounced upon by a beast of prey. Inside, there was no stillness. Mrs. Schuler snored most horribly. He was not sorry when the endless night was over and it was time for him to take his leave.

Not long after O'Donnell's night in the Schuler cabin, it was the scene of a dreadful tragedy. In one of his ungovernable rages, Schuler was beating his wife, when Maggie, who had been out gathering wood, arrived back, and seeing her mother, of whom she was very fond, being ill-used, seized an axe, and, Lizzie-Borden-like, struck her father on the head with it, killing him. She informed the sheriff at once of what she had done. No action was taken against her. Schuler's brutality to his wife was well known, and Maggie was deemed to have been fully justified in killing him in defence of her mother.

After a few months, O'Donnell came to the conclusion that ranching was not his cup of tea. He could never settle down to being a Far Western farmer. For him, it was a case of go (back) east young man.

A spectral young lady in Denver.
From O'Donnell's Twenty Years Experiences as a Ghost Hunter (1916).

A haunted hotel in Boston.
From O'Donnell's Twenty Years Experiences as a Ghost Hunter (1916).

An alluring female ghost makes an appearance near Winnipeg, Canada. From O'Donnell's Twenty Years Experiences as a Ghost Hunter (1916).

A very unappealing Canadian ghost, said to have been fired upon without coming to any harm. From O'Donnell's Twenty Years Experiences as a Ghost Hunter (1916).

5

Hitting The Ghost Trail Home

Looking back, his spell in Oregon had been tough, but a wonderful, never-to-be-forgotten period of his life, sitting at camp fires listening to the eerie, spell-binding tales of the Red Indians and the backwoodsmen. Particularly memorable had been his living for a time in their settlement with the Rogue River Indians, who had been the last tribe to revolt against the invading white man.

He came to understand them and their beliefs. Like some of the ancient tribes in Asia and Europe, the Red Indians of America held that every mountain, rock, river, cave, and tree harboured a spirit. They told him, for instance, that tree hauntings were common in the Western American forests. Sometimes the tree would be haunted by the ghost of someone who had hanged himself from its branches, or who had been murdered within the ambit of its shadow; sometimes it would be by an Elemental, that is to say spirit which had never had human form, was usually frighteningly grotesque in its assumed appearance, and always maliciously disposed.

Then there were those trees which were themselves actually phantoms. They were plainly recognisable, as they were always either very dark and shadowy, or else extraordinarily vivid, emitting violent vibrations and a lurid glow. Their effect on horses was terrible, often sending them downright mad with fright, or, at best, making them feeble, uncertain, liable to shy and bolt for no obvious reason. Certain of these ghost trees were, the Red Indians declared, more evil than any other kind of ghosts, and were frequently responsible for suicides, homicides, and all kinds of diseases. They were not necessarily the ghosts of trees that had once actually lived. Sometimes Elementals assumed the form of trees, just as they would also impersonate animals and humans.

"The Indians showed me a spot in a Californian forest," said O'Donnell, "they said was haunted by a tree ghost, and even though the sun was out at the time, I felt something unpleasantly peculiar in the atmosphere, and was glad to get away from it. "

He was also told certain things with regard to wild animals, such as the fact that "bears were much more susceptible to ghostly influence than any other animal – more susceptible than dogs and horses – and that no bear would ever go near a place that was in the least degree haunted. They had seen many phantom bears and pumas, and they had seen also, at certain seasons of the year, in the Oregon forests, round by Crater and Klamath lakes, the ghosts of coyotes and eagles. Artificial light was the only safeguard they knew of against ghosts, so whenever they slept in a haunted spot they took care to keep a bright fire burning."

Heading back east, O'Donnell did not hit the lonesome trail alone. Shortly before his departure from Oregon, he had met, working at the nearest settlement to his ranch, one Edward Richards, the son of a Hampshire parson, an old public school boy, who, like himself, had discovered that he had no bent for ranching. United by their plight, the two had become friends in adversity, and set out together on the long trek home. They took the transcontinental overlander in stages. First California – San Francisco, Sacramento.

To many people back home in Britain it was unthinkable that America, being so modern in its civilisation, should possess any ghosts at all. But, as O'Donnell was to find, transatlantic ghosts there most certainly were, in abundance, and he had begun to fill his notebook almost as soon as his feet touched the New World soil.

> I only too well realised the possibilities when I was sleeping by myself on the ranch in Oregon, or riding alone through the giant forests of the Cascades mountains. I believe all the loneliest parts of America, the great, bold Rockies, the vast Californian and Oregon forests are periodically visited by ghosts – ghosts of murdered soldiers, of scalp-raising Indians, of tramp suicides – of all manner of evilly-disposed white and red people, and of neutrarians, spirits that have never occupied earthly bodies, and which are as grotesque and awe-inspiring as the fantastically carved boulders and queerly shaped tree trunks with which those parts are so lavishly bestrewn. America, indeed, affords one of the widest fields in the world for the genuine ghost hunter.

Now, en route home, paying his second visit to San Francisco, the old

San Francisco before the earthquake and great fire of 1906, O'Donnell found it a strangely fascinating place – a switchback city of street upon climbing street, terrace upon steep sloping terrace, of quaintly individual buildings, in an atmosphere impregnated with its distinctly own afflatus.

He was the sole visitor in the vast hotel on 117th Street. Clambering up flight after flight of stairs, past mazes of dimly-lighted passages teeming with doors, the blank-faced, tight-shut doors of empty rooms, ascending higher and higher on his way to bed, he felt suffocated by the all-blanketing silence, breached only by the hollow echoing of his own footfalls. He shrewdly suspected the hotel was haunted, but never caught so much as the whisk of a ghost there.

However, hearing of his interest in psychic matters, the owner of the hotel introduced O'Donnell to a Mr. Sweeney, who kept a drug store on Market Street.

"The only experience I ever had with the supernatural took place in this very room," Mr. Sweeney told him. Exactly twelve years ago I engaged the services of a young man called Edward Marsdon. He was very amiable and capable, but highly-strung and hypernormally sensitive. He had been with me about six months when he came into the parlour one evening with a face like a corpse. 'I've poisoned someone,' he gasped.

'Poisoned someone? Good God, what do you mean?'

'What I say,' he replied. 'A young fellow came into the store about an hour ago and handed me a prescription, signed by Dr. Knelligan, of 111th Street. I made it up, and gave it to him. A few minutes ago I found I'd put in salts of lemon instead of paregoric. The young man will die, and I'm ruined for life.'

'We both are,' I said testily. 'Ring up Dr. Knelligan at once and ask him for the young man's address. When you get it, drive round immediately and see if you're in time.'

He rang Dr. Knelligan, got his patient's address, and drove straight round there, only to discover that he had just left and the landlady had no idea where he had gone. Marsdon came back in a state of utter collapse, trembling all over as if he had ague, went upstairs and slammed his door.

About a quarter of an hour later, my wife, the servant, and I all heard Marsdon come downstairs and go out. The servant then went up to his room to make the bed, and hearing her scream out, I ran upstairs to find her standing in the middle of the floor, wringing her hands, whilst

Marsdon was sitting in a chair – dead. Well, from that day on we had no peace. Footsteps which we all recognised as Marsdon's trod up and down the stairs all hours of the day and night, and frequently when I was in the laboratory dispensing medicines I was strongly conscious of some presence standing close beside me, watching everything I did. One day my wife actually saw him. She was going out, and, wanting some money, she called to me. Finding me, as she thought, in the parlour with my back to her, she touched me on the shoulder. The person she had mistaken for me turned round, and she found herself confronted with the white, scared face of Edward Marsdon. A week or two afterwards he was seen again. My wife and the maid met him on the stairs.

Then one morning a young man came to the store to see me.

'I'm the man to whom your assistant gave that unfortunate mixture,' he told me. 'I've just returned to San Francisco and heard all about it. The medicine was perfectly all right. I drank it directly I left here, and it did me the world of good. There was even the suspicion of poison in it. Your assistant was labouring under some extraordinary delusion. If only he'd told my landlady about it when he called, she could have given him the glass I had drunk out of. It would have contained the dregs, and they could have been analysed. I'm told there are rumours afloat that his apparition has been seen several times since he died; not that I believe in such things as ghosts.'

'Whether you believe in them or not,' I said quietly, 'it is a fact that Edward Marsdon has been both seen and heard.

'Then I hope that my visit here today will put matters right, and that his poor wandering spirit, learning that I am alive and well, will find rest and trouble you no more.'

He bade me good morning and was walking towards the door. 'My God!' he cried out, coming to an abrupt halt, 'there he is.'

I looked, and as sure as I am sitting here, Mr. O'Donnell, there was Edward Marsdon, just as I had known him in life, standing on the pavement with his face glued to the window, peering in at us. The expression in his eyes was one of infinite joy and astonishment. I took a step or two towards him with the intention of speaking and he immediately vanished. From that day to this the hauntings have entirely ceased."

During his stay in San Francisco O'Donnell obtained the services of a guide and did a nightly tour of Chinatown, and penetrated to a number of the lesser known subterranean haunts of the city. He also did a bit of freelance writing there.

> My guide piloted me over some of those haunts that have so often furnished writers with a theme. I saw men and women under the influence of opium. They were lying on divans and in bunks, and all kinds of queer places, and they all looked pretty much alike, very stupid, very unhealthy, very dirty. The air was foul and fetid I don't think anyone but a Chinaman could have stood it for very long. Some of the furniture and upholstery had probably cost a good deal of money when new, it was now indescribably dirty, very dilapidated, and simply snowed under with soiled and tawdry cushions and covers in every stage of decay. However, despite all this, some of the Chinese women were not unprepossessing; indeed one or two of them were downright attractive. I asked my guide whether there was any truth in the many stories I had heard of the white slave traffic in underground Chinatown and of the kidnapping of American and European girls for that purpose, and he gave me a significant nod.

Digging around, O'Donnell secured an introduction from a Mr. Lester, whom he met at his hotel, to a man called Hal, who worked as an attendant at a swimming-bath.

'So you want to hear of a haunting in this town,' said Hal, popping a plug of tobacco into his mouth. 'Well, I reckon you couldn't have come to a better place, for there's a ghost right here. Come round again the day after tomorrow, about six in the evening, and I'll give you an opportunity to find out what's wrong with this place. But,' he warned, 'you mustn't go and blab about it to anyone, or let it get into the papers, as that won't do either for the boss, myself, or you!'

Two days later, at the appointed time, O'Donnell duly turned up at the baths.

'Take a swim round and tell me afterwards if you feel any weird sensation,' said Hal.

Nothing happened till he got to the deep end, where an icy chill suddenly ran through him, and he experienced the powerful feeling that something very horrible was lurking directly beneath him. It so startled and shocked him that he made straight for the nearest steps and scrambled rapidly out of the water.

'Did you feel anything?' asked Hal.

'Indeed I did,' said O'Donnell, describing to him, as best he could, the sensation that he had felt, and pointing to the exact spot where it had occurred.

'I reckoned it was there you'd get it,' said Hal, 'that's just where the haunting is. Some years before I came here, a fellow was found lying dead at the bottom of the bath in that spot. It was given out that he had had a fit, but I believe there was always a bit of doubt about it. Suspicion. Anyhow, from that time onwards, those who have bathed over the place where the body was found have complained of exactly the same sensation as you had. And some have said that, when diving, they struck against a body lying at the bottom of the bath, and asked me to come and fetch it up.'

A final tale from O'Donnell's San Francisco sojourn.

He had been out tramping all day along the southern bank of the Bay, and it was late when he got back to the city. As he swung wearily round 117th Street into a narrow thoroughfare leading to the obscure corner of the town in which his finances forced him to live, the last chime of midnight sounded. He was just coming within sight of the end house of a block of low, old-fashioned buildings, when he saw, with something of a shock, the glow of a bright, almost phosphorescent, light emanating from one of its ground floor rooms. He was surprised because when, only that very morning, he had passed the place, noticed that it was to let, and been struck by its air of utter loneliness and past grandeur, and, peeping in through one of its dirt-grimed and cobwebbed windows, taken stock of its unfurnished, dust-strewn state, contrasting so sadly with the splendid oak-panelling of the otherwise mouldering room. Leaning now against a verandah, he looked in and, to his amazement, the room was no longer empty, but richly carpeted, illuminated by countless candles, and filled with ponderous, old-fashioned furniture. In the centre was a long table, covered with a snowy cloth, bearing a profusion of silver dishes containing a cornucopian selection of the choicest food.

Dumbfounded, he saw a door at the far end of the room open and a young and charming girl, dressed à la mode de Marie Antoinette, enter and advance towards the fireplace, where was the cheery glow of a huge log fire. She turned, all smiles, to the window, and her eyes fell on O'Donnell. Instantly her countenance changed. Putting a finger to her lips, she beckoned him to come in. He walked to the front-door. She opened it.

"We are having a fancy-dress dance," she said, "but none of the guests have as yet arrived and I want you to come into the ball-room while I rehearse some of the dance music." She had a slight French accent. "There is no one about but you and I, but someone else will arrive soon. It's not half-past twelve, is it?"

"No, twenty past."

She sighed deeply. "Ten more minutes." Then she sat down at the piano and began to play a Strauss waltz.

A feeling of intense, but wholly unaccountable, fear gradually crept over O'Donnell.

"It's close on the half-hour," whispered the girl. "Listen!"

He listened and heard a door from somewhere in the lower part of the house open and shut. Then the sound of muffled footsteps coming stealthily up the stairs. They arrived outside the door. He saw the doorhandle begin to turn. Slowly, very slowly, the door opened, and on the floor of the room there appeared a black shadow – vague, indefinite, and grotesque. The girl looked over her shoulder at it. O'Donnell caught an expression in her eyes that appalled him. Turning to the piano again, she played frantically, and the faster her fingers flew, the nearer crept the shadow. Suddenly it seemed to shoot right forward, there was a wild scream of terror, a terrific crash, and all was absolute darkness.

O'Donnell groped his way frenziedly to the door. Something came into violent collision with him. He staggered back half stunned. When his brain cleared, he found himself standing in the street, weak with exhaustion, and hatless.

He visited the house next day. The sun was shining brightly. There were plenty of people about. It was as he had first seen it – untenanted and unfurnished, gently decaying. He concluded that he must have dreamt the whole thing. What, indeed, more likely? He had been excessively tired; so worn out that he had felt that he could hardly crawl back to his hotel. Without a doubt, he concluded, he must have dropped off to sleep resting against the verandah.

But there is a slightly disturbing coda. Just out of interest, O'Donnell made a few enquiries. He contacted the owner of the house and he told him the following story. About fifty years before, a very rich French family had occupied the house, and at the coming of age of their daughter they gave a fancy-dress ball. Among those who attended was an Italian, who, being a rejected suitor of the daughter's, had not been invited. Nevertheless he appeared, wearing some grotesque and alarming costume, and when the dance was at its height suddenly overturned a large oil lamp. In no time the whole floor was ablaze, and before anyone could stop him, he had seized the daughter of the house and hurled her into the centre of the flaming mass. Both he and the girl were burned to death.

O'Donnell said that, just out of curiosity, he would like to go into the house and see if its interior bore any resemblance to the house of his dream. The owner said that he would like to go with him. Once inside, he recognised every feature of the house, and, when they went upstairs to the ball-room, there, to his unspeakable surprise, lying in the middle of the floor, was his hat.

It was at San Francisco's International Hotel that O'Donnell made the acquaintance of Captain Harding, the skipper of a trader, who gave him the background to the extraordinary affair of the *Squando*, a Norwegian vessel, aboard which, around the year 1889, a shocking tragedy had occurred as she lay in San Francisco harbour. One night a fearful cry was heard coming from the barque. The following morning the first mate was missing, and bloodstains were discovered on the deck. His decapitated body was later recovered from the harbour, where it was found floating. It seems that there had been long-standing ill-feeling between the captain's wife and the mate, and that this had erupted into his murder by the captain, assisted by his wife. They had first of all plied him with drink, then, when he was alcoholically incapacitated, the woman had held him down while her husband beheaded him. They had then heaved the body overboard.

Captain Harding told O'Donnell that he had met the murderers several times before the crime, and said that the woman was goodish-looking, but with very hard eyes. It was his belief that she and the mate had been carrying on together, and that she, fearing they would be found out, rounded on him, and pretended to her husband that he had been persistently annoying her.

Soon after this murder, the *Squando* had, said Captain Harding, witnessed another tragedy. While at sea, the crew had mutinied and killed the captain who had been appointed in the murderer's place. After this second tragedy the *Squando* acquired a sinister reputation, which was heightened when her next skipper was found dead aboard her in circumstances which could not be accounted for. The death of a fourth captain set the seal upon her as a hoodoo vessel. Seafaring men are notoriously superstitious, and thereafter they had taken into their heads the notion that it was extremely unlucky to sail in her. On her arrival at Bathurst, New Brunswick, in the spring of 1895, every man aboard her deserted.

Apart from being unlucky, the barque was said to be haunted. Learning of this, the Norwegian Consul at Bathurst engaged two strong-headed, stout-hearted night-watchmen to look after her, and sent them aboard with instructions to hide themselves and lie in wait for anyone they suspected of trying on funny tricks. They duly boarded the barque about 9 p.m. and settled themselves down in the captain's cabin. All was reassuringly quiet for the first hour or so. Then, all of a sudden, their complacent vigil was rudely interrupted by the most extraordinary cacophony proceeding from the deck. Rushing forth and scaling the companion ladder, they emerged to find the deck in chaos, covered with a tangled mass of ropes, spars, yards, hand-spikes, and other maritime paraphernalia. Puzzled, they went below again, and, tired, lay down in the captain's bunk. That was when they felt sharp tugs by invisible hands at their sleeves and trousers, followed by the laying of icy-cold fingers on their faces, and the dragging off and flinging around of the coats and rugs with which they had covered themselves. An attempt to light a lantern failed. It was immediately and repeatedly blown out. Next came the voices, belonging to the invisible entities, issuing from all parts of the cabin, whispering hollowly and menacingly, telling them to leave the *Squando*.

It was a bidding that they did not really need. Convinced now that they were dealing with the supernatural, and having no real wish to do so, they had decided to abandon ship. Their resolution was reinforced when, turning round, they saw coming after them with long strides from the direction of the cabin which they had just quitted, the shadowy outline of a man in seafaring costume, but without a head.

Other attempts were made to tame the fierce phantoms of the ghost ship, but they all failed. Finally abandoned, *Squando*, with all her ghosts, was sold to the ship-breakers.

Leaving, not without regret, San Francisco behind, O'Donnell's next stop on the eastward trek was Sacramento. Any American city hotter in the summer, or more bone chillingly cold in the winter, he found it hard to imagine. His chief memory of Sacramento was of buying a pair of braces there – "The very best half-dollar's worth I ever had." He wore them for years and still had them decades later, stowed away in a trunk of mementoes of the long past.

Frankly, the town did not deeply impress him, but one curious thing did happen to him there. He met a man on one of its streets who was so like an old Clifton College master, Mr. Tait, that, in the belief that it was him, he went up to him and greeted him. The man gasped in amazement. "Why, Jupp," he said, "how on earth have you managed it? It's only ten minutes since I left you eating your dinner in the Eagle Hotel on the other side of the town. Have you wings?" The moment he spoke O'Donnell knew he was not Tait, but it took him some time to convince the stranger that he was not Jupp, and when, half an hour later, O'Donnell was introduced to Jupp, he saw clearly how the mistake in identity had arisen, for he did not think it would have been possible to find a more striking likeness to himself, even in his own portrait! The coincidence was made all the more remarkable since there had been at Clifton College, contemporary with Tait, a master named Jupp.

On, eastward of Sacramento, over the border into Nebraska, is Carson City. It was the man who lived there, named Weston, who asked O'Donnell if he would like to see a gully in the Sierra Nevadas, about forty miles south-west of Carson City, that bore a very evil reputation, both for crime and for ghosts. Of course, O'Donnell said that he would. They went part of the way by wagon and the remainder on horseback. As they approached close to the gully, Weston told O'Donnell to dismount. "We'd better leave our horses here," he said, "or we shall have trouble. No horse ever goes through the gully without shying or bolting, generally both."

Having tethered the animals to a tree, they carried on along the forest track on foot. It was about nine o'clock in the evening and the gloom was frightful. Enormous pines towered on either side, obscuring all but the briefest glimpses of the serene, star-laden sky. At length they came to the brink of a precipitous hill.

"There," said Weston, pointing to the descent in front of them, "the gully is down there. Mind how you walk, and keep your eyes well skinned."

Slowly they descended into the ravine. Edging down at a snail's pace, O'Donnell observed how, deep in the gully below, the tree tops did not stir, but remained stock-still, apparently impervious to the stiff night breeze that blew. After narrowly escaping the threats of sprained ankles, posed by the ruts and holes, and concussion from low-hanging branches, invisible in the dark, they eventually reached the bottom of the chasm. There, revealed brilliant in the moonlight, was a scene described by O'Donnell as "a more ghostly and murderous-looking place than, even in my wildest flights of imagination, I had ever conjectured."

The track seemed to expand abruptly, and, on either side, grotesquely fashioned trunks of trees and between them huge misshapen masses of stone, gleamed a startling white.

"According to tradition," said Weston, "either the Sioux or some other tribe of Indians used to offer up human sacrifices on one of these blocks of stone. That seemed to set the ball rolling, for, after their time, several white people, so it is said, committed suicide here, while not a few were murdered. I can vouch for one tragedy at least, because I knew the victim, a bright, clever lad called Edward Hickson, whose parents owned a ranch some twelve or so miles away. He left home early one morning in the fall of the year to attend school, and as a terrible storm came on, suddenly, soon afterwards, his mother, becoming anxious about him, sent a messenger to the schoolmaster to see if he had arrived safely. The reply came in the negative. Edward was not there, and no one had seen him. Much alarmed, the parents, accompanied by search-parties, set out to look for him, but they had little success, for the only traces they could find of him were a pair of bloodstained shoes and a handkerchief, undoubtedly his, close beside the rock over there," and Weston pointed to a great gleaming boulder about a dozen yards from where they were standing. "No other clue was ever discovered, and to this day his fate has remained a profound secret."

"Do you think that the rock was a sacrificial stone?" O'Donnell asked.

"It is recorded so," Weston nodded. "If you examine the top of it in daylight you can see a number of dark marks on it that are thought to be bloodstains, and a groove all round it that is supposed to have been made for catching the blood and allowing it to drain off. It's believed by the Indians to be haunted by a spirit that manifests its presence by making a peculiar sound like a long protracted sigh or shudder – God, what's that?"

As Weston spoke, O'Donnell distinctly heard a sound strangely like that which he had just described, coming, so it seemed, from the rock.

"This is the first time I've experienced the haunting myself," said Weston, "but dozens have told me they've experienced it. I feel convinced that the rock is really haunted by an evil spirit which periodically clamours for blood, and I believe that it is this haunting which is largely responsible for the many crimes and deeds of violence said to have taken place here."

As they were retracing their steps up the hill, O'Donnell heard a faint sound drifting up from the gully. It sounded like the whoops that boys sometimes make.

"Did you hear those whoops?"

"Yes," answered Weston, "and I believe that Edward Hickson's ghost haunts this place, and is the author of them."

At Denver, Colorado, next step on the odyssey, O'Donnell had a pleasant time meeting there one or two relatives of friends of his in England. He had last stayed in Denver in the summer, on his outer, westbound, journey, and the intense heat then, combined with an injudicious consumption of fruit and iced water, had brought on what he euphemistically described as "a mild attack of cholera", which left him with none too favourable an impression of the place. But on this second visit all was changed. The weather was much cooler, he had grown acclimatised, no longer felt himself a stranger among strangers, and, despite the fact that the employment he had managed to secure, doing a bit of freelance journalism was anything but lucrative, he enjoyed his second time in Denver immensely.

The town of Denver had not been built very long. Little more than a mere ten years previous to O'Donnell's visit, it had possessed only one orthodox street, so, in the circumstances of its modernity, it seemed to him just about the last place in the world in which he would expect to come across a haunted house. However... he had been to the Zoological Gardens and was returning by tram when a journalist called Rouillac, whom he had met a few times, hailed him and came running up in great excitement.

"O'Donnell," he said, "I've unearthed something that'll interest you; the case of a haunted office."

The office on Race Street was rented by a Mrs. Bell, a typist, who employed two girls, Stella Dean and Hester Holt. One morning Hester failed to come into the office. "If she's ill, she ought to let me know," said Mrs. Bell. "There was nothing wrong with her yesterday, was there?"

"Not that I'm aware of," said Stella.

Next day there was still no sign of Hester, and Stella was despatched in the dinner-hour to find out what had become of her. She returned looking very white and scared.

"Why, Stella, what on earth's the matter?" asked Mrs. Bell.

"Hester's gone away without telling anyone where she was going. She never returned to her lodgings after leaving here; at least, that's what her landlady, Mrs. Britton, says. And she hasn't written either. I think you'd better call there yourself. I don't like the woman."

Mrs. Bell did so. She interviewed the landlady, who stuck to her story. Hester had, she said, been a singularly reserved girl, and never mentioned her family except when she went away for her annual holiday. She would then ask for all her letters to be forwarded to the address of her married sister. Mrs. Britton gave this address to Mrs. Bell, who wrote off straight away, and received an answer by return of post saying that Hester was not there, and her sister had heard nothing from her for over a month. The one person who would be sure to know her whereabouts would, she said, be her young man, Pete Simpkins.

Without delay, Mrs. Bell set to work to find Mr. Simpkins and hurried off to have a talk with him.

"When did you last see Hester?" she asked.

"The day she left you. I had been out in the country all day, superintending the building of a large farm some ten miles to the east of this city, and I was cycling home along a very unfrequented route when I met a buggy. Two girls were in it, Hester and Stella Dean."

"What!" Mrs. Bell sounded very surprised. "Stella Dean? Are you sure?"

"Absolutely. I can swear to it. It astonished me because I knew they had been on very bad terms. I was engaged to Stella before I met Hester, but I couldn't stand her temper. One day she was so enraged with my dog because it snarled at her, that she seized my walking stick and beat it on the head till it was dead. I found her standing over it white with fury; and feeling that after what I had witnessed I could never like her again, I broke off our engagement there and then. After that I met Hester Holt at the same house where I had first seen Stella, and we at once became friends. Stella Dean did not like it, but she took on more than was necessary, and Hester told me there had been several very painful scenes between them. Indeed, I understood that out of business hours they were not on speaking terms; hence you can judge of my surprise when I saw them driving in the buggy side by side."

"It's all very mysterious," said Mrs. Bell. "If she doesn't turn up soon I'll have to inform the police."

Next day, Mrs. Bell asked Stella if she had gone for a drive with Hester Holt the evening of her disappearance. "No, the last time I saw Hester was when she left here that afternoon," Stella answered. "She said goodbye to me as usual on the other side of the road, and I've never set eyes on her since. Hester and I were always on the very best of terms, and it would be downright mean of anyone to allege otherwise. Besides, I can produce proof to the contrary."

The following day, Hester was still missing, so Mrs. Bell went to the police. They made enquiries, and Pete Simpkins' story about the buggy was corroborated by a witness who had seen the two girls driving to the outskirts of the town that evening. A car proprietor came forward to testify that he remembered Miss Holt hiring a buggy from him, but that she had driven off in it on her own. He had been out when the buggy was returned. His wife had taken the money for it, but it was then dusk and she was unable to swear to the identity of the lady who had paid her. She could only say that Miss Dean resembled her in both build and height.

Asked if she could provide an alibi, Stella produced her mother, very old and decrepit, who stated that she had come home from the office and stayed indoors all that evening.

A week after the vanishing of Hester Holt, Mrs. Bell engaged a new assistant, Vera Cummings. On her second day working in the office, she was busy typing when she suddenly exclaimed: "How is it that I get convulsed with shivers when I sit next to you, Miss Dean?"

"What nonsense. You imagine it," replied Stella Dean.

"No, I don't. I'm going to sit somewhere else." And Miss Cummings moved to the other side of the table.

Mrs. Bell made no comment.

About an hour later, Miss Cummings abruptly observed: "My, Stella Dean, what long legs you have!"

"What in the world do you mean?" was the indignant response.

"Well, there's no one else on your side of the table, is there? And someone's feet keep kicking mine."

"You're dreaming," said Stella Dean.

Mrs. Bell noticed she turned very pale.

Three days later, Mrs. Bell and the two girls were sitting talking. It was coming up to the tea interval and work was just then very slack.

"Who is that tall, good-looking girl, Stella, that I've seen following you into the building several times? Vera Cummings asked.

Stella, her cheeks ashen, asked: "What do you mean? I've seen no one. You've dreamt it."

The next morning Mrs. Bell, Stella Dean, and Vera Cummings all arrived at their work place simultaneously, and went up in the lift together. As they neared their office, they heard the sound of a typewriter. But the office door was locked. Mrs. Bell put the key in the lock. The typewriter continued working furiously. It stopped the minute Mrs. Bell crossed the threshold. There was no one in the room.

That afternoon, complaining of a headache, Stella Dean went home early. It was several weeks before she returned. During her absence the phenomena ceased completely. The morning of her return, Pete Simpkins met her and Vera Cummings outside the building. He was bubbling over with excitement.

"She's come back! Come back, and never sent me a word."

"Come back! Who are you talking about?" Stella was staring at him, anger distorting her features.

Oblivious in his excitement, he continued: "Hester Holt. She's just gone into your place. Didn't you know?"

Stella Dean made no reply. She just pushed past Simpkins and disappeared into the building.

Vera Cummings hung back. She asked Pete Simpkins to describe Hester Holt. "Why that's the girl I used constantly to see following Stella. Where she disappears to is a mystery, but it's only one of the many funny things that have happened since I've been here." She went on to tell him about the feet under the table and the typewriter that rattled away on its own.

Pete Simpkins retailed all this to his friends. Rouillac got hold of it and handed it on to O'Donnell. He wanted him to go with him to the haunted office right away. O'Donnell could not. He had work he was obliged to complete in a given time. They arranged to meet the following week. But when the time came, Rouillac told him: "I'm afraid it's no use. The office is closed and it's impossible to get permission to go there.

What had happened was this: The day after Stella Dean's return, Mrs. Bell was off sick, and Stella and Vera were alone. It would have been at about eleven o'clock that Vera got up to go and get a drink of water. In passing she chanced to look at Stella. She was leaning forward in her chair, staring with an expression of the utmost horror at a despatch-case on the floor which was oscillating violently to and fro. Vera noticed that the case bore upon it the initials "H.H."

"I believe it's Hester Holt," said Vera, "she's dead, and for some mysterious reason her spirit haunts this room."

"Nonsense," came the quick-fire answer. "How can you be so silly! There are no such things as ghosts."

At lunch time the two girls were getting ready to go out. Vera had just put on her hat and was walking to the door when she heard a sharp cry. Stella was standing in front of the mirror. In it was not the reflection of her face but that of a pale girl with two dark eyes glaring fixedly at her. Vera instantly recognised that face. It was that of the girl she had so often seen following Stella – Hester Holt.

Vera was so frightened that she ran out of the room. The door slammed behind her with a tremendous crash. Worried, she tried the handle. It turned. She pressed her hardest, but the door would not open. She called out to Stella. There was no reply. Alarmed now, she ran to the lift and fetched the man who operated it. They both pushed at the door with all their strength. Still it would not open. As they stood wondering what to do, they saw the door handle suddenly turn, and, of its own accord, the door swung gently open. They peered in. Stella was lying on the floor in a dead faint. She died that same night. Some people reckoned that she committed suicide, but her mother said that she had always had a bad heart, and maintained that she had suffered a fatal heart attack.

Rouillac told O'Donnell that he had tried to get permission for them to spend a night in the office, but Mrs. Bell dared not give it. She said that the landlord was furious with her for allowing the report to get abroad that his premises are haunted, and threatened a libel action if he heard anything further.

Hester Holt's body was never found. Not surprising really, for the route which Simpkins discovered the buggy to have taken afforded ample opportunities for concealment of a body – deep ditches, creeks, and crevices covered with a thick and rank vegetation.

And he had one last extraordinary item of information to convey to O'Donnell.

"When Vera Cummings passed by the office this morning, she saw Stella Dean enter it; Stella Dean just as she looked when alive, only very white and in abject terror. She passed right in through the half-open doorway, and, as usual, Hester Holt followed her."

A spectral tree on Tooting Common.
From O'Donnell's Twenty Years Experiences as a Ghost Hunter (1916).

A vengeful ghost makes an appearance to its murderer, who topples down an abyss. From O'Donnell's Twenty Years Experiences as a Ghost Hunter (1916).

6

A Ghostly Goodbye to New York

Sweeping on from Denver, O'Donnell arrived in Omaha. His stay there this time was uneventful. St. Louis yielded the cautionary tale of Mr. Vandergooch.

Ephraim B. Vandergooch was a dentist. He practised dentistry on 6th Street, St. Louis. O'Donnell went to him to have a jumpy tooth filled. In the course of his session in the chair, he asked him if he knew of any haunted houses in the town. Expecting a superior smile, if not an actual sneer, he was surprised when, taking his question seriously, Mr. Vandergooch said that he knew of several haunted places in St. Louis, and that nothing interested him more than really first-hand ghost stories. He then proceeded to tell him of an experience which he himself had had.

"A few years ago, I learned of a haunting in a street of rather older houses than these, close to here; and as the evidence was to a large extent corroborative, I decided to investigate it. It was Christmas time, and the thought of earthbound spirits pacing up and down cold, empty houses, when all around was warmth and jollity, depressed me. I felt that I must, now that an opportunity had come, try to see them, and if possible do something for them.

I set out on Christmas Eve, and I admit that when I left the cheerfully lighted thoroughfare and plunged into the dark silent emptiness of the house, my heart almost failed me. Apart from ghosts there were so many possibilities, and what more likely than that some tramp or criminal had forced an entrance, and was hiding somewhere on the premises. For a few seconds I stood and listened, and then, feeling a trifle more assured, I closed the door gently and advanced cautiously along the wide hall. At each step I took I became more and more sensitive to an atmosphere of intense sadness and desolation – an atmosphere of intense loneliness, loneliness that is without hope – that is perpetual and absolute. It could be felt in all parts of the house, but more particularly, perhaps, in the kitchen, which was built out at the back on the ground floor. I had never been in such a dreary and inhospitable kitchen. The night was bitterly cold and the bare stones sent chilly currents up my legs and back, into my very brain.

To remain in such a hole until morning was assuredly courting pneumonia or rheumatic fever. I looked at the range, it was covered with rust and verdigris. If only it could be lighted! Then I uttered an exclamation of joy, for lying in one corner was a pile of wood – boxes, shelves, faggots, etc., intermingled with an assortment of other rubbish. In my early days I had lived on a ranch out west, and the experience I had had there now came in useful. In a few minutes there was a loud crackling, and the kitchen filled with a ruddy glow. A couple of dresser-drawers served me for a seat, and I was soon ensconced in a tolerably snug position, from which, however, I was prepared to spring at a moment's notice.

The hours sped by, and the silence deepened. At last, just about two o'clock, when I was beginning to think nothing would happen, I heard a door slam somewhere upstairs. This was followed by a series of creaks, and I heard someone cautiously descending the stairs. A great fear now seized me, and had I been able, I should doubtless have beaten a hasty retreat. Instead, I was possessed with a kind of paralysis, which rendered me quite helpless and prevented me from either moving a limb or uttering a sound. The creaks came nearer – down, down, down, until quite suddenly they stopped, and I heard a cough. It was repeated – cough, cough, cough. The cough of a delicate, neurotic woman. At first it simply startled me, it seemed so distinct, so reverberating, so real. Then it irritated me, and then it infuriated me – almost drove me mad. 'God take the woman,' I raved. 'Will she never cease.'

Cough, cough, cough. A nervous, hacking cough, a worrying, grating cough, an intensely silly, murder-instilling cough. I could see the owner of it – upstairs, hidden from me by the impenetrable darkness, and yet quite distinct – a slight, pale, excessively plain little woman, with watery eyes and a quivering mouth. Heavens, how the mouth maddened me! On she went – cough, cough, cough! She was still coughing when I suddenly became aware of a presence close beside me, and I saw from the glow in the dying embers the figure of a man seated at a table in the middle of the kitchen. He appeared to be trying to write, but to be unable to collect his thoughts. Every now and then he paused, dashed his pen down, and clenched his fists furiously. At first I could not understand his behaviour, and then it all of a sudden occurred to me – the coughing, of course. That perpetual noise, the everlasting hacking, it distracted, demented him. I watched him with feelings of infinite sympathy. At last, unable to stand it any longer, he sprang from his seat and dashed upstairs.

I heard him race up two steps at a time. No madman would have raced faster or more nimbly. Then came a strange variety of sounds, a gratuitous course in phonetics; an altercation, more coughing, oaths, bumping, a scream, a thud, a little feeble cough, silence, and then rapidly descending footsteps, a man's footsteps. I did not wait for them. The spell that had hitherto held me limb-tied now abruptly left me, and I fled out of the building – home.

The next day, Christmas Day, I made my report to the owner of the house, and told her exactly what had happened.

'Good heavens!' she exclaimed, ' and he's married Maisie! Swear that you will never tell a soul, no one, not even your most intimate friend, and I will give you an explanation of what you witnessed.' I promised, and she at once began.

'Ten years ago the occupants of the house you've been in were a well-known dramatist and his wife, whom I will call Mr. and Mrs. Charles Turner. Mrs. Turner was exactly like the woman you imagined, frail, small, and very plain; whilst her husband would tally with the man you saw in the kitchen, a tall, muscular, handsome man. He obviously married her for her money, poor soul, for there was nothing in her to attract him, and everyone could see how she irritated him, especially when she coughed. In fact, he often said to me: "You don't know, Mrs. Wehlen, how Eva annoys me. Whenever I am in the midst of my work, trying to concentrate my thoughts, she starts her infernal coughing. I can hear her all over the house – hack, hack, hack."

"She can't help it, poor thing," I replied. "You ought to feel sorry for her."

"Feel sorry for her," he said. "You'd feel sorry for her if you were tormented as I am. I believe she does it on purpose."

Well one evening, to be precise it was Christmas Eve, Mrs. Turner was found at the foot of the staircase with her neck broken. There was no direct evidence as to how she came there, but as one of the stair-rods was found loose, it was presumed that she fell over it, and, accordingly a verdict of accidental death was returned.

Charles Turner left the house directly afterwards, and a few months later married my niece, Maisie. As far as I know, what you have seen has never been seen by anyone else, but coughing in the house has been heard, and it is quite plain to me now that Charles Turner murdered his first wife. I only pray to Heaven he won't serve Maisie the same.'"

But he did.

Mr. Vandergooch told O'Donnell: "Maisie, too, was found at the foot of a staircase with a broken neck. In all probability she had possessed some idiosyncrasy that worried and annoyed Turner; or, possibly, having once taken to murder, he felt he must go on with it, the habit of homicide being, no doubt, just as fascinating as the habit of drugs or drink. Nothing, however, was proven, and, for all I know to the contrary, he may still be alive, still be killing people to appease his hyper-sensitive and outraged nerves."

O'Donnell afterwards wrote:

> This experience of Mr. Vandergooch's made me think; and eventually led me to devoting no small amount of attention to psychology and criminology. From what a variety of influences, it seemed to me, any one act might be induced, and to what innumerable and varied causes any one crime, for instance murder, might be traced. A minute bone pressing on a certain section of the brain, a stomach continually overladen with beefsteak and other animal food, over-excited nerves, the sight of some locality, such as a wood, an object, such as a knife, all may lead to the same thing – the desire to kill; whilst, at the same time, the superphysical, through the agency of some evil spirit continually whispering to its selected victim, the arrestive, the compelling thought, almost enforces any and every sort of crime. Seeing, then, that in every act of cruelty or violence it is more than likely that either one or other of these factors has been at work, is it fair that we should so readily condemn and therewith rest content?
>
> True, it may be, and, I believe it is, expedient to punish the criminal, but surely it is even more urgent that we should make ourselves thoroughly acquainted with his case, so that we may if possible discover the factor that conduces to his crime, and then either destroy or counteract it.

Quitting St. Louis, bucally restored, O'Donnell carried on to New York, where he lodged in a fifty cent hotel in West Quay, not a particularly elevating neighbourhood, but one that boasted several allegedly haunted loci.

It was a fellow-lodger at the hotel, a Mr. Boxer, who took him to one of these haunts, to probe the mystery of the Evil Room. The scene was a small store that supplied seamen's kit, and was owned by a Swede named Jansen. At first he displayed extreme reticence to confide in O'Donnell, but on being assured that he was not representing any of the New York journals and would not connive at the story getting into print, he became more conciliatory.

Jansen and his wife led the way upstairs to the top landing. There, in front of a closed door, stood a large oak chest.

"That," said Jansen, "is the room. We've barricaded it like that to prevent the children going in. When we first came here, my wife and I and our youngest child, Bertha, slept there. But we none of us liked the room and we soon began to have very disturbed nights. I had ghastly nightmares, and so had my wife."

"And Bertha, too," added Mrs. Jansen. "She used to dread being left alone in the room even for five minutes, and used to cry until one or other of us went to her."

"That's right enough," said Mr. Jansen, "and Bertha's never behaved like that since we moved her into another room. Well, we experienced nothing more disturbing than those bad dreams for the first fortnight or so, and nothing happened until we were both aroused one night by hearing Bertha scream. We lit a candle and got out of bed. 'What's the matter,' I asked, 'are you in pain?' 'No, Poppa,' she said, 'not in pain, but so frightened. I kept hearing the bed creak, and I thought one of you was coming out of it to kill me.'

'Why, what nonsense,' I said. 'You've been dreaming again, child.'

Then, turning to my wife, I remarked: 'If she has many more of these nightmares we'd better send for the doctor. Don't you think so?'

My wife made no answer, but suddenly gave a cry and pointed at the bed. 'Otto! Look at the clothes! We never left them like that. What's happened to them?'

I looked. The clothes were all heaped together down the centre of the bed exactly in the shape of a human body, with the face turned towards us. We all three stared at it in open-mouthed silence, and the longer we gazed, the more pronounced grew the features, until they at last became so lifelike, so evil, that my wife and I instinctively shrank back against the child's cot, and tried to hide the thing from her. My wife declares she saw it move.

"It did," Mrs Jansen insisted. "I saw it distinctly shift nearer to us. So did Bertha."

Mr. Jansen nodded. "I know you were both agreed on that point. All I can say is I didn't see it do that, but I started praying, and whether it was the effect of my prayers or not, the clothes gradually became clothes again, and, after soothing Bertha, we scrambled back into bed, feeling rather ashamed we had been so frightened.

The following evening after Bertha had been put to bed we heard her scream again, and we ran up and found her quivering under the bedclothes. She said our bed had begun rattling, as if we were moving in it. On turning to examine it, we found the clothes just as we had seen them in the night, with one of the pillows pressed and moulded into the speaking likeness of a face. As I looked at it, the features became convulsed with such an indescribable expression of hellishness that I backed against the table and upset the light. On re-lighting it, the thing on the bed had disappeared, and the clothes were once again normal.

That same night, some time after we were in bed, I awoke to find myself being roughly shaken by the shoulders. It was my wife, but perhaps I had better let her go on with the story.

'I shook him,' Mrs. Jansen explained, 'because a feeling had suddenly come over me that I must kill Bertha. The very first night we slept in the room I became obsessed with a passionate desire to see someone die, a desire that I can assure you was absolutely novel to me, because I flatter myself that I am naturally kind-hearted and extremely sensitive to seeing other people suffer. Well, the feeling became so unbearable that, fearing I should actually be compelled to kill someone, I awoke my husband and begged him to tie my hands together; which, after some hesitation, he did. Bertha was crying bitterly, and told us she had again heard bed creaks in the room, just as if someone was getting out of bed to murder her. That was the last time we slept in the room. I felt it was a positive danger to spend another night in it, and so we removed into the one we are sleeping in now.'

The room had only been occupied once since. A niece of Mrs. Jansen's, Charlotte, came to stay with them, and as they had nowhere else to put her, she had to sleep there. Three times in succession that night Mrs. Jansen dreamt that Charlotte was creeping down the stairs with some strange weapon in her hand with which she intended to kill Bertha.

"The third dream was so vivid that I awoke from it bathed in perspiration. I told my husband, and he said, 'Well, that's curious, for I thought I heard someone moving about overhead. I'll go and see if anything is amiss.'

He opened the door, and, going on to the landing, discovered Charlotte tiptoeing cautiously down the stairs, holding a long, glittering pair of scissors in her hand, and with an expression on her face similar to that on the face in the bedclothes.

'What are you doing here?' my husband demanded, and Charlotte at once dropped the scissors and began to cry. She told us that no sooner had she got into bed, than she felt as if she were another person. It was just as if someone else's soul had crept into her body. All her old sentiments and ideals vanished, and the maddest and most unholy ideas presented themselves in rapid succession to her mind. A blind hatred of everyone in the house possessed her, and she was seized with the most ungovernable craving to kill. For a long time she fought against this mania, until at last, unable to restrain it any longer, she got out of bed and sought some weapon. Cold hands, she declared, seemed to guide her to the scissors, and armed with them, she crept downstairs, just as I had seen her in my sleep, determined to butcher Bertha first, and then, if possible, my husband and myself.

She pleaded our forgiveness and begged to be allowed to go home first thing in the morning.

'I do not feel I am responsible for my behaviour,' she said. 'I never had the slightest inclination to do anything of the sort before. I'm sure it's that room. There's some sinister influence in it, and if I go back to it, I'm certain I shall do something dreadful.'

She spent the rest of the night on the sofa in the parlour.

After that we locked up the room and had this chest placed against the door, as you now see it."

"Do you know the history of the house?" O'Donnell asked.

"Only that before we came here," said Mrs. Jansen, "there were several deaths. I don't think any of them were actually attributed to murder, though they were all due to rather extraordinary accidents. Originally, I believe, the house was an inn, kept by a woman who bore a very evil reputation, and we have always wondered if the hauntings had anything to do with her."

While based in New York, O'Donnell availed himself of the opportunity to travel up to Boston for a couple of nights, to see the sights and visit some relatives whom he had never met before. It was pure chance that directed his steps to a hotel that bore the, for him, enviable stigma of housing a ghost. It was situated in a rather poor area of the city, and attracted few visitors. Indeed, on the landing where he slept, his was the only occupied room.

It was late when, after a day spent sightseeing and calling upon relatives, he got back to the hotel. The place was dimly lit and silent.

"Am I the last in?" he asked the night clerk.

"Yes, sir. The other guests have gone to bed two hours or more. It's close on one."

The clerk's accent was a give-away. "What part of Ireland do you come from?"

"County Limerick, to be sure. But you couldn't tell I was Irish!"

"At once,' said O'Donnell. "What were you over there?"

"I was working on the roads, and before that I was in the Army – the Inniskillings."

"What date?" He told me. It transpired that he had enlisted in that regiment when one of my uncles was a major in it, and he remembered him well.

They were talking away, nostalgically recalling the long past, when O'Donnell heard a familiar sliding kind of noise, and broke off in mid-sentence. "Surely that's the elevator," he said. "I hope our talking hasn't disturbed anyone."

"I don't think so, sir," he said. "At any rate, I shouldn't trouble myself about it. There was something strange in the tone of his voice, and an odd, furtive look in his eyes as he spoke, that somehow alerted O'Donnell's sixth sense. He walked across the hall, was just in time to see the lift come slowly and softly down, and, to his astonishment, saw that there was no one in it.

"How's that happened?" he asked the clerk. "No one called it, and there was no one in it."

"I can't say, sir." The clerk looked shifty and uneasy.

O'Donnell was late again getting back to the hotel the following night.

As he entered the vestibule, the lift again came slowly and softly – and empty – down. The same porter was on duty.

"Does it come down at the same time every night?" asked O'Donnell.

The night porter looked awkward. "Yes, sir," he muttered, "every night."

"And the reason? There must be some reason. An elevator can't start off unless someone or something starts it."

He was silent.

"I see, there's some mystery attached to it. What is it? Tell me."

For some seconds he remained obdurate, silent. Then, succumbing; "For goodness sake don't let on, sir, because the boss has forbidden any of the staff to mention it, and if he found out I'd told you, he'd sack me at once. This hotel is haunted. Several years ago, before my time, a visitor arrived here late one night and was found by the day porter dead in the lift. How he died was never exactly known; it was rumoured he had either committed suicide or been murdered. It was never found out who he was or where he came from and, as he had no money, he was buried like a pauper. Well, sir, ever since that elevator has taken it into its head to set itself in motion at the same time every night. Sometimes the gates clang, just as if someone were getting in and out. At first I usedn't to like it at all. You can imagine, perhaps, what it's like to know that you are the only person about in a place of this sort – and then to hear the elevator suddenly beginning to descend. However, by degrees, I got accustomed to it, and if that was all that happened I shouldn't mind."

"What else happens?"

"I can't tell you, sir. Would you like a bit of exercise?"

"I don't mind. Why?"

"Will you try the staircase, then, instead of the elevator? Count the stairs and note carefully when you come to the forty-first."

The stairs were narrow and tortuous, the light meagre, and soon O'Donnell was beginning to feel very, very far from his friend the night porter and very much alone in the building, a feeling which increased the further he proceeded, until it became so unbearable that he involuntarily halted. He was on the thirty-ninth step. High overhead was a kind of funnel formed of black, funereal, and apparently never-ending banisters. Below was a similarly constructed pit. A host of eerie shadows came dancing out of the flickering gas-light. As he watched their gambollings he became aware that something, a presence, something he could not see, was standing on the staircase a few steps ahead, barring his way. With a tremendous effort, he struggled on to the next step. Then, the most frightful, the most overwhelming, diabolical terror seized him, and turning round, he tore downstairs.

"Well, you've come back. Couldn't pass it," the porter greeted him. "No one who tries to do so at this time of night ever can."

"What is it?" asked O'Donnell. "What is the beastly thing?"

"I don't know. No one knows," he paused. "This place was once a madhouse, I believe, and perhaps..."

"Thank goodness I'm leaving tomorrow," said O'Donnell, "and as it's a choice of two evils, I'll go up in the lift."

He returned to New York, where, really strapped for cash, he put up at a fifty-cents-a-night hotel kept by a Hungarian, name of Kalowski, in the somewhat insalubrious quarter of West Quay, until, finances improving a shade, he moved over to the Cosmopolitan, in Chambers Street, where he stayed during his final couple of weeks in the city.

Walking, one of his last days in New York, through the Bowery, it nearly was his last day! He narrowly escaped being shot. A drinking saloon fracas escalated to the drawing of firearms stage, and a bullet whizzed out, near enough parted O'Donnell's hair, and embedded itself in a wall.

His golden dream of making his fortune in the brave New World dissipated, O'Donnell shipped for England as a steerage passenger aboard the North German Lloyd vessel, the S.S. *Elbe*. They slipped out of New York harbour on November 13th, 1894. This was to be the ill-fated *Elbe*'s last homeward journey. On her next voyage out she was run into by the *Crathie*, several hundred miles off the east coast of England, and sank with an appalling loss of life.

It was an experience O'Donnell would never forget. For the whole of the first night or two at sea the steerage passengers – men, women, and children – were herded together on the bare boards of the lower deck. No sleeping accommodation was provided. The ship's officers swore at, even kicked, them whenever they happened to get in their way, and the crew did not bother to conceal their hearty contempt for all but the first-class passengers. O'Donnell was lucky. He managed to bribe an engineer to let him have the loan of his cabin, which he shared with his friend and fellow steerage passenger, Edward Richards.

They were given three meals a day, food and drink being doled out to them in tin dippers. The menu fell somewhat short of liner luxurious – Breakfast: tea without milk, and bread and margarine. Dinner: meat or soup, supplemented occasionally by a few prunes. Supper: milkless tea, and bread and margarine.

Most of their time was spent boxed up, hour after hour, below decks, in a stifling atmosphere that reeked of oil, the fumes of bad tobacco, and the odour of packed and none-too-clean humanity, many of whom were constantly vomiting as the ship rolled and pitched. The air down there was loud with screaming children, scolding and squabbling women, swearing and growling men, and the sound of the violent retching of seventy per cent. of them. In the intervals between meals, they were grudgingly allowed short spells up on deck. To make matters worse, the weather was particularly rough, and the voyage took nine days.

There was the odd incident that relieved the gloom of the eternal-seeming sea passage. An Irishman, Patrick Murphy, played a trick on a Polish Jew who had made himself extremely unpopular by his habit of ceaseless chewing throughout the day, and, at night, the constant smacking of his lips, which regularly awoke his sleeping neighbours. Asked what he was playing at, the Pole reluctantly admitted that he was hungry and had been continually snacking from a supply of ham and other food which he had brought with him from his meat stores in Chicago; a confession received with mingled anger and disgust. The next morning but one, the greedy Pole, holding one hand to his throat, rushed, yelling and screaming, up on deck. Thrusting aside any seaman or steward in his path, he accosted the first officer he met. "*Gott in Himmel!*," he shrieked, "look, look, my throat has been cut! An Irishman did it. He drew the blade of his razor right across my windpipe. I bleed to death. Save me! I suffer terrible. Save me!"

"I can't see any blood," the officer grunted. "Take your hand away."

The Pole did as he was told, and immediately received a sound slap on the face. "Be off at once. There's nothing the matter with your throat at all." Giving him another good cuff, and a kick into the bargain, the officer added: "And that's to teach you not to come to me again with such a cock-and-bull story."

Returning to the steerage quarters, tail between legs, the Pole was greeted with roars of laughter. He had been the victim of an ingenious trick. While he was sleeping, Murphy had with one hand drawn the back of a cut-throat razor across his gullet, and with the other poured a tumbler full of tepid water down his neck. Half-awake, dazed, his eye caught by the razor which Murphy had been careful to stain crimson, his elected victim was totally convinced that he had had his throat slit. Anyway, Murphy's action had the desired effect, completely curing the Pole of his offensive chewing habits.

More tragic was another incident.

O'Donnell was on deck one night, talking to a couple of his fellow-passengers, when a uniformed figure, whom he recognised as the captain, passed slowly by, moved to the taffrail and, leaning his elbows on it, stood gazing into the dark sea below.

"The skipper. Wonder what he's doing here?" remarked one of O'Donnell's companions. O'Donnell wondered, too, and asked a seaman.

"That can't be the captain," was the reply. "It looks like him, but I know he's engaged at this moment on the quarter-deck. I can't understand it." The seaman then walked across to the taffrail, said something to the figure who, without seeming to a reply or take any notice of the man, then walked across to one of the deck-houses, and entered it, followed by the seaman.

A few moments later, the seaman emerged and came across to O'Donnell. "The figure you and I saw just now was not the captain at all," he told him, "but his *Doppelgänger*. I followed it in there," he pointed to the deck-house, "and while I was looking at it, it vanished, melted right away into the air."

It was with considerable relief that O'Donnell walked down the gangway and felt the English soil of Southampton crunching beneath his feet.

The Ghost of Smithills Hall, from O'Donnell's Famous Curses (1929).
This stately home is still standing near Bolton in Lancashire, and is still said to be haunted.

The Screaming Skulls of Calgarth Hall, a well-known legend discussed in O'Donnell's Famous Curses (1929).

7

Spectral London in the Nineties

The train which he caught from Southampton, where he had docked and where he had spent a couple of days, steamed into Waterloo. It was a wretched day, cold and wet, and as he watched the teeming masses of rain-sodden people pushing past him, ignoring him, his heart failed him. It all seemed so hopeless. He was a pigmy in a vast city, without influence, without money. Could he reasonably expect ever to find employment here? Could he compete, even for the barest weekly pittance, against these countless hordes, all clearly more experienced and infinitely more valuable in the labour market than he was. He lingered for a long time on the platform and around the station watching, and envying in his loneliness, those merry, boisterous passengers who were driven away in hansoms to the comfort of a home or the luxury of an hotel.

O'Donnell's knowledge of London was strictly limited. Indeed, he had never before been on the south side of the Thames. There had been a few brief visits, when most of his time had been spent sightseeing, and when he was there for his Sandhurst exam, and he had stayed at a private hotel in Cambridge Street, in Pimlico. That was somewhere that funds would not run to now.

He left his luggage in the station cloakroom, made for the first exit he saw, wandered out on to the sloshy pavement of Waterloo Road, and set off in search of a room. The rain was descending in sheets, and splashing up again off the ground. It was not long before the legs of his trousers were soaking. He plunged into a gloomy, subaqueous Stamford Street. The houses that he went into were "grimed with dirt, if there were any carpets they were threadbare, the furniture, of which there was often a superfluity, was dilapidated, and the landladies were mostly on a par with their effects. Some of them in an attempt at 'make-up' had painted their cheeks, while not a few wore cheap jewellery, chiefly in the shape of drop ear-rings, silver lockets and clasp bracelets."

One woman, whom he judged not so unprepossessing, and a trifle cleaner than the others, showed him a fair-sized room on the second floor. Its furnishings included a rickety table, a pair of almost seatless chairs, an insubstantial wash-stand, a yellow grained chest of drawers, and two single beds.

"You can have the room for four shillings a week if you don't mind sharing it with another young feller," the woman told him. "He's very respectable. He's German. A waiter at an hotel in the Strand. You're sure to get on with him. He don't interfere with no one, and he'd be a nice bloke for you to go about with when you've done work."

The allurement of the offer eluded him. He declined and swam off down the watery street.

O'Donnell afterwards wrote: "This certainly took me aback. It was indeed a revelation as to how the poor really live, and concealing my surprise as best I could, I thanked this kind woman – I could plainly see that she meant to be kind – for her offer. But her parting words, 'Why, we never puts less than two in a room and sometimes we puts three or four. We couldn't pay our rent if we didn't,' spoken in a candid and explanatory, though somewhat reproachful, manner, made me feel not only very sad and depressed but also very apprehensive. Indeed, it was some time before I felt I could face another prospective landlady and risk another such setback."

After a thoroughly wet and wearisome hunt, he finally managed to find a place to stay. It was in Tennyson Street, S.E., a very small room, very dark, and very beetle – black-beetles, whole armies of them, parading the floor, scaling the walls, one of them occasionally dropping with a thud so close to him that he sprang out of bed in terror that it had actually landed on the counterpane. Cockroaches scared him as much, if not more than, ghosts. He only stayed in that house three days.

Another wearisome search brought him to an attic room above a little restaurant in York Road. He felt himself wonderfully lucky in finding quarters in one of the few respectable houses in the mean and squalid York Road of the mid-nineties, which he described as being "in the day-time full of frowsily dressed men and women and the fetid steam from the cheaper kinds of restaurants; and at night it was infinitely worse, I have never in any other street in London seen such an endless procession of women of the unfortunate class. They were nearly all German, and their hard, cruel faces should have been a sufficient warning to anyone to give them a wide berth. I haven't the slightest doubt that many of the young men who were foolish enough to be enticed by them were ruthlessly robbed and not infrequently murdered."

Pure benevolent chance had led him to a small café on York Road. As he sat there with a cup of tea, he overheard the girl behind the counter telling another customer that they had two rooms over the café to let. He waited until the customer had gone, then enquired about a room. He was shown one right at the top of the house, up an Everest of stairs. It was to let at a very moderate rental, a few shillings per week. Every day a splendid breakfast of bacon or an egg, toast and butter and jam or marmalade, was served up, never at a cost of more than sixpence, and on Sundays the landlady insisted on his dining with the family, which consisted of a widow, her 19-year-old daughter, and two sons, young men in good situations. They were charming. He had seldom, he said, met nicer people. He felt that he had fallen on his feet.

He now turned his mind to the desperate problem of finding some means of making a livelihood. He had been expensively educated, but that did not seem to stand him in any good stead here and now. Those subjects which he had so zealously studied for the Sandhurst and R.I.C. exams in no wise fitted him for a business career. Eventually he landed a position in a kind of jobbing stockbroker's office in Lewisham. It lasted for a week. His employer was a wizen-faced man, displaying a straggling beard, yards of gold watch-chain, and a strong tendency to bully. The hours were from nine to six, with twenty minutes interval for lunch. The second day he was there, he was kept at the office until after seven, so the following day, by way of retaliation, he took a good hour's lunch break. When he got back, he found his employer showing all the signs of apoplexy. "What do you think I pay you for?" he shrieked, "to eat?"

"You haven't paid me yet," responded O'Donnell. "It'll be time enough to give way to your emotions when you have. You kept me here last night an hour longer than the time agreed. Very good! You get an hour less work out of me today. What's sauce for the goose is sauce for the gander."

He raised a thick, podgy hand. O'Donnell thought he was going to strike him, and hoped he would, for he had always been very fond of boxing, and a scrap with him would have been as nectar. However, he suddenly subsided, and walked out of the room. For the few more days that O'Donnell remained, the pre-arranged office hours were rigidly adhered to. Thus ended, his one and only venture into the world of business.

He decided to invest his tiny capital, plus a small legacy from his godfather, in a course of shorthand and typing lessons at Pitman's School in Chancery Lane, hoping that this might fit him for being taken on as a reporter by one of the London dailies. Meanwhile, he worked hard, learning all he could at Pitman's in the daytime, and grinding away at practice and preparation at York Road in the evenings.

The beginning of 1895, one of the coldest of recorded London Januaries, was cast well in the icy mould of the never-to-be-forgotten savage winter of 1880-81, the Thames being decorated with miniature icebergs and the roads and houses tucked in under an inches deep pall of snow.

The bitter weather, on top of an abortive pubescent infatuation with Alice, a member of Pitman's staff, "one of the prettiest girls I have ever seen... a slender blonde with blue-grey eyes, in a trim sailor hat, tripping daintily along Chancery Lane, parasol in hand," who, sadly, did not reciprocate his feelings, and made him seriously contemplate suicide, until he learned that she had become engaged to somebody else – proving too much for him, he had to shove his shorthand books aside and take to his bed. He went down with a dose of 'flu. His landlady was very good to him, not only sharing her family Christmas dinner with him, but now when he was ill keeping him supplied with nourishing broth and other small invalidish delicacies.

The evening of January 12th, a Saturday, the influenza having subsided, found him feeling considerably improved, though still too poorly to leave his room. He had not been idle though. All day he had persisted with his shorthand studies. Not stopping until around seven o'clock. He had relapsed into serial snoozing until, at midnight, he had abruptly become acutely awake.

The road outside was unaccustomedly still and quiet; an unusually heavy fall of snow, descending after dark, had not been swept away, and deadened the noise of wheels and the sounds of hooves and footsteps. Glancing at his watch, he saw by the reflection of the fire, still glowing ruddy, that it was getting on for 1 a.m. The whole household seemed to be wrapped in slumber. Then... of a sudden... in the street, just below his window, the sound of footsteps crunching on frozen snow. A sort of sixth sense seemed to switch on. In the sound of those footsteps was something that chilled his blood. He felt them to be the herald of the advent of some indefinable horror.

Sitting up in bed, he leant his hand against the window-sill and waited. It was not long before he heard more footsteps in the snow. Lighter than their predecessor's, these he judged to be those of a woman. Next, he heard a sort of burr, as of some heavy object whirring through the air, in a rough male voice, a volley of oaths. A scuffle. A cry cut short. A sequence of groans and terrible gurglings. A whistling. A sound of carriage wheels. Then silence, until the rattling of shutters and the opening of doors proclaimed the birth of a new day.

His landlady, ill and pale-looking, the dark circles beneath her eyes betokening a sleepless night, came in with an early morning cup of tea for him. He asked her if she had heard anything in the night.

"Heard anything!" she said. "I not only heard it all, but I saw it, too."

Her account tallied exactly with the sounds and visual imaginings which had put his own tranquillity to flight. She slept in the basement, in the front room, which was not much below the street level. She had been lying awake when she heard light footsteps coming down the street. They were those of a woman. She came into plain view from the landlady's bed, which faced the window, and when she got exactly opposite the house, pulled up sharp, with a cry of fright. The next instant, a man, who had been hiding in the café doorway, sprang out on her. Knife in hand, he dealt her blow after vicious stabbing blow. Groaning and gurgling, the woman sank to the ground in a spreading pool of blood. "That serves you right for peaching," he growled. "You won't tell no more tales." The man whistled. A cab came up. He and the cabby bundled the woman inside, and drove off with her.

In the morning, O'Donnell's landlady had found blood on the doorstep and the area railings. Neighbours told him that they thought it likely that the woman attacked had been the witness in a recent trial whose evidence had been chiefly responsible for the conviction of a man sentenced to death for the murder of a prostitute in a street close to York Road. The friends of the murderer had sworn to get her.

Asked if they were going to do anything about it, the neighbours replied with an emphatic "No." What would be the good? After all, what they had told him was merely surmise. They had not seen the men involved, and to mention the matter to the police might well mean that they, too, would be subjected to a savage attack.

That was not O'Donnell's only memorable experience at his York Road lodgings. Going upstairs to his room one morning, he had encountered a fellow-lodger, Mr. Ramsey, coming down. Continuing his ascent, he was considerably surprised when Mr. Ramsey suddenly appeared before him again on the stairs, coming down.

"Why, hello!" O'Donnell greeted him. "How's this? You passed me going down only a few seconds ago."

"I didn't, as you can see," said Ramsey. "But are you sure it was I? Because, if so, it means that something serious will happen to me. Whenever a double is seen of anyone in our family, the original is sure to die shortly."

Of course, O'Donnell told him not to worry, that very possibly he had been mistaken. But Ramsey did die, exactly three weeks later.

One wet night, when he was still living in York Road, O'Donnell said goodbye to a friend of his in Adelphi, walked down Villiers Street, and crossed the tram-lines on to the Embankment:

> Besides being wet, the night was cold and dark, the streets were absolutely deserted, and the feebly flickering lamps seemed to cast strangely elongated shadows on the glistening pavements. As I walked hurriedly along in the direction of Waterloo Bridge, I glanced at the river. The tide was unusually high, and the water, which appeared to be almost on a level with the road, where the many lights from Waterloo Bridge fell on it, flashed and sparkled like highly burnished silver; but elsewhere outside the radius of the lamps, it rolled by all black and sullen and shadow-laden.
>
> I had just arrived at Cleopatra's Needle, and was passing by it, when I suddenly heard a whistling. It seemed to come from the river side of me, and there was something so arrestive about it that I at once stood still and listened. After a few seconds it was repeated – a low, soft, and wonderfully seductive whistling, that sounded this time almost in my ears. Determined to fathom the mystery and ascertain its origin, I descended the steps leading on to the little landing-stage or alcove behind Cleopatra's Needle, and searched everywhere. There was no one there, nothing but the shadows of the grim and silent sphinxes that looked extraordinarily ghostly and sinister in the semi-gloom. Again I heard the whistling; it was softer and even more seductive than before, and now there was no atom of doubt but that it proceeded from the water. I immediately leaned over the wall and looked down, down into the sullen, gleaming depths gliding noiselessly by; but I could see no

one. After the lapse of a minute or so, the whistling was repeated, and I felt I must get as near to it as possible, lest any single note should escape me. With this intention, I was leaning over the wall, when a hand suddenly caught hold of me from behind and jerked me swiftly to the ground. I turned angrily round and found myself face to face with a policeman.

"Another second and you would have been over," he said sternly. "What were you trying to do – commit suicide?"

"Why, no," I replied indignantly, "I was merely listening to someone whistling. It is quite the most extraordinary phenomenon I have ever experienced. I could see no one and the sounds seemed to come from the very bosom of the river."

The policeman was an elderly man, and as he stood watching me in the full glow of the street lamp, I fancied I could detect a strange expression creep into his eyes.

"Can you in any way account for it ?" I asked.

"No," he replied, shaking his head, "I can't; but queer things do happen at times along this Embankment and on the bridges... One evening some years ago, before I joined the force, I was walking along the Embankment feeling down and out. I'd come up from the country to look for a job, and as I'd looked in vain for some days, tramping the streets from morning to night, I was getting just about fed up. Well, when I got to this recess, where you heard the whistling, I stopped, something seemed to make me, and peered over the parapet into the water; and, as I did so, I heard a voice, which sounded like a girl's, it was soft and musical, whispering in my ear: "Jump in." I started and turned round, but there was no one there, nothing but that lamp-post...

Well, I moved on, but I hadn't gone far before I felt obliged to come back. I did so, and was leaning over the parapet when I again heard the voice. "Jump in. Jump in." There was something so alluring and persuasive in its tone that I felt I must do as it said. I then looked round, just to make sure that no one was about, and to my surprise and annoyance I saw a young man crossing the road towards me. He came and stood a few yards off, and every time I was about to take the plunge I was obliged to draw back, because I saw him eyeing me. At last, losing all patience, I went up to him and asked him what he meant by continually spying on me. "I don't mean any harm," he said. "It's only because I like company. I'm bent on committing suicide tonight, and as you seem to be inspired with the same idea, I thought we might as well go together."

"No," I shook my head. Life suddenly became dear to me again. "I've had enough of it for one night. I'll have a last look round for work tomorrow, and if I don't find any, you may count on seeing me here at one in the morning. Wait till then." I held out a few coppers to him, exactly half of what I had in my pocket, and, taking them, he promised. The following day I sought for work, but with no better luck, and at 1 a.m., worn out in body and mind, I arrived at the appointed rendezvous. He was waiting for me.

"Hello," I said. "I see you've kept your word. Well I'm going to do it this time."

To my surprise the young man shook his head. "Why, what's up?" I asked, "You're surely not going to back out of it!" "No, it's not that," he said. "Only I took your money under false pretences. I jumped in." And he vanished, completely, inexplicably, and totally vanished. I found myself talking to nothing. That frightened me and I fled – fled like the wind.

"So it was a ghost?" I said. "And the stranger had actually committed suicide?"

The policeman nodded.

His shorthand up to speed, O'Donnell set himself to trying to secure a position on the staff of a newspaper. He wrote to almost every editor in London, but each time drew a blank. He did, however, succeed in soliciting a bit of freelance work, including some interviewing for a weekly journal, *Theatricals*. The first theatrical celebrity he was commissioned to anatomise was Sir Augustus Harris, to whom he introduced himself on the stage at Drury Lane, during the rehearsal of a pantomime, at which Dan Leno was present. O'Donnell must, in the course of the interview, have communicated his own dissatisfaction with the shape his life was taking. Sir Augustus listened to his tale of woe with great courtesy, and told him to go and see Mr. Neil Forsyth, his assistant manager. This he did, with the result that he was offered a small post on the staff of the theatre. He felt obliged to refuse, with gratitude, this kindness, for, apart from the corresponding smallness of the salary, there were other obstacles in the way which made its acceptance impossible.

Before long he had to give up working for *Theatricals*: he had so much difficulty in getting paid. He was, however, getting bits and pieces of freelance work and having the odd short story accepted.

It was a fellow-student at Pitman's, Digby Childe, – "a public school man, one of my sort" – who had suggested the ushering alternative to O'Donnell and told him that he should visit the scholastic agents, Gabbitas-Thring and register with them for teaching work. Schoolmastering, although used as a, somewhat insubstantial, crutch by 'prentice literary men, was not a very popular profession. The generality of its offerings as to pay and conditions were less than seductive. Needs must though.

"You may find Gabbitas a bit of a rough card," Childe warned, "but apart from a few swear words he is not so bad."

O'Donnell reports: "Gabbitas certainly was a rough card, as Childe put it, but improved on acquaintance. When I told him that I had no qualifications beyond the London Matriculation, he said, 'Oh, that is all right. You were at Clifton, and if you are any good at games, those are sufficient qualifications.'

He gave him the names of several schools where there were vacancies for masters to teach elementary subjects, and promised to find him more. He did, and O'Donnell was taken on at Daventry Grammar School. Apart from the miserable salary – £30 *per annum*, out of which he was expected pay all his travelling expenses – O'Donnell felt himself being overworked, as well as underpaid. It was required of him not only to teach all day, but, outside school hours, to supervise early morning and alternate evening preparation, and to turn out on half-holidays to play games with the boys. Luckily, it so happened that he enjoyed sport, so that coaching the boys in cricket and football, and acting as umpire or referee was no great hardship. What, on the other hand, was a great hardship was the total lack of discipline in the school. He shrewdly suspected that the plain fact was that the headmaster lived in fear of losing paying pupils if he were to visit too severe a punishment upon them. What was an even greater hardship, a positive thorn in his side, was the attitude of the headmaster's wife. She seemed to resent his having any authority over the boys, and would openly encourage them to flaunt it. He put up with two terms of this, then left.

A dominie's lot, like that of a Gilbertian policeman, was not a happy one.

The Daventarian purgatory was, however, to transport one great benefice into the life of its suffering temporary citizen.

> I was staying in Daventry when I first met Ada Caroline Bullivant Williams. A friend of my mother's, who was living in a village about twelve miles from Daventry,[1] invited to spend the weekend with her and her husband. I cycled there and met Ada, who came to dinner. I was 23. She was 26. Her portrait, painted by Sheridan Knowles, was exhibited in the Royal Academy and bought by the proprietors of the *Illustrated London News*. Her father, a clever and highly qualified physician,[2] had practised in the West End before retiring and settling in the country.

---

1   Guilsborough.
2   Henry W. Williams, M.D. Born: c. 1837, at Guilsborough, Northants.

Ada studied painting at the Caldron Studio in St. John's Wood. She was a very clever portrait painter. She was also a clever essayist, critic, and writer of verse. She reviewed books for several of the London papers. No words of mine can ever do her sufficient justice. She was as near perfection as it is possible for any human being to be. Honest, kind, beautiful, generous and absolutely unselfish. Her loyalty to me in all the long years we were married never wavered. She was the loving companion in all the trials and hardships, the sorrows and illnesses, that were my lot, and she never murmured or upbraided me, when she would have been fully justified in so doing. If ever there was an angel in flesh and blood, it was she. My first meeting with her, although it is many years ago is almost as fresh in my memory as if it occurred only yesterday. It was not until four years later that we became engaged, and it was rather more than another five before we were married.

There was, too, the yield of a strange psychic experience when, on a spring afternoon in 1896, O'Donnell was riding his bicycle along the main road from Weedon to Daventry. "I became aware of the presence of a cyclist in grey who rode slowly ahead of me. The curious part of it was that a second before I had looked round and the road, a very long and level one, had been absolutely void of life. Now here was someone who had sprung suddenly and noiselessly to life. For some distance we continued our course, until we came up to a large cart which was rattling along in the centre of the thoroughfare, the driver blissfully careless of anyone else's welfare save his own. To my horror my mysterious companion ran with great force right into the back of the cart and, the phantom cyclist disappeared. Not a vestige of either him or his machine was to be seen, and I rode on wondering whether I had been dreaming."

In January, 1896, he wrote to the Bristol publisher, J.W. Arrowsmith, obviously hoping to persuade him to commission a book. "If you will call in some morning – about 10 o'clock is the best time to catch me – I shall be glad to chat with you if you wish it," read Arrowsmith's note of reply, written on January 10th, 1896. No doubt their meeting was cordial enough, but it did not lead to any publication.

Daventry Grammar School well behind him, O'Donnell's was back in London. His *Purgatorio* was Henley House School, in Mortimer Road, Kensal Green. The premises was a corner house with a small garden in front, and a large one, devoid of grass and obviously used as a playground, at the rear. The scholars' entrance was in the basement. The accommodation provided for O'Donnell was not very inviting. He was led along a dreary, stone-paved passage. Off it was a bathroom. The bath was filthy and brimful of loads and loads of books and grubby clothes. At the end of this passage was the room described as the master's study. Its window overlooked the wasteland garden, what small quantity of furniture it contained was dilapidated. The bedroom was in keeping with the other rooms, but with one additional feature: its walls were running with water. O'Donnell remonstrated with the short and scraggy woman servant who was acting as his guide.

"I really couldn't sleep in such a room."

"Oh, them walls is all right," was her response. "It's only sweat on them." She was right. It was.

The headmaster, Mr. Godley, was an elderly man with a pleasant face, who proved as benign and genial as he looked. He never punished a boy and was consistently most considerate to O'Donnell. He had two daughters, very stand-offish at first, but afterwards friendly enough.

The boys ranged from between nine and ten to fourteen years of age. They were middle class and largely Jewish. There was an assistant master, Mr. Turner. He proved a great friend, ever ready to do a kindly act for O'Donnell, and frequently taking preparation for him. He had not had the happiest of lives – sacked from two public schools, equally unlucky at his university, either Oxford or Cambridge, and no more successful as a medical student. A consolation prize: Mrs. Turner was, O'Donnell observed, very pretty. Interestingly, Turner gave O'Donnell to understand that he had been raised with Dr. Neill Cream, the infamous dispenser of lethal pink pills to pale prostitutes.[3]

Over the course of the next few years, O'Donnell was to do several other stints of schoolmastering, none of them turning out satisfactory. Wolverhampton Grammar School was one of the oldest in England. It catered for about 500 boys, "mostly of the middle middle class, with a sprinkling of boys from elementary schools." O'Donnell got on with them very well. They gave him no trouble. The headmaster, Mr. Coldicote, was fish of another kind. "I cannot say that I liked him."

The headmaster at another of O'Donnell's penitential brief stop-overs, Clyde School, Hereford, Mr. Baker, he found a perplexity. "He had been

---

3   Thomas Neill Cream. Born: Glasgow, 1850. family emigrated to Canada, 1854-55. Entered M'Gill College, Montreal, to read medicine, 1872. Graduated 1876. Executed at Newgate, 1892.

a housemaster at Bruce Castle. How he got that post puzzled me, for he was by no means a gentleman, and furthermore he had no degree." The boys were logged on O'Donnell's pupillary spectrum as "lower middle class", and some of them further stigmatised as "very rude and rowdy." In addition there were several Spanish youths, learning English. They were categorised as "not bright." He only stayed there for one term, and was thankful to leave.

One sparkling memory of his time at Hereford was his meeting with the Parrys – old Mrs. Emma Parry and her sons, Joseph and Henry. "Jo and Harry had both been at Winchester, like me, they were on the Foundation of that school as descendants of the nearest kin of William of Wykeham. From Winchester they went on to either Oxford or Cambridge. Joe, for a term or two, was a master at a well known private school. Harry was the master of the Hereford Hunt. Mrs. Parry was a cousin of his mother's, and had been a bridesmaid at her wedding She invited me to spend a few days with her at Harewood, a picturesque old country mansion about six miles from Hereford. While there, we visited several interesting places in the neighbourhood, and enjoyed ourselves very much. They were most hospitable."

Of all the varied assistant-masterships which he had held, O'Donnell was to like least the one which was to prove to be his last. It was at Shirley House School, an academy for the sons of gentlemen, at Blackheath, south-east London. The principal fly in the ointment was... the principal, Mr. S. Storrs, a self-professed Radical, further professing Socialistic leanings, who, the very reverse of liberal, was the most unmitigated snob, forever reminding O'Donnell that whereas he had not been to a university, he, his headmaster, was a Cambridge man. Worked like a slave, for a mere song, and treated in a manner which, even in recollection, made his blood boil, he also found his pupils hopelessly spoilt and tiresome. Moreover, he developed an absolute detestation of the Heath after dark. His only consolations were cricket and writing.

O'Donnell had for some time been afflicted with the *cacoethes scribendi*. He had, in fact, written his first book after leaving Dublin and his visit to Scotland. A crime mystery, based on an unsolved murder committed at Hampton Down, near Bath, in August, 1891, The real-life story is an intriguing one. On Friday, September 22nd, 1893, two boys, Cecil Brand and Alec Emerson, exploring a secluded cave in one of a cluster of disused quarries at Hampton Rocks, on Hampton Down, found the bones of a human skeleton half-hidden under a covering of stones. They proved to be the remains of a slight young woman, estimated age 19 to 21 years, and standing between 5ft. and 5ft. 2ins. in height. Various portions of clothing adhering to the bones included the remnants of an underskirt with figured band, a slip bodice, linen drawers, buttoned, a linen collar, flannel petticoat, and black ribbed stockings. The skull showed fracturing that indicated that she had died from a single blow to the head, delivered with great force.

The discovery of the clue of a bloodstained handkerchief led to the identification of the remains as those of a girl named Elsie Wilkie, who had been a cook in the service of a Mr. and Mrs. James Kerry, at Cheriton Lodge, Oldfield Park, Bath. The girl's real name turned out to be Elsie Adeline Luke; Wilkie was the name of her stepfather, with whom she had been brought up. She said that she came from near London, giving an address which was afterwards thought not to have been genuine. She was, said Mr. Kerry, of prepossessing appearance, well-spoken, knew something of French, and could read music. These were unusual attainments for a domestic servant, and suggested something of a mystery in the girl's background. Mr. Kerry stated that she had been very well conducted in the house, but he had heard of things while she was away from the house that caused him to give her notice. Before the expiration of that notice, she had obtained from him her wages in advance, on the pretence that an uncle from whom she was to receive money having died, she had to go to London. This was on Saturday, August 1st, 1891. She was to have returned on the Monday, but never did. After her departure from Cheriton Lodge, Mrs. Kerry missed a dress and also a portion of her wedding trousseau.

That Saturday, Elsie had actually made her way to the house of Andrew Dillon, at Kingswood Terrace, in Bath. She told him that her employer had gone away for a few days, and asked if he could put her up for a day or two. She was, she said, on board wages. She slept at Dillon's on the Saturday and Sunday nights. On Bank Holiday morning she left the house, saying that she was going for a country walk. She did not return.

A friend of Elsie's, Lucy Isaacs, testified that she last saw her alive in the week before August Bank Holiday, 1891. She was then in good health and spirits. There had been no mention whatsoever of any actual or suspected pregnancy. She had called at Lucy Isaacs' house – 4 Bryant's Terrace, Calton Road, Bath – to collect a photograph of herself, and she had then said that she was going away to be married on Bank Holiday, but she did not say where she was going. The name of her intended was Arthur Coombs. Elsie had often told Lucy Isaacs the same thing before, but she had found her out in so many lies that she did not believe her.

During the inquiry into Elsie Luke's murder, which was believed to have taken place on or about August 3rd, 1891, a great deal of evidence had been taken to show motive with regard to one individual – the said Arthur Coombs. At the inquest, which was opened by the Coroner for North Somerset, Mr. Samuel Craddock, at the George Inn, Bathampton, on September 26th, 1893, and concluded on December 6th, 1893, Coombs deponed that he was not engaged to the deceased, but simply kept company with her. He had severed his connection with her because he had found that she had been telling him "a pack of lies from beginning to end." He had never, he most insistently declared, gone out with her after January, 1891.

Summing up, the coroner said that it was for the jury to reconcile that statement with the sworn evidence of the two young men, Clare and Phillips, that they saw Coombs walking with the murdered girl through the woods leading to Hampton Down; but he added that the sighting in the wood did not bear very much on the case; "at the most, it simply proved that at that particular time Coombs was carrying on an intrigue with the dead girl at the same time that he was absolutely engaged to Miss Sheppard."

And the jury returned a verdict of murder by person or persons unknown.[4]

---

4   At 2.30 p.m. on December 11th, 1893, the mortal remains of Elsie Adeline Luke, contained in a small coffin, covered with a black pall with a white border, were borne from the skittle alley at the George Inn, Bathampton to the lych gate of the parish church of St. Nicholas, on the opposite side of the road. Where it was met by the Vicar, the Reverend H. Girdlestone. The only mourners were two of the police officers involved in the investigation, Police Sergeant Charles Edwards and Police Constable Brunt, and those who had gathered out of curiosity and followed the remains into the church, made up the sole sad sprinkling of mourners. The burial service over, the coffin was taken to a grave on the railway side of the churchyard, and buried next to the tombstone of John Baptiste, Viscount Du Barry, killed in a duel on Claverton Down, in November, 1778. The expenses of decent sepulture were borne by the parish. The last resting place of Elsie Adeline Luke "who was cruelly murdered" has recently received a splendid new tombstone, funded by the estate of the late Lucy Barlow.

This was a rich speculative field for O'Donnell to furrow. He had sold his novel, titled *Escaped from Justice*, to the Fleet Street firm of Edwin J. Brett, but the business ceased publishing the following year, and the book never saw the light of print. It was a great disappointment, assuaged minimally by his having been paid for it.

Every evening, after his work with the boys was done, he used to repair to a room over a library in Blackheath village to ply an industrious pen over his second book, *For Satan's Sake*, a novel. The book dealt with the soul of a suicide, and, grounded in his disappointment with the thwarting of his love for Alice of Chancery Lane, derived much of its substance from his experiences in America and Lambeth's York Road.

Throughout the years of his pedagogy, O'Donnell had made periodic determined, but unsuccessful, escapist attempts. He had, for instance, taken it into his head that he would like to be a war correspondent, and had accordingly addressed letters to the two famous war correspondents of their day, Archibald Forbes and Frederick Villiers, seeking their advice. Villiers, whom he had heard lecture on the Russo-Turkish War at Clifton College, echoed the advice proffered by Forbes, who wrote: "I do not advise you to undertake the vocation of a War Correspondent. That vocation some years ago was full of variety and interest, but now it is trammelled with irksome and irritating conditions."

In his letter, Villiers expressed disapproval concerning the number of men willing to pay their own expenses, just for the excitement of going on a campaign. He said that he would be in Bristol where O'Donnell was when he had written to him, and would be very pleased to meet him and have a chat. Unfortunately, circumstance prevented that meeting from ever taking place.

Any ambition that O'Donnell had entertained of donning a war correspondent's uniform was crucially dampened by these letters, and he speedily abandoned the idea.

Another idea that bit the dust was that of becoming a parachutist! There was at that time a man named Baldwin, who was giving exhibitions with a parachute in and near London. He would ascend in a balloon, with a parachute attached to the side of the basket, and a young girl or youth attached to the parachute. Upon reaching a predetermined height, Baldwin would detach the parachute, and it would come sailing down to earth with its living human freight before a gaping and excited crowd of admiring spectators. O'Donnell wrote to Baldwin and asked him to let him make a descent with one of his parachutes. Baldwin replied that he would be willing to do so on the payment of a hundred pounds, adding that he (O'Donnell) would assuredly get much more than that by the offers he would receive from the music-halls for a parachutist's appearance on their stage. Not having a hundred pounds, he was, much to his regret, not to become a parachutist.

For a short time O'Donnell was tutor to a fifteen-year-old boy in Hampstead. He looked twenty, and could neither read nor write. He had never been to school and was very ill-disciplined. The lad took a liking to O'Donnell, who consequently managed to get him to obey him. He improved, became quite tractable, and anxious to get on with his work. Sadly, O'Donnell could not get on at all with the boy's parents, who were "the last word in snobbishness, regarding tutors in much the same way as people of their ilk in those days regarded governesses." After a few months, O'Donnell resigned.

It was not long after this that he obtained an introduction to the popular author, Guy Boothby, who was then living at Surbiton. Boothy had become celebrated through the publication of his tale "Bid for Freedom", which had been published in the *Windsor Magazine*, and gave a great boom to its circulation. His next book, *Dr. Nikola*, had proved equally successful. Clean-shaven, very good-looking, Boothy was more like an actor than an author. He was extremely kind to O'Donnell, gave him most useful advice regarding writing, and it was inspired by him that he embarked upon *For Satan's Sake*.

While he was still teaching at Shirley House School, O'Donnell was continuing to try to carve out a career for himself as a journalist.

Pursuing a reasonably lucrative line in the shape of interviews with people well known in their respective walks of life, O'Donnell succeeded in arranging a meeting with the explorer H.M. Stanley, of "Doctor Livingstone, I presume," fame. Stanley had proved very interested in what O'Donnell had written to him about the psychic happenings following the Reverend Henry O'Donnell's death. When he arrived at Stanley's house and stepped into his drawing-room, the figure that he saw awaiting him, short and spare, probably in his younger days tough as steel, seemed to confirm all that he had heard of his adamantine qualities. His eyes were the hardest he had ever beheld and his mouth the most determined. He could not espy a soft spot anywhere. But the looks belied the man. He found him quite friendly. He told O'Donnell how the death of Emin Pasha, which took place far inland, was known by natives on the west coast of Africa almost immediately after it occurred. He said that, in his opinion, telepathy, not a drum code, was the only satisfactory explanation for such a remarkably rapid means of communication. To O'Donnell's surprise, Stanley shook hands quite warmly with him when it was time to go, and asked him to pay another visit. Such an opportunity, however, never occurred.

It was only a little while before this mini-tragedy that O'Donnell had made the acquaintance of W.T. Stead.

> I was introduced to W.T. Stead, the editor of *The Review of Reviews*, by Francis Fox, a friend of my family and member of the Reform Club. I went to see him at his office. He struck me as very human; the impression Stanley's exterior had given me was very much the reverse. A bearded man, his greeting was kindly. I was quite a youngster then. He was profound in his belief in ghosts. I asked him if he knew of any badly haunted houses in London. He told me there was one in the north of London, alleged to be haunted by a ghost so terrifying that those who saw it never recovered from the shock. One man who went there alone one night, was found in the morning stretched on the ground under one of the windows, dead. I asked him for the address of the house, but he very rightly declined to give it to me, as he did not want to be responsible for anything that might happen if I held a nocturnal vigil alone in the house.
>
> I saw Stead several times and found him always very kind and helpful. It was a grief to me when I heard that he had perished in the disaster to the *Titanic*.

O'Donnell had managed to persuade Stead to permit him to interview him, for on August 13th, 1898, Stead invites him to "send me a proof of your notes of the interview, and I will look through it, and see if there is anything to which I can take exception."

And, on August 22nd, Stead writes from the *The Review of Reviews'* office, at Mowbray House, Norfolk Street, Strand, London, W.C.:

> Thank you for sending me your interview. Of course you cannot expect me to make any remarks concerning the flattering way in which you speak about me personally. There is one point however to which I must draw your attention inasmuch as you seem to have slightly misconceived what I said, I do not think that you thoroughly caught the illustration which I gave you as to the kind of article that an editor

would be likely to welcome. Mere vamped up descriptions of Havana, Santiago, etc. would not be very likely to find a market with an editor. On the contrary such gazetteer or guide book information he would naturally compile himself.

What you have to do is look up subjects upon which the editor has not got information. With a war seen in advance such a long time the chief points of interest of which can be anticipated in the editorial office quite as well as by an outsider, but the outsider's chance comes when he can pick up information either from books or from travellers about places which suddenly blossom into notoriety without giving the editor time to hunt round and find the copy which he requires. I remember for instance how when Dewey suddenly destroyed the Spanish fleet there was quite a dearth of information as to the Philippines. It has been accumulating ever since, but even at the present moment there are very few persons in London who could tell you practically what the Philippines are and how they are governed.

One other observation I have to make is to be a little more careful of your spelling. Mowbray House is spelt with a 'w', and Russell is usually spelt with two l's.

I return your MS.

A postcard, typewritten, from Stead, dated February 11th, 1899, bears witness to O'Donnell's ready reliance upon him, and Stead's willingness to be of assistance.

Dear Mr. O'Donnell,

I am very sorry to say that I do not know Max Pemberton, and not knowing him, I feel that he would regard it as impertinence on my part to give you an introduction to him. Depend upon it, if your novel has original genius, you will find plenty of publishers only too glad to obtain possession of it.

Yours sincerely,
W.T. Stead.

In November, 1899, O'Donnell was elected an associate of the Incorporated Society for Psychical Research, 19 Buckingham Street, Adelphi, London, W.C. Annual subscription Twenty-one shillings. His relationship with the Society seems to have been uneven. He remained a member for several years after 1899, his name in the Society's records being attached to addresses in Cornwall and Bristol. Thereafter, he vanishes, until 1948, when he took out a subscription for a single year. His book, *The Menace of Spiritualism* (1919), is mentioned in a library catalogue, but otherwise his entire output of books and articles over a period of sixty years were ignored. It has been suggested that this was perhaps a deliberate ploy to save embarrassment on both sides. A society such as the Society for Psychic Research, anxious to reinforce the idea of its scientific respectability, would want at all costs to shun any public association with the writings of Elliott O'Donnell, which smacked of the occult. O'Donnell himself, however, claimed[5] to have been introduced to one of the celebrated founder members of the S.P.R., Frederic W.H. Myers (1843-1901), author of the classic *Human Personality and its Survival of Bodily Death*. He also mentioned meeting, "among the most distinguished in the field of psychic investigation", Dr. Eric Dingwall (1890-1986) "veteran psychic researcher and hostile critic of Borley, noted for what has been described as his crusty scepticism towards many psychic claims."[6]

O'Donnell was very excited when the editor of a well-known weekly offered to pay him £100 if he could get an interview with the German Chancellor of the Exchequer, the French Minister of War, or Boss Croker of Tamany Hall, who at that time was figuring very prominently in America. O'Donnell knew that the first two were well beyond his reach, but thought it just possible that W.T. Stead might be able to help as regards Croker. He could and he did. He gave him a letter of introduction. O'Donnell promptly wrote off to Croker, who was on a visit to Dublin, enclosing Stead's letter. And back came the reply, saying that if he came to Dublin within the next few days, Croker would be pleased to see him.

Off trotted O'Donnell, to break the good news to the editor.

"Oh, I've changed my mind. I don't want to publish an interview with Croker now.", was the unexpected and bitterly disappointing response.

O'Donnell reminded him that he had promised him £100 if he could get an interview. Well, he could.

The editor simply laughed and said, "The promise was not on paper."

It was a salutary lesson, an early warning, as regards the system and morals and pie-crust (made to be broken) promises and vagaries of the Street of Misadventure.

---

5   *Vide: Haunted Britain (1948)* p.192.
6   It is possible that further letters and material regarding O'Donnell's connection with the early days of the Society for Psychical may remain undiscovered in the voluminous archive of the S.P.R. held in the Cambridge University Library.

The Phantom Horseman of Wycoller Hall in Lancashire. From O'Donnell's Famous Curses (1929).

*The family curse of the Keiths in Scotland.
From O'Donnells Famous Curses (1929).*

8

Ghost Writer

For some time, fostered perhaps by the advents of such journalistic treacheries as that of the Croker interview débâcle, O'Donnell had been nurturing a secret desire to go on the stage, and now, while still teaching at Blackheath, had enlisted for a course of thespian instruction at the Henry Neville Dramatic Studio,[1] in Oxford Street, which he describes enthusiastically as "one of the leading training schools for the stage in London."

The Studio was well equipped, and its pride and joy was a lovely miniature theatre, where plays acted by the pupils were performed two or three times a year. Henry Neville, who, before his retirement, had long been one of the principal actors at the Princess' Theatre, did not do any of the teaching himself. He would turn up from time to time, though, to watch the lessons and help with practical criticism, which was always kindly and instructive. He was completely free of any pomposity or actorish egotism. His brother, Fred Gartside, gave O'Donnell his first lesson in elocution, but left soon after O'Donnell joined, his place being taken by G.R. Foss, regarded by O'Donnell as "one of the greatest stage geniuses I have ever met."

His course completed, O'Donnell set off on tour with Eva Dare's *"A Night Out"*. Unfortunately, the company turned out to be run by very unpleasant people. The general manager was Charles Terry, a member of the famous theatrical family. The producer, although, O'Donnell meticulously notes, "a gentleman by birth", proved "an out and out cad, bullying those he deemed he could bully with impunity, and toadying to the management

---

1   Also referred to by him as the Henry Neville Dramatic Academy.

and principals. The stage-manager, who had been a shopkeeper and never could be anything else, used to make love to the pretty girls in the crowd, and if they snubbed him, which they not infrequently did, he would trump up some tale about them to the management, thereby ensuring their dismissal... Despite the tyranny of the producer, who to vent his spleen on some wretched actor or actress who had chanced to offend him, used to call extra rehearsals and bully everyone, the tale-telling of the stage-manager, who used to eavesdrop whenever he could, and thus curry favour with the management at other people's expense... I liked the life."

The travelling he did not like. Early rising every Sunday, the hanging about on railway platforms, frequently in foul weather, and long, wearisome journeys in crowded compartments. Until the nineties, there had been no corridor trains on the Great Western Railway line, and there being no W.C.s on the trains necessitated a frantic rush to find one on stopping at a station. And since no stop lasted for more than a few minutes, and there was usually a number of passengers scrimmaging to get to the conveniences first, it often resulted in one being obliged to wait until the next stop, perhaps with no better luck.

Neither was there, except for the metal foot-warmers, any heating in the old broad-gauge carriages, nor any lighting, other than that provided by oil lamps. In the roofs of all the compartments were circular holes for the lamps. Before the departure of a train, porters standing on the station platform used to toss the lamps up to porters standing on the roofs of the carriages. Since the distance was considerable, and the lamps large and heavy, this was an operation calling for no little dexterity, yet it was seemingly always accomplished without mishap.

Searching for digs in a strange town at a late hour was another omnipresent hazard; and, once found, they could be attended by all manner of annoyances. A howling baby in an adjoining room would hardly conduce sleep. The raspings from next door of an instrument of torture misnamed a piano did little to soothe frayed nerves. Landladies, too, varied. They were not always amiable. Their rooms were not always clean. Their bedding was not always properly aired. On one or two occasions O'Donnell arrived at lodgings immediately after a death, with the corpse still in the house.

The theatres could disappoint; appal even. Filthy, ill-ventilated dressing-rooms, overrun with rats. Small part actors like O'Donnell, had, indeed, a very great deal to put up with for very low pay. The salaries for several of those in the company amounted to only a guinea a week.

One night when the show was being staged at Yarmouth, O'Donnell was disconcerted to hear a man passing his lodgings say in a loud voice that he intended "doing for" some woman. This was followed a few minutes later by screams of "Murder!" He ran out in the direction of the cries and found a hatless, ruffianly man being firmly held by two or three other men. Nearby several women were attending to a woman who had been stabbed, but, fortunately, not fatally.

It was not long after this that O'Donnell was staying in a lodging-house in Coram Street, in Bloomsbury, when one morning he once again found himself listening to loud cries of "Murder!" He tore downstairs. The cries were coming from a room on the landing under his. He pounded on the door shouting, "Open in the name of the law." The cries were becoming even more frantic when the door opened, and a thickset man with a long black moustache and greasy black hair appeared. Looking scared and dishevelled, he mumbled an unintelligible something in broken English. O'Donnell asked him what was going on. He was still mumbling when the landlady, very out of breath, came puffing up the stairs to explain that everything was all right, the man was not harming the woman. She was in the habit of screaming "Murder!" when anything upset her, or she had had a drop too much!

At Worcester, where they had booked no lodgings ahead, after several vain inquiries, he and a fellow-actor found a landlady who said that she was quite ready to put them up if they did not mind sleeping in a room which had recently been occupied by a man who had mysteriously disappeared, leaving all his belongings behind him. Pointing to the river, clearly visible from the window of his bedroom, she said in sepulchral toes, "I have a feeling he's there, deep down in the water." All ended happily, though. The day that O'Donnell and his companion were leaving, the missing lodger walked in as large as life. He had, he said, climbed out of the window in the night to visit friends, and while with them had been seized with a sudden illness which prevented his returning or even communicating with the landlady. A tale that struck the two departing lodgers as decidedly on the thin side.

While the Company was playing at Torquay, O'Donnell had no problem with lodgings; he stayed with friends. They took him on a trip to Babbacombe Bay, the scene of a celebrated murder of 1884. Emma Keyse, an elderly spinster living alone there in a remote villa, The Glen, was found hacked to death. This followed her sacking of her young butler, John Lee. Tried for her murder, found guilty, and sentenced to death, Lee became famous as "the man they could not hang". Three times the hangman pulled the lever, three times the bolt failed and the trap remained shut. Lee's sentence was commuted to imprisonment for life. He was released in 1907, and died in Milwaukee in 1945.

"We were told," says O'Donnell, "by the landlord of an inn near the scene of the murder, that the site of The Glen was haunted by the ghost of poor Miss Keyse, whose harrowing screams could often be heard at night."

The *"Night Out"* tour over, O'Donnell, back in London, settled in at St. James' Road, Brixton. While 'resting' as the theatric euphemism has it, he was scribbling away at his second and third novels – *The Unknown Depths*, based largely on his own life and introducing the subject of Spiritualism, researching for which he had been attending many séances, and *Dinevah the Beautiful*. He was also doing a daily round of the various well-known theatrical agencies in search of work.

A stroke of luck, as he thought, was his running across the manager of a fit-up company who happened to be on the look out for a young man of about his height and build to play second lead in a melodrama he was taking out. Eagerly enough, O'Donnell immediately closed with this offer.

The Company embarked upon a succession of three-night visits to various towns in Wales. The work was hard, for in addition to being a police officer and an Italian waiter, he had to be a young dude and a French porter, and do three lightning changes. The nightly show apart, there were matinées twice a week, and the company was often required to attend morning rehearsals. The Company's funds held out for about four weeks, winding up at Llandudno, where O'Donnell found himself no better off financially than when he had set out from London, and having to pay his own fare back there. In Brixton once more, he picked up his pen, his only sword.

Between skirmishes, he would pay the odd visit to his sisters in Clifton. Petronella and Helena had left a local art school which they had both been attending. Helena went on to study at the Slade and Heatherley Schools in London, with Stanhope Forbes at Newlyn, Cornwall, and then to Paris. She painted in Belgium, Holland and Italy. One of her paintings was hung on the line in the Royal Academy. Petronella took to writing. She contributed many articles to Somerset and Gloucestershire papers and published several volumes of verse. Elizabeth, his step-sister, displayed a considerable natural talent as both a singer and a pianist, and might have made a successful career as either, but her interests were too many and too wide-ranging to allow her the necessary time to devote herself professionally to music.

Whenever he could manage it, he would spend a few summer seaside holiday weeks with his sisters, whose custom it was to take away on holiday with them their retainers – his erstwhile nurse, Fanny, and her sister, Sarah Coldwell – at Bournemouth. In after years, he would recall how a street musician used to sing outside the house where they would all lodge in St. Michael's Road. He would remember, too, the narrow escape they had the day they went in a wagonette to Swanage. Something frightened the horse. It shied and bolted, and was only with the greatest difficulty got back under control. It could have been a very nasty accident. And there was always the Winter Gardens, affording ample entertainment. It was there that he heard Max O'Rell, otherwise Paul Blouët (1848-1903), the author of *John Bull and His Island*, then at the height of his fame, lecture.

It was now that O'Donnell took the unwilling, but, if he wanted to make Ada Williams his wife, mandatory, decision to quit the stage.

Ada, aged thirty was the youngest of the three daughters – her sisters were Catherine (33) and Clara (32). She also had a brother, Henry (28) – of Dr. Henry Williams and his wife Catherine, who lived in a house called Hillside, in the Northamptonshire village of Guilsborough.[2] Her parents strongly disapproved of the stage, and as long as O'Donnell was treading the boards they would never consent to his union with their daughter. His only alternative was to struggle on trying to make a living with his pen.

Some of his journalistic assignments landed him in awkward situations. He was writing for the London *Mail*.

> It fell to my lot to investigate queer advertisements in certain somewhat questionable papers. I remember on one occasion two muscular looking women, who posed as priestesses in a temple dedicated to the Greek God Pan, but whom I had reason to believe were narcotic traffickers, saying when I visited them, pretending that I was greatly interested in

2 Ada was a Londoner, having been born in Fulham. In 1891, she was living, with her father, mother and siblings, at 7 Chapel Place, London, W.1., where her father practised medicine. By 1901, the family had moved to 75 Norfolk Street, Guilsborough. Dr. Williams died in 1917.

their cult: "Don't think you take us in. You're here to pry into what goes on. We don't like pryers. Suppose we sandbag you. How would you like that?"

I told them I should not like it at all; neither would they, because someone was outside with instructions to force an entry if I did not join them in ten minutes. I spoke, and apparently looked, as if I meant it, for they quickly changed their tone, told me a lot of claptrap about their make-believe cult, and made no attempt to molest me. I probably could have handled one all right in a tussle, but two might have proved too much for me, since they were tall, strongly-built women who looked quite capable of sticking me with a knife.

They showed me the room they called a temple. It had what looked like a big box, covered with a black cloth, for an altar, and several stone or marble busts, purporting to be the heads of goddesses, ranged round the room on pedestals. I examined the inscriptions on some of them, and when I saw Saturn, Isis and Griffin, that was quite enough.

On another occasion he visited a person who had described herself as an Omnacea Medium. She proved to be fat, cross-eyed, and looking badly in need of a bath. When he asked her the meaning of 'Omnacea', she said, "A cure for every ill, physical and mental."

"I understand from that," he said, "that you have a cure, a remedy, for all diseases, both of body and mind."

"That is so," she replied. "What's wrong with you? Kidney trouble?"

"No, it's the mind. It's in a state of horrible confusion." And so it was when he looked at her, for he could not make out which of her eyes it was that saw him. Sometimes he thought one, sometimes the other, and sometimes neither. They were the most bothering eyes he had ever seen. It was on the tip of his tongue to ask her why, if she had a remedy for every kind of physical ill, she did not put her eyes straight.

She told him that her terms for curing mental troubles were considerably more than for curing cancer and other diseases.

"You look fairly normal," she said. "I suppose you only get attacks every now and then. You don't get violent, do you?"

"There is that tendency," said O'Donnell. ""I feel it coming over me now." And he glared at her.

That was quite sufficient.

"I don't treat mentals, not when they're in your state," she said, jumping back in alarm. And she slammed the door in his face.

He had another unpleasant experience at a house in a street off the Edgware Road. The advertisement had been for red-haired lady assistants to apply to take part in a thriving, but undisclosed business. The door was opened in answer to his knock by a woman with an exceedingly repulsive, not to say menacing, face. He trotted out his cover story: a sister with red hair who was out of a job and would be very interested to have particulars of the business advertised. The woman invited him to step inside, saying that she could then explain better. As the door closed behind him, she shouted something in a foreign language, and a swarthy, villainous-looking man appeared at the top of the stairs leading up from the none-too-clean passage in which they were standing. The woman pointed angrily at O'Donnell, and, realising that he was in for trouble if he stayed, he made for the door. The woman at once got in front of him. The man came rushing down the stairs. O'Donnell pushed the woman aside, and, discretion defeating valour, made a run for it.

"Joy for everyone at a florin",[3] announced another advertisement that attracted his attention. Following the joyful trail, he arrived at a hall in south-east London, where he handed over his florin for admittance. Inside, raffles were going on. Tickets cost a further sixpence each. He decided that the prizes that he saw would have been dear at a shilling and would have brought anything but joy to the heart of a recipient.

Such trivia made amusing copy, but they brought but little into the depressingly empty coffers. Typical of the kind of unprofitable adventures which befell him was the Valencourt affair.

O'Donnell was minding his own business, quietly drinking a cup of tea in a Waterloo Road café, when a man planted himself at his table. About forty years of age, clean-shaven, lank black hair, muddy brown eyes, sallow complexion. Dressed all in rather seedy black, looked badly in need of a bath, affected a very sanctimonious air, which mixed ill with the sour smell which he exuded. O'Donnell did not take to him.

The man struck up a conversation.

"Do you come here often? Do you live near here? Are you employed?"

O'Donnell frowned. "What business is it of yours?" The man's manner had irritated him.

The man sighed reproachfully. "No business. Only I thought if you were in need of a job I might be able to put you in the way of one."

3   A florin was two shillings in old money, twenty pence in contemporary currency.

O'Donnell was in need of a job. He had not sold any articles or stories for quite a while and funds were reaching a perilous Plimsoll line. What, he wondered, had this man in mind.

"Have you ever spoken in public?" the man asked.

"Never."

The man went on to explain. "The audience would be kindly, homely people, mostly women. It is a blue ribbon meeting. They will all be teetotallers. What I want you to do is take the chair for me and say a few introductory words. I would pay you well."

Then, abruptly, he excused himself. "I can't wait now. I have an engagement. If you meet me at ten o'clock tomorrow morning under the clock at Charing Cross Station I will explain what I want you to say."

Journalistic curiosity prompting his steps, O'Donnell kept the appointment. Looking a little cleaner and a great deal more sanctimonious than the previous day, the man turned up and lead the way to a nearby side street café. There he confessed: he had previously been a great reprobate – drunkard, swearer, wholly irreligious. He owed his reformation to a wonderful dream in which his mother, dead for many years, had appeared to him and implored him to lead a better life.

"That dream made such a deep impression on me that I became a changed man. I ceased to drink and use bad language, and I went to chapel regularly on Sundays. Some months ago I founded a teetotal club, and am now booked to speak at a number of temperance meetings. I need a chairman, someone of good appearance and well educated. All you will have to do is introduce me to the audience, saying what a very different man I am now from when you saw me a couple of years ago., and how the change was wrought through a Heaven-sent dream."

"That might be all right for you," said O'Donnell, "but how should I benefit? I can't waste my time acting as your chairman without remuneration."

"There will," said Mr. Valencourt, for that was the name he gave, Benjamin Joshua Valencourt, "be collections at the meetings. The proceeds of them will go to me, and I will pay you out of them."

On the appointed day, at the appointed time, 2.30 p.m., O'Donnell arrived at Sidmouth Hall, Mark Road, Brixton. The room was about forty feet long; at one end was a platform, on which was a table and two chairs. Facing the platform were rows of chairs. The lecturer arrived soon after O'Donnell. He wore the same black seedy clothes, black shoes and gloves. His lank, black hair was plastered down and shining with oil, the nauseating odour of which was not quite strong enough to conceal the smell of beer.

The audience began to trickle in. Middle-aged and old women in driblets, plainly but not poorly dressed; smugly respectable.

O'Donnell rose to his feet. "Ladies of the Brixton Anti-intoxication Blue Ribbon League, I have much pleasure in speaking to you about our lecturer." Then, turning to Valencourt, "It is your wish, is it not, that I should tell these ladies how very different you are now from when I first met you?"

Valencourt nodded a modest assent.

O'Donnell continued: "Now ladies, you have all heard Mr. Valencourt express his desire that I should describe to you what my impression of him was in what he terms his pre-reform days. Very good, I will do so to the best of my ability. When I first set eyes on him, which was not long ago, I thought I had seldom, if ever, seen anyone as thoroughly revolting. He smelt horribly of drink, bad drink, looked as if he had never washed or had a clean shirt for months; his teeth were black, his breath foul. That, ladies, was what he was like when I saw him for the first time only a week ago, and he hasn't changed a bit. He's a humbug. Don't give him a cent."

Valencourt was choking with rage. He made a savage lunge at O'Donnell, who jumped from the platform and made a quick exit, a babel of highly excited feminine voices ringing in his ears.

There is a coda. "I was taking a stroll along the beach at Bournemouth one day when I saw a small crowd gathered around a man who was apparently selling something. On drawing nearer, I recognised him as the man for whom I had acted as chairman at the temperance meeting in London. He was still clad in a suit of rusty black and still looked as if he very badly needed a bath. He was endeavouring to sell a bottle containing a liquid which he declared was a sure cure for rheumatism, indigestion and various other maladies. I had half a mind to tell the crowd what I knew about him, but resisted the temptation and walked on."

As the year 1899 was winding down, so were journalistic commissions. The slump in the demand for his literary services was surely only temporary, but it was a worry trying to decide the most satisfactory way to sit it out. He was racking his brain to know what to do for the best, when he received, out of the blue, a letter from Cornwall. It was from an old friend of the family. She and her artist husband lived at St Ives, and she suggested that he should come down to Cornwall to act as tutor to her small son and two or three other boys. The work, she said, would not occupy a great deal of his time, and it would leave him free to carry on with his writing.

It was, said O'Donnell, Hobson's choice, and in due course found himself once again engaged in the profession he loathed.

The scullion boy's curse.
From O'Donnells Famous Curses (1929).

*A sinister Gipsy woman puts a curse on a London gentleman,
From O'Donnell's Famous Curses (1929).*

9

The Cornish Ghost Coast

Cornwall beckoned. The idea appealed. Between them, pen and pupils, taken along with his small private income, could add up to matrimony. He waved goodbye to London without qualms. He was lucky to find a suitable apartment at an affordable rent in a good location in the town.

From small beginnings, four or five boys, the numbers gradually increased, and his mind turned towards the acquisition of a premises large enough to house what was in effect a small preparatory school.

For some time he had been watching with interest the progress of a building which was being erected in a commanding position. It was the last house in a terrace and facing it was a steep cliff overlooking a path leading down to the seashore. He was very taken with it, secured the letting, and, in due season, moved in as its first tenant, accompanied by an aged housekeeper, Miss Ellie Bolitho.

It was almost as soon as he took up residence there that O'Donnell realised that there was something amiss. He was occupying a room off the top landing. The housekeeper's room was on the first floor, immediately below. At about two o'clock in the morning, O'Donnell would jerk suddenly awake to hear the sound of footsteps coming up the stairs and along the passage outside his room. Sometimes there would be an accompaniment of heavy breathing and panting. At first, he thought it was his housekeeper walking in her sleep, and the next time it happened he jumped straight out of bed, bounded across, and flung the door open. There was no one there. Just a still, silent, dark passage.

He was not really surprised when Miss Bolitho gave him her notice. She could not, she said go on living any longer in a house that was haunted.

She never got a proper night's sleep because of "the noises", and pointing at a pair of antique Irish antlers that O'Donnell had hung in the hall, she added: "It's them antlers. I know it's them, because every time I pass them I can feel them watching me. They're unlucky and you ought to get rid of them at once. Burn them. I would."

He told her that the antlers were heirlooms, and that she was talking nonsense. But nonsense or not, she was determined to go, and she went.

The next housekeeper he imported from London, Mrs. Webb, a Cockney, middle-aged, very dignified, very practical. She fared no better. Complaining of weird and frightening noises in the night, she soon packed her trunk, and left. In fact, a succession of housekeepers came and went. Only the rackety entity remained in undisturbed disturbing residence.

One night the footsteps halted right outside his bedroom door, and a tremendous bang sounded on its top panel. The following night, before retiring to bed, O'Donnell made up his mind to set a trap. He sprinkled the floor of the passage with alternate layers of flour and sand, and fastened a line of cotton from wall to wall, breast-high, across it. He also placed a small table in the centre of the passage, with a cup of water balanced upon its edge in such a way that at the slightest touch it would fall off. That night the footsteps and the bang came again. He opened the door immediately and saw that neither the flour nor sand showed the slightest sign of imprint or disturbance. The cotton stretched unbroken across the passageway. The cup of water remained, precarious but intact upon the table's edge.

In the holiday period – August and September – he would go to Guilsborough and stay in rooms near Ada's home. They would go out for long walks and drives together, and in the evenings sit talking, laying plans for their united future, or playing games.

Always, when he went off on holiday, he would let his house. One year while he was away, his latest housekeeper, Mrs. Barton, whom he had left in charge, had been so disturbed and alarmed by the outbreaks of nocturnal rumpus that she persuaded O'Donnell's charwoman, a Salvation Army stalwart, to stay in the house and sleep in her room with her. The first night she was there, they were both awakened by footsteps on the landing outside the room. The door handle was then rattled several times. This was followed by a loud crash on the door. The Salvation Army lass prayed aloud, and there was no more noise that night. There was one other occupant in the house, the lady's maid of the family who had rented part of the house but had not yet arrived. She was a spiritualist and informed Mrs. Barton that the place was undoubtedly haunted. She had been visited in the night by something from another world. It had banged on her door and departed when she crossed herself and addressed it. She was sure that it was harmless, but most likely to be of a terrifying appearance.

Not until after he had quit the house, did O'Donnell learn certain strange things which, he thought, might offer some sort of explanation for the phenomena that he and so many others had experienced there. A Mrs. Ashby told him that when passing by the spot on which the house was afterwards built, she saw a very tall figure with a queer round head rise from the ground, walk across the road in front of her with a peculiar swaggering motion, and disappear abruptly over the edge of the cliff.

A woman, whom he met quite by chance in Plymouth, told him how on a visit to St. Ives, about twenty years previously, she saw an apparition on the site later occupied by the house in which he had lived. Her description of what she had seen tallied precisely with that given to him by Mrs. Ashby of what she had seen.

After hearing these things, he came to wonder if perhaps the site had originally been haunted by some kind of Elemental, and when the house was erected that supernatural entity came into it from the outside, losing its way, perhaps, and then disappeared outside, and away over the cliff, as it had before the house was built.

O'Donnell reported odd happenings in another house which he rented in St. Ives. It had been occupied by an eccentric old woman, and her niece, showing him over it made, with a look at the bare and rather gloomy staircase, the scarcely inviting remark to a prospective tenant: "I could never live here. I should always be seeing my aunt. She died in one of the rooms overhead, and I can see her now, coming down those stairs."

He took the house, but never saw the old lady's spectre. He did, however, see a trap door in the ceiling open very mysteriously – since it was completely inaccessible from below. He also found on coming out of his bedroom one morning, a rug spread very carefully on the landing in front of the door.

> At the time about which I am writing there was a field between Paul, a village near Newlyn and Lamorna Cove, that was haunted by a presence which was supposed to belong to the category of Elementals. While

spending a few weeks at Paul, I often used to fish on the quay and rocks at Lamorna, and when returning in the evening generally took a short cut which led me through that particular field. When crossing it I invariably experienced an uncanny sensation, and was glad to get out of it as quickly as possible. I was told afterwards that the field was well known to be haunted, and was shunned at night by the local people.

The hinterland of St. Ives, with its barren patches dotted with great bare rocks of granite, its gaunt hills, dolefulness, isolation, loneliness, and sense of gloom, might well have been far from the abode of any human being. There was a fascinating eeriness about it, a feeling of the near presence of the spirits of the long, long dead denizens of a world primitively remote.

I spent many nights wandering alone in that strange region, resting when weary on a fantastically fashioned boulder or cairn that might well have covered the bones of a long deceased Roman general or British priest. Not once, but on several occasions when resting a while, I saw, or fancied that I saw, shadowy forms emerge from the gloom and glide past me; forms too vague to give a very definite idea of their actual appearance; some that might have been the shades of people who had lived in the locality, and others that gave the impression of something quite distinct from the human race. Some caused me alarm, others filled me with dread; some did not seem to be aware of my presence, others, I sensed, were scrutinising me, although I could not distinguish their eyes.

A short note from W.T. Stead, dated September 23rd, 1901, shows that O'Donnell had still not relinquished his dreams of Fleet Street.

"I should be glad to know what you want me to say to the editor or sub-editor of the London newspapers," he wrote. "I could hardly introduce you by saying that you were introduced to me by Mr. Francis Fox, and that you were headmaster of a small preparatory school at St. Ives. But that is all I could do at present."

Living in Cornwall at this period was Ranger Gull, who, under the *nom de guerre* Guy Thorne, had written an extremely successful novel, *When It was Dark*. He was a reader for the publisher Arthur Greening, and it was at the suggestion of Charles Marriott, author of a novel, *The Column*, which had enjoyed wide popularity, that O'Donnell made contact with him and asked him to look at the manuscript of *For Satan's Sake*, which had been mouldering away in a drawer for the best part of six years. Great was O'Donnell's jubilation upon receiving a telegram from Gull telling him that he had recommended it for publication. He had perforce to practise considerable patience for it was quite a while before the contract arrived, and even longer, a whole year, before, in 1904, it was published.

The appearance of *For Satan's Sake* proved a welcome fillip so far as the reception of his articles and short stories was concerned. In particular, he was pleased that *The Idler* had bought a clutch of his tales. And one of the papers that commissioned his services was the *Weekly Dispatch*, whose editor, Mr. Buley, requested a series of ghost stories founded on fact, and which on publication generated a positive inundation of readers' letters. Indeed, so roseate did the outlook seem, that he decided to give up the loathed profession – he had only a few pupils left anyway, the numbers having inexorably decreased from a maximum of thirty, following upon someone with more capital coming along and setting up a far grander establishment – and devote all his energies to the wielding of the pen.

Thus, crackling with enthusiasm and optimism, faith and hope, he finally married Ada, in 1905. The wedding took place in Guilsborough. The honeymoon at Clifton. The newly-weds then returned to take up residence in St. Ives, where they were to spend the next three years.

Although Arthur Greening said that, despite its having been extensively reviewed, *For Satan's Sake* had not been a financial success, he nevertheless published three more of O'Donnell's novels – *Jennie Barlowe, Adventuress*, written between school hours in Cornwall, in 1906; *Dinevah the Beautiful*, the last of his efforts in Brixton, in 1907; and *The Unknown Depths*, also written while he was living in Brixton, in 1908.[1]

Ranger Gull and Charles Marriott apart, there were a number of writers who were to be found in Cornwall at that time; Fergus Hume, Harold Begbie, and Mrs. Henry Dudeney.

Hume (1859-1932), precursor of the popular detective mystery writers of the twentieth century, wrote, with Gaboriau as his template *The Mystery of a Hansom Cab*, a crime novel which created a huge sensation, was the biggest seller of its day. O'Donnell met him at a gathering of artists and writers at a friend's house. The party over, O'Donnell had returned home and was about to take himself off to bed, when there was a rap at the front-door. It was Hume. He apologised for calling at such a later hour, but explained that he had had the impression when they had met earlier

---

1 Another occult thriller, the *Graphic* commented: "The narrative ranges over every field, from idyllic comedy to such ghastly African horrors as surpass any of Mr. Rider Haggard's boldest flights."

on that O'Donnell was deeply troubled. Having first assured him that that was not the case, O'Donnell invited him to stay on for a while and give them the pleasure of his company. Hume told the O'Donnells that in spite of the enormous sale of *The Mystery of a Hansom Cab*, he had by no means reaped a harvest out it. His share had, in fact, been very limited.

"Many authors I have met," wrote O'Donnell, "who had not acquired anything like the fame that Hume had, have been very swollen-headed. It was not so with Hume. He was extremely nice and unassuming. After he left Cornwall, I received several letters from him, always in the same kindly, friendly vein."

Harold Begbie (1871-1929) they met at Carbis Bay, where he was staying for a short time with his parents. He was celebrated because of his books and his work on the *Daily Mail*. He was editing *The V.C. (The Voice of the Commonwealth)*, a weekly journal to which O'Donnell had contributed several tales. His father, the Reverend M.H. Begbie, had been for two or three years a master at Clifton in the very early years of the school. Mrs. Begbie told of a harrowing experience which she had had in a haunted house in Hampshire. She awoke one night to hear the hollow sounding of a gong, and felt a cold hand on her head, pressing her down. How long she endured this she could not say, but so great was her horror that she was ill for some time afterwards. She had not been told that the house was haunted, nor that other people who had slept in that room had had a similar experience.

Mrs. Henry Dudeney[2] and her daughter visited the O'Donnells several times, and were pronounced by them to be charming.

They met, too, Charles Lewis Hind (1862-1927), editor and well-known art critic, and Mrs. Havelock Ellis. She lived at Carbis Bay. Seldom did she speak about her famous husband. She seemed to be entirely absorbed in her garden and in farming. Far more interested in horses, dogs, and cattle than in human beings, she exuded an atmosphere of fields and stables.

O'Donnell visited A.T. Quiller Couch, "Q", at Fowey. "I was keen to see him as I enjoyed so much his *Dead Man's Rock*, when I was a boy. He was very friendly, but appeared to me to be very nervy and highly-strung, and not as fond of writing as he was of boating and sailing. He was a boy at

---

2   Born Alice Whiffin, (1864-1944). Compared with Thomas Hardy for her portrayals of regional life. Her personal diaries published as: *A Lewes Diary 1916-1944*. Edited by Diana Crook. The Tartarus Press, 1998.

Clifton before my time."

No list of Cornish literary acquaintances would be complete without reference to the genial editor of *The Cornishman*, Herbert Thomas – "A very likeable man, always friendly, he was a poet and a great authority on Cornwall. He reviewed several of my books at length. He always wore a white helmet, no matter what the season. One day, years after I had left Cornwall, my wife and I were in Regent Street, London, when I saw a white helmet looming in the distance. 'Herbert Thomas!' I exclaimed. And so it was, and very pleased we were to see him. He and his wife had tea with us at the Authors' Club, and he regaled us with the latest news of Cornwall."

There were several cliques in St. Ives. The artists whom the O'Donnells knew best were W.B. Fortescue, who was a friend of his sisters, Fred Milner, Hayley Lever, and Leonard Fuller, who played with O'Donnell in several cricket matches. Others who he occasionally met and found friendly were Algernon Talmage, R.A. and Julius Olsson, R.A., who was one of the best marine painters of his day. He was a big, genial man, who walked with a slight limp. Talmage had only one arm. The majority of the artists kept very much to themselves, mixed little with the townspeople. They had their own especially favoured pub where they foregathered in the town, its walls hung with their paintings.

O'Donnell was surprised and delighted in equal measure when he was invited by E.W. Hornung, creator of the immortal Raffles, to play for the Authors in a cricket match, Authors v. the Artists at Esher. He travelled up from St. Ives and was invited, along with Hornung and his wife, to dine with S.A.P. Kitcat and his wife. Their host had been educated at Marlborough, where he was captain of the XI, and had often played with considerable success for Gloucestershire.

The Authors' team was: J.C. Snaith, Captain Doyle, Major P. Trevor, Hesketh Prichard, Sir Arthur Conan Doyle, P.G. Wodehouse, A. Kinross, Lee Trevor, Elliott O'Donnell, G.C. Ives, and E.W. Hornung.

The Artists' were: G. Gascoyne, F.D. Barnes, E.H. Fischer, H.J. Ford, G.H. Swinstead, G. Spencer Watson, L.C. Nightingale, Arthur Bachelor, A. Chevalier Taylor, Frank Baxter, and A. Carruthers Gould.

Snaith was the Authors' fast bowler. Prichard, too, was a very fast bowler, his height being a great asset to him. As he raced up to the wicket, swinging his long arms and grimacing in his zeal to send in a particularly swift ball, he looked positively awe inspiring. Wodehouse also bowled fast, but did not appear so formidable. The star of the match was undoubtedly Fischer, who was rightly eulogised in press and reviews. He knocked 130.

"Had I not been so tired after a very long journey and late going to bed, I think," apologised a self-conscious O'Donnell, "I might have done rather better." He was caught by Taylor for a duck.

The Artists won. 246 to 188.

Wodehouse, whom O'Donnell had not seen for years, subsequently wrote some verses about his ghost hunting in the *Globe*, and also interviewed him for *Ideas*.

All his life very fond of cricket, he admitted that he was never a good all round cricketer. He was, he confessed, a better bowler than batsman. He was a slogger. He was asked to play again for the Authors in a match at Lords, but was prevented from doing so by illness.[3] But he played for the St. Ives town cricket club several times, and when it ceased, he got up scratch teams to play various neighbouring clubs.

Throughout his Cornish years, O'Donnell always got on well with the fishermen. He found them very good fellows, and on more than one occasion when he chatted with them they made him a present of pollock or some other fish. He sympathised with their desire to keep Sunday as a non-working day of rest. The Cornish folk generally, however, he did not at all like.

> Several writers have been credited with introducing to the public none too favourably the Cornish colony amongst whom I lived. If they have done so, I can certainly endorse their sentiments. In no other town that I have been in have I ever met people who laid themselves open to such unfavourable criticism. I lived there nearly eight years, and during that time I received the bare minimum of hospitality. I found the greater number of the inhabitants bigoted and pharisaical, and the townsfolk and labouring people not only extremely ignorant, but very unforgiving and vindictive. That they were still – that is to say at the time I am writing of – in a tribal state was proved by their puerile attitude of hostility to strangers, whom they used frequently to insult and annoy. I signed two petitions relative to the throwing of stones at visitors, which petitions were forwarded to the Home Secretary. The result was nil. The

[3] On May 10th, 1909, C. Aubrey Smith wrote from The Playhouse, W.C.: "The Actors *v.* Authors match is on Thursday, August 26th. I hope the authors' side will be organized by Sir Arthur Conan Doyle. I should imagine the authors will be glad of volunteers – as I fear they will find it difficult to get a side together so late in the season. I could fill up the actors' side 3 or 4 times from applications."

local authorities in dealing with such cases displayed the most woeful apathy, and apparently this state of affairs was irremediable, since the magistrates, with few exceptions, were related to half the people in the town.

With the Art Colony I had very little to do. The few artists I knew at all intimately I liked. I found them congenial and generally sympathetic, though displaying an avidity in criticising authors, which, considering their touchiness with regard to any criticism of their own work, was distinctly amusing; all the same, apart from this and one other harmless peculiarity, namely, an exaggerated and unblushing deference to titles, I found them very good fellows, and nearly all the hospitality I received in the town I received from them. I think I am right in saying there was never a very friendly feeling between the townspeople and the artists. The townspeople looked upon the artists as intruders, 'foreigners', whose ways and habits were diametrically opposite to theirs, especially with regard to the treatment of the Sabbath; while the artists showed a none too well concealed contempt for the townspeople, whom they seemed to regard not only as hopelessly inartistic, but (as being) of an utterly inferior breed.

In most small towns there is a good deal of unkind gossip and scandal, but I really think that in this respect the town I refer to was unrivalled. It seemed to me that the people were never so happy as when saying malicious things about each other, and they meanly victimised those whose limited means would not permit of their taking legal action against them. I have often wondered what made these people so peculiarly unkind.

Peter Underwood, himself a dedicated and widely experienced hunter after ghosts, in a short memoir of Elliott O'Donnell in his book *The Ghost Hunters*, gives an interesting account of an occasion when O'Donnell attempted a personal psychic experiment in the phenomenon known as projection, which is the separation of part of oneself from the physical body and the sending forth of it as an image that might be termed a phantasm of the living.

It was a hot and sultry day. Not the lightest breath of wind. The baking sunlight set a shimmering layer of air above the surface of the Nancledra to St. Ives road. O'Donnell, trudging along it, was suddenly taken with the notion that he would see if he could project himself to his home at St. Ives, where his wife would be having her afternoon tea. He tried to bring a picture of the house before his mind. He did not seem to be able to. Just as he thought he was about to succeed, his concentration seemed to fail, and the picture that he was seeking to build would slip away. He tried again and again, always failing. Then, all of a sudden, he saw it vividly – "the house, the garden gate slightly ajar, the conservatory, a mass of glittering, sparkling colour. He found himself walking along the sun-baked garden path towards the conservatory, passing through it, crossing the hall and then pausing with one hand on the handle of the drawing-room. He heard voices from within the room which he recognized as those of his wife and someone else. He opened his mouth to call out and let them know that he was back when, in a flash, it had all gone and he was out of doors again, tramping along the white and dusty road, with still a couple of miles to go to reach home.[4] It was five o'clock, nearly an hour later, when he finally arrived at his house.

"Whatever have you been doing?" Ada greeted him. "We heard you come back ages ago, and you called out to us, but when we went to look for you, you were nowhere to be found. We've been waiting tea for you ever since."

The experiment had been a success. He was never able to repeat it.

O'Donnell and his wife had moved into another house in St. Ives. It, like the previous one, was new-built. Also like the previous house, it was the last in a terrace. It was surrounded at the rear and on one side by a garden, flanked by a hedge, beyond which were fields that led in almost unbroken succession to the coast. To describe its location as a lonely one would not be right, although the fields were little frequented after dusk. One night the O'Donnells were awakened by a series of the most agonised and heart-rending screams, which, if they could be compared with anything earthly at all, seemed to them like those of a woman in the very direst distress. The cries were so terrible, and sounded so close, indeed, almost in the room, that they were both horribly alarmed, and hardly knew what to say or think.

"Whatever is happening?" whispered Mrs. O'Donnell, catching her husband by the arm. "What is it?"

"I don't know," replied O'Donnell, "unless it's the Banshee, for there's nobody else who could make such a noise."

The screams continued for some seconds, and then died away in one log drawn out wail. They waited to see if the screaming would start up again. It did not. O'Donnell got up and, not without apprehension, went out on

---

[4] *The Ghost Hunters: Who They Are and What They Do*. Peter Underwood. Robert Hale, London, 1985. pp.41-42.

to the landing, where he found several other of the inmates of the house huddling together, discussing with scared faces the terrible disturbance which had brought them from their beds.

A thorough search of the house and grounds having been carried out without the discernment of anything that could possibly have accounted for the screams, O'Donnell adhered to his opinion that it must have been the Banshee, a view which seemed ratified by tidings a few days later that an aunt of his, an O'Donnell in county Kerry, had died within twenty-four hours of the time when the screaming had occurred.

An exceptionally curious story dating from this period of O'Donnell's life centres upon a hotel in Plymouth. He had been working very hard, and feeling in need of a rest, decided to take himself off to Plymouth for a weekend. He arrived there rather late on a Saturday night, and after spending some little time searching for a room in the vicinity of Millbay Station, eventually came upon a hotel the look of which strongly attracted him. In the vestibule he met a member of the hotel staff whose face he seemed to know, and although he had never been in the place before, the building struck him as strangely familiar. He had the very strong impression that he had known the hotel in a former existence. The more he saw of the place and all the incidents and the things that happened seemed to him to be but a reproduction of the past.

> A green parrot in a cage in one of the rooms shrieked out, "William, you old blighter, lend me a sov.,'" and then chuckled just like a human being; a dark-eyed girl clerk smiled at me as I passed her little office in the hall, and then began to hum an old and plaintive English air; and, as I entered the coffee-room, a black and white dog flew at a venerable and bald-headed gentleman and frightened him to such an extent that he scrambled into a chair and shouted frantically for help.
>
> Well, all these scenes seemed to me to be familiar; merely back history. I was conscious of having lived through them once before; I knew and anticipated all that was about to happen.
>
> My dreams at night were strange; I fancied innumerable people glided noiselessly up to my bed, and, after gazing at me intently, glided away, only to make room for others, who came and went in the same manner; and, also, I kept on hearing music of a bygone date, and visiting houses and localities that I felt were once, in some peculiar way, associated with me.
>
> When, on the Monday morning, I left the hotel, I had been so uncannily at home in it that my departure seemed like parting from an old friend.

> The dog barked, the parrot screamed, and the girl in the office smiled, as I bade her goodbye; whilst the official in the vestibule whom I had, it seemed to me, so often seen in the past, beamed all over his face when I told him that I hoped to stay there again.
> But now comes the strangest part of it all. When next I visited Plymouth, a year or so later, that hotel was nowhere to be found. There was no building in the least degree like it in the street in which it had stood, and although I made endless enquiries of endless people, for I remembered every detail concerning it, no one to whom I described it had ever heard of such a place.

He felt, too, that he could never write about St. Ives without reference to the phantom ship that is said to have visited the bay from time to time. He was told by a fisherman who sometimes took him out in his boat, of how once he had been called upon to go to the rescue of a ship to the westward of St. Ives Head that had been burning lights as a signal for help. He and his comrades put out, and when they drew near to the vessel were utterly flabbergasted to see that her masts and riggings were covered with ice, as if she had encountered arctic weather. Curious, too, was the fact that no one was visible on her deck, and when they hailed her there was no reply. But, queerest of all, when the man in the bows of the St. Ives' boat stood up and tried to catch hold of the bulwarks of the strange vessel it suddenly and inexplicably vanished. His hands met nothing, and he would have toppled over into the sea had he not been grabbed in time by one of his mates. It was then that the men realised that what they had seen was the famous phantom ship, and they lost no time in making it back full speed to harbour. The phantom ship is seldom, if ever, seen in St. Ives Bay, except before some local maritime disaster. On this occasion, a few hours later, a great storm blew up and a ship was wrecked at Gwithian, everyone on board perishing.

O'Donnell claimed to have had many encounters with ghosts while living in Cornwall, so it is not really surprising that it was while he was there that he conceived the idea of writing a ghost book. His wife was ill, and in the evening, the schoolroom's harassments abated, he used to sit at her bedside formulating the tales that he would tell.

His first collection of ghost stories was published in 1908. It was a sixpenny paperback, *Bona Fide Adventures With Ghosts*, published by Baker, at Clifton. The book bore the additional description: "A Book to thrill Especially suitable for Xmas." And the rear endpaper advertised its author's services as a lecturer "in London and the Provinces (Cornwall excepted) on his experiences in Haunted houses." These lectures were to be popular events for the next fifty years, and were usually illustrated by his own impressive and unique magic lantern slides.

That same year also saw the publication, by Eveleigh Nash, of his first hardback volume of ghosts. He had sketched out a synopsis, posted it off, and been pretty well immediately commissioned to write the book, which he did in the summer of 1908, having made public his intention of giving up his school. Entitled *Some Haunted Houses of England and Wales*, it was issued, with an extremely attractive pictorial cloth cover, as a companion volume to Algernon Blackwood's celebrated *John Silence*, in the autumn. It created something of a sensation, was extensively and favourably reviewed not only by the London and provincial papers, but by many of the American and Colonial newspapers as well.

"It was the success of this first work of mine on ghostly phenomena," writes O'Donnell, "that made me realise that what I had long hoped for had at last come within measurable distance of attainment. I could give up teaching and devote my time once again, wholly and solely to writing. Never shall I forget with what joy – with what unbounded and infinite joy – I hailed the prospect of leaving for ever behind me all those weary, dreary hours in the schoolroom, where I had been forced to display a patience I never had, and where I had been forced to assume a virtue I never really possessed, namely, a love of teaching."

O'Donnell shed no tears as the train bore him and Ada away from the bays and coves, the romantic rocks and beaches of Cornwall, back to the Smoke, back to the future in London.

*The attractive cover of
O'Donnell's Some Haunted Houses (1908).*

A cartoon in the Penny Illustrated Paper, May 30 1908, making fun of Elliott O'Donnell's assertion that London's busy streets abound with ghosts.

10

Spooks in the Smoke

The winter of 1908 saw Elliott and Ada O'Donnell snugly settled in at a cosy Upper Norwood villa – No.14 Becondale Road. The house, which had a score of years to run before the lease ran out, had been offered to them by O'Donnell's step-sister and ex-guardian, Elizabeth. The couple were delighted with their new quarters.[1]

"Ada was not over-fond of domestic life," her doting husband wrote, "but she loved her home and making it look nice. She had a passion for antiques, and would seldom pass a curio shop without stopping to look at old and quaint pieces of furniture. Modern stuff did not appeal to her, any more than did very new houses. She liked character in houses. Inartistic paper worried her, and she spent days in stripping walls of such and covering them with washable paint of the hue she liked."

It was the same with clothes. "She disliked the term smart, as applied to clothes, and had as wonderful an eye for the artistic in dress as she had in furniture and wallpaper. She hated anything common or in bad style. She was fastidious, but not what could be called faddy."

She was, he said, highly intuitive and an excellent judge of character. She belonged to a Quotation Society, and had an extraordinary faculty for locating quotations. "Among her favourite prose writers were George

---

1 It is slightly puzzling to find the actress, Lily Brayton, writing from the Garrick Theatre, on March 9th, 1911, thanking O'Donnell, whom, incidentally, she addresses as "Miss E. O'Donnell", at 14 Beaconsfield Road, Gipsy Hill, London, S.E. It would seem that, for one reason or another, the O'Donnells had moved out, possibly only temporarily, from 14 Becondale Road, Upper Norwood. A letter from Lydia Yavorska, written from the Kingsway Theatre, on November 24th, 1911, is also addressed to O'Donnell at Gipsy Hill.

Meredith, George Eliot, and the Brontës. Regarding poetry, Mrs. Browning was one of her favourites."

Elliott was never tired of extolling Ada's virtues.

"As one example of her goodness of heart, although she was fond of dancing, she would never dance because I did not dance. So when we went to dances she insisted on sitting it out with me, watching other people whirl round the floor. Never could there have been a less selfish and more considerate wife or woman. Her greatest joy in life was being my companion and seeing people happy. Her views as regards politics and religion were much the same as mine. We preferred to be Independents rather than Party people, as regards the former, and, as regards the latter, Christians, but not denominationally bound. My sister Petronella in her later years was Protestant almost to fanaticism. My step-sister, at one period of her life, was equally High Church. Perhaps that was in a measure the reason for my being neither one nor the other, but a very broad in-between. My other sister Helena's views in this respect closely resembled Ada's and mine."

The O'Donnells' first year in London saw the publication by Nash of *Haunted Houses of London*, with its prefatory *caveat*: "The Ghost Stories narrated in this volume have all been selected expressly on account of their authenticity. I have, however, for the same reasons as those stated in my previous work, given fictitious names to people and places (save where it is stated to the contrary)."

The principal reason for deliberate vagueness, total disguise even, of true identities and localities, harked back to the rumpus over an allegedly haunted house in Egham, its putative revenant, and legal consequences of its public disclosure, played out in the courts in 1904, 1906, and, as subject of slander of title action, in 1907.[2]

The book was in the shops and, after mainly kind reviews, was selling quite well, so it was with feelings of optimism that O'Donnell sat down in his tiny room in Upper Norwood and started work on his fourth book of the supernatural, *Ghostly Phenomena*.

Determined to take full advantage of his new metropolitan status, one of the first things that he had done on coming to London was to set about getting himself elected to the Authors' Club. The membership

---

[2] *Vide: Stephen Phillips: A Biography.* Richard Whittington-Egan. Rivendale Press, 2006. pp.119-122 and J. Bondeson (*Fortean Times* 330 [2015], pp.44-5).

was distinguished. Among the members were Maurice Hewlett, Morley Roberts, Charles Garvice, and Conan Doyle, who was often to be seen playing billiards there.

He had not long been a member when, on going into the library one afternoon, he spotted, seated quietly by the fire, a rather small, not particularly impressive man. He looked to O'Donnell to be, like himself, a new member, who knew no one there, and consequently feeling a bit at sea and lonely. Full of those good intentions with which the road to Hell is said to be paved, O'Donnell diffidently approached him. "Do you write?" he inquired with a friendly smile. The effect of this, as it seemed to O'Donnell, innocent introductory remark was, to put it mildly, striking. Slowly, the little man turned his head towards his intrusive interlocutor, fixed him with an arctic gaze and, in equivalently glacial tones, informed him: "I have just turned down an offer for one of my books of..." he casually named a sum that to O'Donnell was positively stupendous, "yet you ask me if I write!" With a withering glance, he got up from his chair, and walked out of the room. Burking his merriment, a member sitting at a nearby writing-table said: "That was Arnold Bennett."

Another afternoon at the club, O'Donnell was inoffensively dozing, when he was suddenly roused by a little man with a pointed beard. "Excuse me," he said, "but if you nod your head much more I'm afraid you'll dislocate your neck." It was Hall Caine.

Sometimes O'Donnell would invite a few friends to tea in the ground floor lounge at the club. Memorably, on one such occasion, attended by his friend, Dr. Norman, another member, Mr. B., a retired professional man who had created something of a furore with his claim to having established communication with the inhabitants of Mars, came up to their table and showed the party a flower, which, he told them, had been gathered in the Balkans, and was possessed of a mystical magic property: when nibbled it would render the nibbler invisible. A sceptical Dr. Norman suggested that he should demonstrate by taking a nibble at it. Mr. B. promptly obliged. Nothing happened.

"We can still see you," chorused Norman and O'Donnell.

"Ah, you *think* you can," said Mr. B. "You are mistaken. It is the after-vision in the retina of your eyes that gives you that impression. I *am* invisible."

And no amount of argument would persuade him otherwise!

O'Donnell had a set-to there one day with the novelist Morley Roberts, who took him to task about some ghost stories that he had published in the *Tatler*.

"You shouldn't write just to frighten people," Roberts scolded him. "It's not good art."

Leaping, resentful of the corrective way in which he spoke, to his own defence, O'Donnell replied that he thought that people who read ghost tales should expect the possibility of being thrilled, just as they should if they sat up all night in a place that was reputed to be haunted, and he went on to mention some of the stories by highly respected authors about No.50 Berkeley Square and other notorious haunted places, that were far more calculated to frighten their readers than any of his *Tatler* tales.

During those early years in Norwood, much of O'Donnell's spare time was devoted to the investigation of hauntings that came to his notice. A lady who had read some of his books made contact with him to tell him that she had a house in Roehampton which was so badly haunted that she had felt obliged to vacate it, and she asked him if he would spend a night there. He agreed to do so, and, knowing several people anxious to pass a night in a haunted house with him, invited Lady Theresa Muir Mackenzie, Sir C. Aubrey Smith, the well-known actor, Mrs. Osborne Leonard, the celebrated medium and a prominent member of the Society for Psychical Research, and Sir Ernest Bennett, M.P. to accompany him. Unfortunately, the occasion, although socially speaking impeccable, proved far from psychically auspicious. The investigators drew a total blank.

He made psychic pilgrimage to the Mummy Gallery at the British Museum. His expectations were high. "I can honestly say, without any desire to boast, that I believe my experience of spontaneous manifestations in haunted houses is second to none, and that I have so much confidence in my faculty for detecting the presence of the superphysical that I think it would be well nigh impossible for me to err in my conclusions – if a house or a room or a piece of furniture is haunted, I am sure I should know it."

> I visited the notorious mummy case of a lady, name unknown, of the College of Amen-ra at Thebes. According to rumour this case has brought bad luck on all those who have handled or had anything to do with it – one person committing suicide, another going mad and another meeting with a serious accident.
>
> The case in itself seems ordinary enough, though a photograph that has been taken of it (and which can be seen by its side) is presumed by

some critics to possess a very human-like expression, quite different, in fact, to that of its painted and wooden representative.

The face on the mummy case is short, yellow, broad and wholly dollish, the in the photo is certainly much more expressive – the nose being more like a real nose, whilst the right eye positively leers with a blending of malice and good humour. I could not say at the time whether or not I thought the case was under any spirit influence, I am now inclined to think it may be, and for this reason, that on the occasion of my last visit to the department – a dull and dreary afternoon in March – I suddenly and instinctively felt that something had passed through the glass frame containing the mummy case and had planted itself by my side.

I went home and "the presence" followed me, nor was I rid of it for at least a fortnight, during which time I was continually seeing strange dark faces – all of them Egyptian both in colouring and cast of features – peeping at me from behind curtains, or peering down at me from over balustrades, and always with the same baffling and peculiar enigmatical expression in their long and glittering eyes.

Still, even though the case be haunted, I cannot say what by, I can only again surmise that it is under the influence of some particular species of Elemental... I do not for one moment believe that the soul of the original mummy confined in the case has anything to do with the alleged "bad luck," nor that it even has any cognizance of it.

Most probably the case was haunted in Egypt by the same spirit that has clung to it persistently ever since, as spirits often do attach themselves to things, following them from house to house, and from country to country.

Of course, he found it difficult to get very vivid impressions in the large and well-lighted, visitor-thronged gallery of his visitation. Here, alone, at midnight, things might well have been very different.

"Should I not expect those closely-swathed, recumbent figures to slowly shake off their bandages, and reveal the dark and sinister countenances of ages long ago? Would they not turn their eyes, lurid with Elemental glow, in my direction and, rising from their couches, come stealthily towards me?

The mummies of Katebit, a priestess of the College of Amen (Amun), and that of "the lady, name unknown," which he found awaiting him at the British Museum, were by any means the worst haunted. He could "feel the presence of other ghosts, and their name is legion, the very atmosphere is impregnated with them. Some of them move about encased in the bones, wrappings and outer coverings of the dead, others appear in their own guise, sinisterly attractive or diabolically repulsive, whole or in part only, tangible or vapourish, clearly defined or mere masses of pulp, but always incomprehensible, even more so than were once those whose remains they now haunt."

Ghostly Phenomena, which he had written in 1909, was published by T. Werner Laurie in 1910. It was reviewed at length by Andrew Lang, he of the brindled hair, in the *Morning Post*.

It is in this book that O'Donnell supplies a clear definition of what he means by the coinage "Elemental." Some occultists might call such entities Nature Spirits, but O'Donnell named them Elementals or Vagrarians. They are to be met with in lonely places – country lanes and spinneys, empty houses, isolated barns, and on moors, commons, and hill-tops. They may be minute in size, or tall, thin figures with tiny rotund or flat heads. They may be box-headed Elementals, with square or rectangular heads. They may have animal heads. Probably, says O'Donnell, they are the most terrifying of all apparitions, for not only are they horrible in aspect, the expression in their eyes diabolical, but they seem possessed by intense animosity to every form of earthly life.

He provides two illustrative examples of the phenomenon.

One May afternoon when he was a very young child staying with friends in the country, he saw from the nursery window a woman with a long beard rolling about on the lawn as though in great agony. Her face was not like that of a human being. Her head resembled that of some very grotesque caricature of an animal. Her fingers, which she kept opening and shutting, were short and webbed. She vanished instantly when one of the servants entered the nursery.

When he was even younger, night after night he would lie awake watching half a dozen or so tiny, pixie-like figurines flittering about the floor and pirouetting on top of the wardrobe. They, too, were grotesques, with long beards, oddly-shaped limbs and bodies, faces uniformly white and utterly devoid of expression. And when he was twenty, lodging in Dublin's Lower Merrion Street, he met with another Elemental. Above his rooms there were those of a Mr. Charles Clifford, at that time a briefless barrister, but who afterwards enjoyed a high reputation in the West Indies. On a particularly mild September evening, O'Donnell was chatting away with him in his sitting-room, when he suddenly complained of feeling extremely cold and asked O'Donnell if he would shut the window. As he approached the bay window, O'Donnell noticed that the curtain was rustling in a very peculiar way. He was just going to call Clifford's attention to it, when the most odd-looking yellow hand emerged suddenly from behind the curtain, pulling which aside, he was confronted by "the tall, nude, yellow figure of something utterly indefinable. Its head was large and round, its eyes light green, oblique and full of intense hatred." Clifford asked what in the world was the matter, and the moment he spoke, the thing vanished.

The next encounter took place when he was on tour with No.1 Company of *The Only Way*, at Plymouth. He was sharing rooms with an actor called Cornelius. On this Saturday night, Cornelius, who did not appear in the last act, had gone home. O'Donnell left the theatre about an hour later. The streets in the vicinity of his lodgings were silent and deserted. Just as he was turning in at the gate, he saw a tall figure come out of the house. There was something about its strange gliding movement that sent a wave of cold terror through him. He moved aside. The figure halted, and, to his horror, O'Donnell saw that it was exactly like the yellow Elemental that he had seen in Dublin. It remained stationary for about forty seconds, then seemed to dissolve into the mist.

Shortly before he began to write *Ghostly Phenomena*, O'Donnell had locked horns with another Elemental. Hearing that a house near Crystal Palace was rumoured to be haunted, he had requested and received permission to spend a night there.

> The house in question, though furnished, had been standing empty for some long time, and when I entered it alone one evening about nine o'clock, I was at once impressed with the musty atmosphere. I admit that, when the front-door closed behind me, and I found myself in a silent, empty hall, in which the shadows of evening were fast beginning to assemble, my heart beat a little faster than usual. Confronting me was a staircase leading to all the grim possibilities of the upper landings, while a little on one side of it was a dark, narrow passage, from which a flight of unprepossessing stone steps led into the abysmal depths of the basement.
>
> After a few minutes' hesitation, glad even to hear my own footsteps, I moved across the hall, and after examining the rooms on the ground floor, ascended to those above.
>
> All the blinds in the house being down, each room with its ponderous, old-fashioned furniture presented a particularly funereal aspect, to which a startling effect was given by a few patches of brilliant moonlight, that, falling on the polished surfaces of the wardrobes, converted them

into mirrors, wherein I saw the reflections of what apparently had no material counterparts. Here and there, too, in some remote angle, I saw a white and glistening something, that for a moment chilled my blood, until a closer inspection proved it to be a mere illumination on the wall or on some naturally bright object.

My investigation of the upper premises over, I descended into the basement, which, like all basements which have remained disused for any length of time, was excessively cold and damp. There were two cellars, the one opening into the other, both pitch-dark and streaming with moisture, and as I groped my way down into them by the spasmodic aid of my pocket search-light, I could not help thinking of the recent gruesome discoveries in Hilldrop Crescent.[3] In nine cases out of ten the origin of hauntings may be looked for in basements, the gloomy, depressing nature of which seem to have a special attraction for those Elementals that suggest crime. And here, in the cellars, far removed from prying eyes and sunlight, here, under the clammy, broken cement floor, here was an ideal sepulchre ready for the use of any murderer.

Minute after minute passed and nothing happened. The hour of midnight passed, and I anxiously awaited for what I felt every moment might now produce.

About one o'clock the temperature in the cellars suddenly grew so cold that my teeth chattered, and then I heard, as I thought, in the front hall, a tremendous crash as if all the crockery in the house had been dashed from some prodigious height in one big pile on the floor. Then there was a death-like hush, and then a jabber, jabber, jabber – apparently in the kitchen overhead – as of someone talking very fast, and very incoherently to themselves; then silence, and then, what made me sick with terror, the sound of shuffling footsteps slowly approaching the head of the steps confronting me. Nearer and nearer they came, until they suddenly paused and I saw the blurred outlines of the luminous figure of something stunted, something hardly human, and something inconceivably nasty. It rushed noiselessly down the steps, and, brushing swiftly past me, vanished in the furthest corner of the cellar.

Feeling that nothing more would happen now, I ascended the steps, and after a final and brief survey of the premises, walked home, feeling convinced that the phenomena I had experienced were due to a Vice Elemental attracted to the house by a murder that had once been committed there, the body of the victim being interred in one of the cellars. I was not able to visit the house again, and the owner, though acknowledging that what I had seen and heard was a recognised feature of the hauntings, refused to disclose anything further.

[3] The remains in the cellar of that house - Number 39 - of Cora Crippen, wife of Dr. Hawley Harvey Crippen, hanged for her murder on November 23rd, 1910.

Around the time of the publication of *Ghostly Phenomena*, O'Donnell made the acquaintance of Mrs. E.M. Ward, Henrietta Mary Ada Ward, relict of the English painter, Edward Matthew Ward, R.A. (1816-1879), who suffered from depression and died by his own hand, at Windsor, on January 15th, 1879. His son, Sir Leslie Ward (1851-1922), was the celebrated caricaturist of *Vanity Fair*, better known by his pseudonym, Spy. Their meeting came about in this wise. Mrs. Ward's youngest daughters, Enid and Beatrice, were getting up some theatricals, and found themselves short of a male actor. They turned in their difficulty to a woman friend and asked her if she could recommend a suitable man She knew O'Donnell, and wrote to him, with the result that he took part in the play, and came to know the Ward family. Henrietta, who, after her husband's early death had built up a successful career for herself as an art teacher, asked him if he would edit her memoirs. He was only to happy to oblige, and *Mrs. E.M. Ward's Reminiscences*, edited by Elliott O'Donnell, published by Sir Isaac Pitman & Sons, came out in 1911. The book was accorded an excellent reception by the press in general, *Vanity Fair* and the *Weekly Graphic* in particular giving it lengthy and eulogistic notices.

The year 1911 was a literarily busy one, for, O'Donnell also produced a collection, *Scottish Ghost Stories*, for publication by Kegan Paul, a book on *The Meaning of Dreams*, for Eveleigh Nash, and *Byways of Ghostland*, for William Rider and Son.

Scottish Ghost Stories had the misfortune to be published at the same time as M.R. James' *More Ghost Stories of an Antiquary*, and to be reviewed jointly with it, and to its detriment, in the *Observer*, where the innominate reviewer commented: "Beside Dr. James's, Mr. O'Donnell's ghost stories are foolish and feeble things. He does not vouch for these, as for some of his previous ones, as genuine occurrences' but there is still the same suggestion of actuality in the indications of names and addresses. If any of the concatenation of bogles whom Mr. O'Donnell has now expounded in five volumes have any basis in the Proceedings of the Psychical Research Society, they can only commiserate the ordinary ghost on its tameness, sameness, and generally imperfect equipment of horror as compared with the eerie and ingenious spectres of Dr. James."

An interesting passage in *Byways of Ghostland* describes the strange, trance-like state which could suddenly overcome O'Donnell and transport him to lost Edens of the really remote past.

Often as I ramble through thoroughfares, crowded with pedestrians and vehicles, and impregnated with steam and smoke and all the impurities arising from over-congested humanity, I have suddenly smelt a different atmosphere, the cold atmosphere of a superphysical forest land. I have come to a halt, and leaning in some doorway, gazed in awestruck wonder at the nodding foliage of a leviathan lepidodendron, the phantasm of one of those mammoth lycopods that flourished in the Carboniferous period. I have watched it swaying its shadowy arms backwards and forwards as if keeping time to some ghostly music, and the breeze it has thus created has rustled through my hair, while the sweet scent of its resin has pleasantly tickled my nostrils. I have seen, too, suddenly open before me, dark, gloomy aisles, lined with stupendous pines and carpeted with long, luxuriant grass, gigantic ferns, other monstrous primeval flora... I have watched in chilled fascination the black trunks twist and bend and contort, as if under the influence of an uncontrollable fit of laughter, or at the bidding of some psychic cyclone. I have at times stayed my steps when in the throes of the city pavements; shops and people have been obliterated, and their places taken by occult foliage; immense fungi have blocked out the sun's rays... On the Thames Embankment, up Chelsea way, I have at twilight beheld wonderful metamorphoses. In company with the shadows of natural objects of the landscape, have silently sprung up giant reeds and bull-rushes.

Such transformation scenes were not, to O'Donnell's way of thinking, mere visions, or the exquisite fantasies of a vivid imagination. These scenes were not illusions. "Why?" he asks, "have I not imagined other things; why, for example, have I not seen rocks walking about and tables coming in at my door? If these phantasms were but tricks of the imagination, then imagination would stop at nothing. But they are not imagination, neither are they the idle fancies of an over-active brain. They are objective, just as much objective as are the smells of recognised physical objects, that those with keenly sensitive olfactory organs can detect, and those with a less sensitive sense of smell cannot; those with acute hearing can hear, and those with less acute hearing cannot. And yet people are slow to believe that the seeing of the occult is as much a faculty as is the scenting of smells, or the hearing of noises."

Back in the spring of 1910, O'Donnell received a letter addressed to him by the Reverend Henry Hacon, of Searly Vicarage, North Kelsey Moor, Lincolnshire, enclosing a letter which his father had received from the Reverend John Stewart, Rector of Syderstone, near Fakenham, in Norfolk.

Spooks in the Smoke

The old, carefully preserved letter, written from Syderstone Parsonage, on May 22nd, 1833, read as follows:

My dear Sir,

All this Parsonage circle were gratified to learn that you and your family were recovered from the late epidemic. We are very sensible of your kind wishes and shall be happy to see you, at any time your press of business may allow you to leave Swaffham. The interest excited by the noises in our dwelling has become quite intense throughout this entire district of country. The arrivals from every quarter proved at last so utterly inconvenient that we have been obliged to decline receiving any more. We were compelled to draw the line somewhere, and we judged it could not be more sensibly done than immediately after the highly respectable authentication of the noises furnished last Thursday.

On the night preceding and the Thursday, four God-fearing, shrewd, intelligent brother clergymen assembled at the Parsonage, and together with a pious and accomplished lady and a medical gentleman from Holt (of eminence in his profession), joined Mrs. Stewart, my two eldest boys and myself in watching.

At ten minutes to two on Thursday morning the noises commenced, and lasted, with very little pause, till two hours after daybreak. The self-confident were crestfallen, and the fancied-wise acknowledged their ignorance as the sun rose high. Within the limits of any sheet of paper I could not give you even a sketch of what has taken place here. The smile of contented ignorance, or the sneer of presumption, cut but a poor figure when opposed to truth and fact – and the pharisaical cloak that is ostensibly worn to exclude "superstition" may secrete in its folds the very demon of "infidelity."

Arrangements are in progress to detect the most cunning schemes of human agency – but must be kept profoundly secret until the blow can be struck.

The magistrates, clergy, and surrounding gentry continue to arrive at the Parsonage, and offer us their public and private services in any way that can be at all considered useful. The Marquis of Cholmondeley's agent has gone to town resolved to lay the whole business before his lordship, and to suggest that a Bow Street officer should be sent down. I have likewise written to his lordship, who has been very kind to me.

You may rely upon it, that no human means (at whatever expense) shall be neglected to settle the point as to human agency. To attain a right history of the Syderstone noises you must read the details [here the writing is illegible, owing to a blot], that took place in the family of the Wesleys in 1716, their Rectory being at Epworth, in Lincolnshire. The father's (the Rev. S. Wesley's) journal is transcribed by the great and good John Wesley, his son. These noises never could be accounted for.

I have already traced the existence of noises in Syderstone Parsonage for thirty-six years back. I am told that Mr. Bullen, farmer of Swaffham, (with whom you are intimate), lived about that time at Creake (three miles from here), and recollects them occurring then. Be kind enough to ask him if he remembers of what nature they, at that period, were, and how long they continued without intermission. Favour me with the results of your enquiries. I think that but three of the generation then living now survive. The noises were here in 1797. Some ignoramus put the notices of them in the *East Anglian*. In that account some things are correct, mixed up with much that is wrong. However, I have kept a regular diary or journal of all things connected with them, and which in due time shall be published. Get the solution of these questions from Mr. Bullen for me, and, lest we should be wanderers, when you purpose coming over to us, let us know by post the day you mean to visit here.

Kind compliments from all to all under your "roof tree".

John Stewart.

The comparison with Wesley's Epworth is apt. The Syderstone manifestations were, like those at Epworth, poltergeistic. The disturbance began with unaccountable knockings in the middle of the night. Thereafter, it gradually escalated both in violence and protraction, until it was continuing unabated for spans of four or five hours. Other phenomena followed. The plopping and bouncing noise, as of a huge rubber ball, descending unimpeded through succeeding floors from roof to cellar. The metallic clatter of falling showers of coins. The bump and grind, the lift and fall, the push and drag of heavily shifting furniture. The powerful scratching on inner walls of what seemed like lion's or tiger's claws. An intermittent cacophony of moans and groans, creaks and shrieks, rattling iron, sounding brass, clashing earthenware, splintering glass, shivering the household air.

An invisible hand tapping time on the bed's wood to the music of an Evening Hymn, sung by the parson's daughter after she had retired for the night. The incident which befell Mr. Thomas Seppings. He and his wife were invited guests, staying the night. Before bidding his host and hostess goodnight, Mr. Seppings went over to a side table to collect a bedroom candlestick. "Well, I don't suppose we shall hear anything tonight," he remarked. The words were barely out of his mouth, his hand was about to grasp the candlestick, when there came a heavy hammer blow under the table and the candlestick.

The great and the good came to observe. Departed mystified and chastened. The most perfervid prayers availed nothing. The record is silent regarding the date of the cessation or otherwise of the strange affair at Syderstone, but all things come to an end. According to O'Donnell's further inquiries, it ended for sure with the pulling down of the old Parsonage, and the erection of a new and quiescent one in its place.

O'Donnell had home grown (literally) experience of his own with the poltergeist, albeit of milder mien. In his house in Norwood he lost, in rapid succession, two stylograph pens, a knife, and a sash. In each case he remembered laying the articles on the table, having his attention called away by some rather unusual sound in a far corner of the room, and, upon turning back to the table, finding that the article had inexplicably vanished. Just once, he caught a glimpse of the purloiner.

"It was about eight o'clock on a warm evening in June, and I was sitting reading in my study. The room is slightly below the level of the road, and in summer the trees outside, whilst acting as an effective screen against the sun's rays, cast their shadows somewhat too thickly on the floor and walls, burying the angles in heavy gloom. In the daytime one rather welcomes this darkness; but in the afternoon it becomes a trifle oppressive, and at twilight one sometimes wishes it was not there. It is at twilight that the nature of the shadows usually undergoes a change, and there amalgamates, with them, that Something, that peculiar, indefinable Something that I can only associate with the superphysical. Here, in my library, I often watch it creep in with the fading of the sunlight, or, postponing its advent till later, steal in through the window with the moonbeams, and I feel its presence just as assuredly and instinctively as I can feel and detect the presence of hostility in an audience or an individual. On the evening in question, I was alone in the house. I had noticed, amid the shadows that lay in clusters on the floor and walls, this enigmatical Something. It was there most markedly; but I did not associate it with anything particularly terrifying or antagonistic. Perhaps that was because the book I was reading interested me most profoundly – it was a translation from Heine, and I am devoted to Heine. I (was) absorbingly, spiritually interested, when I heard a laugh, a long, low chuckle, that seemed to come from the darkest and most remote corner of the room. A cold paroxysm froze my body, the book slid from my hands, and I sat upright in my chair, every faculty within me acutely alert and active. The laugh was repeated, this time from behind a writing-table in quite another part of the room. Something which sounded like a shower of tintacks then fell into the grate; after which there was a long pause, and then a terrific bump, as if some heavy body had fallen from a great height on to the floor immediately in front of me. I even heard the hissing and whizzing the body made in its descent as it cut its passage through the air. Again there came an interval of tranquillity, broken only by the sounds of people in the road... the quick, sharp tread of the lamplighter, and the scampering patter of a bevy of children. Then there came a series of knockings on the ceiling, and then the sound of something falling into a gaping abyss which I intuitively felt had surreptitiously opened at my feet.

For many seconds I listened to the reverberations of the object as it dashed against the sides of the unknown chasm; at length there was a splash, succeeded by hollow echoes. Shaking in every limb, I shrank back as far as I possibly could in my chair and clutched the arms. A draught, cold and dank, as if coming from an almost interminable distance, blew upwards and fanned my nostrils. Then there came the most appalling, the most blood-curdling chuckle, and I saw a hand – a lurid grey hand with long, knotted fingers and black, curved nails – feeling its way towards me through the subtle darkness, like some enormous, unsavoury insect. Nearer, nearer, and nearer it drew, its fingers waving in the air antennæ fashion. For a moment it paused, and then, with lightning rapidity, snatched the book from my knees and disappeared. Directly afterwards I heard I heard the sound of a latchkey inserted in the front-door, whilst the voice of my wife inquiring why the house was in darkness broke the superphysical spell. Obeying her summons, I ascended the staircase, and the first object that greeted my vision in the hall was the volume of Heine that had been so unceremoniously taken from me! Assuredly this was the doings of a poltergeist! A poltergeist that up to the present had confined its attentions to me, no one else in the house having either heard or seen it.

In my study there is a deep recess, concealed in the winter-time by heavy curtains drawn across it; and often when I am writing something makes me look up, and a cold horror falls upon me as I perceive the curtains rustle, rustle as though they were laughing, laughing in conjunction with some hidden occult monstrosity; some grey – the bulk of the phantasms that come to me are grey – and glittering monstrosity who was enjoying a rich jest at my expense. Occasionally, to emphasise its presence, this poltergeist has scratched the wall, or thumped, or thrown an invisible missile over my head, or sighed, or groaned, or gurgled, and I have been frightened, horribly, ghastly frightened. Then something has happened – my wife has called out, or someone has rung a bell, or the postman has given one of his whole-hearted smashes with the knocker, and the poltergeist has cleared off, and I have not been disturbed by it again for the remainder of the evening."

The year drew to its close on a sad note. O'Donnell's sisters, Petronella and Helena, came to visit him and Ada at Norwood. Helena had been ailing for some time, and it was hoped that a change of air from Clifton would do her good. After leaving Norwood, the sisters went first to St. Ives and then to Penzance. It was there that Helena became very ill, and the doctor who attended her told Petronella that she had cancer. The pair returned to Clifton. And there, On Christmas Day, 1911, Helena died.

THE "HAUNTED HOUSE," BERKELEY SQUARE

The haunted house at No. 50 Berkeley Square.
From Charles G. Harper's Haunted Houses. The house still stands today.

JUDY'S LUNATIC CONTRIBUTOR AND THE BERKELEY SQUARE GHOST.

It was mentioned in *Truth* the other day that Captain MIDDLETON, Lord BEREHAVEN, and Mr. HENRY BULLER wanted to take the famous Haunted House in Berkeley Square, and to investigate the mysteries.

On hearing, dear Madam, of the intentions of Lord BEREHAVEN, Captain MIDDLETON, and Mr. HENRY BULLER to investigate the mysteries of the Haunted House in Berkeley Square, I resolved in the interests of your inimitable journal to forestall these gentlemen, and, should I survive, report to you thereon; so with that intention I called at the house agent's for the key. "What, my dear sir," cried he, "*I* keep the key! Ha, ha! not if I know it!"

But he directed me where to go for it. 'Twas to a weird old man living in a tumbledown house at the back of Mount Street. He handed me the instrument, and then, placing his long skinny hands on my shoulders, cried, with a shrill laugh that went to my very marrow, "He, he! Let me have a good look at you *for the last time*! He, he! Mark ye—FOR THE LAST TIME!"

I thought after this it would be as well if I took little something with me into the house as a ne steadier; besides, the bottle might come in handy a weapon of defence, if necessary, for I was entirely armed. What a different scene—the bright chee tavern, made more so by the beaming smiles of the pr lady who served me—to that to which in a short sp of time I was doomed. But I anticipate.

I need not dwell on how I gained Berkeley Square, turned the key in the rusty lock of the door of the Haunted House, entered, shut it after me, lit my candle, and made myself comfortable in one of the dusty old corners; but will come to midnight, when slowly the door, which I need hardly say I had previously securely locked, opened, and *there entered the ghost!* I found him quite a sociable old person. He said he found it rather dull at times, and that he remembered what whisky was, but that it was not the fashionable drink in his time. He further remarked that he didn't mind if he did.

In fact, he "did" several times. Whether it was the mixing of the spirits I can't say, but by degrees the venerable party began to be quite jolly, not to say boisterous; volunteered a song, sentimental, but sung with a smile; and said if I'd whistle he'd show me how they danced in his days. This I agreed to do, and at it he went, capering about in the most quaint style, and as airily as ÆNEA herself.

It was while performing a rather difficult mo ment that he fell lightly (heavily to a being flesh and blood) to the ground, and gently m muring, "Olorowqueerifeel," commenced to so snore, not loudly, just the ghost of a snore. A now I felt my mission ended, for I had done best successfully to lay the ghost; so, after mak a candlestick of the phantom's mouth, which gap invitingly open, I toddled home to bed. If the man who keeps the key wants it, he will no dou find it somewhere about.

A joke about the Ghost of Berkeley Square.
From Judy magazine, January 10 1883.

11

Spirited Times

At the same time that he was editing Henrietta Ward's memoirs, Elliott O'Donnell was also writing for the *Weekly Dispatch*, having been commissioned by its editor, Mr. Buley, to write a series of ghostly experiences for the paper. The series, the first article of which was published in the issue of Sunday, June 26th, 1910, was prefaced by a *Weekly Dispatch* interviewer's impression of the "Prince of Psychic Investigators".

> I met Mr. O'Donnell at a small hotel within a stone's throw of the British Museum. In appearance he is the very embodiment of mysticism: tall, thin, and pale, with clean-cut, marked features, and dark, piercing eyes that look one through and through in a way which, although somewhat disconcerting, is far from disagreeable or unpleasant. In fact, Elliott O'Donnell's manners are the essence of good form, and a slight imperiousness in speech and gesture is in accordance with his general bearing.
>
> An odd mixture of Sir Henry Irving, to whom he bears a strange resemblance, Edgar Allan Poe, and Camille Desmoulins,[1] of a Roman patriot and an ascetic dreamer, of real flesh and blood and of some curious eerie spirit that might well belong to one of the lonely castles or misty moors about which he loves to write – his is indeed a personality that would at once make itself felt anywhere and in any circumstances. Though his hair is grey, and there are many lines on his forehead, his face has at times an expression of such extreme youth that it is quite impossible to guess his age. I hazarded thirty-nine, and found he was considerably younger.
>
> He has Protean qualities, as one gazes at him he appears in a dozen

---

1   Camille Desmoulins (1760-1794) French Politician. Friend and supporter of Danton. Played a prominent part in the French Revolution. His advocacy of clemency angered Robespierre and he was guillotined.

characters. I alternately saw in him the quiet scholar, the reckless soldier, the intrepid explorer, the tragic actor, the devoted husband, the generous friend, the detective, the barrister, the artist, most markedly the artist, to his fingertips, and over and above all the cool, determined, unflinching investigator of haunted houses.

The articles appeared, ten of them, each of which was accompanied by a highly atmospheric illustration, every Sunday until August 28th, and the writing of them involved making trips all over the country – and the odd non-psychic adventure.[2]

Trepidatiously, he trod the enshrouding dust and gloom of a menacing old house in Brighton. He had entered illicitly through a slightly open window. One minute he was groping his cautious way in a pitch-black room with seemingly never-ending walls, the next he was crashing to the floor, having stumbled over a large, soft object, and found himself rolling over and over, clawing and clutching at some foul, unsavoury, but totally material, tangible mass. Contriving to disengage himself, staggering to his feet, disoriented in the dark, he struck with trembling hands a match. Crouching on the floor in front of him he saw a long, thin, scraggy creature – bloodless face, matted hair, clad in filthy, string-bound rags.

The creature spoke. "I sleep here every night. This is my house." The voice was that of a woman.

"Then you are the ghost," said O'Donnell.

"I soon shall be, for I've eaten nothing for two days."

O'Donnell drew a package – some biscuits, bread and cheese, the snack he had brought to sustain him through his night watch – from his pocket and handed it to her. She seized it, voraciously crammed the food into her gaping, fleshless jaw. Then, when she had finished the last crumb, turning with a snarl said, "Get you gone and leave me here. I tell you this is my

---

2   The articles were as follows: (1) The Man Behind the Door. Locus: Brockley Road, London, S.E.4. (2) The Lady With the Evil Face. Locus: Shepherds Bush Road, London, W.6. (3) The Ghost of the Choking Woman. Locus: Piccadilly, London, W.1. (4) The Woman With the Invisible Face. Locus: Victoria Street, London, S.W.1. (5) The Secret of Berkeley Square. Locus: London, W.1. (6) The Man in Evening Dress and the Face at the Window. Locus: Church Road, London, S.E. (7) The Phantasm of the Radiant Child. Locus: Adelaide Road, London, N.W.3. (8) The Black-Framed Portrait. Locus: Tugela House, Blackheath Village, London, S.E.3. (9) The Woman in White and the Spotted Dog. Locus: Woodbine Cottage, Sydenham, London, S.E. (10) The Strange Disappearance of Rachel Rossiter, Gipsy. Locus: Dovedale Farm, near Penge.

house. Get you gone, or I'll spit at you."

Not wishing to be spat upon, the ghost hunter vanished, vanquished.

Unbelievably, a virtually identical misadventure awaited him a couple of hundred miles north, at Manchester. The house was in every way different. It was in good repair, fully furnished, and anything but sinister in appearance. Fast-fading sunshine was filtering in through the drawn Venetian blinds when he arrived in the early evening for his vigil at the allegedly haunted house. The atmosphere was non-hostile, and as he wandered from room to room he was, at first, completely at ease and unworried, but the intense silence began at length to tell upon his nerves. He was on the staircase leading to the top storey when he fancied that he heard an alien noise, and so taut-strung was his state that, a sudden wave of faintness overcoming him, he had to clutch the banisters to prevent himself from falling. Recovered, his head no longer swimming, he opened a door at the stair head and walked into a large room that communicated with two other rooms, the doors of both of which stood ajar. He had passed through the first room and was about half-way across the second when he suddenly felt one of his ankles being gripped. Shocked, it seemed to him as though all the blood in his body had dried up, and he hovered again on the verge of fainting. He forced himself to look down and was horrified to see a skinny hand and arm protruding from under the dressing-table. He struck at it with his stick, kicking out vigorously at it at the same time. With terrible howlings there now crawled out from beneath the dressing-table, a long and lanky idiot boy. He was, it transpired, the son of one of the servants of the rich and somewhat eccentric old lady who owned the house, but who, believing it to be haunted, had decided not to live there. His mother used to visit the boy, sole tenant of the otherwise deserted house, every evening, to make sure that he was all right, and bringing him food. This particular evening, the lad had hidden with the intention of playing a prank on his mother, and giving her a fright. The servant lost her post, and the old lady, reassured by O'Donnell's laying of the "ghost", returned to take up residence in her no longer haunted house.

The following week O'Donnell was in Liverpool, from where he had received a letter from a woman saying that her daughter, Emily, was being tormented by a phantom man who appeared in her bedroom every night at the same time, approached her bed on tiptoes, grabbed the bedclothes, pulled them off, and walked away with them. Spirit lights were constantly seen in the room, and sometimes figures like angels would be there.

Accepting her invitation to pay them a visit, O'Donnell, ascribing to the discretion better part of valour maxim and taking a friend with him, made his way to the house, which was, he said, situated in a crescent close to Clayton Square. This was obviously a deliberate misdirection, a masking of the true location, for there was never any crescent in the vicinity of Clayton Square. The family were waiting for O'Donnell and his companion in the drawing-room. Having been regaled with detailed accounts of all that was alleged to have happened, they were escorted to the haunted bedroom, were the young woman about whom the phenomena centred was sitting. As soon as the electric light was switched off, she began to see spirit lights. O'Donnell saw nothing. No man appeared. He decided that the phenomena were subjective and that it was a case of hallucination. He advised the girl's mother that it would be a sound idea to consult a good general practitioner.

Months later, O'Donnell ran into a young London doctor to whom he had mentioned the affair.

"You remember the Liverpool case of the young lady whose bedclothes used to disappear, and you thought was hallucination? Well, you were mistaken. Since I saw you, I've become acquainted with the doctor who attends her, and he told me that while he was there one day the bedroom door opened, and in walked a young man. He says the girl immediately exclaimed, 'Here is the man who haunts my room at night. For goodness sake, Doctor, do something.' Whereupon, the man, muttering some words in German, abruptly left the room. My doctor friend immediately ran after him, but he was nowhere to be seen, and although the house was at once searched, no trace of him could be found."

O'Donnell was confessedly perplexed, but hazarded: "It may be a case of projection. Someone who knows the girl and wishes to torment her is experimenting in visiting her in his immaterial ego. I have heard of similar cases. The image she sees may be, and very likely is, merely an assumed one. I incline to the idea that the ghost in this case was a phantasm of the living, rather than a phantasm of the dead."

The series assignment for the *Weekly Dispatch* completed. O'Donnell took a brief holiday, visiting for the first time Matlock and Harrogate. The Harrogate sojourn turned into something of a busman's holiday, for he discovered a haunted house there – "a modern edifice of a great height, situated about ten minutes' walk from St. James' Hall."

He went there alone, and on entering the premises was aware of an almost death-like air of stillness, contrasting oddly with the life and gaiety of the streams of ultra-fashionable people heading for the Spa Concert, the theatre, and the Valley Park.

But this house – this forsaken house, void of furniture, of everything, save the soft summer evening sunlight, the shadows, and my presence – how different! As the hours passed by and darkness came on, I began to be afraid. No amount of experience in ghost hunting will ever enable me to overcome that awful, hideous fear that seizes me when I see the last glimmer of daylight fade, and I realise I am about to be brought into contact with the superphysical, and that I must face it – alone.

Noises in empty houses I have noticed usually commence in the basement, and I was not at all surprised when presently I heard a faint tapping proceeding from one of the kitchens. This was followed by a long spell of silence, and then one of the stairs creaked. My heart gave a big thump, and I gazed expectantly into the darkness before me, but there was nothing to be seen. Silence again, and then more tapping, and more creaking. Something then tickled my hand, and a moment later my finger touched a black-beetle. In an instant I was on my feet, for I dread beetles more than I dread ghosts, and, on my striking a light, I found the whole floor swarming.

As I could no longer tolerate the idea of remaining in the hall in the dark, I lighted four candles, and, placing them on the floor, sat in the midst of them. It was only eleven o'clock by my watch. Half an hour or so passed, and then I received a start. A door opened and shut downstairs, and bare footsteps pattered their way along the stone passage and up the wooden stairs. The nearer they drew, the more intolerable became my suspense.

What should I see? A white-faced, glassy-eyed phantasm of the dead, or some blood-curdling, semi-human, semi-animal neutrarian. Which would it be? I confess, I would have given all I possessed to be out in the road, but, as is usually the case with me when in the presence of the superphysical, I was quite powerless to speak or move.

Then, to my unfeigned astonishment, instead of anything grotesque and awful, there appeared before me a little fair-haired girl, clad in a much-soiled pinafore and without either shoes or stockings. Though not actually crying, she appeared in great distress, and feeling around on all sides, as if anxiously searching for someone, she ran past me, and commenced to ascend the stairs.

Picking up a candle, I followed her. The pattering of her poor, chilled feet spread their echoes far and wide through the vast deserted house. On and on we went, the little thin legs leading the way, till when she ran into a room facing me, and slammed the door. I immediately followed, but the room was quite empty. There was no only a particularly vivid beam of moonlight, and a virile and overwhelming atmosphere of sadness.

During the next few days I was told a story that fully accounted for the hauntings.

It appears that about thirty years before my visit to the house a little girl had lived there with her father and step-mother. Her nurse, to whom she was very much attached, being summarily dismissed by her step-mother, she became ill, and very soon died, so it was rumoured, of a broken heart.

He was commissioned to write a second series for the *Weekly Dispatch*, and a further seven articles appeared therein between February 19th, and April 2nd, 1911. This second series,[3] too, seems to have been a considerable success, and a positive maelstrom of eager readers' letters came torrenting in to the *Weekly Dispatch* office. To be fair, he had asked for it! He had let it be known to the paper's readership that he was always anxious to hear of fresh cases to investigate, and that he "earnestly hoped that readers of the *Weekly Dispatch* would introduce him to a new collection of ghosts who visit the glimpses of the moon."

A little unexpectedly perhaps, there is an undeniable vein of *snobismo* running blue through the green of O'Donnell's Irish blood. He indulges it; he identifies with the blue-bloods – "Among other prominent members of society who sat up with me" – he cites the Duke of Newcastle, "who was opposed to spiritualism, but took a keen interest in hauntings."[4]

3 The articles were as follows: (1) The Man With the Scissors and the Everlasting Grin. Locus: Devon. (2) The Limbless Body and the Grey Nurse. Locus: Near Felixstowe. (3) The Mystery of Lipscombe Manor. Locus: Near Ealing, London. (4) The Vampire Hand of Crompton Court. Locus: Near Worcester. (5) The Grey-hooded Monk and Skeleton Woman of Barque Abbey, Near Durham. (6) The Black Cat and the Man With the Tongue. Locus: Aytoun Street, Manchester. (7) The Coughing Woman. Locus: Regency Square, Brighton.

4 O'Donnell dedicated his book *The Menace of Spiritualism*, published by Werner Laurie in 1919: "By Permission to His Grace, the Duke of Newcastle." This was, in fact, the first of his many books to bear a dedication. Thereafter there were no further dedications until the 1940s and 1950s. In 1945, he dedicated his novel, *Murder at Hide and Seek* (Eldon Press): "This Book is dedicated to Nora Jeffery", and in 1948, *Haunted Britain*, was dedicated: "To Nora Jeffrey (sic). In 1951, *Ghosts With a Purpose*, bore the dedication: "To the Memory of My Many Friends who have passed on." His 1952 novel *The Dead Riders* (Rider & Company), is dedicated: "To Christian Leslie", *Dangerous Ghosts*, 1954 (Rider) is: "To Nora", *Haunted People*, 1955: "To Christian", and finally, in 1956, *Phantoms of the Night*, is: "In fondest memory of my wife".

The house to which His Grace, the Hon. Arthur Lambton, and several other friends had accompanied him was in the vicinity of Redcliffe Square, off the Brompton Road, South Kensington. The party distributed themselves, at about midnight, in different places, "some in the hall, and some on the staircase, and the lights being lowered, we sat waiting and listening for the alleged phenomena." But alas, despite the aristocratic presence, no supernatural presence deigned to manifest itself. A loud scream from one of the ladies perched on the staircase seemed to herald psychic success. When the light was at once switched back on, the tremulant visionary declared, hand on heart, that she had suddenly seen a skeleton face peering at her through the landing window. The owner of the house expressed great astonishment at this, as no such thing had ever before been witnessed in her demesne. "However," O'Donnell apologetically explains, "when it transpired that the lady who had seen the skeleton face was a prominent member of a certain 'sisterhood' in Kensington that had figured in a recent sinister case, none of us were surprised that she had seen what she had seen. We were only surprised that she had not seen something far worse."

In August, 1913, an impressive letter arrived on O'Donnell's breakfast table. It brought the compliments of Lord Curzon of Keddleston, and the tidings that he would like to hold a vigil in a house reputed to be haunted, and that he had been told by the Hon. Everard Feilding that he [O'Donnell] might know of one. He did. He suggested B. Grange,[5] in Somerset, where he had himself on several occasions held nocturnal vigils.

Curzon asked O'Donnell to meet him at the Atlantic Hotel, in Weston-super-Mare in order to discuss arrangements for the occasion. Now Curzon was not only very self-consciously top drawer, but had had a uniquely distinguished career, which included his occupancy of the office of viceroy and governor-general of India. He had, moreover, a reputation for sharp-tongued formidability and pomposity. It was not, therefore, without some quaking that O'Donnell proceeded to the appointment, and was ushered into his presence. "I had been told he was cold and reserved, and apt at times to be very sarcastic and pungent, but I did not find him so. To me he was extremely affable and considerate, without that air of superiority and condescension I have experienced in people of far less eminence. He was most friendly and courteous."

---

5   This name, selected by O'Donnell, masks the true identity of the house.

O'Donnell suggested that they should take a dog with them, because he had found that dogs often act as psychic barometers, showing restlessness and alarm at the advent of the supernatural. He also advised that they should include a professional photographer in the party. At the dinner which preceded the expedition, Curzon showed himself to be by no means devoid of humour. He asked O'Donnell what was the usual *de rigueur* costume for ghost hunting, and whether or not he could sense the presence of the supernatural. But he never revealed what he really thought about ghosts, whether he believed or not in their existence.

At about 10 p.m. Lord Curzon, a handful of his friends, O'Donnell, the photographer, and a dog made their way to the Grange. The party went directly to the haunted room. There, they grouped together. O'Donnell sat facing the corridor, others sat on chairs alongside of him, the dog settled itself comfortably on the floor, the photographer, his flash primed in readiness, hovered, the very picture of alertness. At first there was a smattering of talk. It was soon submerged in a silence broken only by a normality of night noises – the jarring and creaks of windows, floors, and doors, the hootings of an owl. O'Donnell sensed nothing ghostly, neither did the dog, fast asleep. There were a couple of times when O'Donnell fancied that he heard the muffled echoings of distant footsteps and was conscious of a certain tenseness among the watchers, but the moments passed, brief punctuations of optimism in a wearisome wilderness of failure. Shortly after 2 a.m. Curzon opined that, as it was long past the traditional witching hour, and there seemed little prospect of anything happening, they should call it a night. No one disagreed.

They went to the house again the next night. It proved a discouraging encore of nihility.

Third time lucky? Following the twin disappointments, an admirably persistent Lord Curzon asked O'Donnell if he knew of any other haunted house in the vicinity of Weston-super-Mare. O'Donnell mentioned one in Bristol, near the Clifton Suspension Bridge. Curzon enthused. Arrangements were made. His lordship suggested that, as well as a dog, they ought perhaps to have a lady accompany them. He had heard that ladies were often clairvoyant. The only likely lady that O'Donnell knew was Mrs. Green Armitage, a novelist of more than local renown. He telephoned her. She was happy to come. Most conveniently, she happened to have a dog. O'Donnell also imported Bligh Bond, of Glastonbury Abbey fame, who had held a previous vigil in the house, and had some interesting information to impart.

The house was situated in a terrace and dated back to somewhere around 1780. The last tenant had, when he went to view it one day before taking it, seen a woman dressed all in black standing in one of the rooms. She had her back to him and, obviously unaware of his presence, seemed to be arranging her hair under her hat. He was about to approach her, when, she simply vanished. Thinking that he had been the subject of some kind of hallucination or illusion, he dismissed the matter from his mind, and in due course rented the house. He and his wife and their little boy had not been living there long when one evening his wife, son, and another lady were startled by a strange, ominous cry that seemed to pass right through the room. On another occasion, the little boy and his brother saw a lady in black holding a small boy by the hand standing in the doorway staring at them. They called out to their mother. She ran upstairs to them, but the lady and boy had disappeared. There were other phenomena. Every night about the same time footsteps were heard running up the stairs from the hall to the first floor landing, where sounds like the winding of a big clock were heard. After that, the footsteps would ascend to the next floor. Arriving there, they would run across the landing to the bathroom, the door of which would be heard to open and slam shut. From within the bathroom would come the sound of them bouncing about on the floor.

A hospital nurse who once stayed there, hearing what she took to be a clock on the landing being wound, and curious as to who would be doing such a thing in the middle of the night, peeped out of her bedroom door and saw something that gave her a nasty shock. A weird shadowy figure was bounding, two or three steps at a time, up the stairs in complete and eerie silence. She could only see its back, no face, but the thing gave her the impression of being very evil and grotesque, more like some huge, horrible ape than a human being. She heard it open and shut the bathroom door, and start bounding all over the floor.

Another phenomenon, reported to occur in the daytime, was that of footsteps, accompanied by heavy breathing, coming up the stone steps leading from the cellar to the passage on the ground floor. On one or two occasions an indistinct shadowy form was glimpsed rushing along the passage and disappearing into the kitchen. A voice calling out "Henry!" was heard, seemingly coming from the chimney in one of the rooms.

The clocks were striking eleven as Lord Curzon, Elliott O'Donnell, Bligh Bond, and Mrs. Green Armitage and her dog, bent their footsteps towards the house of evil repute. With so liberal a menu of recorded psychic items before them, the outlook seemed hopeful. The place certainly looked haunted. Dilapidated. Most forlorn. Cobwebs festooning the ceilings. Paper peeling from walls. Window-panes cracked and broken. Doors and floors covered in places with huge, repulsive-looking spreads of fungi.

The optimistic investigators distributed themselves – Lord Curzon and Mrs. Green Armitage on camp stools at the head of the cellar steps, the dog beside them. Bligh Bond and O'Donnell in a room on the first floor. All was quiet until... at about 1 a.m. the door of the room where Bligh and O'Donnell were on watch began slowly to open. Heart fluttering, jaws tight clenched, O'Donnell inched across to the door... and there stood Mrs. Green Armitage's dog. Bored with the hall, adventurous and inquisitive by disposition, it had made its way upstairs for a prowl, to see what was going on.

And that was the sum and apogee of the night's phantasmagoria. The vanquished ghost hunters trooped crestfallen back to their hotel just after 2 a.m.

Next morning O'Donnell took Lord Curzon to see the Clifton Suspension Bridge, fully expecting that he would, as most visitors did, express a measure of admiration for it. "Not at all wonderful. Not to be compared with a bridge I have seen in India," was his lordship's unexpected and unwelcome verdict. O'Donnell's chagrin was redeemed by Curzon's cordial subsequent letter thanking him for his services as ghost hunter in chief.

It was getting on for twelve months since, in October 1912, he had brought out his last book, *Werwolves*, published by Methuen.

The *Scotsman* had accorded it a distinctly hostile review. "Having in several volumes harrowed the souls of nervous and weak-minded readers with tales of ghosts and haunted houses, Mr. Elliott O'Donnell turns to the yet more grisly and hair-raising subject of werewolves, a class of anomalous beings with which he conjoins the allied races of vampires and ghouls. In all three of these tribes of night-prowling monsters bred of mediæval ignorance and superstition, he professes to be a believer, although he is hard put to find a theory to explain the "wolfman" that will stand either on four legs or two, and one cannot help suspecting that he has his tongue in his cheek alike when he is propounding the basis of his belief, and in producing the illustrative examples drawn from the different countries infested with wer-wolves. It may be added that the stories, apart from being otherwise most unconvincing, are most inartistically told."

This was manifestly a most unfair criticism; treating it as a five-shilling shocker. The book was clearly the product of extensive scholarly research, documenting the state of werewolf lore and belief in the British Isles, France, Belgium, the Netherlands, Germany, Austria-Hungary, the Balkan Peninsula, Spain, Denmark, Norway, Sweden, Iceland, Finland, Russia, and Siberia. Anyway, undeterred, O'Donnell, clearly concerned that the upper class British lad of parts should be forearmed against possible future encounter with lycanthropic danger, presented the School Library of Eton College and that of Cheltenham College also each with a copy of the book.

His mind turning again to fiction, O'Donnell approached William Rider, the Aldersgate Street publisher.

"Dear Mr. O'Donnell," he replied, "I have read the synopsis with much interest. It sounds most thrilling, and I think should make an interesting book. I should be pleased to see you Thursday or Friday next week sometime between 3.15 and 5 o'c. As regards the title, the only titles I can think of at the moment are: *The Black Magicians; In League With Hell; In League With Darkness; An Astral Alliance; An Infernal Pact*. The word "Hell" seems to specify evil too definitely, I am afraid. I think it important to have the title a terse one; *Byways of Ghostland* seemed to appeal. If we had some such title as *In League With Darkness* we might have on the outside of the book two hands clasping each other to suggest the idea, one hand being black. I think I could suggest some more tips which would help you in your narrative from past *Occult Reviews*."

The novel came out in 1912, as *The Sorcery Club*.

With an eye to the main chance, O'Donnell scribbled off a hopeful note to the celebrated actress, Marie Tempest, who replied, writing from the Prince of Wales Theatre: "If you will be good enough to send me a copy of the book, I will read it with pleasure, and let you know at once whether I think there is anything in it which would suit me." Nothing came of it.

Now, in November, 1913, William Rider & Son published O'Donnell's fifteenth book, *Animal Ghosts or, Animal Hauntings and the Hereafter*. In it, he set out the stall of his beliefs.

"If human beings, with all their vices, have a future life, assuredly animals, who in character so often equal, nay, excel human beings, have a future life also. Those who in the Scriptures find a key to all things, can find nothing in them to confute this argument. There is no saying of Christ that justifies one in supposing that man is the only being whose existence extends beyond the grave... It is to testify to a future existence for animals and to create a wider interest in it that I have undertaken to compile this book; and my object, I think, can best be achieved in my own way, the way of the investigator of haunted places. The mere fact that there are manifestations of 'dead' people (pardon the paradox) proves some kind of life after death for human beings; and happily the same proof is available with regard (to) a future life for animals; indeed there are as many animal phantasms as human – perhaps more; hence if the human being lives again, so do his dumb friends. Be comforted then, you who love your pets, and have been kind to them. You will see them all again, on the soft undying pasture lands of your Elysium and theirs."

Nor was it only dogs and cats and horses that peopled O'Donnell's psychic Ark. Rabbits and hares, and goats and pigs, and bulls and cows were also there. And, more exotically, elephants. Lions and tigers, and a virtual aviary of birds – ravens, crows and magpies, vultures, eagles, owls, and the red-breasted robin.

Lest you should be tempted to deem this calumnious as regards the cheery, red-breasted, decorative icon of so many merry Christmas cards, give ear to the Super-tramp, W.H. Davies' carolling of him.

> Since I have seen a bird one day,
> His head pecked more than half away;
> That hopped about with but one eye,
> Ready to fight again and die –
> Ofttimes since then their private lives
> Have spoilt that joy their music gives.
>
> So when I see this robin now,
> Like a red apple on the bough,
> And question why he sings so strong,
> For love, or for the love of song;
> Or sings, maybe, for that sweet rill
> Whose silver tongue is never still –
>
> Ah, now there comes this thought unkind,
> Born of the knowledge in my mind:
> He sings in triumph that last night
> He killed his father in a fight;
> And now he'll take his mother's blood –

The last strong rival for his food.

No sooner was the manuscript of *Animal Ghosts* away than the industrious O'Donnell had picked up his stylograph and inked the first words on virgin-white paper that would increase and multiply to become the thick press of pages making up the script of his next work, *Haunted Highways and Byways*.

Shortly after arriving in London, he joined the Irish Literary Society, whose premises were then in Hanover Square. His fellow-members included Miss Eleanor Hull, the historian and folklorist, Percival Graves, author of "Father O'Flynn", and Plunket Greene, the well-known professor of singing at the Royal Academy of Music, who, was an old Cliftonian. Elliott and Ada frequently had tea there, took part in the play readings, and went to lectures. Occasionally, O'Donnell would himself deliver a lecture before the Society.

O'Donnell was a clubman through and through, and over the years became a member of many clubs. For a brief time he belonged to the Press Club. He was also a member of the Whitefriars, which met once a week. He greatly enjoyed the luncheons there, and appreciated the opportunities it provided for his making contact with so many well-known people in the literary world. He was enthusiastic, too, about the Faculty of Arts. Its quarters were in a street just off Golden Square, and it included in its membership many well known in all branches of art, as well as a number of people from various embassies. He gave several talks on his usual subject, ghosts, there, and remarked that one could always be sure of a good audience. But, without a doubt, the most eccentric of his social haunts was the Freak Club, in Mayfair, which he joined in 1912. The proprietor was an American, and he had managed to attract a membership of some of the most peculiar characters that O'Donnell had ever encountered in either this or the other world!

There was, for instance, an old gentleman, a respectable retired professional man, who, of his charity, O'Donnell simply designates Mr. Jones.

"I came upon Mr. Jones one day crawling down the staircase of the club. I asked him if he was ill. 'Hush,' he said in very solemn tones. 'I am a bear.' He explained later on that every now and then he was under the impression that he was subject to metamorphosis, and when in that state he believed himself to be a bear. He fell in love with a tree in Green Park, and used to talk and croon to it. When it was either cut or blown down, he was greatly distressed, and put on mourning. He was talking one evening to a well-known magician, also a member of the club. After the magician left, Mr. Jones suddenly cried out: 'My watch has gone. I know who's taken it.' I asked him who, and he said: 'One of the little imps that I saw behind the magician. They are his familiars.' I told the magician what Mr. Jones had said, and he was much amused. A day or two afterwards, Mr. Jones came to me in the lounge and said, 'I've found my watch. It was in the lining of my coat. No human agency could have put it there. It was the magician's imp.' And he firmly believed it.

It was only occasionally, however, that he behaved in a very odd manner. He was mostly apparently very rational. He was not particularly interested in the supernatural, but on one occasion he did ask me to take him to an allegedly haunted flat in Brunswick Square. The woman in whose flat the psychic disturbances were said to be taking place, was a lady of artistic temperament and open mind. So, having rearranged the furniture and turned out the light, we settled down for the murdered gentleman – the alleged ghost was that of a man named Molyneux, who had been murdered in the house – to pay us a call. In the centre of the room sat four persons round a small table and round them sat an outer circle, the members of which all joined hands. No one spoke. Presently, one of the sitters saw a green light in the room. Everyone was thrilled, and disappointment was evinced when the light was found to be due to a luminous wristlet watch one of the sitters was wearing. Shortly afterwards, a lady with the faculty for seeing things informed me that she saw a large eye near the ceiling. We all looked and saw the eye. It was elliptical in shape and it showed dim and uncertain. Then someone saw a light somewhere else, but before it could be investigated Mr. Jones made noises like a dog barking, began to bump the table with his fists, and told us that some ghostly fingers were at his throat. He made such harrowing, gurgling moans that I was alarmed, fearing he was in a fit, and announced my intention to switch on the light. He begged me not to, however, and presently commenced barking again. Several of the sitters said that they felt a cold wind, and two people declared that they saw spirit faces. One of the faces was beautiful and the other that of a corpse. There was an eeriness in the room that affected most of the people to such a degree that they clamoured for a light. Consequently, I switched it on. When Mr. Jones had got back into something like the nearest approach to a normal person, he expressed his opinion that the beautiful face was that of a girl who had murdered Molyneux, that she was as lovely as she was evil, that it was her spirit that had tried to strangle him, and that the corpse face was that of her victim, Molyneux. He told us that the extraordinary sounds which he had made were due to metamorphosis, on this occasion not ursine, but canine. I think most of us felt that the flat really was haunted, and that Mr. Jones was possibly right. During the night I tried, as I generally do, to get into communication with whatever spirit might be present, but there had been no response."

Apropos the eccentrics of the Freak Club, O'Donnell amusedly recalled:

> An elderly retired medical practitioner came to see me one morning. He told me that when he was in India he had seen fakirs do very wonderful things. "They have great mesmeric power over animals," he said, "and can walk through a tiger-infested jungle without being harmed. No savage beast will molest them. Your book, *Animal Ghosts*, shows you have great sympathy with animals and suggests to me that you are on the same psychic plane with them and, like fakirs, could be in close contact with lions and tigers without being attacked. To prove I am right, I want you to accompany me to the Zoological Gardens one day and enter a tiger's cage. I can arrange that. Should the tiger resent your intrusion, I will hypnotise it so that it won't touch you. It will be a most interesting experience, I assure you."
>
> "No doubt," I said, "a more interesting one for you and the tiger than for me. I take it that you, too, are very fond of animals. Isn't that so?"
>
> "Why, yes," he replied. "However do you know?"
>
> "Intuition," I said. "Why not see if you are on the same psychic plane as a tiger? You enter a tiger's cage, and if it looks as if it is about to eat you, I will put my mesmeric power to the test, and will it to be great pals with you. How about that?"
>
> The idea did not appeal to him at all. He shook his head. He much preferred his own proposition. So, as we could not agree, we parted somewhat abruptly. and I saw him no more.

A distinctly less desirable companion was a man, betrayed by a very sly face, who one day sought O'Donnell's company at the club. After a few commonplace remarks about the weather and such topics, he launched into an account of how he had stumbled upon the quasi-alchemical secret of how to transform common stones into gems. He showed him a handful of glittering red cubes, and said: "Look at these. They were once common pebbles, and what are they now?"

"Glass," responded O'Donnell, and he was right. The man was arrested not long after for palming them off as rubies.

Then there was the member who told O'Donnell that he was an expert in concentration and could, through sheer will power, move objects without touching them. O'Donnell suggested that he should demonstrate his powers with his umbrella. The man said that conditions were not right for the amount of concentration that that would require, but offered to experiment with matches. He proceeded to put two matches horizontally on a table, a little distance apart and parallel with one another, and then placed a third match vertically across them. Sitting about a yard from the table, he then concentrated. After a while, the match that was lying on the two matches slowly moved, and, slipping off them, assumed a horizontal position midway between them. It was a feat that completely perplexed O'Donnell.

He was impressed by the psychic abilities of a woman member who made no pretence of being either a psychometrist or clairvoyant, but who nevertheless exhibited a most remarkable faculty. With her eyes bound over with a thick bandage, she could, simply by running them through her fingers, tell correctly the colour of each of a variegated series of ribbons. She was watched too closely for any trickery to have taken place.

The fact is, the club seems to have been a magnet for all sorts of oddments. There was a woman with elephantine ears, who was a man hater. Whenever she met a member of the masculine sex, she would snort and curl her lips at him scornfully. There was a girl who harboured a great aversion to the aged of her own sex. When she clapped eyes on any old lady in the street, she would make diabolical faces at her. There was a bald-headed man who was always mistaking someone else's hat for his own. There was a black-bewhiskered man who was forever accusing people of purloining his umbrella. There was an old man in short trousers who would not eat or drink anything without asking first aloud the permission of his Chinese spirit guide.

To keep the balance, there were, however, a number of very sane and charming members of both sexes. That O'Donnell and his wife frequently visited the club, and found it most entertaining, is hardly surprising.

The Curse of Rudesheim, featuring a huge, monstrous crab. From O'Donnell's Famous Curses (1929).

The cursed Bishop Hatto is devoured by mice inside the mouse-tower he had built to protect himself in such an eventuality, from O'Donnell's Famous Curses *(1929).*

12

The Ghostly Dogs of War

As ordained, *Haunted Highways and Byways* issued forth from the publishing house of Eveleigh Nash early in 1914. In it – Chapter VIII. The Swing – O'Donnell, looking back to his fledgling dominie days and dropping an interesting identificatory clue, writes: "Towards the end of the last century there was a preparatory school for young gentlemen in Blackheath, kept by the Rev. Samuel Twining, M.A. I am careful not to omit the M.A.; Mr. Twining was inordinately proud of it, and in the event of his still being alive – which is quite possible, since only fifteen years have elapsed from the time I write about – I should not like to hurt his sense of dignity. The school was much the same as all other schools of its kind, saving, perhaps, that the teaching was, if possible, of a rather more mediocre order, the boys greedier, more spoilt, more uninteresting, and the assistant masters worse paid – the headmaster more obviously 'running the show' as a purely money-making concern."

And there you have part-payment, at least, of a rankling old debt.

The book as a whole is very much the mixture as before: 13 chapters, 219 pages, of jolly good creepy yarns, couched in some cases in beguilingly fictive form, but not lacking its interspersed passages of serious, informative psychic discussion.

Away from the writing-desk O'Donnell's saga of club land memberships continued in bewildering plethora. He joined the Gipsy Club. It was a one night a week club. Its premises consisted of a single room. It was furnished with a table, a chair, and a piano. There was no carpet. People brought their own rugs to sit on. It was either that or bare floorboards. The entertainment could be described as 'home-made'. People sang, recited, told funny stories. One man sang the Arrow Song every week. Another, a professional acrobat, turned spectacular somersaults. O'Donnell regaled them with ghost tales. Sometimes there would be organised games or competitions. They tended to be of the vintage of Addison and *The Spectator*. Old games revived included hoodman blind, shoe the wild mare, and bob apple. On one occasion a troop of real Gypsies came and sang; and on another, buskers collected from outside theatres. Owing to the constant increase in the number of members, the club needed larger premises, and moved for a time into a basement in Lower Regent Street. O'Donnell ceased to be a member when it left its original home, and did not know what became of it after it quitted Lower Regent Street.

The basement was taken over in 1915 by the Studio Club, of which O'Donnell was one of the first members. Others were Sir Jacob Epstein, Sir A.J. Munnings, P.R.A., Augustus John, C.R. Nevinson, Edgar Jepson, and Ursula Bloom. He used sometimes to see George Grossmith and Heather Thatcher dancing there. There were frequent cabarets at the Studio, and fancy-dress dances. On one occasion a member who had a small menagerie brought a little alligator to the club and let it loose on the floor. The poor little thing seemed very scared, as did, to O'Donnell's immense amusement, a certain tall, lanky university professor, who at once drew up his feet and very perceptibly shivered.

Another club that caught O'Donnell's fancy was the Ham Bone, in Ham Yard, in Soho. The premises had formerly been mostly used for stabling. There was a fairly large room on the first floor for dancing, and there were lofts above it. Its members came mostly from the art world. One of them had a large collection of armour, and, both clad in mail, he and a friend used to have a combat one night a year in the loft of the club. One night they invited O'Donnell to the unrolling of an Egyptian mummy in a studio in St. John's Wood. Badger Moody, a well-known and popular Chelsea artist of the time, was there, and made no bones about the fact that he regarded the unrolling as unlucky, and was loathe to take part in it. One evening not long afterwards, Elliott and Ada were sitting in the Ham Bone Club lounge when they saw a painting by Moody, which was hanging on one of the walls, suddenly fall without any apparent cause. Moody died that same night.

After the demise of the Ham Bone Club, O'Donnell joined the Arts and Letters Club. Debates were sometimes held there. One on nudism was very keenly argued. O'Donnell spoke against it, as did the majority of the members present, and its advocates were resoundingly defeated. One of the most hectic debates was on the subject of pacifism. A long-haired, dyspeptic-looking youth roused O'Donnell's ire to the pitch of flame, arguing that men should not forcibly resist invaders, even when they saw them violently assault and about to rape their sisters and wives.

He also joined the Artists' Film Club, in Wardour Street, and produced his play, *Conditionally*, there one night. A fellow-member was Bombardier Billy Wells, the famous boxer, whose magnificently muscled torso used to be exhibited as he ritually struck a gong at the opening of many British films.

Sitting one evening in the lounge of another establishment, the Motley Club, of which he was a short-lived member, O'Donnell noticed a man, a complete stranger to him, drinking at the bar. It was a case of Dr. Fell. O'Donnell did not like him. In fact, he took an instant dislike to him, which was apparently reciprocated, for, as he left the room, he glared at him and made a very rude remark. He was a peer, the son, O'Donnell was informed, of a very wealthy tradesman who had obtained a title through his usefulness to the government. Some nights later, the peer was leaving the club, when, all the evidence indicating that he had been imbibing rather too freely, he tripped over the foot of a young and pretty lady. Picking himself up in a fury, he threw a thoroughly insulting remark at her. Thoroughly athletic and muscular, she promptly punched his head and her companion gave him a good kick. He slunk out of the club like a whipped cur and was never seen there again. It should in fairness be added that he was a guest, not a member.

The Irish Club in Charing Cross Road was a favourite place. It was not, like most of his clubs, an art club, but it was very Bohemian. It was devoid of any décor and gave the impression of bareness. The carpeting was worn to the verge of threadbareness, the furniture also showed signs of much wear and tear, but no one minded. It was a friendly, homely place, and Sam was beloved by all. It was open every day of the week. Well-known actors were often guests at the dinners. Occasionally members suffered from 'friendly fire' – noses and eyes suffered from flying furniture when Irish tempers boiled over – but Sam always intervened before any serious injury could be sustained. Every Sunday there was a concert there, the performers being all professional or fringe-professional. The genial owner was bald-headed Sam Geddes. He invited Elliott and Ada to a concert there. They enjoyed it so much that O'Donnell became a member there and then. The membership was all male, so Ada was not eligible.

While still a member of the Irish Club, O'Donnell also enrolled in the membership ranks of the Four Provinces of Ireland Club in Russell Square. Here there were Sunday night concerts of a high order, and on Saturday nights there were dances. On St. Patrick's Night there would be a grand banquet at either the Café Royal or some equally well known restaurant. Hibernians, eminent and otherwise, crafted speeches overflowing with Irish wit and wisdom, Irish bands played Irish airs, Irish eyes and feet were dancing. It was here, too, that he convoked a gathering of the O'Donnell clan in the fine concert room. Irish pipers played the clan march, a professional singer delivered with due panache the famous song "O'Donnell Abu", and Elliott addressed the assemblage with an account of the history of the clan. Next day they were filmed in Russell Square Gardens by British Movietone News, and O'Donnell repeated on camera a brief version of his clan history.

For a short time O'Donnell was a member of the Bolton Club, in Denman Street, most of the members of which were film and stage actors, and the Oasis Club, in Dean Street. It was while he was on his way to the latter club one evening that a well-dressed woman suddenly ran across the street, kissed him, and was gone round a corner in a trice. When he got to the club he felt in his pocket for his wallet. That had gone too.

O'Donnell used to pay visits, too, to three public-houses – the Fitzroy, the Duke of York, and the Marquis of Granby – which were favourite meeting places of members of the art world of the day. At one of them he met Nina Hamnett, a clever sculptor and painter, who wrote a book, *Laughing Torso*, which created a great sensation. She took him one evening to a club in Bloomsbury, where he met well-known people of all kinds – writers, painters, explorers, airmen, soldiers, society girls, actors and actresses. He found there art and beauty, glamour and entertainment. He was enchanted. He became a member. But it was not long before change and decay set in. The more eminent members left. People of less and less note filled their places. The club soon fizzled out.

In May, 1914, Elliott and Ada rented a studio in Montparnasse from an artist friend. During their stay in Paris they were enchanted to meet Maude Gonne, still beautiful although no longer in her prime, at a literary evening at the Bergsons',[1] and they were charmed by her. They also met James Stephens, author of *The Crock of Gold*.

Either on that or another occasion, I walked back to our quarters with Stephens, who carried a cudgel as a protection, he said, against apaches. He knew an artist who had been attacked by several apaches and might have been badly injured but for the timely appearance of the police. He was emphatic in his dislike of England, yet he was living, so I learned, in London at the time of his death.

One evening I was returning home after a literary gathering at a friend's studio, when a short, thickset man emerged from a doorway and, lowering his bullet-shaped head, came at me like a battering-ram. Avoiding him by stepping quickly aside, I struck out, caught him a biff on his head and toppled him over. He was probably half drunk. Not wanting a tussle, I did not wait to see if he got up.

On another occasion when Ada and I were returning home from visiting friends in Passy, a smartly dressed girl snatched my wife's handbag from her and sped away like the wind. I tore after her and was close at her heels when she turned and threw pepper in my face. Some of it got into my eyes and blinded me. Before I was able to see again, the girl was out of sight. Fortunately, there was nothing of much value in the bag, which was old, so we did not bother to report the theft. Had it happened in England, we should probably have done so, but from what we had been told about strangers in Paris, like ourselves, reporting petty thefts to the police, we thought it wiser to say nothing about such a trifling loss. It was lucky only a little pepper got into my eyes, but small as the quantity was, it smarted dreadfully.

We were visiting some of our friends one day in the Ile Saint Louis, when one of them asked us if we would like to go to a fancy-dress dance. It was to be in a hall let for dances and other entertainments and was restricted to members of the art world – artists, writers and actors. Neither Ada nor I cared for dancing, but we thought it would be amusing to watch the others. It was a subscription dance, but our friends very kindly said that, as their guests, we would have nothing to pay except for the hiring of clothes. They told us where to get them. My wife went as a nun and I as a monk. Everyone had to be masked until one o'clock, when all masks had to be taken off. There were to be no present day dances except waltzes. Our friends drove us to the hall. It was not large. There were not more than about a hundred people, and when we arrived

---

1 Henri Bergson (1859-1941). French philosopher. Professor of philosophy at the Collège de France. Exercised a profound influence on modern literature. He believed the source of knowledge to be *a priori* and not empirical. His metaphysics were close to those of Heraclitus.

the dancing had begun. As one might have expected at an art world dance, the dresses were very striking, and some of them highly original. Julius Caesar was waltzing with a *vivandière*, Juno with a Punchinello, the witch of Endor with Henry VIII, a fishwife with a skeleton, Robin Hood with Helen of Troy. There were columbines, Harlequins, Follies, May Queens, pierrots, men in armour, amazons, dogs, cats, Bacchantes, Pan, monkeys, Blue Beard, nymphs, elves, a leg of mutton and a Mad Hatter. I never saw such a queer variety of dresses. A mazurka, in which there had been about eight couples, had just finished when a Pierrette wearing a maroon domino came to me and to my surprise, said, "Roger, why did you not tell me you were in Paris, bad man."

"I'm afraid you are mistaken, " I replied. "My name is not Roger."

"Oh, I'm very sorry," she stammered. "I thought you were Roger." She pulled up short, giving me the impression that she had not finished what she meant to say, and walked away, mingling with the crowd.

Espying one of my Ile St. Louis friends close to me, I told him about the girl mistaking me for someone whose Christian name was Roger. He did not know of any Roger except Sir Roger Casement, whom he met two or three years ago in Paris, but had not seen since. Whether Casement was in Paris then I never found out. I had never seem him. One of my near relatives, when she was a young girl, had danced with him at a ball in Dublin and had found him charming.

We were disappointed in the Paris shops and did not think them as good as we had expected they would be, except for those in the Rue de Rivoli and one or two other streets. We did not think they compared at all favourably with the London shops. Perhaps it was our bad taste. We went to the Bon Marché and some of the popular cafés.

We went one day to Rambouillet, a veritable beauty spot, and saw in the forest the Dog's Pond, which a few years afterwards acquired a sinister reputation owing to the dismembered remains of a girl and the body of a murdered young man being found close to it. It was not far from the forest that Landru, the notorious French Bluebeard lived and was believed to have murdered some of his many women victims.

We went of course to Fontainebleau. It was in Fontainebleau Forest that Henry IV of France, when hunting there, saw the much dreaded apparition said to haunt it. It warned him of his death at the hands of the assassin Francis Ravaillac. The ghost was believed to be that of a hunter killed in the Forest of Fontainebleau in the reign of Francis I. In the sixties of the last century, the Forest acquired for a time an evil reputation on account of the murder of Sidonia Mertens, a woman of light habits and much wealth. Her body was found in the Forest. A woman named Matilde Frigard, who had been seen entering the Forest with her, was arrested, and tried for strangling her to death. The motive was robbery. Frigard was found guilty with extenuating circumstances, and consequently escaped capital punishment. It was not improbable that her good looks were largely responsible for saving her life. She was a very handsome woman. After the murder, the Forest had for some time an increased reputation for being haunted. I was thrilled at visiting a locality so famous in the annals of ghost-lore, but neither saw nor sensed anything in the least degree supernatural.

I had been given a letter of introduction to an official of the National Library of Paris, and I worked there quite a lot while I was compiling a new book. I did not find the library officials very helpful or obliging.

We did not enjoy our stay in Paris very much. The French people, with a few exceptions, were not very friendly. The weather was bad, and cold for the time of year.

We were preparing to leave France when war was declared against Germany. We had been led to believe that the French were a highly emotional people, but we saw no sign of great emotion in Paris on that historical occasion – no waving of national flags, no mass meetings, nor did we hear any shouting, cheering, or demonstration of any kind. Except for a number of cuirassiers that rode solemnly past us in the street, we saw nothing unusual. Everywhere seemed to be much the same as usual – dull and ordinary.

A French journalist assured me that the coming war would doubtless see two myths exploded, namely, the invincibility of the German army and the might of the British Navy. He was right about the former, but entirely wrong about the latter.

The O'Donnells left France and returned to England the day after the declaration of war, and were escorted across the Channel by one or two warships. They reported overhearing during the crossing the following conversation between an English passenger and a pretty, daintily dressed young American woman, whose husband had not been able to leave Paris.

"Are you not anxious about your husband?" the English passenger asked. "Supposing the Germans bomb Paris."

"Oh, we must not think of anything so dreadful," was the reply. Then added: "But in a war there are always risks, and, well, his life is insured, and I have taken care to have everything I value with me."

On reaching England, Elliott and Ada stayed for two or three weeks in Folkestone. They were there when England declared war. The declaration was greeted with great enthusiasm. A number of men linked arms and marched around the town singing "Red, White and Blue", "Rule Britannia" and other patriotic songs.

After leaving Folkestone, they returned briefly to their house in Upper Norwood, then let it, and went off to share with a friend a maisonette on the upper floor of a house in Red Lion Square, Holborn.

The house turned out to be haunted. O'Donnell was alone in the flat one May evening, sitting in his bedroom. The two floors below were let out as offices, and were unoccupied after six o'clock. It was a beautiful evening of golden sunshine, the window was open and the sound of children playing outside in the square came drifting up. Suddenly, his ear caught a different kind of noise, that of heavy footsteps coming slowly and wearily up the uncarpeted stairs, seeming to his mind to herald the approach of an old, decrepit man. He wondered who it could be, for he was expecting no one. He heard the steps cross the landing. He got up, and going out of the room looked down the stairs. Saw no one. Then, as he stood there nonplussed, the steps suddenly began to descend, and he followed behind them, right down to the ground floor and along the passage to the front-door, where they abruptly ceased.

His wife also had a weird experience in that house. At about eight o'clock one evening, as she was going downstairs to the front-door, there was a thud just behind her, as though some heavy object had fallen from a height on to the stairs, and it frightened her so much that she did not dare return upstairs alone, but waited in the hall until Elliott came home.

O'Donnell subsequently heard that the daughter of the caretaker, who lived in the basement, had often seen the phantom of an old man on the stairs, and in other parts of the building. Also, the people who took the flat after the O'Donnells and their friend had vacated it, told him that they had several times heard mysterious footsteps on the staircase. He made enquiries, but was unable to ascertain that any tragedy that might conceivably have accounted for the haunting had ever taken place in the house.

Elliott and Ada were living in Red Lion Square when the Bosche, as the Germans were referred to in the First World or Great War of 1914-1918, dropped the first bomb on London from a plane. O'Donnell would never forget the instant panic among the Holborn Italians. They rushed out into the square's garden, some barely clad; and for some totally inexplicable reason they climbed trees in the garden and lamp-posts in the road. It was a ludicrous sight.

Classified medically as C.3 because of his varicose veins, O'Donnell, rising forty-three, took a job as a censor, in which post he continued until ill-health forced his resignation.

One day O'Donnell and his wife saw a girl leaning against the railings of a nearby house in the square. Thinking she might be ill, they asked her if she was all right. She had, she said, had a bad shock and was feeling faint. As she seemed a respectable, nicely spoken girl, they invited her into their flat to rest a while, and gave her some brandy. Sufficiently recovered, she had a passing strange tale to tell.

She told them that, in need of a job, she had answered an advertisement for someone of superior education, with some nursing experience, to look after an invalid. A letter invited her to come for interview to a house in Holborn. She arrived at the appointed time at what proved to be a dilapidated mansion, detached, and in a kind of cul-de-sac. The door was opened by a smartly-dressed woman who led her across a gloomy hall to a back room, and subjected her to a positive cross-examination. She had then told her that the post she had come about was a peculiar one that required someone with courage and great patience. She warned her that the first sight of the person she would have to look after might shock her, but there was nothing to fear if she had steady nerves and kept a firm hold of herself. She was then escorted to a room at the rear of the basement. A dark curtain covered the window, which was barred. Seated on a chair facing the door was a figure in a red dressing-gown. Its head was covered with patches of thick black hair, as was its face, the skin of which was greenish-grey and scaly. The nose was a bulbous mass of flesh, with something like a frill round the end of it. There was only one big, staring yellow eye. The half-open mouth displayed a few long, yellow, jagged teeth. There was nothing to determine the creature's sex. It was so altogether non-human and revolting that the girl had recoiled, and when the thing rose from the chair and came slowly towards her, long arms outstretched as if to embrace her, she had turned, run up the stairs, across the hall and into the street, never pausing until she was out of sight of the house.

Feeling much better, she thanked the O'Donnells, and left. A ship in distress that passed in a night, they never saw her again. Elliott and Ada left Red Lion Square and moved to Earl's Court, where they were to share a flat again with the same friend.

One of the books upon which he had doubtless been working, and hard, while he was in Paris, *The Irish Abroad: A Record of the Achievements of*

Wanderers From Ireland, was published by Sir Isaac Pitman & Sons, in 1915. A hefty, 400-page book, it was a meticulous enshrinement of the notable attainments of Irish *émigrés* who had exchanged the shamrock-sprinkled green turf of their native heath for the stony shores, and occasional gold-paved streets of alien lands – England, Scotland, Wales, Spain, Portugal, France, Belgium, Germany, Austria, Switzerland, Italy, Scandinavia, Russia, India, Australia, New Zealand, South Africa, Canada, the United States, the British Colonies.

They left their marks as literary men – Richard Steele, Laurence Sterne, Oliver Goldsmith, Richard Brinsley Sheridan, William Hazlitt, Oscar Wilde, W.B. Yeats; as actors – James Quinn, Charles Macklin, Edmund Kean; in politics – Edmund Burke; in the Army – Arthur Wellesley, Duke of Wellington; in the law – Lord Russell of Killowen, Lord Chief Justice of England, and who, as counsel, defended Mrs. Maybrick in the celebrated Liverpool murder trial of 1889; in the Church – Archbishop James Usher; in medicine – Sir Hans Sloane, eminent physician and virtual founder of the British Museum. Nor must we omit from this roll of honour the Ladies of Llangollen, Lady Eleanor Charlotte Butler and Miss Sarah Ponsonby.

"There are some nations," wrote O'Donnell, "that retain their individuality no matter what vicissitudes they undergo. The Jews are one, the Irish are another." Especially interesting in this context is his account of the hibernian refugees fleeing the potato famine in the nineteenth century and landing in Liverpool. The hardships borne by them were appalling. Between 1845 and 1849 more than 10,000 of the 60,000 who came died within six months of disembarkation. They lived, crammed twenty to thirty in a single room, generally a cellar, deep down, dark, ill-ventilated, and full of rats and cockroaches. They died in shoals, and so dilatory were the authorities in the matter of the disposal of their bodies, that, for weeks on end, the corpses remained in the cellars where they had died, decomposing alongside those who still survived.

In 1916, the second fruit of his pen at this time, a fascinating slice of autobiography, *Twenty Years' Experiences as a Ghost Hunter*, came from the Fleet Lane publisher, Heath Cranton. Eric Russell in his *Ghosts* (Batsford, London, 1970) is critically somewhat harsh: "The style harks back to that traditional style of the story-teller in which the narrator introduces another narrator who may introduce another and yet another, so that the nub of the matter is found at last in the inner box of a Chinese puzzle out of which the reader extricates himself only with difficulty. But O'Donnell handles the complex business with immense confidence and gusto, creating a vivid, swiftly moving narrative which hustles the reader on from marvel to marvel, giving him no time for reflection and the scepticism that might arise."

And does one detect a certain cynicism? "Infallibly, if O'Donnell seeks a ghost, he finds it whether it is noonday upon a San Francisco street, night in the Welsh mountains or upon Wimbledon Common. Some of the tales might have come straight from the *Arabian Nights*: an elaborate banquet, complete with revellers, appears and disappears in an empty house: a character has what appears to be djinns at his service. Other stories have the dank chill of the German forests, creations which the Brothers Grimm might have envied, or possess the whimsicality of Perrault.[2] All seem to be original, most are related as personal experiences."

"Of late years," O'Donnell writes, "the increase of interest taken in things psychical, particularly among the more educated classes, the classes that were at one time incorrigibly sceptical has been enormous. I believe this to be mainly due to the fact that people are not satisfied with the scriptural declaration of another world. They want proof of it – that is to say, absolutely authentic and corroborative evidence that it exists – and they feel that they can only obtain such evidence by witnessing superphysical manifestations themselves.

Psychical Research Societies, perhaps, convince them even less than the Bible. And naturally, for the scientist, even though he be titled, can hardly hope to accomplish in one generation what theologians, of an equal if not superior intelligence, have attempted and failed to accomplish throughout the ages.

Hence, I am of the opinion that one can learn more from one spontaneous ghostly manifestation in a haunted house than from a thousand lectures, or a thousand books. Experience is the only medium of conviction, and so long as people are without a personal experience relating to another world, they can never really believe. The boy in rags and tatters may be far more conversant with – may know far more about – a future life than the

---

2   Charles Perrault (1628-1703). French author of a collection of fairy-tales, *Histoires et contes du temps passé*, published under the name of his son, Pierre Perrault, in 1697. Translated into English by Robert Samber as *Mother Goose Tales*, in 1729.

most learned professor at the university. But no one can logically claim to be an absolute authority on the Unknown; the most any of us can do – even those of us who have actually seen and heard spirit manifestations – the rest do not count – is to speculate. When we attempt to do more, we label ourselves fools.

Of all the professions, none, I believe, is more interested in this question of another world than the theatrical. I have a great many friends amongst actors and actresses, and I find them not only keenly interested in my work, but always ready – even when working hard themselves – to share my vigils in a haunted house.

Only the other day, at a concert given by the Irish Literary Society in Hanover Square, I was introduced to Miss Odette Goimbault, who recently delighted London audiences by her impersonation of the child Doris in *On Trial* at the Lyric Theatre. When a very small child she lived with her mother at Thornton Heath. A lady died of consumption in the flat immediately beneath, and after the burial. Odette, though previously very fond of staying up late, used, every night, at precisely seven o'clock, to beg her mother to take her upstairs to bed, declaring in a great state of terror and with tears in her eyes, that she saw an old man with only one leg standing in a corner of the room shaking his stick at her. When once she was taken out of the room her fears subsided.

But stronger even than its hold upon the theatrical profession is the stand that psychism has taken with regard to the present war. Ever since the fighting began I have heard speculations raised as to whether our soldiers at the Front have been witnessing ghostly manifestations or not. So far, I must own that I have elicited very little reliable evidence on this point, but the circumstances have established at least one interesting fact, and that is, that to the man in the street the question of another world has at last become a matter of some importance.

The wife of a very eminent official at the War Office told me a few weeks ago that officers who took part in the Dardanelles Expedition assured her that figures believed to be ghosts were on several occasions seen gliding over the ground after an engagement, especially where the dead bodies of the Turks lay thickest. The same lady also told me that when a certain regiment formed up after a brilliant charge, in which it had suffered very severe casualties, some of the gaps in the ranks were observed to be filled by shadowy forms – forms which disappeared the moment anyone attempted to touch them.

Neither my informant nor any of the soldiers from the Front that I have met have been able to give me any information as to the alleged superphysical demonstrations in the sky during the retreat from Mons."[3]

In January, 1917, with Ada's consent, Elliott accepted a tiny part in Louis N. Parker's three-act play, *The Aristocrat*, at the St. James' Theatre. A story of that favourite of dramatists, The Terror – the French Revolution – in which George Alexander played the lead, ably supported by Genevieve Ward, and Dennis Neilson-Terry and Mary Glynne as the young lovers.

O'Donnell remembered: "Mr. Vivian Reynolds was the producer. One cannot speak too highly of the management. My dressing-room, which I shared with several other small-part actors like myself, was well lighted and heated, and everywhere was scrupulously clean and orderly. Reynolds was very strict at rehearsals, and it was necessary as some of the crowd needed firm handling. Dame Genevieve Ward and Helen Rouse were much liked by us small fry because they were always so pleasant and different from some of the stars, who did not deign to notice us. Lady Alexander, if she chanced to meet any of us, was always very charming. I was very nervous at the dress rehearsal because I had made myself up and was not sure the red wig I wore had been properly fixed. We had to come down to the footlights in turn to be scrutinized by Sir George Alexander, the author of the play, and other bigwigs who occupied the front row of the stalls. I quite expected to hear scathing criticism when it came to my turn to be viewed, but to my surprise, Sir George exclaimed, 'Fine,' and I retraced my steps, greatly relieved and much elated."

It was not long before he found writing and having to be at the theatre every night too much of a strain, and, though he thoroughly enjoyed being at the St. James' and made lasting friendships with some of the cast, after a few weeks he resigned.

In those war-time days there was a bit of spy mania about, and, like many others, O'Donnell was fired with the desire to ferret out spies. Walking along Clifford Street one day, he stopped and gazed into the window of a

---

3 The phenomenon of the so-called Vision of the Angels of Mons has since been established as having been the admitted invention of Arthur Machen (1863-1947) who wrote a story in the London *Evening News* of September 29th, 1914, called *The Bowmen*, in which St. George, in company with an army of the English mediæval Agincourt bowmen, appeared in the sky at the critical moment to cover the British retreat from Mons.

beauty shop. As he stood there, there emerged from the shop's doorway a fine looking woman with white hair, wearing an eighteenth-century costume. She asked him if he was interested in beautiful things, and invited him in to inspect some. The beautiful things proved to be her assistants, in similar costume to herself. She said that she would be very pleased to see him and any gentlemen friends of his, particularly army officers, at one of the parties that she frequently gave in her flat in Park Lane. She spoke with a foreign accent, as did her girls, and that, together with the whole set-up, made O'Donnell extremely suspicious. He told a friend of his who was in close touch with Intelligence about the lady, and soon after heard that she had been either deported or interned as a spy.

He also reported a woman posing as a masseuse in a street off Regent Street, as well as several other people who he thought to be acting in a suspicious manner.

One of his sister Helena's friends, the wife of a Field-Marshal, gave him an introduction to "Room XYZ", that is to say, to Intelligence, and from time to time he would mention people he believed to be engaged in espionage. He must have had a shrewd eye, for it nearly always transpired that the people who aroused his suspicion were already being watched.

The bombing of London during the Great War was, of course, insignificant as compared with that of the Blitz of the Second World War. O'Donnell was there during sixteen air raids, warnings of which were given by men on bicycles blowing bugles. He and Ada were in their house in Norwood when an enemy plane flew over and dropped a bomb on nearby Sydenham, completely destroying two houses and killing their occupants. And he was at a séance in Bayswater when a bomb fell in the garden, fortunately without exploding. Several more bombs were dropped that night. One fell on a house where a friend of theirs lived. It came through the roof and exploded in the room in which she was sitting. She was horribly mangled and died within a few hours.

He was investigating a case of reputed haunting in central London with the Duke of Newcastle one night when there was a raid. Anxious to get home as his wife was alone, he promptly ended the vigil and tore off to Victoria Station. The streets were in darkness and he had difficulty finding his way; it was crowded with people waiting for trains. They were singing hymns. There was no panic, although every now and then there was the sound of an exploding bomb.

In the spring of 1917, he enlisted in the United Arts Rifles, which was one of the first Volunteer Corps to be formed, and was composed entirely of members of the art world. Inaugural meetings were held at the Bath Club and Earl's Court Exhibition. Lord Desborough presided. Among those present were Sir Arthur Pinero, Sir Edward Poynter, Arthur Bouchier, Henry Arthur Jones, Sir John Lavery, and Sir Edward Elgar. Some six hundred men – painters, actors writers and musicians enrolled. At first their 'uniform' consisted of white sweaters and they drilled at Earl's Court. They were then transferred to the grounds of the Royal Academy and later to the Imperial College Union. The white sweaters gave way to light green uniforms. Finally succeeded by khaki. For a time the men drilled without arms. They were then issued with .303 Martini carbines, and ultimately with 1914 rifles and bayonets.

They used to drill outside the Albert Hall and in Hyde Park. One day when they were practising skirmishing and were ordered to lie down, O'Donnell's breeches, which were very tight, split. On being ordered to rise, he pleaded inability because of ladies being near at hand watching them. The sergeant-major, speedily realising his plight, which caused much merriment, instructed him to cover the exposed area with a handkerchief, and after they had been dismissed O'Donnell went down Exhibition Road to South Kensington Station. He was standing on the platform there waiting for a train and his bandaged rear quarters attracted the interested attention of a number of people. An old lady glanced at it, shuddered, and quickly averted her gaze. A sympathetic middle-aged man said, "I trust the wound does not hurt you a lot." O'Donnell assured him that it did not.

In April, 1917, O'Donnell wrote to Lord Northcliffe soliciting journalistic work. "I am very sorry that I have no work likely to suit you just now," he replied. "Owing to their reduced size my newspapers are at present over rather than under-staffed."

By 1917, most of the very famous men had either left or elected non-combatant members. Younger men had joined the regular army and gone off on active service Among the men whom O'Donnell knew best were C. Aubrey Smith, stage and film star, who in his younger days played cricket for Sussex and was popularly known as "Round the Corner Smith", and E. Cranton, who was a partner in the firm Heath Cranton, which had published his latest book. O'Donnell played cricket against the Actors' Orphanage School in an eleven captained by C. Aubrey Smith. Unfortunately, rain stopped the game, and he could not wait for tea, as he had to go on sentry duty that night on Grosvenor Railway Bridge.

He went on duty at 8 p.m., had two hours on and two hours off all through the night, finishing at eight o'clock in the morning. There were three posts allotted to the sentries; one was under the south end of the bridge, close to the river, one on the bridge above, and the third at the north end of the bridge, which, nearest to the guard-room, was thought the easiest. The post under the bridge was regarded as the worst, as the sentry there was far from aid if attacked by anyone desirous of blowing up the bridge. This night O'Donnell was on duty at the post on the bridge, the second worst. When at their posts they always longed for something exciting to happen, but it very seldom did. They had to challenge everyone and make them show their passes. O'Donnell anticipated some difficulty with railwaymen, but he had none, finding them always civil and pleasant. Their guard-room was the Grosvenor Road Railway Station. Before the war it had been derelict for a long time. They rested there when off duty, and there was a gas stove there on which they boiled water for tea and coffee, and fried bacon. In addition to sentry duty there were route marches, fatigue duty at Tadworth Camp, shooting at Rainham and Runnymede ranges, inspections by various generals, including Lord French. He remained in the United Arts Rifles until the end of the war, and said that he enjoyed every moment he was in it.

War brought its medallic moments of pride: his brother, Henry, who commanded a brigade, was at the Battle of the Somme; but, conversely, for him, as for so many others, it imported its terrible tally of sorrows. Ada's father, Dr. Williams, died. Many old Cliftonians, among them several of his great friends, died on the battlefield. And, from another generation, there were his former pupils. "I had never liked teaching, and am afraid my pupils spent more time at cricket and football, boxing and going on fishing expeditions with me than they did at lessons. My main idea was to encourage them to be manly and healthy. And some of them," he wrote with a heavy heart, "were killed in the 1914 war, fighting for their country." He was deeply aware of the culling of the flower of England's youth, and to the end of his long life he would, at the drawing down of blinds, remember them.

The wicked Queen Elfrida whips Edward the Martyr at Corfe Castle. From O'Donnells Famous Curses (1929).

13

Ghosts and Ghouls

The guns were silent. A new decade. A land fit for heroes. Those who had survived the slaughter sought to fill the sad, accusatory silence with the carefully orchestrated merriment of roaring 'twenties' parties. O'Donnell was not proof against the tempo of the times. Typical of the new era was the Italian Ball, held at Covent Garden, on April 28th, 1920. *The Times'* Court Circular of April 23rd heralded the event "in aid of the Italian Hospital in London, promises to be a great success. Princess Helena Victoria has promised to attend." O'Donnell was there, fancy-dressed as a friar, rubbing shoulders that Wednesday with the Duchess de Sangro, wearing the 16th-century Italian costume of Adelaide of Savoy, Duchess of Burgundy; Countess Curzon of Kedleston, wearing an Italian Renaissance dress; and, in diverse fancy finery, Baroness Henri de Rothschild, the Duchess of Rutland, Lady Diana Cooper, the Marchioness of Blandford, the Marquess of Northampton, and the Marquess of Worcester.

The sort of parties that O'Donnell delighted to throw were somewhat different. He referred to them as his "freak gatherings". The genesis of these queer parties is interesting. It all began when a friend of his told him of a haunted maisonette of which she knew near Lancaster Gate, and suggested that he ought to give one of his weird parties there. Having succeeded in getting permission from the people who rented it, he, Ada, and their friend Charles Marriott set to work preparing the place. They made use of every part of the basement, except, the kitchen, scullery, bathroom and coal cellar. Paintings of skulls, cross bones, and horrible demons covered the wall of one of the ground floor rooms. An electrician friend agreed to illuminate the place with ghostly blue light. The arrangements completed, the invitations went out.

The entertainment was styled "Dante's Inferno", and tickets printed on blood-red paper, bearing the legend "Come to Hell", went out to the press. Press and friends alike wore fantastic ghostly attire – white ladies, skeletons, Elementals, one enterprising representative of a popular daily newspaper came as the ghost of jazz! Between the periods of general dancing there were star turns. The daughter of the well known expert on historical costume, Herbert Norris, danced an appropriate solo under the watchful eye of her instructor, Novikof, famous partner of the illustrious Pavlova, who was there with her. The actress, Phyllis Calvert, danced a fairy solo to the air of *Spring Time*, and a great sensation was caused when a beautiful girl rushed into the room closely pursued by a masked ruffian, who cut off her head with a gleaming scimitar. This 'dreadful crime' was most realistically staged by a magician friend of O'Donnell's.

At midnight the partygoers were requested to descend to the basement, in turns and alone, to walk along a dimly-lit passage. As they went, skeleton hands came out of dark corners and clutched at them, and hideous heads floated terrifyingly in the air about them. There were screams and groans, and the repeated faintings of certain of the ladies cost O'Donnell quite a lot in brandy! Nor was the terror confined to the fair sex, for one member of the press was loud in his exclamation of horror on seeing a tall figure in black, with a cowl that only partly concealed its fleshless face, suddenly spring out on him from the larder, the disturbed dishes in which suggested that the spectre had been sampling the earthly foods. Several well known professional magicians had put their skills at O'Donnell's disposal. Great was the surprise and consternation of one of them, when, in the act of terrifying a guest, he suddenly felt an icy hand clutch him round the neck. O'Donnell had not told him that there was a lesser known but extremely clever member of his vocation secreted in a cupboard.

Soon afterwards it was O'Donnell's turn to be at the receiving end of an unanticipated shock. A man who happened to be staying in the house, arriving home truculently drunk, took an immediate and violent dislike to one of O'Donnell's guests, and chased him with a carving knife. Thinking that it was another item in the programme, the onlookers just stood by cheering vociferously. Fortunately, the inebriated one was seized and disarmed in time, and what could have been a real tragedy averted. He was last seen hurling empty whisky bottles at the window, under the impression that he was seeing fiery-eyed cats.

The following day's newspapers contained wonderfully high-coloured journalistic views of the affair.

"Guests, attired as weird spectres, danced in a ballroom upstairs, dimly lighted to represent one of the infernal regions. Flames appeared to spring out from the walls, the red glow of a burning furnace cast a baleful light over the thronged rooms. Dancers costumed as skeletons danced with partners representing Death; Mephistopheles partnered Helen of Troy; ghosts and Elementals frequented uncanny corners; thrills and sensations lurked in almost every nook of the house.

Downstairs, in the nethermost regions, was a realistic hell, and guests were permitted to explore the various chambers of horrors in parties of two and three. Eerie figures, enacting the silence of Death, piloted the visitors from one sensation to the next. Horror followed upon horror. Not a word was spoken.

With a tingling sensation creeping up one's spine to the nape of the neck, one groped through dark passages, stumbled over what felt like a prostrate body.

'Hold my hand,' came a woman's whisper, 'I'm scared to death,' – and suddenly, as a stupefying smell of opium half suffocated one, the light went up on a Chinese drug den. Men and women lay huddled around in tiny bunks. At a small table sat a Chinaman trying to keep pace with the clamour for more dope. There was an altercation: 'No monee, no dope,' wheezed the Chinaman to a half-drugged white man. Li Chang turned to fill a half-drugged woman's pipe. The disappointed man reached out a hand; he clasped something shining, there was a loud report – and the den-keeper fell shot in the back.

It was too realistic a scene for one guest. She fainted – and when the brandy, real dope this time, came quickly, others wondered why they had not thought of it first!

Farther on, there was to be seen, through Cagliostro's original crystal, the ghost of the house, presented by Mr. Charles Marriott; and another scene found some demon, amidst ear-piercing shrieks, thrusting burning coals into the eyes of a real live girl.

During an interval in the dancing Li Chang presented an alarming illusion in the middle of the ball-room, when he chopped off the head of one of the girl dancers."

Screams from the Inferno occasionally drowned the jazz music of the ball-room above, where the tall figure of Dante (Mr. O'Donnell) moved majestically among his guests.

Within a year of the party several of the people present met with tragic endings. One man blew his brains out in a taxi,[1] a lady and her husband went raving mad, and at least four other people died suddenly and unexpectedly.

To his great delight, in December, 1920, O'Donnell was elected to membership of the Savage Club, whose premises were at Nos. 6 & 7 Adelphi Terrace, W.C.2. Founded in 1857, this was one of the leading gentlemen's Bohemian clubs in London. Its membership was, in the main, drawn from the categories of art, drama, law, literature, music, and science. Two explanations are offered for the origin of the Club's name. The first, is that it was named "in frolicsome humour" after the friend of Dr. Samuel Johnson, Richard Savage (c.1697-1743), actor, playwright, and poet, who killed a man in a brawl, and died a poverty-stricken death in a Bristol debtor's prison. The second, tells of a waitress, who, when instructed by the barman at the Club's first home – the Crown Tavern, Vinegar Yard, Drury Lane – to take a round of drinks to the noisy company roistering upstairs exclaimed, "What! I'm not serving that bunch of savages!"

Another of O'Donnell's gazetteers of ghosts had appeared in 1919, *Haunted Places in England*, published by Sands. It was rapidly followed, in 1920, by *More Haunted Houses of London*, a sequel, brought out by Eveleigh Nash eleven years after their publication of his *Haunted Houses of London*. The earlier volume had contained some fascinating tales. The malicious creature that haunted a house in Earls Court Road. Invisible, it proclaimed its presence by the production of a really terrible odour. Attending to her toilet in the bathroom, a woman felt two damp and fetid hands steal cautiously up her back, and force open her jaw. She fainted. Coming to, she found her upper set of false teeth missing. Three months later, her husband found them locked up in an iron safe to which no one but himself had a key, and which had not been opened for at least a year. The teeth were wet and warm. The grand house in Cheyne Walk, Chelsea, where the hatched-faced, eyeless woman, with the long, yellow, spidery

---

1 A Major Rowlandson shot himself in a taxi at three minutes to 3 p.m. on August 3rd, 1934, in order to die before the expiry of a £50,000 life insurance policy. Although the date does not fall within the period specified, it seems likely that Rowlandson may have been one of the guests at the Inferno party.

fingers strokes your face in the night. The orange-haired homicidal horror, the phantom footman of Ealing. The ghostly phenomena reported in *More Haunted Houses* are of spectres less spectacular, still riveting enough though – the door that would never keep shut, the phantom teeth of Knightsbridge, the figure on the stairs.

Among the many fascinating tales of the supernatural connected with the historic county of Hertfordshire is the legend of Minsden Chapel. The haunting is said to take place on Hallowe'en. The manifestations usually begin with the tolling of the lost bells of Minsden, and as the sound dies away the figure of a monk is seen under the ivy-covered arch on the south side. With cowled head bowed, he walks silently up steps no longer visible, and disappears. After a moment strains of sweet music fill the air, but almost as soon as the hearer is aware of them, they die away into an all-pervading silence.

On a Wednesday afternoon in 1907, two young men, Thomas William Latchmore and Reginald Leslie Hine, knapsacks, packed with camera, plates, various assorted items of photographic paraphernalia, and a collapsible wooden tripod, on their backs, set off from Hitchin, in Hertfordshire, for the hamlet of Langley. A couple of miles through the southern outskirts of the city, they arrived at the Royal Oak, Chapelfoot. From there they headed off along a track that led up to where, nestled in woodland atop a small hill, stood the ruins of the fourteenth century chapel of Minsden. The mission upon which they were bent was a strange one. They were planning to photograph a ghost – the hooded shade of a monk which had for many years been reputed to drift in eternal anguish about the crumbling ruins of the chapel. The photograph which they obtained that day created a sensation. It had, moreover, been critically examined on behalf of the Society for Psychical Research and pronounced not to be the result of any fakery or abnormality of the plate.

It was in 1923 that O'Donnell, after hearing about the photograph from a friend, went off to interview one of the two young photographers, Thomas Latchmore, who showed it to him and explained how he had gone to Minsden that day simply to take some new pictures of the ruin for his files.

"I noticed nothing unusual at the time. It was only when I was back in my studio developing the plates that I noticed this strange image on one of them," he told O'Donnell. "I do not claim it is a ghost. It may only be due to some freak of light and shade, but it is extraordinary, is it not?"

O'Donnell agreed. Clearly believing that he was on to a great story, he contacted the *Daily Express* and told them of his desire to hold a nocturnal vigil at the ruins on Hallowe'en, one of the nights when the ghost orbit is believed to be at its closest point to the living.

The *Express* liked the idea, and at 10.30 p.m. on the evening of October 31st, 1923, accompanied by H.V. Morton, Wyndham Lewis, and a well known spirit medium named Mrs. Everett, O'Donnell set forth.

> We arrived at Minsden Wood shortly before midnight... I wanted my companions to separate, in order to perform the spells appropriate for the occasion and in the working of which Mrs. Everett was an expert. She had brought with her a witch's costume which she had donned before leaving Hitchin, and its effect on the few people we had passed on our way to the ruins had been electrical. Nothing, however, would induce the newspapermen to separate, and they all remained huddled together under one of the arches, waiting with bated breath for whatever might happen. Nothing daunted, Mrs. Everett sat on the cold, damp soil and kept up a dismal chanting which was well calculated to draw even the most bashful of All Hallowe'en ghosts from its lair.
>
> Nothing came, however, and we were all beginning to despair of experiencing any phenomenon when suddenly one of our number, with a loud ejaculation, pointed to a white light shimmering through the naked branches of a tree.
>
> "It's come at last," someone whispered and, on advancing toward the tree, all agog with excitement and awe, we saw what looked like a figure clad in the white costume of a nun standing in the centre of one of the arches. Our camera was at once directed towards it and, doubtless, some of us were anticipating the taking of a picture that would thrill the world. For my own part, I had doubts when someone suggested it might be an illusion of the moonlight, and so, to our intense disappointment, it proved to be naught, so far as we could judge, but a curious and distinctly eerie effect of moonbeams and shadow. It was the only thing approaching a ghost that we saw and, when 4 a.m. arrived, we decided to vacate the grove agreeing that, if it was not haunted, it ought to be, for a more eerie spot none of us had ever been in.
>
> Tramping wearily along the high road, which was now shrouded in fog, we were startled by flash-lamps being shone on us and the stentorian voices of four members of the Hertfordshire Police bidding us to halt in the name of the law. It then transpired that the booking office at the Welwyn railway station (a few miles distant) had been broken into some hours previously and a shot fired at an official, and the police wanted to

know what we were doing prowling about the highroad this early in the morning. My explanation that we were looking for a ghost produced peals of satirical laughter and a search was forthwith commenced to see if we possessed firearms. However, as luck would have it, for one of us did happen to have a revolver on him, the search was cut short by the opportune arrival of Mr. Latchmore. Having the lady of our party to look after, he had not been able to keep up with us, and his corroboration of our ghost story resulted in our immediate release. Thus ended my first expedition to the haunted ruins.

"I visited the ruined chapel three times," O'Donnell was to write to Reginald Hine. "My second visit was alone, and I did feel extraordinarily uncanny at times. I was conscious of something close beside me, scrutinizing me, although I neither saw nor heard anything... On the whole I am inclined to think there is truth in the legend."

In 1925, O'Donnell, undaunted by previous failures, paid his third Hallowe'en visit to Minsden, accompanied by "a stalwart Colonel and two friends."

> We had barely arrived amid the ruins before there was an explosion under our very noses, and a sudden blaze of white light. Magnesium wire! Hoaxers! The Colonel gripped tight hold of his stout ash cudgel. A few minutes later. More explosions and more lights, first in one part of the ruins and then in another. Led by the Colonel who, cudgel in hand, made a rush forward, we ran to a spot among the ruins whence the loud explosions had proceeded, and there we found a white sheet on the ground, with one end fashioned like a hood. Feeling that nothing further was likely to occur that night we returned home, the Colonel disappointed that he had not been in time to give the wearer of the sheet the cudgelling he so richly deserved.

In 1930, Latchmore gave O'Donnell a second interview, and now admitted for the first time that the image on the celebrated photograph was not the result of a spontaneously manifesting and recorded phantom nun, but of a carefully planned experiment. He had read of a new method of producing such 'spirit' photographs, and it was to try it out that he had arranged for a friend of his to don a hooded white sheet and pose for a timed exposure in front of the ruin. The likelihood is that the cowled figure on Latchmore's historic photograph is none other than his friend Reggie Hine.

The late Reginald L. Hine, F.S.A., F.R.Hist.S., industrious local historian, bibliophile, antiquary, man of letters, and country solicitor of Hitchin, who lived in the village of Willian, will be for ever associated with Minsden Chapel. He fell in love with the place, researched its history, purchased a lifetime's lease on the ruins from the vicars of Hitchin, and spent many hours of quiet, contented contemplation there. It was here that, in 1943, he completed the final chapter of his book, *Confessions of an Un-Common Attorney*. Six years later, on April 14th, 1949, at the age of sixty-five, he committed suicide in strange circumstances, calmly stepping in front of a train while in the middle of a conversation with a friend at Hitchin railway station. His ashes were scattered at Minsden Chapel, and, at the entrance, by the eastern apsidal aisle, his widow, Florence, had set an inscribed memorial stone, grown now sorrowingly obscure, embowered in the undergrowth grasp of the twisting fingers of bramble and ivy.

Despite the enormous number of séances which O'Donnell attended in his long lifetime, the only one at which he was positive that something supernatural occurred was one that he attended on May 29th, 1924. An Authors' Club friend of his, whom he calls Colonel R., who had been with the British Expedition to Tibet, in about 1906, told him that he had had in that country but one experience that might be considered to be in any degree of a psychic kind. He and a friend had been visiting a lama one day when the lama had suddenly told them the year in which each of them was going to die. Colonel R. was to die in 1924, and his friend in 1910. On May 27th, 1924, O'Donnell met Colonel R. in Wardour Street and invited him to come to a séance that he was holding on May 29th in a reputedly haunted flat in South Kensington. He promised to come.

At about half-past ten on the evening of Thursday, May 24th, O'Donnell was seated with about ten other people round a deal table in the kitchen of the South Kensington flat. They were all listening to a professional medium, who was supposed to be under control, conversing with one of the company, and to knocks that were taking place at intervals. Glancing towards the open doorway, O'Donnell saw standing in it a tall figure all in black. It seemed to him to resemble a man wearing a top-hat, but he could not see the face with any distinctness. While he was staring at it, two of the ladies present, Miss Myra Smith and Miss Shanahan, declared almost simultaneously that they saw it, and Miss Smith seemed so perturbed that O'Donnell suggested that the lights should be turned on. This was done, and the figure was no longer visible. No one other than O'Donnell and the two ladies seemed to have seen it. He did not think that the apparition had anything to do with the medium, whose so-called psychic faculties had by no means impressed him. She seemed to be wholly ignorant of the presence and made no comment on it. The man at whom the figure seemed to be looking was Colonel R. He died a few days after the séance. His death was quite sudden and unexpected.

In December, 1924, Rider published, price five shillings, *Ghosts Helpful and Harmful*, described in the *Scotsman* as "A collection of episodes which prove, in the writer's opinion, that denizens of the spirit world take an active interest in what is going on in the material world, and on occasion intervene, from motives good, or otherwise."

In it, O'Donnell told of how his aunt, Mrs. Warren, had been the recipient of the good offices of a helpful ghost. Her husband was a captain in the army and she was quartered at Meerut at the time of the Indian Mutiny. She was actively preparing for flight, when the door burst open, and to her horror in rushed a Sepoy. A ferocious looking ruffian, in dishevelled blood-stained uniform, he stared at her with black, gleaming eyes. In one hand he was carrying what looked like a butcher's cleaver. It was dripping with blood. He grinned horribly and stood gloating over O'Donnell's aunt. In an agony of anticipation, she clasped her hands, and prayed more fervently than she had ever prayed before, and as she did so, she distinctly felt some concrete body brush against her and the wooden plank of the floor on which she was standing vibrated and shook, as if trodden upon by some very heavy person. The effect on the Sepoy was positively electric. He had been advancing towards her. He stopped dead in his tracks, staring straight in front of him, horror-stricken eyes wide-open. Then, turning on his heels in a flash, fled. Mrs. Warren was convinced that he had seen the, to her invisible, figure that she had only felt brush against her. To her dying day she remained convinced that it was to the advent of some awe-inspiring spirit that she owed her deliverance. Later on, she fell into the hands of the notorious Nana Sahib, but he treated her with the greatest courtesy and consideration.

Of indisputably harmful intent was the bed-haunting ghost of Bruges. Two travellers to Belgium for a West End London firm decided to put up for a night at an hotel situated in one of the oldest parts of the ancient city of Bruges. The bed provided in their shared room was a large and impressive-looking double one. At about one o'clock in the morning the man sleeping on the right side of it was awakened by a dreadful gurgling sound. It seemed to be coming from his slumbering companion. Sitting bolt-upright in some alarm, his attention was caught by a large mirror directly opposite, shining in the moonlight. In it, he could see the reflection of the bed, but... wait... what was that? Bending over the left side of it was a tall, shadowy figure, cowled and habited like a monk. Its face hidden by the big, black hood, it was clutching his bedfellow by the throat, strangling him. He jumped out of bed and switched on the light, and instanter the monkish intruder vanished.

O'Donnell had always been fascinated by the out-of-the-ordinary, the fantastic, the bizarre. Back in 1900 he had hunted up one of the original members of that strange little band of mystics who called themselves the Ghost Circle.

It was one night in the eighteen-eighties that three men met, quite by chance, in what was said to be a badly haunted house in Cricklewood, North London. Their meeting resulted in their founding what later developed into a small, very exclusive company of people, neither spiritualists nor scientific investigators, but just ordinary people interested in ghostly phenomena. There was no entrance fee, no subscription, no collection at meetings, which took pace at the houses of the members of the Circle, as there was no fixed headquarters. Always at meetings a skeleton sat in a chair opposite the chairman. Investigations of alleged haunted places were carried out by members, the results of which were, however, never made public. The Ghost Circle ceased to exist at the beginning of the twentieth century.

One of the strangest of the clubs that O'Donnell became aware of was the C.C.C. or Cory Coffin Circle, which flourished briefly in London in the eighteen-nineties. It had no headquarters, and met weekly at the home of one of the members, who always during the meeting sat in his or her coffin. The member who acted as host provided tea or coffee. No alcohol was permitted. Membership was open to both sexes, and to people of any religion. The one essential qualification was belief in a future life. At the end of each meeting the Coffin Song, which had been composed by a lady member, was sung. When a member died, all his fellow members were expected to attend the funeral and place a wreath of white flowers on the grave.

Stashed away among O'Donnell's posthumous papers for the year 1921, is a short note from 3 Temple Gardens. "Thank you for your letter which is interesting," it says. "For the moment it is quite impossible for me to make any appointment to see the documents you refer to, but I could do so some time next week. I will write you again." It is signed, Edward Marshall Hall.[2]

Curiosity led O'Donnell to insert in a London newspaper a request for information concerning man-hating feminist organisations. He received many replies, most of them anonymous. Furnished with sufficient testimony as to the existence of a few secret ultra-feminist clubs of very pronounced nature, in April, 1922, he gave a talk at the Scala House on the Menace of Cults of Male Hatred. The talk was widely advertised, and the large hall was packed. O'Donnell was careful to confine his remarks strictly to ultra-feminist organisations, never mentioning the word 'woman' or alluding to politics. He was nevertheless subjected to a furious attack by an obvious ultra-feminist who declared that men were promoted reptiles, that their age was ending, and that the sooner there were none left the better it would be for the world. She used such disgusting language that the chairman ordered her to leave the hall. Many of the people present, including not a few women, demonstrated their disapproval of her conduct by hissing her as she stalked out of the hall. The talk created a great sensation. There were long accounts of it in the *Daily Telegraph*, *Referee*, and other Sunday papers. Under the big headline "Sex Hatred", and the byline Elliott O'Donnell, the *Manchester Evening News* published, Saturday, April 8th, 1922, a whole page article.

Hearing that Aleister Crowley, who, mainly because of his dabbling in Satanism, had already acquired the reputation of being a very bad man, and who was later to become notorious as the Master Therion, the Beast 666, had a temple in Chelsea, where he practised his evil cult, O'Donnell, accompanied by two friends, went along there to see things for himself. The so-called temple was simply a room, in the centre of which was a table, or altar, draped in black and covered with Cabalistic signs. On the table were two tall black candles. Fronting the table, and just a few feet from it, were two boxes like sentry-boxes, their fronts covered with green drapery. On pedestals around the room were ranged busts supposed to represent the Hierarchy of Hell – Asmodeus, whom the angel Raphael bound in Egypt, Pytho, prince of lies, and other devils. Crowley, tricked

---

2 Sadly nothing has emerged to throw any further light upon the subject to which this relates.

out in black robes, made a dramatic entry. Advancing with slow, measured steps to the table, he knelt before it, muttering words that were quite unintelligible to O'Donnell. He then rose and read from what he called "The Book of Mysteries". He followed this by walking majestically around the room, pausing in front of each of the busts to utter prayers to them before stabbing them all over with a knife. The climax of these absurdities came when he stood in front of the table and pretended to cut his chest and apply a lighted taper to the supposed wound. From time to time while these various activities were proceeding, females robed in green garments emerged from the sentry-boxes to pay silent homage to the High Priest (Crowley) and the Hellish Hierarchy. When the performance was over, Crowley requested those who wished to be initiated into the cult to remain behind, the rest to leave. O'Donnell and his friends needed no second bidding. All that had happened struck them as very stupid and unhealthy, and Crowley as a mediocre showman, utterly devoid of anything psychic or spiritual: in other words, a very undesirable humbug.

By 1925, when he brought out *Ghostland*, published by Cecil Palmer, O'Donnell was living at 6 Upper Phillimore Place, Kensington, W.8. In it, he warns of the dangers of ghost hunting. "I do not think ghost hunting is a pursuit to be recommended. Apart from the ghostly dangers, there is the risk to one's general health. Going into an empty house at night and waiting there in the dark in constant expectation of one knows not what is bad both for body and mind, and, even in the case of the strongest people, sooner or later it is sure to tell. I do it, partly, because, at this stage, I cannot help myself, the quest of the Unknown attracts and fascinates me, and, partly, because I set out on this mission with a definite purpose, which, as yet, has not been, and, most likely, never will be, fulfilled. My object, primarily, was to find out something definite with regard to another world, and, if possible, offer some kind of consolation to the poor ghosts, who would appear, for the time being, at any rate, to be exiled from it... I have on several occasions spoken to what I have believed were ghostly entities, but I have never obtained any communication from them. Neither, do I believe, and this I repeat very emphatically, has anyone else – at least, not on any authentic and corroborative evidence, the only evidence that normal, open-minded individuals can accept. Hence, as I have so often said before, the most that those of us who are sane and honest can do at present is to speculate."

And he had previously written: "I am often sorry, extremely sorry, I was ever brought into contact with the Unknown. I did not go out of my way to seek the superphysical – it came to me. And it has never given me any peace. I feel its presence beside me at all times. In the evening, when I am writing, the curtains that are tightly drawn across the closed windows slowly bulge, the candlestick on the mantel-shelf rattles, a picture on the wall swings out suddenly at me, and, when I go to bed and try to sleep, I frequently hear breathings and far-away whispers. Some of these 'presences' no doubt have been with me always – most probably they were with my ancestors – whilst other have attached themselves to me in my nocturnal ramblings. My wife, who was a confirmed disbeliever before our marriage, has long since thrown aside her scepticism, and for a good reason. She has had many startling proofs of the power the spirit has of making itself manifest. The night a near relative of mine died both she and I heard a loud crash on the panel of our bedroom door, and I, though I only, saw a hooded figure standing there. Also, besides having heard the banshee, my wife has seen objects moved by superphysical agency, seen them fanned by a wind that is apparently non-existing, had small stones and other articles thrown at her, and heard all sorts of queer, unaccountable sounds – laughs, sighs, and moans…

My last experience occurred only a few days ago, as I was sitting on the stairs of a haunted house near Ealing. I had applied to the landlord for permission to spend the night there, and, pending his reply, had obtained the keys from the agent, in order to see what the house was like by daylight. Having just finished jotting down some notes – a memorandum of something I had suddenly thought of – I paused, still holding the pencil in my hand, whilst my note-book lay open on my knee. I had not sat thus for more than a minute, when, with a thrill of surprise, I felt the pencil suddenly taken from my hand, and, looking down, I distinctly saw it, of its own accord, scrawl right across my book. Whether what I afterwards found written in my note-book was written by the spirit that haunted the house, or by a projection of one of my own personalities I cannot say; neither can I, myself, nor anyone to whom I have shown the symbolic writing, tell what it means.[3] I might add that it is my one and only experience of spirit-writing, and also that it was my one and only experience in the haunted

---

3   Amid a jumbled line of symbolic shapes only the following three inscripts are intelligible: "March 28 12".

house near Ealing, as I did not succeed in getting leave to spend a night there.

It is March 28th, midnight, and as I pen these concluding words,[4] my mind reverts to the symbols and the date March 28th, twelve o'clock. Suddenly I hear footsteps – distant footsteps on the road outside – coming in the direction of the house. I glance at my wife, wondering whether she hears them too. She is asleep, however, and, as I covertly watch her, I see a look of terror gradually steal into her face. Clicking steps. They come nearer and nearer. They stop for a moment at our door, and then – thank God – pass slowly on. I look out of the window – the road is absolutely deserted, but from close at hand the sounds are wafted to me – click, click, click, fainter, fainter, fainter – until they abruptly cease."

---

4   This passage is being quoted from the final chapter of his *Twenty Years' Experiences as a Ghost Hunter*.

GHOSTS
HELPFUL & HARMFUL

ELLIOTT O'DONNELL

FIVE SHILLINGS NET.

The cover of Elliott O'Donnell's book Ghosts Helpful and Harmful, with a portrait of its rather awkward-looking author.

14

Phantasmal Gore

Sitting beside the glimmering fire one childhood evening, watching with apprehension the shades of night falling fast, and shadows, dark and mysterious, creeping forth from various objects in the room, young Elliott listened, eyes wide, heart racing, while Miss Milward, a native of Worcester whom his mother employed to do needlework, recited to him the blood-curdling details of such murderous horrors as the tale of Kate Webster, a Victorian bogeywoman, who, in 1879, in a villa in Park Road, Richmond, struck down, cut up, and boiled her mistress, Mrs. Thomas. Miss Milward told him that when staying with some friends at Twickenham, she had often seen Kate Webster, who used to do occasional charring for the people next door. "Her face," she said, "frightened me dreadfully. I didn't know anything about her then, of course, but whenever she looked at me, I felt as if nothing would give her greater pleasure than to wring my neck. If your mamma will let you come home with me one day, I will show you something that will interest you, something we treasure very much indeed."

Having obtained the necessary permission, he went with Miss Milward to her house. He had not been in her parlour many minutes before, without any apparent reason, his attention was attracted to an armchair that seemed to stand out conspicuously from the rest of the furniture. No one sat in it while they had tea, but suddenly it creaked.

"There!" Miss Milward exclaimed. "Did you hear that, Master Elliott? That chair, which is the surprise I had in store for you, belonged to Mrs. Thomas and came out of the house where she was murdered. My Twickenham friends bought it at the sale of her effects, Now, whenever I hear that chair creak, I feel sure that either Kate Webster or Mrs. Thomas is sitting in it."

"Whether Miss Milward's – or rather Mrs. Thomas' – chair really was haunted, I cannot say," comments O'Donnell, "for I never went to her house again." What he could, and did, say, was that he had it on good authority that Mayfield cottage, the house where Mrs. Thomas met her horrible end, "has never been disturbed by any ghostly phenomena."

Although he was only a child of seven at the time of the crime, he was, 46 years later (in March, 1925), to edit a full account of the case, *Trial of Kate Webster*, in Hodge's classic *Notable British Trials* series.

Harry Hodge, the publisher, wrote to him from 12 Bank Street, Edinburgh, October 26th, 1922: "There is no hurry about Kate as it will be some time before we start setting-up. As regards the German books – they are rather horrible, both as regards text and illustrations, and I don't think they are quite what you would like to ask your wife to read! You know how beastly and how thorough the Germans can be. These books are a sample of it – but they are intensely interesting. I shall, of course, be delighted to lend them to you, but I think it right to give you this warning first. As regards Church and Porter – the alibi is somewhat difficult to follow in the evidence at the trial. That is why I think you should assist the reader in your introduction."[1]

O'Donnell's 82-page Introduction was carefully fashioned and rich in detail. And he concludes: "It may interest the reader to learn that I have been in correspondence with a lady who, with her people, went to live at 2 Vine Cottages in 1897. She tells me that the house had then stood empty for some long time, for, although the copper Mrs. Thomas's remains had been boiled in had been removed and the house altered, no one would live there. My correspondent further states that, in spite of some trouble at first with servants, on account of the murder, they were quite comfortable in the house and," he characteristically cannot resist adding "not troubled by any ghostly disturbances."

He dedicated the book to Sir Harry Bodkin Poland, K.C., who had, under the Solicitor-General, Sir Hardinge Giffard, K.C., been Counsel for the Crown. Poland had written to him, "I shall be much pleased to have the Kate Webster trial dedicated to me."

Elliott O'Donnell was sixteen and still at school at Clifton College when

---

1 John Church and Henry Porter were prosecution witnesses, both of whom Kate Webster accused of having committed the murder. John Church had a solid alibi. There was not a shred of evidence against Porter.

Saucy Jacky was plying his Ripper's knife in Whitechapel in the autumn of 1888, but he well remembered in after years "the thrill I got at hearing news-vendors shouting out 'Another horrible murder in Whitechapel'." In 1895, when he was living in London, he made a point of visiting all the Jack the Ripper murder localities, and had interesting conversations with people who had actually lived there throughout the time of the terror. They told him that in the places where the slaughterings had taken place appalling screams and groans were sometimes heard at night.

In Buck's Row, where Mary Ann Nichols had been slain, a huddled up figure like that of a woman, emitting from all over it a ghostly light, was frequently seen lying in the gutter.

When he was lodging in York Road, O'Donnell got to know a Whitechapel costermonger named Mullins, who used to come in for meals in the café there. Mullins told him of how, on the night of October 1st, 1888, he was walking along Hanbury Street, where Annie Chapman had been murdered, on his way home. It was about one o'clock in the morning, and the place seemed deserted. When he came to the part of the street by Number 29, where Chapman's body had been found on September 8th, 1888, he was startled to feel a hand suddenly seize hold of his shoulder. He spun round thinking it must be a policeman. There was no one there. Scared, he had hurried on home as fast as his legs would carry him. On two further occasions, in January and February, 1889, respectively, at the same time and in the same part of Hanbury Street, he had again felt the hand. "Heaps of others who live in Hanbury Street," he told O'Donnell, "have felt it too."

"This," said O'Donnell, "proved to be correct, for on my visiting the unsavoury locality and making inquiries, I was able, after much trouble, to ferret out from the chary and none too communicative inhabitants information to the effect that, both the ghostly hand as well as other phenomena – inexplicable lights and noises – were still periodically experienced."

The ghost of Lizzie Stride was also said to have been heard. About a month after her murder, on September 30th, 1888, a Whitechapel tradesman was walking up Berner Street towards Commercial Road, when he heard a series of the most harrowing moans and groans, the source of which he found it quite impossible to locate. Thinking that Jack the Ripper had been at his work again, or that someone had been taken violently ill, he drew other pedestrians' attention to the sounds. He was about to knock at the door of one of the houses, when a woman in the crowd that had collected called out, "It's no good knocking there, them sounds don't come from that house, they're in the street here; we've often heard them since poor Lizzie was done to death close to this spot."

The Ripper's last victim, Mary Jane Kelly, discovered on November 9th, 1888, was reputed to haunt the scene of her terrible death and grotesque mutilation, No. 13 Miller's Court, Dorset Street. A woman in black was often seen entering the house and looking out of its window, while strange sounds were heard proceeding from it.

O'Donnell was a man of thirty-eight, when, in 1910, little Dr. Hawley Harvey Crippen paid the supreme penalty for the murder of his wife and interment of her filleted remains in the cellar of 39 Hilldrop Crescent, their Holloway home. It seemed to be the end of the affair, but the ghost of the hanged man is said to walk. O'Donnell himself had never seen the wraith, but confesses that he always experienced the psychic prodromal syndrome – similar to the epileptic aura – of pins and needles in ice-cold hands, in the vicinity of the house in Hilldrop Crescent.

The very next year, actually on New Year's morning, 1911, the stabbed and battered body of an East End Russian Jewish property owner, Leon Beron, known habitually to carry large sums of money about his person, was found in some bushes near the bandstand on Clapham Common. Another Russian Jew, Steinie Morrison, was found guilty of his murder. A number of people reported seeing and hearing weird things when passing by the spot on the Common where Beron's corpse had lain. One man told O'Donnell that he was taking his dog for a run one evening, and when they got close to the place where the crime had been committed, the dog ran into some bushes and started barking excitedly. The man went round to the other side of the bushes, and saw there the shadowy figure of a man standing still as a statue in the moonlight. It faded away in a few seconds. The dog wagged its tail, barked, and seemed greatly pleased by the figure's exit.

An old Clapham cabman confided to O'Donnell that one night a week *before* the killing of Leon Beron, he was crossing the Common at about half-past twelve, commenting to himself about the extraordinary stillness of everything and the fact that there was no sign of any human being about, when he saw a light of a bluish colour on the spot where the murder was in the future to be discovered. Wondering whatever it could be, he had walked towards it. He had covered a dozen or so yards when it faded out, but, a moment or two later, appeared again. It was at first very faint, then suddenly burst into a flash, strong enough to bathe everything around it in a lurid, ghastly glow. He examined every inch of the surrounding ground and bushes, but there was nothing that in any way explained the cause of the light.

"The cabman's tale so fascinated me," O'Donnell admitted, "that I visited the Common several nights in succession, and although I did not see anything that was unaccountable, I certainly heard something – namely, a curiously ominous noise, something betwixt a cry and a wail, which seemed to me to be neither human nor animal, and to come from the exact spot where the body of the murdered man had been found. Now, although I felt sure that it was a manifestation of the superphysical, in order to assure others, I thoroughly searched every adjacent space that could possibly afford cover for anyone playing a trick, and, as I had anticipated, I found no one, and nothing that could in any way explain the occurrence."

It was part of Elliott O'Donnell's psychic credo that certain places do undoubtedly have certain effects on certain minds; possibly minds which are a trifle abnormal. There is something in some specific localities that begets crime and vice. And it is not perhaps altogether unreasonable, he thinks, to suppose that the effect is not produced entirely by physical surroundings, but by that something behind the physical surroundings. He has in mind, for instance, that two-mile stretch of lonely shingle between Eastbourne and Pevensey Bay known as the Crumbles. It was here, in the holiday month of August, 1920, that Irene Munro, a 17-year-old Scottish-born London typist was battered to death for her handbag, stuffed with her holiday money, and buried in the Crumbles' sand by two young local layabouts, Jack Field and William Gray.

O'Donnell had conducted a psychic stake out on the Crumbles, making his way at half-past eleven one night to the spot where Irene's body had been found. Just as he was drawing close to the place, the figure of a man arose from the ground and, very pale-faced, and walking eerily on tiptoe, advanced towards him. For a moment or so a thoroughly startled O'Donnell actually quaked, but was quickly reassured by a very non-ghostly voice. The man, indisputably a somewhat weird character, confesses that he comes often to Eastbourne, and every visit feels impelled to make his way to the Crumbles.

"There is a rumour," he tells O'Donnell, "that the ghost of either Field or

Gray is to be seen here on certain nights. It is dressed in a check suit, and has a very white, evil face. Many people have told me about it. I have never seen anything, but I have heard things. Hark, what is that?"

O'Donnell listened. He heard close to them a sound like the moaning and sighing of the wind, very, very sad and plaintive, yet, at the same time, ominous.

"I have experienced that sound," said the stranger, "in absolutely sultry weather, when there has been hardly a breath of wind stirring. Do you know what I think it is? I think it is a spirit, but not the ghost of poor Irene Munro. It is a spirit that tempts people to murder. I have felt that way myself when I have stood in this spot and listened to it."

Involuntarily O'Donnell edged away.

"Oh, it's all right," he laughed. "I know how to overcome it. I shan't kill anyone – at least not yet. But, seriously, very strange and evil thoughts, such as I have experienced nowhere else, have assailed me here, when I have been listening to that noise, and it makes me wonder how far Field and Gray were really responsible for the crime they committed. I wonder whether they may not have been prompted to commit it by this horrible influence which I myself have felt. Their minds, probably much cruder and less disciplined than mine, would not be able to resist the influence as I have done. What do you think?

"I think what you suggest is highly probable. Certain localities and houses no doubt suggest crime and vice."

The stranger bade O'Donnell goodnight and speedily disappeared in the darkness, leaving him feeling very far from comfortable listening to the sound of his retreating footsteps, his quick tip-toeing across the shingle. As he stood there alone, an ice-cold feeling suddenly ran through him, and he felt, distinctly felt, some strange, uncanny presence pass close to him. He did not wait any longer. He made immediate tracks for his hotel in Eastbourne.

Four years went by. Then, in April, 1924, murder came again to that precise area of the Crumbles. Patrick Mahon took his *de trop* pregnant mistress, 37-year-old Emily Kaye, to a bungalow facing that forlorn beach, and there murdered her, striking her down, it was thought with an axe, and thereafter dismembering her, burning some parts of her in the fireplace, and boiling others in a variety of pots and pans.

O'Donnell wrote:

The house on the Crumbles in which Miss Kaye was murdered had long been reputed to be haunted. In the early part of the summer of 1924 I was dining one evening with an old school-fellow of mine, and in the course of conversation we touched on the Crumbles crime, which happened just then to form a very general theme for discussion.

"Do you know," he said, "we, that is to say, myself, and wife, and family, once lived in the house. We took it for several weeks, a few summers ago, and we had not been in it many hours before we discovered it was haunted. Regularly, every night, soon after we went to bed, we used to hear someone cross the floor of the front bedroom and go along the short passage leading to the kitchen. And once something was actually seen. A lady friend of ours, who was sleeping in the bedroom leading into the room in which Mahon was believed to have killed Miss Kaye, woke one night to see a figure in naval uniform step into her apartment through the window, cross the floor, and make off in the direction of the kitchen. She heard his footsteps retreating along the passage, and they sounded just like the footsteps she had heard on previous occasions, when she had seen nothing."

My friend went on to tell me that, on making inquiries about the house, he was informed that, according to certain rumours, many years previously, a tragedy had taken place there. It was said that a coastguard (whether officer or man was not stated) had been found dead in one of the rooms, under circumstances that very strongly suggested foul play. More than that my friend was unable to ascertain; but he said that although the house appealed to them all in many respects, there was something about it they did not quite like, and which they could only describe as something that was more than gloomy.

Well, it was this conversation with my friend that made me resolve to visit the place myself, and to experience, if possible, anything in the way of ghostly phenomena that it might have to offer. Accordingly, I discussed the matter with an editor whom I knew would be interested, with the result that he rang me up shortly afterwards and asked me to go to the Crumbles by the very first train I could catch.

I now quote from the report I subsequently published in the weekly paper that he edited.

'Tonight, or rather last night (for I am penning these lines in the early hours of the morning), I enjoyed the privilege of sitting alone for several hours in the room where the last of the great Crumbles crimes is popularly supposed to have been committed. Let me detail my experience from the beginning.

I arrived at the house at about seven o'clock in the evening. The weather was gloriously fine, and the Crumbles all aglow with sunshine. Anything less ghostly-looking than the bungalow then, viewed from the exterior, could not be imagined. Nor, despite the great open space confronting it, did it strike me as at all lonely.

Immediately in its rear, within a few yards of it, in fact, was a row of small houses, bungalows, one and all teeming with life, while in front of it, looking over its garden wall, were sightseers galore.

Then I entered. I viewed, in turn, the range where parts of the body had been burned, a room where parts of the body had been found, another room where the body, *in toto*, was believed to have been dragged, the room in which Mahon and his successive ladies slept, and finally the room in which the murder is generally believed to have been committed. The sun was still high in the west when I reviewed these respective apartments, and I received no impression, saving the pleasant one of how charmingly picturesque, quiet and peaceful the house was, as a whole. In the murder room nothing could be more artistic than the yellow wall-paper, the red-brick fireplace, and the black oak corner cupboard, all designed, no doubt, to enhance the effect of the low ceiling, the old-world windows, and the quaint doorways. I seat myself at a table – the very writing-table, presumably, whereat the letter that figured at the trial, the letter with the strange signature, was written – beside a window overlooking the front garden. Gazing out of this window, I see a small grass-plot; a white wall; and beyond, a great stretch of open, desolate ground – the Crumbles. A little to the left, a Martello tower; to the right, nothing. In the room on my right is another window, also overlooking the Crumbles, and on my left, a doorway through which I can see the room where the murderer slept. The shadows deepen; and, as they do so, the sightseers cease their peeping and, somewhat hastily, so it seems to me, commence to retreat, quickening their footsteps as they cross the Crumbles. Sounds, too, diminish, and despite the near proximity of the houses at the back of the one I am in, I can hear little, only the occasional bark of a dog, the distant hoot of a motor, the far-off whistle of a train. At intervals I experience an almost absolute silence, and it is then that I begin to realise how quiet the Crumbles can be. And now, for the first time, I get a suggestion of something ghostly in the atmosphere.

I have in my pocket a small mirror; it comes from the Hebrides, the true home of second sight and all that is uncanny. I have had it with me on several of my ghost hunts, and it has rarely failed to demonstrate to me the presence of the Unknown by emitting a strange, pale blue light. I take it now and stand it upright against the red-brick fireplace, where Mahon is supposed to have burned the head of his victim. I go back to my seat, his seat, and watch, and presently... there it is, an unmistakable pale blue flame emerging from the mirror. It moves slowly in the form of a small candle flame to the left, finally halting in the doorway opening into the passage. I get up at once, and going to the door, throw it open and walk into the passage, and, as I do so, my right hand undergoes a sensation like 'pins and needles' and then feels as if it had been suddenly thrust into a bucket of icy-cold water. I have had the same experience when passing through the tunnel in which Miss Money was killed,[2] in my present quarters, near the British Museum, which witnessed a suicide in January last [1923], and in various other places, and I have come to regard it as a kind of tragedy indicator, a sure indicator of the spot where something peculiarly dreadful has occurred. My instincts tell me now, as I stand still in the passage, that there was no struggle, not the vestige of one, and that it was here that Miss Kaye received the fatal blow, delivered in true coward fashion from the rear. I go back into the room, and there I see shadows, not the same shadows I saw before, but new shadows, shadows I have ever seen in places where grim and harrowing happenings have taken place. I now sense a feeling of concentration in the atmosphere, which previous experience has warned me is the prelude to a climax, and I am preparing to meet it, when I hear sounds of very human voices from the other part of the house, and my vigil abruptly ends.

O'Donnell sums up: "That that part of the Crumbles where Irene Munro was murdered and the house where the murder of Miss Kaye occurred, is haunted, I think one may regard as certain. I can vouch for the genuineness of at least one of the ghosts, namely, that in naval uniform, as the story can be corroborated by my friend and his family, and I have the utmost faith in their integrity. I believe, too, I saw and heard and felt something, but belief is not, of course, evidence. Still, apart from my own experience, there is what the stranger told me and local rumour and opinion. Hence, I think one may take it as a fact that the Crumbles, in and around the spot where I walked, is haunted, not by one ghost but by several, and that the ghostly influence there is for the most part evil. I believe that Field, and Gray, and Mahon were all seriously affected by it, though Mahon's past suggests that he more than met it half-way. I do not think that this influence emanates from the apparition in naval uniform seen by one of

2 On September 24th, 1905, the badly mutilated body of Mary Sophia Money, a 22-year-old bookkeeper who worked for Bridger's, dairymen, of 245 Lavender Hill, Clapham Junction, was found in the mile-long Merstham Tunnel, on the Brighton & South Coast Railway. That she had been murdered was evidenced by the fact that she had been gagged with her own scarf, rammed so tightly in her mouth that the police had difficulty in removing it. No one was ever charged with the crime, the motive of which may have been sexual.

my friend's party, but from something that is very much more sinister and *outré*. At least, such was the impression I received, while I was waiting and listening."

Another seaside locale that can boast an uncanny coincidence of corpses is Yarmouth. In September, 1900, Herbert John Bennett strangled his young wife, Mary Jane, with a bootlace on the beach. The sands of time had run a mere dozen years more, when, in July, 1912, there came once again to Great Yarmouth's South Beach, a strangler, who, shoe-lace in hand, cruelly despatched 18-year-old Dora May Gray. Her killer was never found. O'Donnell discovered that in 1844, there had been an atrocious murder on the same sands, and in October, 1852, a young woman named Mary Anne Proudfoot had been decoyed on to the beach one night by a former lover, who tried to murder her by means of a pitch-plaster, and failing in that due to her struggles, next set to work to throttle, in which endeavour he was happily foiled, her loud screams capturing the attentions of a passing rescuer in the nick of time. This criminous quartet had lent the locality a pretty poor reputation, and O'Donnell says that when he visited there in 1899 the rumours of its being haunted were well established. Indeed, he recalled that when he mentioned to his landlady that he had been for a stroll along the North Denes she had remarked, "Lor' that's an unpleasant place for a ramble. I wouldn't go there by myself for anything you could offer me." He asked her why not?

"Why not? Why, because for one thing it's so lonely, and for another it's haunted. Yes, haunted. You needn't laugh. They did say when I was a girl that a ghost in the shape of a very nasty-looking black dog used to be seen there and on other parts of the beach before something dreadful happened. My father, for one, said he saw it a night or two before poor Mary Proudfoot was set upon by Sam Howth and nearly killed; and it was seen there, too, just before another woman was done to death, I forget her name. No, I wouldn't venture there alone after dark, for all the money in Yarmouth."

There was a trio of old Victorian Bloomsbury murders which fascinated O'Donnell.

The first took place on Christmas Day, 1872, when Elliott was just ten months old, in the street that changed its name to Great Coram Street. The house, No. 12, was a boarding-house. The victim was a 27-year-old part-time chorus girl, part-time prostitute, Harriet Buswell aka Clara Burton.

She was found in the second-floor back, lying on the bed, multiply stabbed, her throat cut, a half-eaten apple on the wash-stand beside her, which, had this not been before the days of the triumph of forensic dentistry, might well have snared the murderer by his bite. As it was, this her last, literally, client, and bloody despatcher, was never found. Suspicion ran deep in the tracks of a German clergyman, Dr. Gottfried Hessel. But the good Pastor Hessel sailed safely away from these shores dentologically unassailed.

Five minutes to the north of Great Coram Street lay Burton Crescent, scene of the second murder. It, too, shed its old identity, to become Cartwright Gardens. Here, at No.4, in December, 1878, the diamond merchant's widow, Mrs. Rachel Samuel, aged seventy-four, was found lying dead in a pool of blood in her basement kitchen. She had been battered to death with a heavy piece of wood, studded with nails, that had formed part of a hat-rail. Strong suspicion attached to a former servant, Mary Donovan, but her trial never progressed any further than Bow Street Magistrates' Court, where the case against her was dropped.

The third case, the murder that came to light in 1879, that of Miss Matilda Hacker, spinster of sixty years, especially interested O'Donnell because one of his aunts knew Miss Hacker. The house in question, a boarding-house, was No.4 Euston Square. It was situated at the north end of the square, a few paces from Eversholt Street. It, too, took on a subsequent new identity as the gardens in front of Euston Station. It was in the coal cellar there that her decomposed remnants were unearthed. They revealed death by strangulation. A 24-year-old maid-servant in the house, Hannah Dobbs, from Bideford, who had been seen in possession of a large sum of money after Miss Hacker's disappearance in October, 1877, was arrested, and put to trial before Mr. Justice Hawkins. For lack of evidence, she was found not guilty.

Edward Austin Creed was the 46-year-old manager of an old-established cheesemonger's of Messrs. Lowry & Company, Provision Merchants, at the corner of Leinster Terrace and Craven Hill Gardens, in Bayswater. On the night of July 28th, 1926, after the assistants had gone home at the end of the day's work he had stayed behind at the lock-up shop to wash his hands. That would have been at about 7.10 p.m. Later that evening, P.C. Watts, a policeman on the beat had detected a strong smell of gas emanating from the grating of a cellar beneath the shop. Shining his lamp into the cellar and on to a flight of steps leading down from the shop, he saw within its beam a man's foot, just visible protruding from the stairway. Watts, assisted by another constable, forced the shop door open. On his back, halfway down the cellar stairs, they found Mr. Creed. He lay on his back, his jacket off, his shirt-sleeves rolled up. His face, head and left arm were covered with blood, and he was dead. Marks in the sawdust on the floor indicated that he had been murdered, by repeated blows from some heavy instrument, his body dragged along the ground and tossed down the cellar stairs. For no apparent reason, three gas-jets in the cellar had been turned on, but left unlit. The motive had clearly been robbery, for between thirty-five and forty pounds had been stolen from the shop safe. The crime was to remain unsolved.

It was to the scene of this lethal malfeasance that O'Donnell repaired on the night of the third anniversary of the murder, July 28th, 1929, a Sunday. He went at the behest of the Allied Press in Manchester, who wanted him to spend a night in the shop to see if anything ghostly happened, and if he could form some hypothesis therefrom as to the actual committal of the deed.

"At closing time the present manager locked me in, leaving me with the cat (a pretty tabby with a white patch on its chest) that was in the shop on the night of the murder, as my sole companion. I confess I felt far from comfortable when I heard the key turn in the shop door and the footsteps of the manager die away in the distance. I did not realise till then, perhaps, that as I was locked in the shop, whatever happened I should have to stay in it until the manager arrived the next morning with the keys to release me.

Though it was light outside, the drawn down door-blinds and closed shutters made the interior of the shop rather dark, and, despite the voices and footsteps of the passers-by and the continual sound of traffic, a curious sense of loneliness and solitude seemed to hang about the place. I was glad the little cat – I am very fond of cats – was there to keep me company. Having assured myself no one was concealed in the basement, I re-ascended the staircase and took up my position at the cashier's desk, which commanded a full view of the main body of the shop. The cat came to me and, perching itself on the desk at my elbow, looked at me with wondering green eyes, as much as to say, 'In the name of all that's curious, what are you doing here tonight?'

As the streets gradually grew quieter and the gloom in the shop increased,

I let my mind wander to the night Mr. Creed was murdered. It was generally supposed the deed was done a few feet from where I was sitting – that is to say, in the fore part of the shop; for there were bloodstains behind the street door and also on the counter. The supposition most commonly put forward in the press was that Mr. Creed opened the door to some person or persons just as he was preparing to depart. One thing is certain: Mr. Creed was taken unawares; had this not been so, he would probably have given his assailant a pretty bad time, since he was very strong and a fine amateur boxer. I went over all this as I sat at the desk waiting. Waiting for what? Anything that might happen. Every now and again I left off reading, and, switching off the electric light by my side, sat in the gloom and talked to the cat.

As the hour grew later, the noises in the street grew less frequent, fewer people and vehicles passed, and a stillness, the stillness of night, presently became perceptible. More for the sake of exercise than anything else, I went down into the cellars again, and as I crossed the floor of the first cellar, I was conscious of a change. the place before had seemed ordinary enough, but there was now an uncanny feeling about it. This feeling was not so profound in the cellar beyond. It was now eleven o'clock, and I telephoned to my wife in Bloomsbury, to wish her goodnight and say everything was all right up to then. Amid the silence and loneliness, which were becoming more and more noticeable every minute, her familiar voice sounded very welcome.

An hour passed, the voices and footsteps in the street had practically ceased, motors still passed hooting, but only at intervals, and a hush, broken only by the sonorous ticking of the clock high up on the wall near me, reigned throughout he building.

Suddenly there was a loud clanging noise in the nearest cellar, just as if a bar of iron had been thrown or let fall on the cement floor. The cat heard it, too, for with a wild bound it leaped on to the small window-ledge, high up on the wall to my left. I had never seen a cat so scared, and I thought it would jump out of the window, which was slightly open, into the street below. When it did not do so, I own I felt much relieved, for I should have greatly missed its company. I was somewhat scared too, because the manager had told me for a fact that there were no rats, and even if there had been I do not think that they could have accounted for the noise I heard. Pulling myself together, however, I descended once more into the basement and searched around. Again, an uncanny feeling, much stronger this time in the nearest cellar, and not so strong in the adjoining one; but no one and nothing to explain the noise.

After I had resumed my seat at the cashier's desk, I noticed a sudden lowering of the temperature, which might, of course, been entirely due to the lateness of the hour. It was now raining, and the wind moaned and howled round the shop, occasionally blowing with almost hurricane force.

I passed the hours alternately reading and waiting. While I read, of course I kept on the electric reading lamp by my side, otherwise, and for the greatest part of the night, I sat in darkness. Periodically the wind beat the rain with great violence against the windows, and periodically, during a lull in the gale, everything was very still. Only, at long intervals, the sound of a passing motor. The cat descended from its perch and resumed its seat by my side.

About one o'clock, during a quiet spell, the handle of the shop door was tried. With all my faculties at once on the alert, I rose noiselessly from my seat and listened. Again a cautious turning of the handle, but no footsteps. I felt, however, that something had entered the premises. Though I neither heard nor saw it, I was conscious of it moving past me in the darkness and heading for the cellar steps. I switched on the reading-light, but no one, nothing, was visible. The cat, however, was once again high up on the window-sill, a picture of feline terror.

From now onwards a series of strange things happened.

Again and again I heard curious noises in the nearest cellar, then whisperings at the bottom of the staircase, and footsteps, which came stealthily up the stairs towards me. This gave me the most unpleasant thrill I had so far experienced, and I had to struggle hard with myself to stem off a downright panic. Not knowing what I might see – for the idea flashed through me that the murderer had taken it into his head to visit the spot where he had committed the murder on its anniversary, as murderers are supposed sometimes to do – I turned on the reading-light again, and, gripping hold of the telephone at the same time, prepared to defend myself. The whispering and footsteps at once ceased.

Dropping the telephone, and armed only with my electric torch, I now went to the head of the stairs and peered very apprehensively down them. No one was there. Feeling a trifle more courageous now, I went down the stairs and searched the cellars. I looked everywhere, but could discover nothing that could in any way explain the noises. When I came back to my seat the cat was once again sitting on the desk, and it seemed delighted to see me. Turning out the light, I was sitting listening to the rain and wind, which had suddenly got up again and was shrieking like a dozen lost souls, when suddenly I saw a man standing on the floor of the shop directly in front of me. His profile was turned towards me, and he appeared to be in the act of talking to someone. I switched on my electric torch, fully prepared to see him immediately vanish, but he did not; he remained. He was a rather short, thickset man, with a nose placed somewhat prominently on his face; he had a moustache and was bareheaded. While I was looking at him, the cat panicked and bounded once more on to the window-sill. I turned on the reading-light, and when I looked for the figure this time it had gone.

Unconsciously I glanced at the clock; it was just two o'clock. I switched off the light and again sat in darkness. Suddenly there was another clanging sound in the cellar, more whisperings, and steps on the stairs. This time I was too afraid to move; I simply sat and listened. The steps came right up. I then heard sounds of something heavy being dragged across the floor of the shop right past me. I was next conscious of a presence on the floor of the shop, directly in front of me, leaning on the desk and peering stealthily at me. I received the impression of a man, wiry, pale-faced, and intensely vicious. After the lapse of some minutes there was a noise as of someone placing his hand on the desk and searching about for something. It was all so evil and so horribly near me that I switched on the reading-light. I saw no one, nothing, only the main body of the shop, with the counter on one side.

Unable to bear being in the dark, I now lighted up and made notes of what had happened in a book I had brought with me. I also devoured some biscuits and tried to entice the cat down with one. He preferred to remain where he was, however. Once more I switched off the light, and almost immediately heard the cautious movement of a hand, again on the desk just in front of me. This time I got a very vivid impression of a rather dirty, coarse hand, with muscular fingers and ugly spatulate nails. It was a young hand, and might have belonged to someone in the twenties or early thirties. Then there was another clang in the cellar, a single cough, and I saw behind the counter the same figure I had seen previously in the body of the shop. I was moving myself to speak and address it when it disappeared. A few minutes later there was another clang, louder than any of the former clangs in the cellar, and another cough. Afterwards... silence.

A feeling that I must go down into the cellar now came over me, and, electric torch in hand, I very fearfully proceeded to do so. Nothing that could in any way account for the sounds was apparent, but I was conscious of something horrible there, something that at once reminded me of the vicious presence I had felt opposite me when I was seated at the desk. I felt, as I stood peering around me, that it was in the cellar that Creed was taken unawares and that it was there that the first blow was struck. A picture of the crime rose rapidly before my mind's eye. I saw, mentally, the victim bending over a basin of water in the act of washing his face; then the murderer, rather slim and of medium height, came out from a shadowy background and, stealing up behind him, hit him on the head with an iron bar. Dazed, and realising that in his weakened condition he stood no chance against his armed adversary, Mr. Creed, dodging his assailant, succeeded in staggering up the staircase into the shop, and almost to the door of it before his relentless antagonist overtook him and struck him another and even more terrible blow. Two more blows and he was a battered corpse. His murderer now proceeded to drag him to the staircase, and there he left him. There the picture ended.

The dawn was now breaking, or had broken, and, although the grey of early morning had a very uncanny effect, making certain of the objects in the shop appear strangely and startlingly unreal, I felt the ghostly influences that had been present during the long hours of darkness were no longer there. At half-past six footsteps and voices approached the shop door, and to my joy a key was inserted. Seldom had I been more pleased to see a fellow-human.

I believe that I experienced on that night, the anniversary of the murder, a ghostly re-enaction of it, in part at least, and I believe the owner of that wiry, repulsive hand was the actual assassin.

There is a curious sequel. On the Thursday following my vigil, wanting to get into communication with the shop again about something, I rang up the manager at about 2.30. At first there was no reply. After a while, however, the exchange informed me I was through.

'Hullo,' I said, 'are you such and such a number?'

'Yes,' a voice I did not know replied, "Lowry's Stores."

' Is that Mr. ----- ?' I said.

'No,' came back the answer, and there was a cough, exactly the same cough that I heard in the cellar during my nocturnal vigil. It was peculiarly individual. There was no mistaking it. After it, there was absolute silence.

The following day I rang up the place again and informed the person who answered of my experience the previous day.

'What time did you ring up?' he enquired.

'Half-past two,' I replied.

'But you couldn't have done so,' he said. 'We always close at one o'clock on Thursday, and there was no one here.' "

Kate Webster, from the Illustrated Police News, May 3 1879. The bottom right panel depicts the attempt to steal Mrs Thomas' furniture from the murder house.

The execution of Kate Webster, from the Illustrated Police News, August 2 1879.

A postcard showing Dr Crippen's house at No. 39 Hilldrop Crescent.

A postcard showing the haunted Crumbles murder bungalow, where Patrick Mahon murdered Emily Kaye in 1924.

The Crumbles Bungalow—Scenes after the Tragedy

A memorial card to the Crumbles murder, perhaps issued by the person exhibiting the murder bungalow for money, in front of crowds of gawping Londoners.

Three haunted murder houses investigated by Elliott O'Donnell: No. 12 Great Coram Street, where Harriet Buswell was murdered in 1872, No. 4 Burton Crescent [today Cartwright Gardens] where Rachel Samuel was murdered in 1878, and No. 4 Euston Square, where Matilda Hacker was murdered in 1879. None of the murder houses stand today, and none of the murders was solved; the Great Coram Street and the Euston Square hauntings can both be confirmed from the contemporary press. Reproduced from J. Bondeson, Rivals of the Ripper (History Press, 2016).

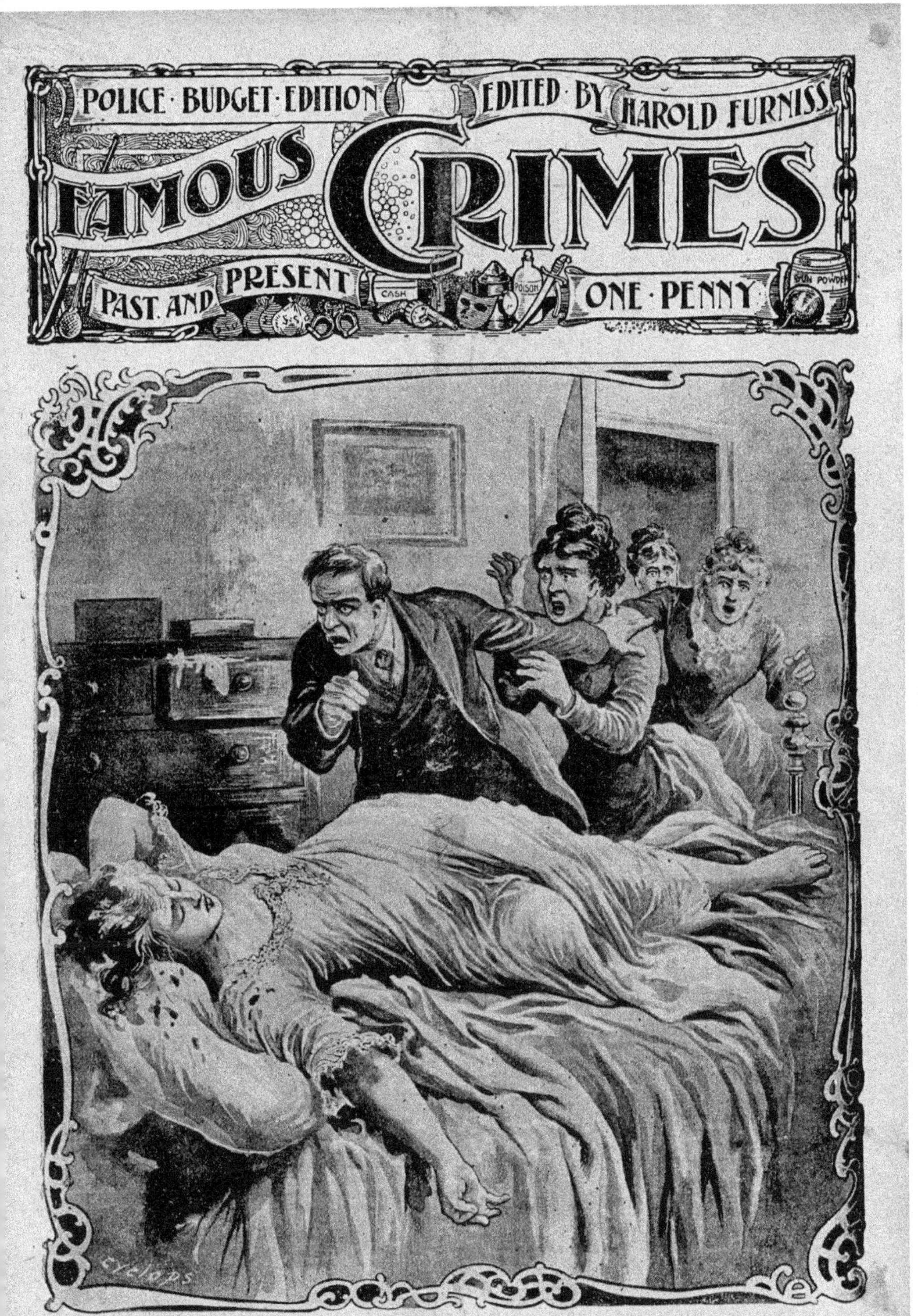

THE DISCOVERY OF THE MURDER IN GREAT CORAM STREET.
Vol. I.—No. 13.

The Great Coram Street murder of Harriet Buswell is discovered.
From Famous Crimes Past & Present. Reproduced from J. Bondeson, Rivals of the Ripper (History Press, 2016).

The discovery of the murder of Mrs Samuel at Burton Crescent, from the Illustrated Police News, January 4 1879. Reproduced from J. Bondeson, Rivals of the Ripper (History Press, 2016).

The Euston Square murder house and the remains of Miss Hacker, from the Illustrated Police News, May 24 1879. Reproduced from J. Bondeson, Rivals of the Ripper (History Press, 2016).

The grocer's shop at No. 36 Leinster Terrace, where the shopkeeper Edward Creed was murdered in 1926, from the Illustrated Police News, August 5 1926. The shop was haunted for many years, and Elliott O'Donnell stayed there overnight and experienced many uncanny phenomena. Other people also experienced the ghost, and the shop was eventually demolished; a small restaurant of modern design today stands on the spot.

15

Dreads and Drolls

She is the wailing woman of Ireland, the ghost who, says Elliott O'Donnell, "terrified me more than any other when I was a child, and which I still dread more than any other." She is the Banshee, whose voice is horrendously, cacophonously unique.

Banshees are Irish family ghosts, and they follow those families, families at least a thousand years old, to whom they are attached to the ends of the earth. The haunted family may be in poor circumstances, living not in a manor house but a hovel. No matter. All that does matter is that the family should be of genuine Celtic Irish origin, or even older extraction; its lineage will more than suffice. Really ancient families, such as the O'Neills of Ulster, the O'Briens of Thomond, the O'Donnells of the North and Trough, the O'Rourkes of Brefni, and some dozen or so more, scattered by the winds of chance to the four corners of the globe – there's an Irishism if there ever was one – are typical banshee prey. And she will never leave or forget them till the last member has been gathered to his fathers in the churchyard.

There is not just one single entity known as *the* banshee. There are many, each clan possessing, or being possessed by, a banshee of its own.

In form, the banshee is infinitely variable. She may manifest as young and beautiful, or old and hideous; very tall and thin, or dwarfish. Her mien may be sorrowful and kindly, or malignant, gleeful, and hellish. The benevolent banshee prognosticates a family death with wailing, moaning and wringing of hands. The malevolent variety greet the shadow of impending tragedy with signs of unholy joy, laughing and clapping their hands. Unlike the Victorian concept of a good child, the banshee is as a rule heard but not seen.

The O'Donnell banshee has been touched upon by many writers. Mrs. Craik refers to it in her novel, *John Halifax, Gentleman* (1857), in some detail in the story of the Doona Saan of White-Goat Glen, but her description of it does not in any degree tally with those given by members of the O'Donnell family who believe that they have actually seen it.

The wailing of the banshee, O'Donnell testifies, "is indescribably weird and unearthly. I heard it before the death of my aunt, Mrs. Hewson, of Kerry, sister of the late Colonel John Vize O'Donnell of Trough, Co. Clare, who was the head of our branch of the old Northern O'Donnells in Ireland. One night my wife and I were awakened about twelve o'clock by a series of the most agonising and heartrending screams. They were so terrible and sounded so near to us, almost, in fact, in the room, that we were both horribly frightened, and immeasurably relieved when, after continuing for some seconds, they died away in one long drawn-out wail or sob. Two or three days later, I heard that my aunt was dead. She had died within twenty-four hours of the time the wailing and screaming had occurred."

Interestingly, in his *Family Ghosts and Ghostly Phenomena*, O'Donnell cites the evidence of an ancestor of mine, Sir Jonah Barrington, as regards the banshee.

> It was during the viceroyalty of Earl Hardwick that Lady Barrington met Lord Rossmore at Dublin Castle. Lord Rossmore was then old, but, apparently, sound in health. He liked entertaining and used, constantly, to invite his friends to stay with him at Mount Kennedy. Amongst others he invited Sir Jonah and Lady Barrington, and they went. What happened after they retired to rest on the night of their arrival is best narrated in Sir Jonah's own words:
>
> "Towards two in the morning, I was awakened by a sound of a very extraordinary nature. I listened; it occurred first at short intervals; it resembled neither a voice nor an instrument; it was softer than any voice and wilder than any music, and seemed to float in the air. I don't know wherefore, but my heart beat forcibly; the sound became still more plaintive, till it almost died in the air; when a sudden change, as if excited by a pang, changed its tone; it seemed descending. I felt every nerve tremble; it was not a natural sound, nor could I make out the point from whence it came. At length I awakened Lady Barrington, who heard it as well as myself. She suggested that it might be an Aeolian harp, but to that instrument it bore no similitude; it was altogether a different character of sound. My wife at first appeared less affected than I, but subsequently she was more so.
>
> We now went to a large window in our bedroom, which looked directly

upon a small garden underneath. The sound seemed then obviously to ascend from a grass plot immediately below our window. It continued; Lady Barrington requested I would call up her maid, which I did, and she was evidently more affected than either of us. The sounds lasted for more than half an hour. At last a deep, heavy throbbing sigh seemed to come from the spot, and was shortly succeeded by a sharp, lone cry, and by the distinct exclamation thrice repeated of 'Rossmore, Rossmore, Rossmore!'"

Sir Jonah goes on to say that he will not describe his own feelings, because it is beyond his power. The maidservant was so terrified that she fled from the window, and it was with great difficulty Sir Jonah could persuade Lady Barrington to return to bed. Lady Barrington asked Sir Jonah not to tell anyone about what they had heard for fear they should be laughed at.

In the morning, at about seven o'clock, Sir Jonah's servant Lawler, tapped at their door and said, 'Oh. Lord, Sir!'

'What is the matter?' Sir Jonah asked impatiently.

'Oh, sir, oh, sir,' Lawler ejaculated; but before he could explain the reason for his agitation Lord Rossmore's footman came hurriedly along and informed Sir Jonah that Lord Rossmore, on his return from Dublin Castle, whither he had been unexpectedly summoned the preceding night, had gone to bed, in, apparently, good health, but that at about half-past two his valet, who occupied the room next to him, hearing him make a strange noise, ran into his room and found him on the point of death. He died, in fact, before his valet had time to summon any of the household to his bedside.

It would thus appear that Lord Rossmore was actually dying when Sir John and Lady Barrington and their servant had heard the ghostly sounds, and his name pronounced three times; and Sir Jonah remarks that he found it impossible to account for the phenomena on natural grounds. The haunting, I would add, being obviously due to a banshee, Lord Rossmore, though neither an O' nor a Mac, must have had a true Irish strain in him.

Sir Jonah Barrington, who was born at Knapton, Queen's County, lived at Dunran, about fifteen miles from Dublin. Dunran is in the centre of the Golden Belt of Ireland, that is to say the lovely district, about thirty miles in length and from four to seven in width, commencing near Dublin and ending a short distance beyond Avondale.

I have, of course, quoted the testimony of Sir Jonah Barrington with regard to the banshee, partly because the testimony of a man of wealth and social standing, as well as of unquestionable sanity and honour, such as he will undoubtedly carry weight with, and possibly convert, at least some of those who have hitherto scoffed at and attributed all stories of the banshee either to imagination or cats; especially if such scoffers should happen to be English, since, if I may be pardoned for saying so, the English, as a race, are peculiarly attracted and influenced by money; their prejudices in favour of or against people and anything connected with them being often attributable, respectively, to their possession or lack of money.

It is not, however, only among the English that we find scepticism with regard to the banshee; there is a growing tendency among a certain section of the Irish today to deride all references to it. The reason for this may, I think, lie in the fact that banshees are generally regarded as the monopoly of old Irish families, and old Irish families' 'descendants' as they are often contemptuously styled, are by no means popular in modern Ireland.

Although banshees have figured repeatedly and extensively in works of fiction, and in stories based on the slenderest of testimony, it is O'Donnell's contention that there is nevertheless much corroborative and authentic evidence to prove their existence.

In 1920, O'Donnell published his monograph, *The Banshee* (Sands, London), which devoted 255 pages to a meticulously impressive study of the subject. On the spine and title page of this volume his name is misspelt, "Elliot". This curious error is to be found also in the cases of *Ghostly Phenomena, The Irish Abroad, Twenty Years' Experiences as a Ghost Hunter, Haunted Places in England, The Menace of Spiritualism, More Haunted Houses of London*, and *Ghostland*.

The year 1926 was that in which O'Donnell made his début as a broadcaster with the B.B.C.'s 2LO.[1]

He also seems at this period to have made another attempt to interest a well-known actress in the possibility of making some use of his work. His choice fell this time upon Miss Lillian Gish, whose secretary replied on November 16th, 1926: "I am requested to acknowledge, with thanks, your very kind letter of October 26th. As you probably know, Miss Gish is at present under contract to Metro Goldwyn Studios, and the choice of her stories for screen production lies with the executives of that company. Should you, however, care to send her the synopsis of your book, she will

---

1 His broadcasts included: February 13th, 1926. 10 p.m. *Some Queer Happenings*. June 23rd, 7.40 p.m. *St. John's Eve*. July 22nd, 7 p.m. *Sea Mysteries*. August 31st, 7.40 p.m. *Strange Cases of Mistaken Identity*. December 2nd, 7.40 p.m. *Old London Inns*. And, on May 17th, 1927, at 7 p.m., *A Night in an American Forest*.

be most happy to read it and let you know her opinion regarding its screen possibilities."[2]

In 1927, O'Donnell bought the Red House at Guilsborough. He described it as "an old, queerly constructed house on two levels, with a secret passage in one of the walls, stabling, and an old-world garden in the rear." It was rumoured to be haunted. At one of his lectures at a London club, he chanced to meet a woman, who, so he was informed, was very mediumistic. When she heard that his home was said to house a ghost, she expressed such a keen desire to pay it a visit that Ada invited her to come and hold a séance there one evening. It was arranged that she should come on June 22nd, and that the séance should be held on Midsummer Eve.

The moment the visitor crossed the threshold she declared: "I can feel the house is haunted. I will contact the ghost tonight, find out why it is earthbound, say comforting things to the poor restless soul, and it will never haunt again. I anticipate no difficulty in persuading it to rest in peace and trouble you no more. It is not harmful or horrible, like so many of the ghosts I have encountered. No ghost has ever frightened me, nor ever will."

What she said was overheard by an artist friend of the O'Donnells, who was frankly sceptical regarding the supernatural and fond of practical joking. He resolved to put the mediumistic lady's vaunted courage to the test. The house being very full, she (Mrs. X.) was having to share a room with Mrs. D. At about midnight, the jocular artist tapped along the corridor leading to the ladies' room as if he were wearing high-heeled shoes, stopped at the door, rattled the handle and groaned and moaned. No one spoke. All within the room was hushed.

In the morning, Mrs. D. said that they had had a dreadful night. The ghost had made spine-chilling noises at their door. O'Donnell told her that it had been his artist friend pretending to be the ghost, and asked her not to mention it to Mrs. X., who, she said, had been terribly frightened. Mrs. X. was far too scared to remain in the house, and hurried back to London directly she had had breakfast. O'Donnell was amused to read in a London paper a few days later how Mrs. X. had stayed in their house, had seen the ghost, and had persuaded it to return to its grave and never haunt them

2   It is likely that the book upon which O'Donnell was pinning his hopes was *Strange Sea Mysteries*, which had been published that November, and which contained among its 41 stories several of potentially filmic potential.

again.

Philip Allan published O'Donnell's *Ghosts of London* in February, 1932. Typical of the reception accorded to it is the review in February 22nd's *Daily Mail*. "(It) deals largely with his own experiences of the weird and ghostly, though it also contains accounts by witnesses of supernatural manifestations which they have encountered. It is a book to read, and full of interest to others than Londoners. Mr. O'Donnell himself is apparently very susceptible to ghostly influences, or perhaps ghosts are not so shy of him as they are of ordinary people. A queer story is that of the last night spent by an official and his wife in the old Newgate Prison which was demolished thirty years ago. They were sitting in the kitchen, said the official – When suddenly we heard the bell from the condemned cell ringing. The bell was in the corridor and could only be rung by someone within the cell pulling the lever, and as we were alone in the building we were not a little startled. They went to the cell and 'could see the bell swinging violently to and fro... We opened the cell door. No one was there.'"

An intriguing paragraph in the *Daily Mail* of July 8th, 1932, intimated that "Mr. Elliott O'Donnell, author and lecturer, has invited several mediums, and others interested in psychic matters, to spend this weekend at his home at Guilsborough, Northamptonshire, to investigate strange local manifestations. 'We shall hold a séance,' he told a *Daily Mail* reporter last night, 'and hope to visit another house in the neighbourhood where the figure of an angel is reported to have been seen. We may also visit crossroads near Naseby where three witches are said to have been hanged in olden times.'"

Over the years of his residence in London, O'Donnell met quite a number of well known people. About a year after his arrival in the capital he saw Bernard Shaw at a gathering of the Authors' Society, and was invited by him to the New Reform Club in Adelphi Terrace. Those were the days before Shaw was quite at his peak, and he was "unaffected, natural and affable. I told him I was thinking about acting again, and he advised me to abandon the idea. At that time he certainly did not seem to regard the stage as a very promising career for young men. When I bid him goodbye he said, 'Not goodbye but *au revoir*. We shall meet again,' and patted me on the shoulder. Some years afterwards when I chanced to meet him again, he was very abrupt in his manner and did not seem to recollect ever having seen me before. During the First World War he was generally believed to hold pacifist views. In one of the Bohemian art clubs to which I belonged there was an author who had achieved notability in writing about tramps. He professed to having spent a considerable time on the roads in order to become acquainted with tramps and find out how they lived. He was a keen pro-warite and was furious with Bernard Shaw. He showed me a thick cudgel and said he intended to give Shaw a good hiding with it, should he ever come across him out of doors. Apparently, he never came across Shaw in a place suitable for the deed; or, if he did, he thought better of it, for I never heard of Shaw ever being molested by him."

It was at a meeting of the Authors' Society too that O'Donnell met Rider Haggard, and he was charmed by his friendly manner and found him extremely likeable. Two other writers that he met in those long past days were L.T. Meade and Dr. Beaumont, who wrote in collaboration a most exciting series of *Stories from the Diary of a Doctor*, in the *Strand Magazine*.

He was introduced to W.B. Yeats by Lady Muir Mackenzie, who belonged to one of O'Donnell's psychic clubs, and was a keen believer in the supernatural. "Yeats told me how he had held a nocturnal vigil in a haunted house in Ely Place, Dublin, but had drawn a blank owing to the reputed ghost disobligingly not manifesting. Yeats struck me as being a sincere believer in the occult."

Elinor Glyn came with a friend to a talk he gave in London in the autumn of 1933. She talked to him afterwards and invited him to her flat to tea. He met there her sister, Lady Duff Gordon, who gave him a vivid account of the sinking of the *Titanic*, in which she had been a passenger. She explained how she managed to get away from the vessel just before it sank, and described her horror on seeing the ship go down – it was broken in half – and the strange, awesome feeling she experienced on finding herself in a boat that was a mere speck amid the vast space of water all around it. Fortunately, the sea was calm. She had, she told him, had a premonition of the disaster.

His volume on *Family Ghosts* made its appearance that August. "The Gael and the Celt, as might be expected, have contributed more to this hair-raising record than their Anglo-Saxon-Norman neighbours", commented the *Daily Mail* in a brief review, "but the English phantoms are sufficient both in quality and quantity to satisfy the most ardent nationalism. They take a bewildering variety of forms – birds, fishes, bats, trees, bells, ducks, monks, nuns, and dogs. Mr. O'Donnell will remove many misconceptions about banshees. He has heard his own family specimen. Surely that should be sufficiently authoritative for anyone!"

A fleeting visit back to Dublin in 1933 proved both impressive and tinged with sadness, for he found the glitter and glamour of past years had, like his youth, softly and silently vanished away. But, if duller than the Dublin of his student days, it was a cleaner, healthier, purer place. It gladdened his heart to find none of the extreme poverty of the old city. He missed the horse-drawn vehicles serviced by liveried footmen, but there were no barefoot, ragged children and no old women sitting on doorsteps smoking clay pipes. Scarlet uniforms had been replaced by green.

For all its great changes, he felt at home in Dublin, visiting some of his old haunts, meeting some relations who still lived there, and especially shaking by the hand again Dr. Sparkhall Brown, who had been on the staff of Dr. Chetwode Crawley when he was at Ely Place, forty years ago.

He forayed further afield later that year, when he and his wife went to America. The purpose of the visit was a lecture tour, addressing audiences in the States on the subject of ghosts. The representative of a New York lecture agency predicted that it would be a novelty that would prove very successful.

Elliott and Ada embarked at the Gladstone Dock, Liverpool, on December 15th, 1933, on the White Star liner S.S. *Georgic*, and arrived at New York just before Christmas. They found the Customs a great nuisance, being kept waiting there for ages, and charged what he regarded as an immense amount for his lecture lantern. Coming events were casting their shadows before them.

The day after their arrival, it snowed heavily. O'Donnell made his way to the office of the lecture agency, where he found the principal far from cordial, or even pleasant. Moreover, he was the broker of bad news. The present state of depression in America was such that some of the lectures that he had anticipated booking had been cancelled, among them the one at Hollywood. Sad news, as he had hoped to make use of the introduction to Marion Davies which he had been given by Elinor Glyn.

The following day, his American publisher took him along to a Dutch Club in New York, where, to his surprise and consternation, he was asked to speak – "I was half frozen with the cold and feeling none too well after the long sea voyage. Moreover, I knew no one present and everything was strange to me. I asked to be excused: it was of no avail. Compelled to speak,

Dreads and Drolls

and without the slightest idea of what to say, I got up, said a few words, and sat down. The next day my agent was furious with me. He said he had been told that I had given a talk at a club without his permission, and that the audience had declared that I was inaudible and uninteresting. I explained that I did not give a talk, but only said a few words. He would not listen, and said I had let him down badly."

The first lecture proper of O'Donnell's tour was somewhat less than a success, too. It was to a ladies' club at Troy, in New York State. When he arrived at the club there was no one there to greet him. By degrees the members filtered into the premises. No one spoke a word to him. At last the chairman arrived, late. She took no notice of him either. He sat alone in an obscure corner. At the conclusion of the reading of the minutes of the last meeting and the business of the club had been discussed, the chairman introduced him very briefly as the lecturer. Elinor Glyn had advised him to talk to American audiences in a very precise and professor-like manner. He tried to do so. The long rows of well-dressed women sat cold and poker-faced, like so many robots. They evinced not the slightest interest, paid him no attention. He found it hard to keep on talking. When he had finished, there was no applause, no proposal of a vote of thanks, no tea, not even a glass of water. He was ignored, and slunk out of the room dispirited and disgusted.

O'Donnell's agent, on hearing that his lecture to the Troy club had been very disappointing, was again furious with him, and even angrier when a Detroit club that had booked him cancelled on the strength of bad reports from the Dutch and Troy clubs.

His next ordeal was at a club in Buffalo. The lecture room was vast. It was packed. Over a thousand people, many in outlandish fancy dress. It was a local electioneering day. On the dais with him were the mayor and corporation. After the mayor and one or two others had harangued the assemblage, O'Donnell was introduced. His reception at Troy in mind, he spoke with less restraint and precision, just managing to hold a restless audience.

With confidence hardly boosted by his first two experiences, he next faced a club in Chicago. He arrived at that toddlin' town at 6 a.m. in a snowstorm, didn't know where to go, ended up, very comfortably as it turned out, at the Y.M.C.A. The lecture was at the Drake Hotel, at that time one of the largest hotels in America. The audience, too, was large, all women. Throwing what remnants of precision and restraint remained to the wind, he this time achieved modest success. Some applause, some tea, and one of the ladies took him for a drive.

Next stop Toledo. Nice start there! Warned by the hotel manager to lock his door at night and put a chair against it. Much rowdiness in the town, he explained, and he had had a good deal of trouble. O'Donnell was cautioned about the perils of the streets at night. He escaped unmauled, even by his lecture audience. In this, as in all his talks after Troy, he had dropped formality in favour of a friendly and familiar manner, and it went down well. He took, too, to asking them if they preferred to hear about hauntings not too alarming, or the reverse. They always chose the reverse. So he let himself go and plied them, Pelion upon Ossa, with horror upon horror. Result: applauded to the ceiling.

When, with great relief, he came to the end of his contract, he went to Baltimore. Ada did not accompany him because of her aversion to railway travelling. He stayed for a few days at an hotel in Charles Street. He thought Baltimore delightful and fell in love with it on sight. He spent time with his kinsmen who lived there. He saw with pride Elliott Street and O'Donnell Wharf, both named after his great-grandparents, and his great-grandfather's grave, which was close to that of Edgar Allan Poe. He was shown over the Peabody Institute by its librarian, Mr. Diehman, and made a temporary honorary member of the local University Club. He was invited to dinner by a lady who was a friend of the famous American actress, Mrs. Brown Potter. Unfortunately, he had no evening clothes with him, but was offered the loan of some. The intention was good, but the fit was not; the gentleman who kindly made the loan was shorter and stouter than the tall and willowy O'Donnell. He borrowed an evening shirt from another well disposed benefactor, but quite forgot about a tie and collar until it was shortly before time for him to dress. He then dashed frantically out of the hotel, and, luckily, was just in time to get to a hosier and hatter's before it closed. Returning in triumph, he was dismayed to find that he had omitted to buy studs, and ended up having to have his collar pinned on. When he reached his hostess' house, he begged her to excuse his appearance, saying that he would not have dreamt of coming thus had he not been so anxious to meet her. She was most amused by his pinned on collar, which he feared might come adrift at any moment, and at his very short and baggy trousers, which made him look and feel like a circus clown.

He stayed a night or two in Washington, where he called upon another of his American relatives, Mrs. Hinckley. He met with great courtesy at the National Library, and noted that, as regards quick service and convenience for writers, it compared more than favourably with the British Museum.

Boston was the only other town that he visited outside those which were on his lecture circuit. He gave an informal talk on ghosts at the house of a Harvard professor, and was accorded a very genial reception. He thought Boston at night, with its many lights and wonderful dome-shaped buildings, exceptionally lovely.

Great pleasure was afforded him by a letter written by Mrs. Maud Briggs Knowlton, Director of the Currier Gallery of Art, 192 Orange Street, Manchester, New Hampshire, on February 2nd, 1934.

> My dear Mr. O'Donnell,
>
> I am enclosing the press reviews of your lecture, delivered at The Manchester Institute of Arts and Sciences, Manchester, N.H., January 31, 1934.
>
> To write you that it was not only a most thrilling talk, but also one quite different in theme from the general run of lectures that have been delivered at the aforesaid institution, would be to once more reiterate the verdict of many of those, whose privilege it was to listen to your talk. May I also add that your sincerity in relation to your subject was a vital force in holding the attention of your audience during the entire evening, and the reluctance with which those, who had remained to ask questions of after the close of the lecture, departed, is proof positive, that your talk was of unusual interest to them.
>
> I trust that your return journey to New York was a pleasant one and wishing you the best of success in your work and thanking you for the most entertaining evening, believe me,
>
> > Yours very sincerely,
> > Mrs. Maud Briggs Knowlton, Director.

The long winter at last ended, he and Ada settled in at Apartment 61, 420 West 119 Street, were able to see more of New York. A great deal of their pleasure in that city was owed to the authorities of Columbia University. Not only did they permit him to read in the University library, a privilege which he much appreciated, but they also allowed him and Ada to take tea in Philosophy Hall and to entertain their friends there. During term time the O'Donnells went most Sundays to the University Chapel. "The sermons," he noted, "were always extempore and full of interest. The preachers did not gabble all the time about sin and penitence, but, without being a bit less reverend, spoke in a really intelligent and interesting way on a variety of topical subjects. The singing was extremely good, the choir being composed of highly trained University graduates of both sexes. The girls looked charming in their very becoming habiliments."

He was asked to give a talk – "I ought to have asked you whether you were willing to give it without remuneration," wrote the Columbia University Librarian – to the Columbia Woman's Graduate Club, and was somewhat intimidated by the idea of telling ghost stories to such a learned company. He need not have been. The talk, which he gave them at 4 o'clock on the afternoon of March 13th, was very well received. One of them, the headmistress of a girls' school in Riverside Drive, asked him if he would give her pupils a talk on haunted houses. He said he thought that he might frighten them. She laughed and said, "There's not much fear of that. It would take a lot more than ghosts to scare them!" Thus emboldened, he went along to the school, which was in an hotel, had tea with the girls, and afterwards told then hair raising tales of hauntings in England. They loved it, and when, several days later, he was broadcasting at Radio City, they came along to hear him and waved to him from the observation gallery.

The size of Radio City, where he was invited to broadcast by the National Broadcasting Company of New York, staggered him. He thought it stupendous. The studio from which he went on air was on about the thirtieth floor. He took part in nine plays, of which he was the joint author. Billed as 'The Original Ghost Man of England', he spoke at the beginning and end of each play. They were put out at 11 p.m. All the members of the cast were professionals.

He later recalled: "I had an awful few moments on one occasion. Sometimes when the script was too long lines had to be blue-pencilled. This was apt to be somewhat confusing. One night when I had to read my opening speech, owing to the blue pencilling I got all mixed up and panicked, I was dreadfully perturbed at the time I took to find the right place and feared the director would be very wrathful. At the conclusion of the play I said to one of the cast that I was afraid I had held up the play. To my great relief, he said he had not noticed any hold-up; if there had been, it was nothing to worry about. During rehearsals there were sometimes people watching up in a gallery at the rear of the studio. At the conclusion of the plays I had to walk home through Central Park. The gloom, stillness, loneliness and feeling that behind each bush or tree a horrible ruffian might be lurking, in readiness to pounce out on me, was a trifle alarming. I was, however, extremely sorry when my contract with N.B.C. ended. The pay was good and I had never experienced a rebuff or unpleasant word. Ada came to some of the rehearsals and sat in the gallery."

On one occasion he was asked to address a community in Jersey City. He had no idea until he arrived that he was expected to tell ghost stories in a church. When he voiced his reluctance to do so, the minister smiled and said: "The congregation have expressed their desire to have you here. You will find the church packed." And it was. He spoke for no less than two hours, relating harrowing cases of hauntings in England, some of which were closely associated with dreadful crimes. The audience all sat tensed, drinking in every word. They would have kept him there much longer, but he was anxious to get back to Ada, who was not with him at that talk, although she attended most of those that he delivered in New York.

He was made an honorary member of the Chemistry Club, the British Schools and Universities Club of New York had 'pleasure in extending the privileges of the Club' to him, and he was asked to lecture at the New York Authors' Club, at departmental stores, and in private houses. He told them all about Britain's Kate Webster and their own Belle Gunness.[3]

Through the kindness and courtesy of the American Irish Historical Society, he was able to hold, at its fine room at 132 East 16th Street, a meeting of the Clan O'Donnell. Ada and Elliott were invited by some of their American acquaintances to share their box at the Grand Opera House. Lily Pons was the prima-donna. Elliott had the misfortune to be seated behind a tall lady with a big head and a mass of hair, and in consequence was able to see little of the stage. Rather more successful was their sharing with another friend of a box at Madison Square Garden Circus. His complaint there was that the arena was too big, and too many performances all going on at the same time was distracting. He and Ada also thought that some of the acts were thoroughly dangerous. American audiences, they decided, seemed to like best performances that were not without a measure of peril to life and limb.

---

[3] Belle Gunness 1860-? Is thought to have faked her own death in 1908. Norwegian immigrant. Settled on a farm at LaPorte, Indiana, in 1901. Known as the Lady Bluebeard, she was a mass murderess, killing many spouses, children and suitors. Motive: financial gain.

On March 21st, 1934, he was the invited guest of The Booksellers League to a dinner at the Aldine Club. 200 Fifth Avenue, New York, where he delivered an after dinner speech on "Ghosts".

The O'Donnells' stay in America came to an end in September, 1934.

Between 1926 and 1936 a steady stream of books kept flowing from O'Donnell's stylograph – twelve books in ten years. Of these, only four were the customary logs of supernatural happenings – *Confessions of a Ghost Hunter* (Thornton Butterworth, 1928), a volume of spooky autobiographical reminiscence; *Ghosts of London* (Philip Allan, 1932), a ghostly gazetteer of famous phantoms and historic haunts of the capital; *Family Ghosts* (Philip Allan, 1933), a psychic menagerie of birds and bats, cats and dogs, of monks and nuns, and drummers and 'cauld lads', make their baleful appearance; and *Spookerisms* (Universal Publications, 1936), a curious little 91-page paperback.

In 1926 he embarked on a different tack, branching off into dealings with the generally non-supernatural but nonetheless mysterious, with *Strange Sea Mysteries* (John Lane, The Bodley Head), which told seamen's yarns of remarkable happenings at sea; tales of sea-serpents, of harrowing experiences in whirl-pools and water-spouts, and of startling deeds on ships; this was followed in 1927 by *Strange Disappearances* (John Lane, The Bodley Head), including that of Urban Napoleon Stanger, of Whitechapel, and little Eliza Carter, of West Ham; *Famous Curses* (Skeffington, 1929), a gathering of the traditional tales and legends of curses pronounced upon family mansions and their occupants, and other persons and places designate; also in 1929, *Fatal Kisses* (John Hamilton); *Great Thames Mysteries* (Selwyn & Blount, 1930); *Women Bluebeards*, brought out in 1931 by Stanley Paul, was a garland of lethal ladies, mistresses of feminine wiles of deceit, intrigue, and cruelty; and *Strange Cults and Secret Societies of Modern London* (Philip Allan, 1934).

Elliott and Ada were staying in Bloomsbury for a week in the winter of 1937, when he was suddenly called upon to face what he described as the greatest sorrow of his life.

"Ada had been to a theatre one evening and was seemingly perfectly well. In the morning she went out to buy a newspaper and on returning complained that she had lost the use of one of her legs. I tore off to a doctor, and I knew by the look in his face when he saw her that it was serious. It was a stroke. She died in the Cranford Nursing home, 26 Harborough

Road, Northampton, and was buried, as had been her wish, within a few yards of the grave of her parents.[4]

Parting with loved ones is not the tragedy in youth that it is in age. In youth, time is a healer; in age, time very often never heals. Work alone helped me. I had to write to live. A curious thing happened after Ada's death. Just before she was taken to the nursing home, she wrote some words on a sheet of paper. I put that sheet carefully away in a drawer. The day prior to her funeral, I suddenly saw the sheet lying on my study table in front of me. I had not put it there and no one else could have done so because I was alone in the house."

---

[4]   In her will she left effects to the value of £924 11s.

Sketches concerning the disappearance of Urban Napoleon Stanger, from the Penny Illustrated Paper, October 14 1882.

Eliza Carter, from the Penny Illustrated Paper, February 18 1882. On the mysterious 'West Ham Disappearances', see J. Bondeson, Rivals of the Ripper (History Press, 2016).

16

Lonely Road

Elliott O'Donnell was now sixty-five years of age – a widower.

"After the death of my wife I could not bear living alone in the house in the country where we had been so happy; it felt so different and I was so terribly lonely. I missed her dreadfully. I have never ceased missing her, and never shall. No woman could ever have been a better wife or a more lovely character. I don't think any man could have suffered more than I did. Had I not been obliged to work, I think I should have gone mad and probably destroyed myself. I was more than once on the verge of it."

He had twenty-eight years left to live.

Mercifully, he survived that Priestleyan dangerous corner. He sold the Red House and returned to London. But London was never again to him the London it was when Ada was with him. He took rooms on the ground floor of a house in Bloomsbury. The place had recently been occupied by a man reputed to belong to a satanist cult and to practise black magic. O'Donnell sensed something horribly evil in the atmosphere of the house the moment he entered it, and was constantly conscious of sinister eyes watching him and following his every movement. The feeling became so intolerable that he surrendered his tenancy and sought quarters elsewhere.

His salvation was an avalanche of work. The *New York American Weekly* commissioned a series on famous hauntings in Great Britain; the *Newcastle Sunday Sun* ordered a run of articles on the white slave traffic in England.

By dint of bribery and adroit pumping of women contacts in West End pubs and clubs, he was able to glean enough inside information to put together a pretty solid dossier. A large percentage of the foreign prostitutes working in England belonged, he discovered, to Continental syndicates.

On arriving here, the girls would be met by agents of the syndicate who had husbands in waiting lined up for them. These would be men, who, for a handful of ready cash, were ready to waltz them off to the Registry Office and provide them with British citizenship. They would be provided, too, with luxurious commercial love, or lust, nests in Mayfair, and an aproned foreign acolyte or maid to pamper her. They would be furnished also with jewellery and beautiful clothes, and tuition in the ways to cater for the tastes of all kinds and conditions of liberally paying clients. They were further supplied by the syndicate with pornographic books and photographs for sale at exorbitant prices. They made a lot of money, but incurred considerable overhead (if that is the right word!) expenses; large rentals for their flats, substantial remuneration for their maids, a hefty slice of the profits to the syndicate. So long as they remained big earners, all was well, but directly they ceased to attract well-heeled clients, perhaps because of fading looks, they would be ruthlessly discarded, with warnings of dire consequences should they betray any of the syndicate's sacredly guarded secrets.

The syndicate also devised, when it could be safely done, subtle ways of recruiting pretty English girls. Bogus hospital nurses, bogus social workers, and bogus fine, upstanding gentlemen, well-dressed and chauffeur-driven in splendid shiny motor-cars, were snarers of the girls. Given doped cigarettes, spiked drinks, or hypodermic injections, rendered helpless, they were transported to Buenos Aires or some other South American port, where the promised days of paradaisical lucrative employment soon turned to a life in chains to shame and misery, or prematurely ended in the grave.

Very useful to O'Donnell, too, in so far as his journalistic work went, was an introduction by one of his friends who had been "a very distinguished member of the C.I.D. at Scotland Yard", to the C.I.D. at Limehouse, and a detective there who took him on two tours of Chinatown.

> There were doss-houses with rooms horribly bare and comfortless, containing beds, if such they could be styled, for a dozen or more people, and little else. Anything more drab and forbidding I had never seen. We saw Chinese restaurants of the poorest kind, and public-houses frequented by women so bloated and ill-formed that they hardly looked human. Some of them glared malevolently at me with their little black slit eyes, as if they would have liked to scratch and kill me.

I asked my conductor if the police were ever attacked when in such awful places, and he said very rarely, that the people there knew too well the consequences if they dared to molest a policeman.

He showed me the house in which Billie Carleton, the popular actress who doped, lived and met with such a tragic end. He took me down dark alleys, almost too narrow for two to walk abreast, into squares composed of squalid houses, and into cut-throat cul-de-sacs suggestive of all kinds of lurking horrors.

He told me that dreadful crimes were not so frequent in the East End of London as people imagined, that they occurred more frequently in the West End; and that regarding murders there were very few the perpetrators of which were not known to the police but who could not be arrested owing to lack of sufficient evidence. He mentioned one in which the identities of both victim and murderer were unknown to the police. It was the one where part of a woman was found in Brighton and the rest of her in King's Cross Railway Station.[1]

I well remember the murder of Georgina Hoffman in her flat in Dover Street in February, 1939. I was at a concert at the Four Provinces of Ireland Club one evening, sitting next to a journalist who was on the staff of a London paper. I was talking to her when she had a telephone call to tell her to go at once to Dover Street, where a murder had been committed. The next day I read particulars about the murder in the morning papers.

The girl was a prostitute and had been warned by her friends not to go with Arthur Mahoney, a sailor, the man who murdered her. It was a particularly atrocious murder as the poor girl was shockingly mutilated. One of her friends told me that she had had a presentiment of something terrible happening to her. The murderer was arrested, tried, found guilty and sentenced to death. This was later respited on the grounds of his insanity, and he was removed to Broadmoor, where he died sixteen months later.

In the autumn of 1939 O'Donnell had a flat at 20 Colville Terrace, Bayswater. It was then, for the one and only time, that I (the author) spoke

---

[1] On Sunday, June 17th, 1934, an offensively odoriferous trunk that had been lodged in the left luggage office of the cloak room at Brighton Station and was causing a nuisance there, was forced open by the police and found to contain the decomposing, decapitated, dismembered body of a woman. The next day, a porter in the left luggage office at King's Cross Station, his attention drawn by its unpleasant odour to a cheap brown suitcase, opened it, and found therein two legs and two feet, a second instalment, as it were, to the first discovery. The murder, which has gone down to posterity as Brighton Trunk Crime No.1, was never solved.

to him. He had just brought out from Quality Press, *Haunted Churches*. One critic greeted it, not without affection: "That staunch apostle of the queer, Mr. Elliott O'Donnell, is an author made of different stuff. His *Haunted Churches* is as full of macabre horror as an egg is of meat. His friendly and sometimes ingenuous style relieves it of morbidity. 'Exhaustive and patient researches' on his part have added zeal to his pen; so obviously does he enjoy himself among the mysteries that I can picture him tackling the next haunted church on his list with the zest with which a hungry schoolboy opens a birthday hamper of dainties from home. In the case of ghost books I find it difficult not to be sceptical. With Mr. O'Donnell I find equal difficulty in having the heart, or lack of it, to be sceptical, lest I should hurt the feelings of so kindly an enthusiast. Yet the whole idea of 'something accursed and strangely horrible' (the phrase is the author's) haunting sacred precincts seems to me to take as much explaining away as the presence of a lightning conductor on a church steeple. If God's House is not free from the presence of the Devil and things diabolical, here indeed is a theological tangle which Mr. O'Donnell, though writing much of the Devil (whom he is given to calling 'His Satanic Majesty'), makes no attempt to unravel. None the less, I commend his account of grimly supernatural goings-on in churches in or near London, in most of the counties in England, in Scotland and Wales, and even the Isle of Man. The Eastern Counties seem particularly full of ecclesiastical eeriness, the churchyards specialising in animal ghosts – werwolves, wertigers, and foxwomen. 'I have seldom heard of a case of a werdog,' he tells us. But a considerable number of his apparitions are 'horrible' headless dogs. I doubt whether I would find a headless dog so very horrible; at least it could not growl and yap at me. A strange story is told of the church of Perranzabuloe, in Cornwall: An old lady poking about one day in the churchyard found some good teeth, presumably false. Pocketing them, she took them home and put them on her dressing-table. She was awakened abruptly by sounds under the window, and presently a voice called out, 'Give me my teeth. Give me my teeth...' Badly scared, she leaped out of bed and threw them on to the road. Directly she did this, she heard queer footsteps patter away in the direction of the church. When she searched the road outside there was no sign of any teeth. Perhaps the teeth had a non-ghostly owner. And, by the way, at what point do footsteps sound 'queer'? What constitutes their abnormality? Hearing of supernatural phenomena in Bristol Cathedral, Mr. O'Donnell organised an all-night vigil. Among those who accompanied me was Miss Jean Colin, one of the prettiest and most charming Principal Boys I have seen at the Prince's Theatre. I can imagine few more delightful companions than Miss Colin for whiling away the small hours in a haunted cathedral. Besides, all members of the theatrical profession know when the ghost walks."

The clouds of war were gathering, and O'Donnell attended lectures in Notting Hill prior to qualifying as an air raid warden. Not being in dire need of the small weekly sum of money that a warden received, he became a part-time warden only, and was subsequently extremely glad that he had done so, as paid wardens were often confined indoors and compelled to do work which he would have found very irksome. As it was, he was assigned to a post near to his flat, and did only night time duty, which was mainly out of doors.

"I was fortunate in having as my chief warden an artist, who was deservedly popular, and with whom I have always maintained a very cordial friendship. From what I heard about some of the posts, the chief wardens were inclined to be very dominating. I was at the post when the declaration of war with Germany was reported on the wireless. A few days afterwards, the ominous wailing of a siren gave warning of a raid. I was only partly dressed as it was very early. Hastily putting on my remaining garments and a helmet, I rushed out of doors, to find several of my fellow wardens already in the street blowing their whistles (in those early days of the war we all had whistles) and shouting to people to keep indoors. The people were very calm. There was no panic, no one seemed at all scared; possibly those who might have been scared stayed indoors. One old man who was smoking his early morning pipe told me he was an old soldier who had served under General Graham in Africa. He asked me to have a cup of tea with him. I thanked him and expressed my inability to, as I was strictly there on duty.

The air raid warning proved to be groundless and it was not for some time that the bombing of London actually began. When that happened there were few nights without an alert warning. High explosive and incendiary bombs fell thick and fast in many London districts, and some in close proximity to my post. The idea entertained by so many young people that elderly people were invariably rattled by the raids was, in my experience, quite erroneous. Most of the wardens at my post in London were middle-aged and elderly, and I never saw one of them, even when heavy bombing was in close proximity to them, at all rattled. They never hesitated to get into remnants of buildings directly after a bomb had fallen, and when there was imminent danger of being crushed by falling masonry, to search for anyone still alive.

My chief warden had a novel way of encouraging us when an alert sounded; he used to whistle Chopin's Funeral March! My sole work as a part-time warden was patrolling the streets, sometimes alone but more often with another warden. People had always to be told to blackout all windows. Usually they were quick in complying, but occasionally we had a little trouble, principally in one or two streets of ill-repute. I remember in one such street nearly every night that I was patrolling a woman who had had one over the eight used to lie in the gutter outside the public-house in which she had been imbibing, shouting and screaming with all her might. Bombs! She did not care a bit for them, nothing scared her. All she wanted to do was remain where she was, undisturbed and bellowing, which she certainly did.

A young Welsh workman, who made no attempt to blackout, was very abusive when we spoke to him and declared in no choice language that he hated London and everyone in it and hoped the Germans would destroy it.

In some cases people could not blackout sufficiently because they lacked the means; they had no money with which to procure the necessary materials. Occasionally, someone, usually girls, would go away for a night or weekend, and leave a light burning in a room where there was no blackout.

I had to leave my flat unexpectedly and return temporarily to my former quarters in Bloomsbury, but I still continued to go to my post in Bayswater. I went there early in the evening and, unless there was a raid or I was needed for something else, I left about two in the morning. Usually I walked all the way back to Bloomsbury, a long distance. I did so because I disliked going by the Tube railway. Its platforms were crowded every night by people who slept in bunks, if there was room for them; if not, on the bare stone platform or staircases. The smell from such a crowd herded together so deep underground was nauseating, and consequently I much preferred being in the open. Groping my way along street after street in the dark, for there were no lights anywhere, was none too easy, and, familiar as I was with the way, I occasionally went astray. Sometimes I was caught in a sudden raid. Guns boomed, bombs fell and shrapnel showered down all around me. Luck favoured me; I was never hit. I rarely encountered anyone going either to or from the post. There was something almost uncanny in the sepulchral darkness, absence of human beings and stillness, except when there was a raid.

Owing to my half-sister and ex-guardian needing me, I had to leave London and go to Clifton, where she was still living.[2] For some months I alternated between London and Bristol, and came in for plenty of bombing in both places. I was staying in Little Russell Street, Bloomsbury, when doodlebugs fell in Drury Lane and Smithfield, killing many people and destroying several buildings. The sight of a doodlebug as it came roaring and rumbling through the sky was very nerve-trying, and there was always the dreadful anticipation of it suddenly stopping when seemingly directly overhead and hurtling down. The rockets were perhaps even more destructive, but I did not find them so harrowing. Their advent was so swift and sudden, and except for a momentary hissing and swishing as they sped downwards, they made no noise till the frightful blast which announced their hellish, death-dealing contact with the ground.

In Bristol I experienced some of the worst of the many raids. One night I was in Alma Road when there was a heavy thud. A high explosive bomb had fallen close by, completely destroying two houses and killing the inmates of one of them. During another raid I extinguished an incendiary bomb which fell in my sister's garden. That same night a dozen or more incendiary bombs fell in her road, at one end of which a warehouse was in flames and, close to the other end, All Saints' Church. The sky over Bristol rendered ruddy by the flames of the many burning buildings, presented a lurid inferno, not soon forgotten by those who witnessed it."

O'Donnell was now staying with his step-sister, Elizabeth, and felt very fortunate to have living next-door, at No.22 Alma Road, Joseph Norgrove, well known in the West country as a poet and as an authority on butterflies and moths, and his artistic, versatile and charming sister, Mrs. Nora Jeffery.

Although he had taken up his abode in Bristol, O'Donnell never ceased visiting London, where the chief attractions were its delightful literary salons and the company of his much valued friends, included among whom was Anton Dolin, the well-known ballet dancer. But, not possessing a car, and finding travelling there by train rather too expensive, he did

---

2   Still at Sherborne Villas, 24 Alma Road.

not manage to get there very often, which was a sore grievance. In March, 1940, a letter was addressed to him from one "Brother Savage" to another.[3] Brother Savage Frank Whitaker, former acting editor of *John O' London's Weekly*, wrote: "I am anxious to propose Mr. Harry Price, the psychical research man, for membership of the club, and I am in a little difficulty because the member who was going to second him, Professor C.E.M. Joad,[4] has just resigned and is therefore ineligible to do so. I have shown Price the list of members and he tells me that he used to know you some years ago. I am therefore writing to you on my own responsibility to ask if you would feel able to add your name to the proposal form." O'Donnell apparently did feel able to comply with Whitaker's request, for on April 26th, 1940, he received the tidings that Harry Price had been duly elected.

Elliott's sister, Petronella, died at Burnham-on-Sea, where she had lived for many years, in 1942. He wrote of her: "A natural blonde, she was very attractive in her youth. Genial and light-hearted, she had the happy knack of making friends wherever she went and was beloved by many in Clevedon and Burnham. Like Helena, she had an art training, but forsook painting and took to writing poems. Several volumes of her verse were published. She had a long, painful illness and bore it heroically, writing for the press until a few days before she died. Named Petronella after an ancestress, she was buried, at her earnest request, in the cemetery of Burnham Parish Church, within a short distance of the sea she loved so much. She was very fond of me and I of her, and her death was a great grief to me."

Just three years later, in 1945, his step-sister Elizabeth passed away. "Of her I cannot speak too highly or ever be grateful enough to her for all the kindness she showed me. The owner of considerable property in London and the Midlands, she was extremely generous and ever ready to help anyone in real distress. She was a devout churchgoer, but by no means bigoted. In her youth, though not handsome, she was attractive, with dark

---

3   All members of the Savage Club are known to each other as "Brother Savage".

4   Cyril Edwin Mitchinson Joad (1891-1953). Philosopher. After the Dragon School, Oxford, Blundell's School, Tiverton, and Balliol College, Oxford, where he gained a first in *literæ humaniores* (1914), joined the labour exchanges department of the Board of Trade. Became head of philosophy at Birkbeck College, University of London, in 1930. Involved himself in psychic research with the object of "demystifying the allegedly supernatural", and became a close friend of Harry Price. Author of many books on popular philosophy and a leading member of the panel of the B.B.C.'s programme, *The Brains Trust*.

hair and eyes, a fine figure and very lovely hands, like those of my mother. She was very musical and fond of the theatre. She lived to a great age and died peacefully."

A letter from Ivor Montagu reveals that in April, 1942, O'Donnell was hard at work finding out all he could about theatre and cinema in the Soviet Union. "There is no need for you to introduce yourself to me," wrote Montagu in reply to his research letter. "I read your books while still a schoolboy, and actually remember meeting you yourself when you came to our school sports ground one day; it must be about 28 years ago."

The war ended. O'Donnell continued to live in Bristol – from 1948 to 1956 at 8 Oakland Road, Redland. From 1961 to 1962 at 49 Trelawney Road, Bristol. His pen, which had been pretty well inactive since 1939, came resolutely back to life in 1948, when Rider published his *Haunted Britain*, which was the mixture much as before. It was dedicated "To Nora Jeffrey." [sic] He also began to lecture again.

The lecture platform had played quite a considerable part in his life. The first time that he ever addressed an audience was when he spoke to the Theosophical Society in Bath. His subject was "Hauntings in the West of England". And he read the manuscript which he had composed with somewhat laboured attention to expression and composition. For the first few minutes he was very nervous, but then settled down, felt more at home and gained confidence. The talk was well received and heartily applauded.

It was a long time before he plucked up the courage to lecture extempore. It was an American artist, Snow Gibbs, who came to one of his talks who advised him that it would be better if he did not read his lectures. He was absolutely terrified of breaking down when he faced the first audience he had ever spoken to without reading the talk. He managed, however, to get through the ordeal without any very obvious halting or hesitation, and the difficulty once overcome lecturing without reading soon became relatively easy. But even after many, many years' experience, O'Donnell was still always a little nervous when he rose to speak.

"I have lectured to a great variety of audiences, in all kinds of places – hotels, private houses, shops, stores, libraries, halls, parks, homes for the blind, famous schools, ships, cinemas, theatres; and to societies, clubs and universities. I never enjoy a meal on these occasions, as all the time I am eating I am fearful of forgetting half my talk. Such a catastrophe has, however, never yet occurred. I have only twice broken down. Once when I was asked quite unexpectedly to speak at a school house supper. I rose, uttered a few words, could not think of anything further to say, and sat down. The other time was when I was speaking before a large audience at a club in the West of England. I was not halfway through my talk when I clean forgot what I was talking about. I stammered out my regret at not being able to continue, and sat down horribly abashed.

At a talk I gave in the auditorium of Selfridge's, Miss Margot Graham, the well-known film star, kindly took the chair for me. I was in the middle of relating a particularly harrowing haunting when something close to me gave a loud ominous crack that startled everyone. It proved to be the glass tumbler on the table in front of me that, with no apparent cause, suddenly cracked without anyone touching it. During the same year I gave a talk on ghosts at Harrods. At both these stores there were large audiences.

I much enjoyed the talks that I gave to Rugby, Marlborough, Uppingham and Aldenham. The boys were always extremely well behaved and appeared to be interested in all I said. At Rugby I stayed a night in the house of one of the masters, and after my talk in the Big School he said that the boys in one of the dormitories wanted me to tell them more about my ghostly experiences. So I acquiesced and told them enough ghostly horrors to give them the worst of nightmares. Not a hair on any of their young heads rose, however, and they kept me talking till the housemaster interposed and rescued me. I could not help comparing the fortitude they displayed regarding ghosts to that of the children in the village where I once lived, whose mothers angrily declared that the mere hearing of my writing about hauntings had terrified their offspring to such an alarming degree that they dared not venture out of doors alone in the dark. I have given talks to girls' schools, too, but I have never felt quite the same amount of ease in speaking to girls as I have in speaking to audiences of boys. Boys seem to evince their feelings more openly than girls do. I can tell better if I am interesting them.

When I was asked to give a talk on ghosts at a Bristol cinema I hesitated. I had considerable qualms as to whether I could hold such a mixed audience, few of whom might be interested in the subject. I felt more than a little apprehensive when I climbed up the steps on to the narrow space between the screen and the edge of the stage. The manager introduced me, and then, screwing up my courage, I launched forth, fully expecting numerous interruptions. I was very agreeably surprised. Apart from a little coughing and scraping of feet there was silence, and I succeeded in holding the audience. I received quite a number of letters afterwards from people who had been present, expressing their interest in what I had said.

A harrowing incident occurred when I was in a train bound for York, near which town I was to lecture. The train was about to leave a station en route when a queer little man in a long brown overcoat got into the carriage and plumped himself down by the window on the seat opposite me. He had black hair and whiskers and large, round brown eyes. He had no luggage and no paper, and I had nothing to lend him. He sat motionless, his eyes staring vacantly in front of him. He gave me a creepy feeling; he looked so mad. There were only the two of us in the carriage; it was a non-corridor train and stopped at nearly every station. After a while, he rose from his seat suddenly and began to open the door. Feeling sure that he was a lunatic and about to jump out of the train, I sprang up, gripped hold of him, and tried to pull him back. Though so little, he was very strong, and a desperate struggle took place. All the while he kept jabbering in a language I did not understand. Despite my efforts, the door was gradually opening when, to my infinite relief, we stopped at a station. The little man got out, and it transpired that, far from wanting to commit suicide, he had been wanting merely to free his coat, which had stuck in the doorway when he got into the train and closed the carriage door. He had tried to tell me this, but, being a foreigner and knowing only a few words of English, he had not been able to make me understand.

I have twice given talks on ghosts in churches in London. One of my talks was in St. Bartholomew's, in Smithfield, reputed to be haunted by the phantom of Father Rahere, the founder of the church, whose footsteps are alleged to be heard at times pacing up and down the ambulatories. Prior to the talk, I had spent a night in the church with two psychical researchers. For about an hour I was shut in alone, but nothing ghostly occurred, although I felt at times the near presence of the supernatural.

The other London church at which I spoke was St. Peter's, in Windmill Street.[5] I was not feeling well at the time and before my talk I went to my club, which was not far from the church, and had a single glass of sherry. I happened to mention this to a friend within the hearing of a lady member of the congregation, who spread the rumour that I drank. There could not

---

5   This talk took place on June 23rd, 1940.

be anything more untrue, as any of my friends can testify. Although not a teetotaller, I am very abstemious and rarely drink anything alcoholic. Consequently I was very indignant on being told what the woman had said about me. It is a great pity that people who go to church or chapel, and pride themselves on being good Christians, do not always behave as such, but are addicted to saying scandalous things likely to do other people serious harm.

I always enjoy giving talks to women's clubs. At a dinner at the Lyceum Club, in London, a lady narrated an interesting case of what was apparently a phantom of the living. Some friends of hers, in the south-west of Ireland, had a room in their house which they believed to be haunted by the apparition of a little boy in a sailor suit. He was often to be seen in the afternoon, racing round the bedstead. The inmates of the house had become so used to seeing him that they were no longer afraid. There was nothing in the least degree evil in the appearance of the ghost. So far as they were able to ascertain there was nothing in the history of the house, no known tragedy, to account for the haunting. One day an elderly gentleman came to the house and asked if he might see over it. He said he had lived in it in his childhood, and had a great affection for it even yet. Permission being willingly granted him, he went from floor to floor, manifesting extreme interest. When he came to the haunted room, he said: 'This was my nursery. I frequently dream I am chasing my little sister round the bedstead, like I used to do when a small boy.' The lady of the house, struck by the strange coincidence, enquired if he had ever had such a dream during the day. 'Yes,' he said, 'when I take an afternoon nap.' She then asked him if he had a photograph of himself as a little boy. His reply was in the affirmative and, on his return to his home, he sent her a photograph of himself in a sailor suit. The moment she saw it, she identified it as the ghost, as did all the other members of the household who had seen the supposed apparition.

At a lecture I gave at the Caxton Hotel, London, a lady told me of an amusing experience she had once had. For some time she had been afflicted with an optical illusion in the form of a well-dressed woman, who came at a certain hour every afternoon and sat in a chair in her drawing-room. She could never properly discern the face of the intruder. Becoming very worried, she consulted a Harley Street specialist, who advised her to sit in the chair immediately after it was occupied by the spectre. The lady took his advice, so implicitly and literally that one day in the dusk of a late afternoon she seated herself in the chair a moment after the supposed spectre had occupied it, when, to her great dismay, she found herself perched on the lap, not of a ghost, but on that of a real flesh and blood person – a visitor.

I was haunted for some time by a very queer man, who used to come to my lectures. He had grey hair, a beard, and a very white face. He wore black clothes, and never spoke. He was always alone, and if anyone chanced to sit near him they always quickly moved to another place. My curiosity aroused, I enquired the reason, and was told that he gave people the feeling that they were sitting next to a corpse, and that he smelt like one. He certainly looked more dead than alive. I never learned his name or how he found out when and where I was lecturing. He was – and remains – a mystery man.

I am very fond of animals and have spoken many times on their behalf. I once spoke in Hyde Park. It was in April, and the wind and dust were very trying. When I said how very sad it was to part with dogs we were very fond of, and that I believed we might meet them again in the Hereafter, someone in the crowd cried: 'You won't meet them again. Animals have no souls.' A lady at once said: 'How do you know? Dogs have a much better chance of a happy hereafter than many men who are far worse than any animal.' That created a regular babel of angry male voices. I at length managed to restore order and told the disturbers to clear off, which they did. I thanked the lady who had spoken, and said I fully agreed with her. In my opinion, the law is far too lenient with regard to cruelty to animals. Every year one reads in the newspapers of shocking cruelty, chiefly by boys, and the punishment awarded them by magistrates is generally trivial. I have given much time and more money than I have been able to afford in speaking on behalf of animals, but I don't regret it."

The cover of O'Donnell's Phantoms of the Night (1956).

17

The Twilight Zone

Never one to let the grass grow under his feet, O'Donnell did not vegetate after settling back in Bristol. He continued scribing and spectre hunting with an energy that would have done credit to a twenty-year-old, never mind a man of getting on for four times that age.

Its coming to his ears that a maisonette in the vicinity of Broadmead had garnered the reputation of housing a ghost, he made it his business to contact the lady who lived there. She confirmed that she had frequently heard ghostly footsteps come from the bathroom and ascend a staircase leading to the top floor, where there were several bedrooms, in one of which she and her baby slept, and seen the apparition of an old woman in a brown garment, with a very evil face, enter the room and steal menacingly towards the baby's cot.

Accompanied by a representative of the local press and members of a Bristol sound recording service, he held a night vigil in the maisonette. Wires connected a microphone to a van outside, thus enabling the lady in the maisonette to communicate with two people in the van, who would record any noise that might be heard.

O'Donnell took up a position outside the bathroom, the lady and her baby were, with a friend, in the room on the floor above with the child in the cot.

About 2 a.m., O'Donnell fancied that he heard something moving in the bathroom, the door of which he had carefully closed. He opened the door at once and scanned the room with his electric torch. There was nothing visible to account for what he had thought that he heard. Almost directly afterwards, there was an appalling scream and the sound of a thud. Everyone rushed to the room with the baby, where they found the lady of the maisonette on the floor in an apparent dead faint.

On recovering, she said that she had seen the ghost of the old woman with the evil face enter the room and make for the baby in the cot. It was then that she had screamed and fainted.

The night passed without anything further happening, and O'Donnell came away with an open mind.

Bristol in olden days contained many convents and monasteries, and several buildings erected on their sites have, from time to time, been said to be haunted. He felt it possible that the house containing the maisonette might have been built on such a site, which could account for the haunting.

Some months after his rather less than satisfactory experience in the maisonette, O'Donnell spent a night in a haunted house near Brislington. The phenomena complained of were mainly the mysterious disappearance and reappearance of various objects, inability to sleep comfortably in one of the bedrooms, owing to sensing there the presence of something alarmingly ghostly, the manifestation of a phantom woman on the hall staircase, and a feeling of intense dread when on a certain stair.

Mrs. B., the lady of the house, gave as a possible, if not probable, explanation of the eerie happenings, a strange story, the gist of which was that the owner of the house had stipulated when letting it to Mrs. B. that one room, containing a trunk, should be kept undisturbed and locked. Mrs. B. had promised to respect this demand, but had not kept her word. She had disturbed the contents of the room, and this infringement had led to the haunting, which had begun soon after the death of the owner of the house. It was her phantom, said Mrs. B., that she had seen on the staircase.

Accompanied as before by a representative of the local press, O'Donnell held vigil in the house. At his suggestion, Mrs, B. and a friend sat that night in a room on the ground floor. They experimented with a planchette. O'Donnell stood on the staircase, which was seemingly the worst haunted place.

He experienced nothing definitely awesome when he stood on the stair of dread; simply a rather creepy feeling, which was only to be expected after what he had been told. He was still there when a cry from the ground floor made him dash down to find out what had happened. Mrs. B. said that when she was holding the planchette, invisible hands snatched it from her and threw it on the ground. She and her friend appeared to be much agitated. The planchette was certainly lying on the floor near the table, and both ladies assured him that no one had put it there.

After a few minutes, when the press man and O'Donnell were in a room next to the one in which Mrs. B. and her friend were sitting, they heard a commotion and someone cried, "Come. Come at once!" They rushed in and found the two ladies very perturbed. They said they had seen a gruesome luminous something enter the room. Whatever it was, it had vanished before O'Donnell got there. They were undoubtedly badly scared. He stayed with them until they had largely recovered from their fright, but before leaving he suggested that they should get a clergyman to try to exorcise the ghost.

"They took my advice and got a local parson to come to the house. News of his advent becoming known, a large crowd, including a number of photographers, collected outside the house. I asked Mrs. B. to let me know if the attempt to exorcise the ghost had been successful, but I never heard from her, nor learned anything further about the haunting. How much of it was due to her fancy I cannot say. I certainly never heard or saw anything ghostly while I was in the house."

The *Daily Mail* of January 3rd, 1948, bore witness, if that were needed, to Elliott O'Donnell's continuing fame and prestige as ghost huntsman *extraordinaire*. Under the headline "Ghostly Forms in the Tax Office", it informed its readers: "The Inland Revenue authorities in Bristol have been asked by Mr. Elliott O'Donnell, investigator of ghosts and crime, if he can stay the night in their taxation office at Oldbury House, St. Michael's Hill, Bristol, to find out if it is haunted. The house was built in the 17th century and there have been many reports of eerie happenings there."

History is silent as to the result of his application, but, knowing the prevalent mentality of government offices and officials, that the requested permission would be granted seems unlikely.

He had, back in March, 1933, similarly applied to the Central Criminal Court, London's Old Bailey, to spend a night there. His letter drew the following response from the Keeper of the building: "I am in receipt of your letter of the 1st inst. Your request is somewhat unusual, but it can no doubt be arranged. Would you give me a call one day when you are next in London and we can discuss details. The building is patrolled every night by watchmen – I only mention this in case it might be a circumstance which would spoil your research."

Five years seem to have elapsed. On January 5th, 1938, the Keeper writes: "Dear Mr. O'Donnell, I have enclosed you an official permit to visit here to assist you in your research, and I note your undertaking not to exploit it by any publicity. On your arrival will you explain to the night watchman exactly where and what you propose doing – as they have to patrol the building during the night. Could you let me know the time you propose arriving at the building."

History is again silent as to the outcome.

It was around this time that an old friend, Dr. Eric J. Dingwall, resurfaced. He wrote, on May 9th, 1949, from 19 Grange Court, Cambridge:

> Dear O'Donnell,
> Good! Would tea with me at the Univ. of London Club, 21 Gower St. (opp. School of Tropical Hygiene, Malet St.) do at 4.30 p.m. on May 25 (Wed.) I shall probably be at The B.M. [British Museum] till 4.15 that day. Let me know. Good to hear from you. I want all the dope and have some too!
>
> Yrs.
> Dingwall.

Dr. Dingwall (1890-1986), who was also a friend of the author's, was affectionately known as 'Dirty Ding', because, as an honorary assistant keeper in the department of printed books in the British Museum, he had charge of the locked cupboard of erotic material. He had an expert knowledge of the medical and scientific literature concerning normal, abnormal, and criminal sexual behaviour, and, regarding the latter, would give lectures to the police. The author of such disparate volumes as *Artificial Cranial Deformation*, *Male Infibulation*, *The Girdle of Chastity*, *How to go to a Spirit Medium*, *Ghosts and Spirits in the Ancient World*, *Some Human Oddities*, *Very Peculiar People*, and *The American Woman*, he was also a veteran psychic researcher. He had investigated spiritualism with the great illusionist and escapologist, Houdini, and debunked Borley Rectory, the so-called most haunted house in England.

In 1948, after decades of having been lapsed, O'Donnell decided to apply for renewed membership of the Society for Psychical Research, and wrote on this score to Dingwall, who replied:

> My dear O'Donnell,
> <u>So</u> ashamed about your letter which got buried just as I was leaving for the Continent and only turned up today. Yes, do send the S.P.R. form.

Of course I will second it for you.

No, thank you! Am too old for vigils in churches. We are not all able to keep young like you! Wonderful man!

Yrs. ever,
E.J. Dingwall

He was duly elected, but it would seem, that he maintained his subscription for only a single year.

A final letter from Dingwall is worth quoting. It was written from "My new address – Pine Hill, Crowhurst, Sussex, on April 5th, 1956.

My dear O'Donnell,

You miracle! That shows what the young in heart can do. I was quite horrified at your letter with all your mishaps and here you are perking up again and hale and hearty. I am pleased, and well done, well done!

I have left Cambridge as you can see as it was getting me down and have moved here where I share a house. Can't you get someone to live with! I wish you could, but I know that now it is pretty hopeless.

I have no news. Black Magic is in the news and I almost wrote to you recently to ask if you ever heard of THE SHINERS, a sort of sexual black magic group operating in Cambridge about 1892 or thereabouts, or perhaps a bit later.

If ever I am in the Bristol area I'll look you up. I don't suppose you are ever down this way. This house is out of the world buried in a pine wood. The few neighbours that we have think the Devil has arrived in the person of your old friend who sends all the very best.

From
Dingwall.

That great historian of the London theatres, W. Macqueen-Pope, wrote, on December 6th, 1951, in reply to a letter which O'Donnell had written to him regarding the Man in Grey, the ghost at the Theatre Royal, Drury Lane.

"The spectre is that of a dandy of the late eighteenth century, young, slim, and handsome, wearing a three-cornered hat over a curled and powdered wig, a long grey riding cloak, knee-breeches, and buckled shoes. He was seen in 1938 by a woman cleaner. He was seen by the entire cast of Ivor Novello's *The Dancing Years* in 1939. When, more than a century ago, Drury Lane was partly rebuilt, a hollow wall concealing a bricked-up room was revealed at the left side of the stage. Huddled on its floor were the remains of a skeleton of a man with a knife in his ribs."

Macqueen-Pope had a theory as to how this old tragedy had come about. The young bloods used to be allowed on the stage of the old Drury Lane Theatre, where they would sit smoking, drinking, and ogling the girls. "I believe that this young man had a girl-friend in the theatre. She was probably a favourite of the manager. The young man was ordered out. He refused to go. He became a nuisance. In the ensuing brawl he was stabbed and his body was walled-up in the little pass-door passage which had known his nightly travels from the stage to the back of the auditorium."

"Thanks for your letter of the 3rd inst. Sent over to me from Theatre Royal, Drury Lane, on the staff of which I am, and whose historian I am too," wrote Pope. "I fear a night vigil would be of little use so far as the Ghost is concerned. He is a day time visitant. Never yet has he been seen before 9 a.m. or after six p.m. Between those hours... his visitations are quite frequent although irregular. Nor does anyone know who he is. All sorts of psychic societies have visited the theatre with me. When next you are in town I should be glad to see you."

O'Donnell's *Ghosts With a Purpose* was published by Rider in 1951. Here, announced the blurb, "the well-known author of over forty books on ghostlore and the macabre, has collected numerous authentic cases which demonstrate that ghostly phenomena are not always without purpose, that some times they do occur for a very definite reason."

And he certainly supplied a fine selection of the phantasmic – benevolent ghosts warning of danger; malevolent ghosts luring people to their doom; apparitions of the dead; spectres whose appearances were peculiar to certain nights in the year; those hooligans of the spirit world, poltergeists; hauntings leading to legal proceedings; the actual presence of a ghost in court during a murder trial; heads without bodies; bodies without heads; phantom hands; phantom feet; animal ghosts; haunted clocks; phantom coaches; phantom ships; banshees, "fetches"; corpse candles; ghosts haunting trees and pools. Equally diverse are the locuses – Bloomsbury, Chelsea, Hyde Park, Norwood, Essex, Yorkshire, Staffordshire, Warwickshire, Leicestershire, Wiltshire, Gloucestershire, Devonshire, Edinburgh, Dublin, and the Isle of Man.

It was a case of ghost hunters with a purpose in 1952, when, according to the *Sunday Dispatch* of May 11th, under the direction of "Mr. Elliott O'Donnell, the ghost hunter and psychic author", Bristol University students, guided by the spirit of a dead nun, were searching for buried treasure under a seventeenth-century house on St. Michael's Hill, Bristol.[1]

After two table-rapping séances at midnight in the house, which was built on the site of a mediæval convent, Mr. O'Donnell was lead to an old well which had lain undiscovered beneath the cellars for perhaps more than four centuries. There, in a dark cobwebbed corner of what must have been the crypt of the convent, the students, stripped to the waist, dug down into the clay and rubble that filled the old shaft. At a depth of five feet, Cliff Perriam, geology student and scrum-half of the University Rugby team, struck solid brick.

Taking it in turns in the two-and-a-half-foot diameter shaft, Bill Ripley, studying chemistry, Bill Bingham (history), and Doug Phillips, who is to be a veterinary surgeon, helped us to scrape away the remaining soil. They laid bare what appeared to be a brick-and-stone wall. It had a hollow ring, and is believed to conceal the entrance to a secret passage described at the séance.

The haunted house on St. Michael's Hill is built on the ruins of the Convent of St. Mary Magdalene, founded in 1174 and destroyed by Henry VIII. For the past seven years the woman who owns it and her young daughter have been troubled by strange happenings. Violent vibrations shake the walls at night. Doors slam suddenly. The daughter of the house frequently finds her nylon stockings mysteriously knotted next morning or the buttons of a coat or blouse done up, apparently by no human agency.

Last week I watched the séance which led to the treasure hunt. Mr. O'Donnell, the owner, her daughter, and five friends sat in a circle in near-darkness with hands placed before them on a heavy deal table. As the clock of St. Michael's church struck midnight the table began to vibrate, then to move.

"Have you a message for us?" asked Mr. O'Donnell.

The table lifted and rapped once, signifying "Yes".

Mr. O'Donnell: "Who are you, who wishes to speak to us from the other side?"

Slowly rapping through the alphabet, the table topped at the letter 'S'. Then, "S... I... S..." until it spelt out "Sister Mary."

Letter by letter a strange story seemed to be unfolded. Ever recurring was an emphatic instruction "D... I... G" and "Jewels corner of passage."

This is the story the table purported to tell: Sister Mary, a nun, killed Sister Angela at the corner of a secret passage beneath the convent. She buried jewellery under he floor there. Later, in remorse, she threw

---

[1] Article by *Sunday Dispatch* reporter, Anthony Hunter.

herself down another well. She has haunted the area since, can find no rest until her bones are recovered and buried and the treasure is dug up and sent to a church in Italy. At this point the table 'went dead' and would move no more. The whereabouts of the two wells in the cellar were minutely described.

Down went the party into the cellar and beneath an old flagstone was discovered the shaft of the second well, said to lead to the secret passage. Mr. O'Donnell decided to act at once. With pickaxes, crowbars, and cold chisels the students assembled at the house early yesterday. (Saturday). A massive flagstone had to be lifted from the top of the well before they could scoop out the rubble and clay. After probing the brick surface, which seemed slightly curved, as if it were the top of an arch, the treasure-seekers decided to suspend operations until an expert could examine the brickwork."

O'Donnell manifested in London on Hallowe'en, October 31st, 1952, His presence was announced by the *Daily Graphic*, November 1st: "In London last night, the night of the ghosts, was phantom-hunter Elliott O'Donnell, up from Bristol to talk to the Three Arts Centre. Subject? Ghosts, of course. He has written more than 50 books about them. Mr. O'Donnell has heard many ghosts, but admits that he has seen few. Now he is planning three ghost hunts in London. One of the ghosts is said to be that of a woman murdered in a Chelsea house; a man who runs up and down a staircase in Red Lion Square; and a woman who was murdered in the next-door house in the square last century."

In 1954, Elliott was eighty-two. Between then and 1958, he would produce five more books, published consecutively, one per year, by Rider. The first of these was *Dangerous Ghosts*. Dedicated "To Nora" [Jeffery], it presented a very comprehensive variety of ghostly phenomena that are "physically, mentally and morally dangerous."

Next came *Haunted People* (1955). The book dealt with haunted royalties, haunted historical people, haunted non-historical people, haunted families, and people haunted by dreams.

Phantoms of the Night, which appeared in 1956, was dedicated "In Fondest Memory of My Wife." Arranged geographically, it was a gathering of good yarns, English, Scottish, and Welsh, woven into the expected felicitous pattern of exciting psychic incidents, and carried the conscientious *caveat*: "The contents of this book vary as regards evidential quality, but in all there is a factual foundation."

The year 1957 brought *Haunted Waters*. Here the rivers, lakes, pools and wells of England, Ireland, Scotland and Wales are scanned for the phantoms and legends that rise like spray about them. "Primitive man," says O'Donnell, "gazing at a rushing river, cataract, deep, still lake or pool experienced... a feeling of awe such as, he reasoned, could only be produced by something more than the mere physical. Hence he derived the notion that such waters harboured the types of spirit likely to cause such an impression. Calm, sun-lit waters, causing a more pleasing effect, he came to regard as harbouring kinder and less repellent and forbidding spirits. The brook, leaping down the hillside, like a gambolling child, winding its sparkling way amid flowering meadows, created visions of gay and charming fairies. Lakes, pools, and rivers all had in the course of time their own peculiar species of spirit... To the mind of Early Man water acted not by laws of force, but by life and will. He believed that the rush and calmness of water, its cruelty and kindness, its power to work him weal or woe, to give him food or cramp and drown him was not due solely to the physical but to the superphysical, that all the actions of water were due to beings of another world, and to gain their goodwill he worshipped them; not satisfied with merely praying to them he offered them sacrifices of animals and human beings. Though water-worship has ceased, there is still a lingering credulity in Peg Powler, the English Lorelei, that haunts the Tees and other North Country rivers; in water wraiths that haunt certain English lakes and pools; ghost lights that hover over Welsh waters prognosticating death; glaistigs that haunt Scottish streams; and ghosts of various kinds that haunt the lakes and rivers of Ireland. Nixies, spirits that lure people to death by drowning, would seem to be ubiquitous. Certain wells are reputed to have magical qualities; there are holy-wells, into which people still drop pins, nails and rags, praying that their wishes may be granted."

And, finally, in 1958, *Trees of Ghostly Dread*. This was, in effect, his last book, for others, subsequently issued and bearing his name on their spines, were no more than anthologies. In it he wrote: "To the mind that is at all imaginative there is often something very ghostly in the appearance of trees in the dusk; their fantastically fashioned, knotted and gnarled branches can bear such an unpleasant resemblance to bony arms with long, curved fingers outstretched, as if in readiness to pounce on one. The rustling of the leaves as a breeze stirs them sounds like whispering voices, and the singing and moaning of the wind like the crying and wailing of lost souls. Shadows of trees on moonlight nights assume strange shapes that sometimes seem to bear little or no likeness to the trees themselves or to any surrounding objects. Should the night be still, there is something solemn and mysterious in the prevailing hush, a sense of brooding and concentration in which the trees play a prominent part. They give the impression that they and everything around them are momentarily expecting the advent of something startlingly weird and supernatural... who can wonder if throughout the ages there has been a credulity in haunted trees and woods."

In the December of 1957, shortly before Christmas, Kenneth Allsop, book columnist of the *Daily Mail*, who was in process of reviewing *Haunted Waters*, travelled to Bristol, to the flat at 8 Oakland Road, Redland, to interview O'Donnell.

Allsop wrote: "Until I picked up a book entitled *Haunted Waters*, by Elliott O'Donnell this week, it had been my impression that ghosts nowadays were having a struggle to keep body and soul together. I can't think when I last saw a poltergeist hogging the headlines. Most haunted houses clank only with the teacups of atomic energy research staffs. A real old-fashioned ghoul Yule seems to have died out with Dickens. Now at the patter of the tiniest invisible feet the Society for Psychical Research are round there with slide-rules, tape-recorders, and truth drugs to put the oldest-established spook out of business, and every cub psychiatrist learns how to exorcise incubi during his first fortnight on the Freud course. I would certainly have said that these brightly lit technological times were lean ones for the whole occult industry. Then along comes this packed dossier of ghost intelligence from Mr. O'Donnell, who is 86 and who is designated by his publisher as Britain's No. 1 Ghost Hunter.

Curious, I obtained Mr. O'Donnell's previous book, *Phantoms of the Night*, and my quick impression of the two was that barely a day goes by that Mr. O'Donnell is not shouldering his way through clammy crowds of the things somewhere up and down the country. This being the seasonal time, I thought I would go down to Bristol and see how the chase was going nowadays with the No. 1 Ghost Hunter. At this point I should say that I don't think I believe in ghosts. I once at the behest of a newspaper sat up all night in a candle-lit almshouse, and a most enjoyable assignment it was, since the poltergeist was after the 20-year-old granddaughter, who kept hearing noises and hurling herself into my protection. On the other hand, I have had two rather stranger experiences, one at Borley Rectory

('The most haunted house in England') and the other at Belsen, on the site of the death-camp.

To get back in the swim, I took Mr. O'Donnell's two books with me down to Bristol and dived into the steaming psychical stew. I didn't find them entirely convincing. For instance, that spot described in 'The Haunted Thames' chapter is only a skull's throw from Fleet Street, and the reported 'unearthly groans and hellish mocking laughter' was obviously only a nearby night news-editor reading copy. As for the story of the haunting of a house in Wigan by a dead murderer, I point blank don't believe that a ghost is going to hang around in Wigan.

When I arrived at Mr. O'Donnell's flat we didn't immediately get to grips with the supernatural. We talked about his family ('all wild and reckless') but that led inexorably to the subject. Among his forebears, he mentioned, were Charlemagne and Niall of the Nine Hostages. His grandfather commanded a privateer, the *Death or Glory*. His father, an adventurous parson, was murdered in Abyssinia.

'It was the start of my interest in the occult,' he continued, 'for the night before his death the family banshee was heard in our home.'

Mr. O'Donnell was a baby then, but when the banshee called again some years later – the head of the line had died in Ireland – not only he but his wife and six others heard it: 'Like a woman wailing inside the house, then drifting outside.'

On the table between us while we talked was a curious bottle containing a crude ivory carving of the crucifixion, with a wooden cork shaped as a cardinal's head.

'That has been in the family over 300 years – our talisman against evil spirits. At séances misty figures have been seen emerging from it.'

I looked closely, but the misty figures remained bottled.

I put the flat question to him: 'How many ghosts do you believe you have personally seen, heard, or felt?'

'I have had an uncountable number of probable psychic experiences,' he replied, 'but those which could not possibly be explained away number eight.'

Apart from nude figures with animals' heads, and immensely tall gargoyles met beside graveyards and in domestic settings, Mr. O'Donnell had also had corroborated experiences of seeing distant friends beside him – 'projection' cases. He has also on three occasions projected himself out of his body.

'Once in Chelsea without moving I concentrated on a woman I didn't much like across the room, and suddenly she cried out: "Stop it! I saw you move out of yourself and coming across to clutch my neck. It was dreadful!"'

He had been telling me of the 'extraordinary wild parties' he used to give in London in the '20s, between ghost-jaunts with Lord Curzon and the Duke of Newcastle, and at first I thought the Chelsea incident was just one of those parties. But he continued: 'Another time as I walked across the moors back to my house in St. Ives I managed to project myself ahead – saw myself entering the house miles away. When I *really* arrived my wife, who was entertaining friends to tea, was astonished. "But we all heard you come in earlier, walk up the hall, and stop outside the door," she said.'

His only dire danger came not from a ghost but from a fear-crazed colonel who, mistaking Mr. O'Donnell for the shade they were tailing, drew his revolver and opened fire at him. Fortunately, his hand was shaking so much that Mr. O'Donnell survived.

Nowadays his time is occupied lecturing and writing, and he said nostalgically: 'Haven't seen a ghost for years.'"

Elliott suffered "an irreparable loss", in January, 1963, by the death of "my dearest friend, Nora Jeffery", known in her youth as the Rossetti girl, on account of her remarkable resemblance to the red-haired young woman of Dante Gabriel's paintings.

He was invited in 1959 to edit for the London publisher, W. Foulsham, an anthology entitled *Ghosts: Stories of the Supernatural*. Of the 27 stories of which it was comprised, seventeen were in fact by him.

This was followed in 1964 and 1965, respectively, by two further Foulsham publications, in neither of which, however, the aged Elliott had a direct hand. The first, *The Screaming Skulls and Other Ghost Stories*, being a collection of 38 of his previously told tales, selected and arranged by Harry Ludlam, the author of a biography of Dracula. The second, *The Midnight Hearse and More Ghosts*, was a collection of a further 37 previously told tales from the files of Elliott O'Donnell, again selected and arranged by Harry Ludlam.

It would be a mistake to think that O'Donnell's interest was exclusively confined to the province of ghosts. In *Who's Who*, he listed his hobbies as "investigating queer cases, inventing queer games, and frightening crooks within the law. Walking and talking." He was fond of the theatre and, when he had the opportunity, would always go to musical comedies and to some dramas. He never cared for dancing, but liked to watch ballet. In his youth he had been a keen cricketer. His favourite recreations in his later years were "watching a public school cricket or rugger match." When young, he used to box a little. Now, he was very interested in reading accounts of international boxing. He did not care for cards or billiards and did not smoke. He had tried to once or twice in his younger days, but it did not agree with him and he had not persisted. As regards politics, he elected to be a freelance. That was his position also so far as religion was concerned. He had been brought up in the Church of England, and was nominally a Christian, but preferred not to restrict himself to any one denomination. What counted most in his view was how you treat other people. He believed that so long as you do not intentionally say or do anything that may harm them, and are not wilfully unkind to animals, you are on the right road to a better world when you leave this one, and to a worse one if you behave to the contrary.

The cover of O'Donnell's The Screaming Skulls (1964).

The cover of O'Donnell's The Midnight Hearse (1965).

The cover of O'Donnell's Casebook of Ghosts (1969).

THE DENNIS WHEATLEY
LIBRARY OF THE OCCULT

THE SORCERY CLUB
Elliott O'Donnell

In 1974, O'Donnell's novel *The Sorcery Club* was reprinted as part of
Dennis Wheatley's Library of the Occult. In his Introduction to the novel, Wheatley
wrote that he had met O'Donnell only once, and not particularly liked him.

18

Passing the Gate

Vitæ summa brevis spem nos vetat incohare longam.

They are not long, the weeping and the laughter,
Love and desire and hate:
I think they have no portion in us after
We pass the gate.

They are not long, the days of wine and roses:
Out of a misty dream
Our path emerges for a while, then closes
Within a dream.

Ernest Dowson.

"As one grows old... losses increase... friend after friend dies. The hearts that used to throb so joyously when we met have ceased to beat; hands that grasped us so warmly lie cold and clammy in the grave. We are too old to make friends like the friends that knew us in our early days. New friends, however kind, can never be quite like the friends we knew so well in the days of long ago.

I lost my brother, Brigadier Henry O'Donnell, C.M.G., in 1928. Popular in the Army and with all who knew him, he was a staunch friend of the British Legion and was given a full military funeral. A house in Bexhill is named after him.

I felt the death of my old nurse, Sarah Coldwell, and her sister, Fanny. They were devoted to my sisters and myself, and were with us from the time we were all children until they died. Like so many of the Irish families in older days, we regarded those who served us faithfully as friends more than as servants, and entertained great affection for them.

The deaths of my sisters and brother left me the last of my generation and, with so many of my oldest friends gone, I feel at times very, very lonely.

I am greatly looking forward to the possibility of seeing once again those I have liked and loved and who have passed on, most of them long before me.

I shall have no regret in leaving this world."

That leave-taking took place on Saturday, May 8th, 1965, at the Grosvenor Nursing Home, Victoria Road, in Clevedon, Bristol. He was ninety-three years old.

Once, talking to Peter Underwood at a meeting of the Ghost Club, he said: "Ghosts? I can't say I really know a great deal about them; perhaps I will know more when I become one, and then I'll try to contact you."

Sadly, he never did manage to do so.

Perhaps the best way is for *us* to contact *him*. And there is no better way to do that, than to recall him in characteristic full flow, happily retailing the charismatic moment of fulfilment in a successful ghostly investigation...[1]

"It was horribly dark and lonely, and although on the former occasion I did not feel the presence of the superphysical, I did so now, the very moment I crossed the threshold. Striking a light, I looked around me: I was in the damp and mouldy den that served as a kitchen; outside I saw the moon reflected on the black and silent water.

A long and sleek cockroach disappeared leisurely in a hole in the skirting as I flashed my light in its direction, and I thought I detected the movement of a rat or some large animal in the cupboard at the foot of the stairs. I forthwith commenced a search – the cupboard was empty. I must have been mistaken. For some minutes I stood in no little perplexity as to my next move. Where should I go? Where ought I to go if my adventure were to prove successful?

I glanced at the narrow, tortuous staircase winding upwards into the grim possibilities of the deserted hall and landings – and – my courage failed.

---

[1] This extract is taken from his account "No. – Southgate Street, Bristol", contained in his first ghost book, *Some Haunted Houses of England and Wales*. Eveleigh Nash, London, 1908.

Here, at least, I was safe! Should the Unknown approach me, I could escape by the same window through which I had entered. I felt I dare not! I really COULD not go any further. Seized with a sudden panic at nothing more substantial than my own thoughts, I was groping my way backwards to the window when a revulsion of feeling made me pause. If all men were poltroons, how much would humanity ever know of the Occult? We should leave off where we began, and it had ever been my ambition to go – FURTHER.

My self-respect returning, I felt in my pocket for pencil, notebook and revolver, and trimming my lamp I mounted the stairs.

A house of such minute dimensions did not take long to explore; what rooms there were, were Lilliputian – mere boxes; the walls from which hung the tattered remnants of the most offensively inartistic papers were too obviously Jerry built; the wainscoting was scarred, the beading broken, not a door fitted, not a window that was not either loose or sashless – the entire house was rotten, paltry, mean; I would not have had it as a gift. But where could I wait to see the ghost? Disgust at my surroundings had, for a time, made me forget my fears; these now returned reinforced: I thought of Miss Rudd's comparison with a morgue – and shuddered. The rooms looked ghastly! Selecting the landing at the foot of the upper storey, I sat down, my back against the wall... and waited.

Confronting me was the staircase leading up and down, equally dark, equally ghostly; on my right was what might once have been the drawing-room, but was now a grim conglomeration of bare boards and moonlight, and on my left was an open window directly overtopping the broad expanse of colourless, motionless water. Twelve o'clock struck, the friendly footsteps of a pedestrian died away in the distance; I was now beyond the pale of assistance, alone and deserted – deserted by all save the slimy, creeping insects below – and the shadows. Yes! the shadows; and as I watched them sporting phantastically at my feet, I glanced into the darkness beyond – and shivered.

All was now intensively suggestive and still, the road alone attractive; and despite my spartonic resolutions I would have given much to be out in the open.

The landing was so cramped, so hopeless.

A fresh shadow, the shadow of a leaf that had hitherto escaped my notice, now attracted and appalled me; the scratching of an insect made my heart stand still; my sight and hearing were painfully acute; a familiar and sickly sensation gradually crept over me, the throbbing of my heart increased, the most inconceivable and desperate terror laid hold of me: the house was no longer empty – the supernatural had come! Something, I knew not, I dare not think what, was below, and I KNEW it would ascend.

All the ideas I had previously entertained of addressing the ghost and taking notes were entirely annihilated by my fear – fear mingled with a horrible wonder as to what form the apparition would take, and I found myself praying Heaven it might not be that of an ELEMENTAL.

The THING had now crossed the hall (I knew this somehow instinctively) and was beginning to mount the stairs.

I could not cry out, I could not stir, I could not close my eyes: I could only sit there staring at the staircase in the most awful of dumb, apprehensive agonies. The THING drew nearer, nearer; up, up, UP it came until I could see it at last – see the shock-head of red hair, the white cheeks, the pale, staring eyes, all rendered hideously ghastly by the halo of luminous light that played around it. This was a ghost – an apparition – a *bonâ fide* phantasm of the dead! And without any display of physical power – it overcame me.

Happily for me, the duration of its passage was brief.

It came within a yard of me, the water dripping from its clinging clothes, yet leaving no marks on the flooring. It thrust its face forward; I thought it was going to touch me, and tried to shrink away from it, but could not. Yet it did nothing but stare at me, and its eyes were all the more horrible because they were blank; not diabolical, as Miss Rudd had described them, but simply Blank! – Blank with the glassiness of the Dead.

Gliding past with a slightly swaying motion, it climbed upstairs, the night air blowing through the bedraggled dress in a horribly natural manner; I watched it till it was out of sight with bated breath – for a second or so it stopped irresolutely beside an open window; there was a slight movement as of someone mounting the sill: a mad, hilarious chuckle, a loud splash – and then silence, after which I went home.

I subsequently discovered that early in the seventies [the 1870s, that is] a servant-girl, who was in service at that house, had committed suicide in the manner I have just described, but whether or not she had red hair I have never been able to ascertain."

Appendix

List of Stories by Elliott O'Donnell

Haunted Houses of London

1. No. – Baker Street, W. (The Clock that Struck Thirteen.)
2. No. – Earl's Court Road, S.W. (The Invisible Horror and the Frantic Ringing at the Bell.)
3. The Parks of London (The Woman of the Mist, etc.)
4. No. – York Road, S.E. (The Murder in the Snow.)
5. No. – Hibbert Road, Ealing (The Orange-Haired Footman.)
6. B––– Lunatic Asylum, S.E. (The Jabbering Head.)
7. 'Pitcraigie House,' Wellington Road, St. John's Wood ('Two Women Fair With Golden Hair.')
8. The Oriental Department of the British Museum (Katebit, the Notorious Mummy Case that inevitably brings bad luck, and Other Haunted Relics.)
9. The Gliding Dachshund of W––– Street, ETC. (The Silent Parrot, and the Black-and-Tan Mongrel.)
10. The Moving Staircase, ETC., of Wandsworth, S.W. (The Chattering Woman and the Awful Head of Wandsworth, S.W.)
11. No. – Chesham Square, W. (The Heavy Footsteps on the Stairs.)
12. Leicester Square, Piccadilly, Jermyn Street, Museum Street, ETC. (The Case of the Moving Brain, etc.)
13. 'The White House,' near Penge, and No. – Adelaide Road, Hampstead (The Woman With the Paraffin Can.)
14. No. – Edgware Road, W. (The Fatal Teeth.)
15. No. – Cheyne Walk, Chelsea, S.W. (The Eyeless Woman With the Spidery Fingers.)
16. Theories, Speculations and Enigmas

Ghostly Phenomena

17. "Elementals"
18. Phantasms of the Living and Dead. Death Warnings and Dreams.
19. The Hauntings of the Old Sydersterne Parsonage (1833), near Fakenham, and a Personal Experience in Sydenham.
20. Suggestions and Hypotheses

Byways of Ghostland

21. The Unknown Brain
22. The Occult in Shadows
23. Obsession, Possession
24. Occult Hooligans
25. Sylvan Horrors
26. Complex Hauntings and Occult Bestialities
27. Vampires, Were-wolves, Fox-Women, etc.

List of Stories by Elliott O'Donnell

28. Death-Warnings and Family Ghosts
29. Superstitions and Fortunes
30. The Hand of Glory; The Bloody Hand of Ulster; The Seventh Son; Birth-Marks; Nature's Devil Signals; Pre-Existence; The Future; Projection; Telepathy, etc.
31. Occult Inhabitants of the Sea and Rivers
32. Buddhas and Boggle Chairs

Scottish Ghost Stories

33. The Death Bogle of the Cross-Roads, Pitlochry
34. The Inextinguishable Candle of the Old White House
35. The Top Attic in Pringle's Mansion, Edinburgh
36. The Bounding Figure of ---- House, neat Buckingham Terrace, Edinburgh
37. Jane of George Street, Edinburgh
38. The Sallow-Faced Woman of No. – Forrest Road, Edinburgh
39. The Phantom Regiment of Killiecrankie
40. "Pearlin' Jean" of Allanbank
41. The Drummer of Cortachy
42. The Room Beyond. An Account of the Hauntings at Hennersley, near Ayr
43. ----- House, near Blythswood Square, Glasgow. The Haunted Bath
44. The Choking Ghost of ---- House, near Sandyford Place, Glasgow
45. The Grey Piper and the Heavy Coach of Donaldgowerie House, Perth
46. The Floating Head of the Benrachett Inn, near the Perth Road, Dundee
47. The Hauntings of ---- House, in the Neighbourhood of the Great Western Road, Aberdeen
48. The White Lady of Rownam Avenue, near Stirling
49. The Ghost of the Hindoo Child, or the Hauntings of the White Dove Hotel, near St. Swithin's Street, Aberdeen
50. Glamis Castle

Haunted Highways and Byways

51. The Corner of the Wall
52. How Eliza Came Home
53. The Ghost of the Bridge of B---
54. The Garden of Shadows
55. The Yarmouth Sands Hauntings
56. The Haunted Field
57. The Spotted Head
58. The Swing
59. The Strange Happenings at D--- Bungalow
60. "Dago's Ghost"

61. Train Ghosts
62. The Red Stag
63. The Phantom Football Player

More Haunted Houses of London
64. The Door That Would Never Keep Shut
65. The Phantom Teeth of Knightsbridge
66. The Two Ghost Houses of Red Lion Square
67. The Man Behind the Door
68. Atmosphere
69. The Figure on the Stairs
70. Nights in Hyde Park
71. Hauntings in Other Parks and Commons
72. Two Christmas Eves
73. A Hampstead Haunting
74. The Haunting of B--- School
75. Miscellaneous Hauntings

Ghosts Helpful and Harmful
76. The Man With the Scythe
77. Summoned to Save
78. The Brown Ghost of Hoddesdon
79. The Haunted Inn at Portsmouth
80. Saved by a Ghost Dog
81. The Lift Ghost
82. A Benevolent Phantasm of the Living
83. A Haunted Church
84. Saved from Suicide
85. A Strange Warning at Sea
86. The Haunted Bridge of Arran
87. Saved from the Tide
88. Finding a Packet of Letters Through a Dream
89. A Vital Warning in a Dream
90. A Dual Warning in Sleep
91. The Beag-Bbeul or Littlemouth
92. The Voice of the Unseen Again
93. The Ghost That Wanted to pay its Debts
94. The Book that would not be Lost
95. The Experience of Lord Chedworth

List of Stories by Elliott O'Donnell

96. A Ghost at the Telephone
97. Cured Through a Dream
98. Saved From Death by Their Mother's Ghost
99. The White Hand of Draycot
100. The Fatal Dice
101. The Supernatural in the Mutiny
102. The Guilsborough Ghost
103. A Benevolent "Trash"
104. Ghosts versus Burglars
105. The Ghost of Bedlam
106. The Crumbles Ghosts
107. The Shadow on the Wall
108. The Demon Horse of Upper Mayfield
109. The Strangling Ghost of Malta
110. The Ayah's Ghost
111. A Strangling Ghost in Bruges
112. Some of My Own Experiences
113. A Maida Vale Haunting
114. A Haunted Bed in Hampshire
115. The Haunting of No. – Berkeley Square
116. Malignant Heads
117. The Phantom Coach of the Vizes
118. The Phantom Coach of Caistor Castle
119. The Langley Hall Coach
120. The Bloody Coach of Doneraile
121. The Calverley Ghosts
122. Peg Powler
123. The Headless Hob of Hurworth
124. The Eleven Ghosts of Skellaw Wark
125. The Clock That Struck Thirteen
126. The Haunted Tree in Hyde Park
127. The House with the Evil Tree, near Guilsborough
128. The Case of the *Squando*
129. The Pig-Faced Phantom of Chelsea
130. Crippen's Ghost
131. A Wicked Ghost's Romance
132. Epilogue

Ghostland

133. My Earliest Experiences of Ghostland
134. Some Strange Tree Hauntings
135. More Uncanny Happenings in My Childhood
136. Irish and Other Fairies
137. On Clocks
138. On Bells and Candles
139. Corpse Candles and Other Hauntings
140. On Sympathy and Early Experiences of Projection
141. On Elementals and Curses
142. On Scottish Fairies
143. Further Irish Experiences
144. Some Queer Happenings in the United States
145. Mainly on Doubles and London Park Ghosts
146. More Park and Some Common Hauntings
147. The Hauntings of the Thames Embankment and Some Recent Cases
148. Still Further Cases and a Final Word

Ghosts of London

149. The Tower of London and Bethlehem Asylum
150. St. James's Palace, the Green Park and St. James's Park
151. Berkeley Square and Red Lion Square
152. Bloomsbury
153. Bloomsbury (continued) and Westminster
154. Lincoln's Inn, The Temple, Greyfriars, Charterhouse, St. Bartholomew's the Great, and Newgate
155. Hyde Park
156. Blackfriars and Highbury
157. Holland House, London Bridges and Chick Lane
158. Bird Hauntings and Blackheath Ghosts
159. Spring-Heeled Jack and the Brompton Road
160. Haymarket Theatre, Ham House and Cranford House
161. Club Hauntings and Some Strange Happenings in Soho and Bloomsbury
162. The Thames and Kilburn
163. Highgate, Hampstead and South Kensington
164. Barnes Common, Bethnal Green and St. Anne's Churchyard
165. St. Paul's and Cripplegate
166. The Cock Lane Ghost
167. Stockwell, Wandsworth Common, Chelsea and Ghostly Clocks

List of Stories by Elliott O'Donnell

168. Enfield Chase, South Mimms, Cheshunt, etc.

Family Ghosts

169. Phantom Birds
170. Fish, Bat and Tree Ghosts
171. Ghost Trees
172. Phantom Ivy, Bells and Clocks
173. Hauntings by Phantom Monks and Dogs
174. Phantom Monks and Nuns, and the Haunting of the Radclyffe Family
175. English Phantom Drummers
176. The Hauntings of Berry Pomeroy and Rainham
177. Phantom Cars, Coaches, Armour-Clad Knights and Cauld Lads
178. The Drummer of the Airlies
179. The Phantom Light of the St. Clairs and Pearlin Jean
180. 'Green Ladies', 'White Ladies' and Other Ghosts
181. The Grey Man and Phantom with the Silver Bracelet
182. Glamis Castle and the Haunting of the Lyon Family
183. Fyvie and Closeburn
184. The Gwyrach-Y-Rhibyn
185. Haunted Welsh Bridges and Ghosts that follow Families
186. Banshees
187. Banshees, Phantom Coaches and the Cathach of the O'Donnells
188. The Haunting of the Bourbons and Bonapartes
189. More French Family Ghosts and the White Lady of the Hohenzollerns
190. The White Lady and the Black Lady
191. Scandinavia, Polish, Russian and Italian Ghosts
192. American Ghosts and Conclusions

Haunted Churches

193. London's Haunted Churches
194. Haunted Churches Near London
195. Haunted Churches Near London (continued)
196. Haunted Churches Near London (continued)
197. Haunted Midland Churches
198. Some Leicestershire Haunted Churches
199. Warwickshire and Shropshire Hauntings
200. Herefordshire and Worcestershire Church Ghosts
201. Hauntings in Notts, Oxfordshire and Yorkshire
202. Yorkshire Haunted Churches (continued)

203. More Yorkshire Ghosts
204. Durham and Lancashire Church Ghosts
205. More North Country Hauntings
206. Haunted Churches in the Eastern Counties
207. Haunted Churches in the South of England
208. Haunted Churches in the South of England (continued)
209. Haunted Churches in the West of England
210. Haunted Churches in the West of England (continued
211. Welsh Church Ghosts
212. The Churchyard Where the Grass would not Grow
213. Haunted Churches in Scotland
214. Haunted Churches in Scotland (continued)
215. More Scottish Church Hauntings
216. Isle of Man Ghosts
217. American Haunted Churches

Haunted Britain
218. Windsor Castle and Its Ghosts
219. Hampton Court Palace
220. The Tower of London Ghosts
221. Haunted Churches and Hospitals
222. Some Haunted London Theatres and Other Buildings
223. Other London Hauntings
224. More London Hauntings
225. More London Hauntings
226. More London Hauntings
227. Ghosts at Cross-Roads
228. Bath and Other West-Country Ghosts
229. A Somerset Haunting
230. Clifton Hauntings
231. Some Bristol Ghosts
232. Ghosts on Wheels
233. Richmond Ghosts
234. Spring Heel Jack
235. Tyneside and Wear Valley Hauntings
236. Yorkshire Ghosts
237. More Yorkshire Ghosts
238. Yorkshire and Lancashire Ghosts

239. More Lancashire Ghosts
240. Still More Lancashire Ghosts
241. Vampires and Other North-Country Ghosts
242. Midland Ghosts
243. Midland and East of England Ghosts
244. Haunted Pools
245. Haunted Lakes, Pools and Wells
246. Mystery Water, Haunted Streams and Lakes
247. Haunted Trees and Woods
248. Some Personal Experiences
249. A Sussex Haunting
250. Some South of England Hauntings
251. Seaside Hauntings
252. More Seaside Hauntings
253. Hauntings of and by Inanimate Objects
254. Moor and Hill Hauntings
255. Screaming Skulls and Haunted Inns
256. More Personal Experiences
257. Ghost Nights: Theories and Obsessions
258. Theories

Ghosts with a Purpose
259. A Ghost Returns to Pay Its Debts
260. A Famous Compact
261. An Execution Justified by a Ghost
262. The Corpse Candles of Whinny Park
263. The Man With the Sickle
264. A Royal Phantom
265. The Ghostly Experiences of a French Actress
266. The Clock's Warnings
267. The Clock and the Ring
268. The Haunted Suicide Cell of New Orleans
269. The Three Knocks
270. Spirit Writing Detects Murder
271. The Ghost With the Baby
272. The Ghost With the Mark of the Cow's Hoof
273. Famous German Generals and the Unknown
274. The Ghosts in Grey

275. The Cemetery, a Warning to Evildoers
276. The Evil Lady and the Phantom Coach
277. The Strange Experience of a Medical Student
278. Purposeful Animal Ghosts
279. Was it Projection?
280. Purposeful Phantoms on St. Mark's Eve
281. Messengers from Another World
282. Ghosts of an Old County Hall
283. The Ghosts of Woolacombe Sands
284. A Very Dangerous Ghost
285. Humorous and Sad
286. Mostly Dangerous Ghosts
287. Bridges and Heads
288. Law and Ghosts
289. Coming Events That Cast Shadows Before
290. The White Hand of Draycot
291. A Ghost Appears in Court
292. Knockings and Tappings by Denizens of Another World
293. A Warning Against Premature Burial
294. The House With the Trunk
295. Naughty and Treasure-Guarding Ghosts
296. The Radiant Boy and Other Appartitions
297. Fetches and Queer Death-Warning Apparitions
298. Crime and the Supernatural
299. Haunted Caves and Pools
300. Omens and Ghosts
301. Two Haunted Dublin Houses
302. Two Persistent Ghosts
303. Chiefly Continental Hauntings
304. Tree and Other Ghosts
305. Ghosts and Warnings of Various Kinds
306. Revenge and Ill-Treatment as Causes of Hauntings
307. Some American Ghosts
308. More American Ghosts
309. Mostly Foreign Hauntings

Dangerous Ghosts
310. The Unseen Danger

List of Stories by Elliott O'Donnell

311. The Menace of Blackness
312. The Menace of the Indefinable
313. Hoodoo
314. The Candle
315. The Phantom Ape of Hampstead
316. A Cardiff Haunting
317. A Newcastle Haunting
318. The House of the Crazy Fancies
319. The Phantom Butler
320. The Old House of Urrard
321. Edinburgh Ghosts
322. The Strange Experience of a Minister
323. A Haunted Inn
324. Two Haunted Houses
325. The Haunted Corridor
326. The Leering Death's-Head
327. The Evil Countess
328. Noisy and Violent Ghosts
329. Christmas and Noisy Ghosts
330. The Vengeance of Ghosts
331. The Vengeance of Ghosts (continued)
332. Haunted Graves and Coffins
333. Isle of Man Horrors
334. Nasty Sea Phantoms
335. More Nasty Sea Ghosts
336. The Haunted Orkneys
337. The Moaning Cave
338. The Black Cave of Death
339. Hill and Moor Ghosts
340. The Eildon Hills
341. The Pentlands and Haunted Churches
342. Haunted Bridges
343. The Brockley Combe Ghosts
344. The Mysteries of Saddell and Neidpath Glen
345. The Mocking Ghost of Whittingdon Common
346. Evil Love
347. Possession
348. Perkes the Obsessed

349. Riders from Hell
350. Possession and Poltergeists
351. The Girl in the Coffin
352. The Grey House of Horror
353. The Man in Flannels
354. Terror in the Far West (America)
355. A Haunted Family (America)
356. The Ghosts of Whooping Hollow (America)
357. A Ghost Embraces (America)
358. Fantastic and Dangerous Spirits
359. The Shapeless Horror near Braemar
360. The Monster of the Morar Mound
361. The Horror of the Pool
362. Some North-Country Hauntings
363. Homicidal Ghosts
364. Very Unusual Hauntings
365. Fearsome Heads
366. The Death's-Head of Mary King's Close
367. A Phantom Skull Haunting
368. Summary

Haunted People
369. Napoleon I and His Familiar
370. The Haunting of the Royal Family of Denmark
371. Haunted Naples Royalty
372. Haunted British Royalty
373. The Haunted Stuarts
374. The Haunting of Caisho Burroughes
375. The Haunting of Mr. Towes
376. The Haunting of the Marquis de Precy
379. The Haunting of Manoury
380. The Haunting of the Marquis Locarno
381. The Haunting of Oliver Cromwell, Protector Somerset, Cardinal Beaufort, Mozart, Dr. Bostock and the Baron de Guldenstubbe
382. The Haunting of Lord Lyttelton
383. The Haunting of Lord Middleton
384. The Haunting of Philippe de Levis, Lord of Mirépoix
385. Two Very Unpleasant Haunting Ghosts
386. More Hauntings by Doppelgängers

List of Stories by Elliott O'Donnell

387. A Great Glasgow Mystery
388. The Haunting of Squire Lighte's Groom
389. Haunted by a ~Duchess
390. Haunted by a Phantom of the Living
391. The Ghost Who Nursed a Baby
392. Haunting Husbands
393. Haunted by Candles and Corpses
394. The Haunting of Miss Sophy Hunt of Liverpool
395. Spirit Interposition in Scotland
396. The Haunting of Martin Flammarique
397. Seen in a Mirror
398. The Haunted Hand-Gate
399. Haunted by West Country Ghosts
400. The Haunting of Robert Dean
401. A Strange Encounter
402. People Haunted by Familiar Spirits
403. A Strange Nocturnal Adventure
404. The Dancer of Death
405. A Haunted Dentist
406. The Haunting of the De Prestons and Gordons of Fyvie
407. The Haunting of the Ancient Family of Malachy
408. The Death Knell
409. The Bog-Oak Chest
410. The Haunting of a Hampstead Family
411. A Family Haunted by a Phantom Man in a Wig
412. Number Ten Burking Place
413. Haunted by a Dream-Man with a Red Scar
414. A Dream With a Dual Purpose
415. An Allegorical Dream
416. The Dream of a Member of a Scottish Hell-Fire Club
417. The Room of the Haunting Dreams
418. The Murderer's Haunting Dream
419. The Room Beyond
420. Foreseen Marine Events
421. Comments, Theories and Suggestions

Phantoms of the Night

422. Some Somerset Ghosts
423. More West of England Ghosts

424. Some Bristol Ghosts
425. The Haunting of Hinton Ampner Manor House
426. The Amorous Ghost of Hove
427. The Room of the Lingering Thoughts
428. The Haunting of Greendale Hall
429. In the Corridor
430. The Haunting at Cheshunt
431. The Sarratt Ghost
432. Cumnor Hall and Edge-Hill Hauntings
433. Two Lovely Ghosts
434. The Haunting of the Old Manor House of Creslowe
435. Demon Tables
436. The Haunting of Manorbere Hall
437. Apparitions Appearing at the Time of Death
438. The Haunting of Holly Lodge
439. The Ghost of the Old Boar's Head Tavern and Other Hauntings
440. The Haunting of Benjamin Mullings
441. A Theatre Mystery
442. No – Berkeley Square
443. The Bumping Ghost of Chelsea
444. Chelsea, Thames and St. James's Street
445. The Chick Lane Ghost
446. A Telephone Mystery
447. Some Hauntings in the North
448. Tyneside and Other Hauntings
449. The Dead Hand and the Laughing Ghost
450. The Footsteps on the Stairs
451. The Hauntings at Littledean and Doncaster
452. Some Hauntings in the Eastern Counties
453. The Phantom Knocker
454. The Phantom Leash
455. The Hauntings at Clifton Park and Dundee
456. Ghostly Happenings in Angus
457. The Bed of Terror
458. A Medley of Welsh Ghosts
459. Rudolf the Accursed
460. The Haunted Earrings
461. A Ghostly Advent

462. Theories

Haunted Waters
463. Water Has Its Own Spirits
464. The Haunted Thames
465. The Stowaway
466. The Phantom Policeman
467. An Epping Forest Mystery
468. The Ghost of the Grinning Woman
469. A Sinister Severn Haunting
470. The Haunting of Dipdale Hole
471. The Strange Disappearance of John Harper, Cripple
472. The Mystery of Lydia Atley
473. The Riddle of the Skeleton
474. The Featureless Horror
475. Monks of Death
476. New Forest Hauntings
477. The Phantom Pond
478. Ghostly Horrors of the Dartmoor Rivers
479. A Norfolk Millpond Mystery
480. The Headless Woman of the Churnet
481. A Derbyshire Pretty Ghost
482. Seen in a Mirror
483. Some Yorkshire Water Hauntings
484. Ghost Lights of the Trent
485. The Phantom Riders
486. Ghosts of the Tyne
487. The Hauntings of Wearedale
488. The Haunted Eden
489. The Punt and the Haystack
490. Hauntings of the English Lakes
491. The River of Ghostly Stealth
492. The Fifth Stepping-Stone
493. The Valley of the River of Death
494. Some Scottish Loch Hauntings
495. The End of the Ravine
496. Some Scottish River Hauntings
497. The Woman in Red

498. Stag-Headed Men of Hate
499. Some Irish Lake Hauntings
500. A County Limerick Haunting
501. The Phantom Haze
502. A Haunted Jamaican Lava Stream
503. Escaped From Justice
504. The Haunted River Morgue
505. The Figurehead on the Mast
506. The Mystery of the Blonde Woman
507. The Hand on the Door
508. A Horrible Fate

Trees of Ghostly Dread

509. Introduction
510. Herne's Oak
511. The Cadenham Oak
512. An Oak of Ill Omen
513. The Ghost of the Windy Oaks
514. The Withered Scottish Oak
515. Haunted Ash Trees
516. The Haunted Christmas Tree
517. Laurel Tree Hauntings
518. The Fatal Cherry Tree
519. The Glastonbury Thorn
520. Yew Trees
521. The Shrieking Mandrake
522. Elm Trees
523. The Evil Garden
524. The Haunting of Millow Grange
525. Possibly Metamorphosis
526. The Green Lady
527. Apple Trees and the Supernatural
528. The Warnings of the Old Beech Tree
529. The Key and the Bible
530. The Haunted Shrubbery
531. The Ghost of Glyndale Hall
532. The Ghosts of Whittlebury Forest
533. Saved by a Ghost Dog
534. The Phantom Headlights

List of Stories by Elliott O'Donnell

535. The Haunted Navity Wood
536. The Phantom Horseman of Bickford House
537. A Haunted Forfarshire Grove
538. The Haunted Glen
539. The Screaming Phantom of Mannheim Forest
540. Projection in a Wood
541. The Ghost of the Frozen Highway
542. The Haunted Avenue
543. Cromarty Ghosts
544. The Haunted Copse
545. The Phantom Forest
546. Silky and Her Ghost Dog
547. The Phantom Rider on the Grey Horse
548. The Phantom White Mare
549. Horrors in the Valley of the Derwent
550. The Haunted Caravan
551. The Drunkard's Warning
552. The Jingling Bells
553. The Sinister Danmark Tree
554. The Swing in the Grove
555. The Last Night of the Carnival
556. Hyde Park Ghosts
557. The Woman of Sorrow
558. Betrothed to a Spirit
559. The Phantom Piper
560. The Fatal Viol
561. Trees, Ghost Dogs and Phantom Hunts
562. Continental Phantom Hunts
563. The Phantom Swaers
564. Marietta the Werewolf
565. The Haunted Wood and Signal-Box
566. Called to the Rescue
567. A Painter's Occult Experience
568. A Ghost's Gratitude
569. A Case of Exorcism
570. The Ghost in the Ring
571. Coming Events Cast Grim Shadows

The Midnight Hearse

572. The Choking Fingers
573. For God's Sake Take It Out!
574. The Midnight Hearse
575. The Headless Spectre
576. The Haunted Crossroads
577. The Vanished Suitor of Shooter's Hill
578. The Nurse's Return
579. The Disappearance of Mollie Phillips
580. The Room of Sighs
581. The Winged Thing
582. The Master of the Sarah Emma
583. The Pool of Horrors
584. The Weeping Tomb of Kilmallock
585. The Terror of Pitlochry
586. The Staircase and the Pit
587. The Canal Torso Mystery
588. Haunted Churches
589. The Black Monk of Newstead
590. Poltergeists and Other Puzzles
591. The Ghosts of Birchen Hall
592. The Man Who Came Back
593. The Night Hounds
594. The House of the Blue Lights
595. Compacts With the Dead
596. The Strangling Oak of Nannau Woods
597. The Murders on the Crumbles
598. Phantom Vehicles
599. The Dance of the Bat
600. White Ladies: And the Headless...
601. Phantoms of the Living
602. Castle of Horrors
603. Phantom Hand in the Jungle
604. Strange Sounds: And the Seven Whistlers
605. The Phantoms of Dunlobin
606. The Stranger in the Fog
607. The Fairy Rock
608. Banshees and Other Death Warnings

List of Stories by Elliott O'Donnell

The Screaming Skulls and Other Ghosts

609. The Veiled Ghost of Highgate
610. The Screaming Skulls of Calgarth Hall
611. The Fifth Stair
612. The Fatal Phantom of Eringle Truagh
613, The Grey Horror
614. The Ghost of Fred Archer
615, The Haunting of the Gory Hotel
616. The London Villa of Ghostly Dread
617. An Unsolved Mystery
618. The Haunted Buoy
619. The Man in Boiling Lead
620. The Creeping Hand of Maida Vale
621. The Man on the Landing
622. The Legend of Cooke's Folly
623. The Mauthe Dog
624. The Phantom Drummer of Cortachy
625. The Ghosts of the Beeches
626. The Phantom Clock of Portman Square
627. Horror in Skye
628. Ghosts and Murder
629. A Haunted Hampstead House
630. The Haunted Quarry
631. The Spectres of the Gables
632. Pearlin Jean of Allanbank
633. The Haunting of Allum Court
634. The Ghosts of the White Garter
635. The Nun of Digby Court
636. The Phantom Lady of Berry Pomeroy
637. The Haunting of St. Giles
638. The Phantom Drummer of Fyvie
639. The Phantom Rider
640. My Night in Old Whittlebury Forest
641. The Fourth Tree in the Avenue
642. A Night Vigil at Christchurch
643. The Haunted Stream
644. The Castle Terrors
645. The House in Berkeley Square

646. Will-'o-the-wisp and Corpse Candles

Casebook of Ghosts
647. The House of the Bloody Cat
648. My First Ghosts
649. The Cry of the Banshee
650. The Eyeless Woman
651. The Highbury Horror
652. Nights of a Ghost-Hunter
653. The Dead Man's Hand
654. The Death Bogle: And the Inextinguishable Candle
655. The Orange-Haired Footman
656. The House on the Cliff
657. The Midnight Bride
658. The Phantom Dachshund
659. The Floating Head
660. Rebecca of Bedlam
661. The Strange Affair at Syderstone
662. Jane of George Street
663. The Letter
664. The Headless Cat
665. Hunting Ghosts in America
666. The Vanished Secretary
667. The Sudden Dead
668. The Beautiful Spoiler
669. The Hand of Promise
700. The Hindu Child
701. Phantoms From My Notebook
702. The Red Fingers
703. The Listener
704. The Lady in White
705. From the Cellar It Came
706. The Sign of the Werewolf

Great Ghost Stories
707. The Veiled Ghost of Highgate
708. The Screaming Skulls of Calgarth Hall
709. The Fifth Stair
710. The Fatal Phantom of Eringle Truagh

List of Stories by Elliott O'Donnell

711. The Grey Horror
712. The Ghost of Fred Archer
713. The Haunting of the Gory Hotel
714. The London Villa of Ghostly Dread
715. An Unsolved ~Mystery
719. The Haunted Buoy
716. The Man in Boiling Lead
717. The Creeping Hand of Maida Vale
718. The Man on the Landing
719. The Legend of Cooke's Folly
720. The Mauthe Dog
721. The Phantom Drummer of Cortachy
722. The Ghosts of the Beeches
723. The Phantom Cock of Portman Square
724. Horror in Skye
725. Ghosts and Murder
726. A Haunted Hampstead House
727. The Haunted Quarry
728. The Spectres of the Gables
729. Pearlin Jean of Allanbank
730. The Haunting of Allum Court
731. The Ghosts of the White Garter
732. The Nun of Digby Court
733. The Phantom Lady of Berry Pomeroy
734. The Haunting of St. Giles
735. The Phantom Trumpeter of Fyvie
736. The Phantom Rider
737. My Night in Old Whittlebury Forest
738. The Fourth Tree in the Avenue
739. A Night Vigil at Christchurch
740. The Haunted Stream
741. The Castle Terrors
742. The House in Berkeley Square
743. Will-o'-the-wisp and Corpse Candles
744. The House of the Bloody Cat
745. My First Ghosts
746. The Cry of the Banshee
747. The Eyeless Woman

748. The Highbury Horror
749. Nights of a Ghost-Hunter
750. The Dead Man's Hand
751. The Death Bogle: And the Inextinguishable Candle
752. The Orange-Haired Footman
753. The House on the Cliff
754. The Midnight Bride
755. The Phantom Dachshund
756. The Floating Head
756. Rebecca of Bedlam
757. The Strange Affair at Syderstone
758. Jane of George Street
759. The Letter
760. The Headless Cat
761. Hunting Ghosts in America
762. The Vanished Secretary
763. The Sudden Dead
764. The Beautiful Spoiler
765. The Hand of Promise
766. The Hindu Child
767. Phantoms From My Notebook
768. The Red Fingers
769. The Listener
770. The Lady in White
771. From the Cellar It Came
772. The Sign of the Werewolf

Ghost Hunters

773. The Bridge at Midnight
774. The Mummy of Amen-Ra
775. The Rectory Horrors
776. The Haunted Husband
777. Houses of Terror
778. The Trees of Fear
779. The Miller's House
780. More Spectres From My Notebook
781. Mr. Wyeth and Mr. Neal
782. A Bargain With a Ghost
783. Old Jeffrey

784. Phantom Dogs and Cats
785. The Residents of Ramhurst
786. The Murderer's Return
787. The Wailing Banshees
788. Banshees Abroad
789. "It Happened To Me"
790. The Cursing Psalm

Ghosts

791. The Horrible Red Sisters
792. The Churchyard Bride
793. The Ghostly Horrors of Rainford Hall
794. The Ghosts of Hampton Court Palace
795. The Visionary Prediction of Mrs. Porteus
796. The Tower Ghosts
797. The Ghost of Berry Pomeroy Castle
798. The Ghosts of Danton Hall
799. The Strange Case of Camilla Flint
800. The Cries in the Old Churchyard
801. The Tragic Story of Mary the Ghost Maiden
802. The Mystery of the Lightship Annabelle
803. The Pan Night Mystery
804. The Ghost on the Stairs
805. No – Berkeley Square
806. The Hoodoo Theatre
807. The Potterdene Ghosts

Spookerisms

808. The Ghost With the Matches
809. The Death Rider of the Fatal Quarry
810. Seen in the Mirror
811. The Phantom Procession
812. The Haunted Street Crossing
813. The Unlucky Corner
814. The Phantom Cyclist
815. The Sporting Ghost
816. St. Agnes's Eve
817. The Door That Would Open
818. A Night in a Morgue

819. The Haunted Clock
820. The Phantom Leg
821. The Ghost Ship of St. Ives
822. The Hooded Phantom of the Dibleys
823. The Ghost With the Missing Finger
824. The Chest Ghost
825. The Ghost in the Billiard Room
826. The Haunted Cupboard
827. No – Berkeley Square
828. The Phantom Barrel
829. The Film Studio Ghost
830. The Haunted Bed
831. The Ghost in the High-Heeled Shoes
832. A Portsmouth Horror
833. The Phantom Char
834. The Ghost House of Dartmoor.

Some Haunted Houses of England and Wales

835. The Green Bank Hotel, Bardsley
836. No. –– Southgate Street, Bristol
837. Mulready Villa, Near Basingstone
838. No. –– Park Street, Bath
839. The Minery, Devon
840. Thurlow Hall, Near Exeter
841. The Guilsborough Ghost
842. Wolsey Abbey, Near Gloucester
843. No. XYZ Euston Road, London
844. Panmaur Hollow, Merioneth
845. Catchfield Hall, The Midlands
846. Burle Farm, North Devon
847. Carne House, Near Northampton
848. Harley House, Portishead
849. The Way Meadow, Somerset
850. No. –– Hackham House, Swindon
851. The Screaming Woman of Tehiddy
852. Park House, Westminster.

Bibliography

1892.	*Escaped from Justice.* (Novel: Unpublished)
1904.	*For Satan's Sake* (Novel: Greening)
1905.	*The Unknown Depths* (Novel: Greening)
1906.	*Jennie Barlowe, Adventuress* (Novel: Greening)
1907.	*Dinevah the Beautiful* (Novel: Greening)
1908.	*Bona Fide Adventures With Ghosts* (Paperback: Clifton, Baker)
1908.	*Some Haunted Houses of England and Wales* (Eveleigh Nash)
1909.	*Haunted Houses of London* (Eveleigh Nash)
1910.	*Ghostly Phenomena* (Werner Laurie)
1911.	*Byways of Ghostland* (Rider)
1911.	*Mrs. E.M. Ward's Reminiscences* (Edited: Pitman)
1911.	*The Meaning of Dreams* (Eveleigh Nash)
1912.	*Scottish Ghost Stories* (Kegan Paul)
1912.	*The Sorcery Club* (Novel: Rider)
1912.	*Werwolves* (Methuen)
1913.	*Animal Ghosts* (Rider)
1914.	*Haunted Highways and Byways* (Eveleigh Nash)
1915.	*The Irish Abroad* (Pitman)
1916.	*Twenty Years' Experiences as a Ghost Hunter* (Heath Cranton)
1917.	*The Haunted Man* (Novel: Heath Cranton)
1918.	*Fortunes*
1919.	*The Menace of Spiritualism* (Werner Laurie)
1919,	*Haunted Places of England* (Sands)
1920.	*The Banshee* (Sands)
1920.	*More Haunted Houses of London* (Eveleigh Nash)
1920.	*Spiritualism Explained* (Paperback: Pearson)
1924.	*Ghosts Helpful and Harmful* (Rider)
1925.	*The Trial of Kate Webster* (Hodge)

1925. *Ghostland* (Cecil Palmer)
1926. *Strange Sea Mysteries* (Bodley Head)
1927. *Strange Disappearances* (Bodley Head)
1927. *For Satan's Sake*. Reprint. (Benman's, London)
1928. *Confessions of a Ghost Hunter* (Thornton Butterworth)
1929. *Famous Curses* (Skeffington)
1929. *Fatal Kisses* (John Hamilton)
1930. *Great Thames Mysteries* (Selwyn and Blount)
1931. *Women Bluebeards* (Stanley Paul)
1931. *Rooms of Mystery* (Philip Allan)
1932. *Ghosts of London* (Philip Allan)
1932. *The Devil in the Pulpit* (Novel: Denis Archer)
1933. *Family Ghosts* (Philip Allan)
1934. *Strange Cults and Secret Societies of Modern London* (Philip Allan)
1939. *Haunted Churches* (Quality Press)
1945. *Murder at Hide and Seek* (Novel: Eldon Press)
1945. *Dread of Night* (Paperback: Pillar, Dublin)
1946. *Haunted and Hunted* (Grafton, Dublin)
1946. *Caravan of Crime* (Paperback: Grafton, Dublin)
1946. *Hell Ships of Many Waters* (Paperback: Grafton, Dublin)
1948. *Haunted Britain* (Rider)
1951. *Ghosts With a Purpose* (Rider)
1952. *The Dead Riders* (Novel: Rider)
1954. *Dangerous Ghosts* (Rider)
1955. *Haunted People* (Rider)
1956. *Phantoms of the Night* (Rider)
1957. *Haunted Waters* (Rider)
1958. *Trees of Ghostly Dread* (Rider)
1959. *Ghosts*, Edited. (Foulsham)
1964. *The Screaming Skulls* (Foulsham)
1965. *The Midnight Hearse* (Foulsham)
1969. *Elliott O'Donnell's Casebook of Ghosts* (Foulsham)
1971. *The Hag of the Dribble* (Robert Hale)
1971. *Elliott O'Donnell's Ghost Hunters* (Foulsham)
1983. *Elliott O'Donnell's Great Ghost Stories* (Foulsham)

Index

Note: Writings by Elliott O'Donnell (EO) appear under title; works by others under author's name

2LO (radio station), 228

Aberystwyth, 22
Abyssinia, 6–8
Adams sisters, Catherine and Mary, 18–19
Afghan War (1878–81), 13
Aldine Club, New York, 238
Alexander, Sir George, 189
Alice (of Chancery Lane), 104, 115
Allsop, Kenneth, 264–6
American Irish Historical Society, 237
Angels of Mons (legend), 189n
Animal Ghosts (1913), 171–2, 175
animals: ghosts of, 216, 244; in the hereafter, 171–2, 253; psychic sensitivity, 74, 168
Argo (steamboat), 50
Arkiko (village), Abyssinia, 7
Arran, Isle of, 55
Arrowsmith, J.W., 110
Artists' Film Club, Wardour Street, 179
Arts and Letters Club, 178–9
Ashby, Mrs. (of St. Ives), 133
Authors' Club, 137, 146–8
Authors' Society, 230, 231
Avenue, The, Clifton, 17, 18

'B. Grange' (house), Somerset: vigils at, 167–8

Babbacombe Bay, Torquay, 123–4
Baker, Mr. (headmaster at Clyde School), 111–12
Baker & Son (publishers), 142–3
Baldwin (balloonist and parachutist), 115–16
Baltimore, 234
Banshee, The (1920), 228
banshees, 9–10, 17, 140–1, 205, 225–8, 265
Barlow, Lucy, 114n
Barrington, Sir Jonah and Lady, 226–7
Barton, Mrs. (St. Ives housekeeper), 132–3
Bath murder case (1891), 112–14
Bayswater murder case (1926), 217–18; vigil at murder site, 218–23
Beaton, Cardinal, 31–2
Beaumont Dr. Edgar, 231
Becondale Road (No. 14), Upper Norwood: O'Donnells move into, 145; poltergeist activity, 157–9; Petronella and Helena visit, 159; EO lets, 184; and air raids, 190
Begbie, Harold (and wife), 136
Begbie, Reverend M.H., 136
Bell, Mrs. (Denver typist), 84–8
Bennett, Arnold, 147
Bennett, Sir Ernest, 148
Bennett, Herbert John, 216

Index

Bergson, Henri, 181n
Berner Street, Whitechapel, 209–10
Beron, Leon, 210–11
Beryl, Sarah, 14
Bingham, Bill, 261, 262
birching machine, 34
Blackheath: Shirley House School, 112, 177
Blackrock, near Dublin, 27, 45
Blackwood, Algernon: *John Silence*, 143
Blanche, Addie, 26
Bligh Bond, Frederick, 168–9, 170
Bloom, Ursula, 178
Bloomsbury, 123, 180, 216–17, 241, 246–7
Blouët, Paul (Max O'Rell), 125
'Bocarthe' (house), Perth, 52, 54
Bolitho, Ellie, 131–2
Bolton Club, Denman Street, 180
Bona Fide Adventures With Ghosts (1908), 142–3
Booksellers League, The, New York, 238
Boothby, Guy, 116
Borley Rectory, 258, 264–5
Boston, Massachusetts: haunted hotel, 96–8; EO gives talk on ghosts, 235
Bournemouth, 125, 129
Bouverie, Nelly, 14
Bowery, New York, 98
Brand, Cecil, 112–13
Brayton, Lily, 145n
Brett, Edwin J., 115
Bridlington Quay, 25–6
Brighton, 162–3
Brighton trunk murder (1934), 243 & n
Brislington, Bristol: haunted house, 256–7
Bristol: air raids, 247; Colston Hall, 13, 14–15; Grosvenor Nursing Home, Clevedon, 270; Prince's Theatre, 14, 26; psychic investigations, 168–70, 244–5, 255–7, 260–2, 270–2; street entertainment and traffic, 15–16; visit by Prince of Wales, 12; *see also* Clifton; Clifton College; Durdham Downs
Bristol Cathedral: vigil at, 244–5

Bristol Mercury, 5
Bristol Volunteers, 12
British Museum: erotic material cupboard, 258; Oriental Department, 148–50
British Schools and Universities Club, New York, 237
Britton, Mrs. (Denver landlady), 84–5
Brixton, 124, 128–9
Broadmead, Bristol: vigil at, 255–6
Bromhead, Lieutenant Gonville, 13
Brown, Dr. Sparkhall, 38, 232
Bruges: bed-haunting ghost, 201–2
Brunswick Square, London: haunted flat, 174–5
Buck's Row, Whitechapel, 209
Buffalo, New York, 233
Buley, Ernest, 135, 161
Bullen, Mr. (Swaffham farmer), 156
Bullen, Julia, 14
Burton Crescent, Bloomsbury (*now* Cartwright Gardens), 217
Buswell, Harriett, 216–17
Byways of Ghostland (1911), 153–4, 171

Caine, Hall, 147
Calvert, Phyllis, 194
Cambridge University Library: SPR archive, 119n
Campbell, Charlie, 40
Carleton, Billie, 243
Carson City, Nebraska, 82
Carter, Eliza, 238
Cartwright Gardens, Bloomsbury (*formerly* Burton Crescent), 217
Casement, Sir Roger, 182
Caxton Hotel, London, 252
Central Criminal Court, London, 257–8
Central Hotel, Broadway, 57
Central Park, New York, 236–7
Chapman, Annie, 209
Chemistry Club, New York, 237
Cheriton Lodge, Bath, 113
Chetwode Crawley, Dr. W.J., 38, 41, 232
Cheyne Walk, Chelsea: haunted house, 196–7

Index

Chicago, 59–61, 233–4
child ghosts, 164–6, 252
Childe, Digby, 108–9
Chinatown, Limehouse, 242–3
Chinatown, San Francisco, 76–7
Church, John, 208
Churchill, Lady Randolph, 57
Churchill, Lord Randolph, 56–7
Clapham Common, 210–11
Cleopatra's Needle, Victoria Embankment, 106
Clifford, Charles, 150–1
Clifton, Bristol: The Avenue, 17, 18; Buckingham Vale, 18; Leeshome dame school, 18–19; Sherborne Villas, 5, 9–11, 17–18, 45, 247; Victoria Rooms, 12; Wellington Park, 4
Clifton College: EO at, 20–1; sporting notables, 30–1; schoolmaster lookalike, 82; Reverend Begbie at, 136
Clifton Suspension Bridge, 170
Clyde School, Hereford, 111–12
Cold Ashby, Northamptonshire, 4–5
Coldicote, Mr. (headmaster at Wolverhampton Grammar School), 111
Coldwell, Fanny, 13, 18, 19, 45, 125, 269–70
Coldwell, Sarah, 13, 17–18, 23–5, 125, 269–70
Coldwell, Tom, 13
Cole, Albert, 18
Colin, Jean, 245
'Colonel K.' (bogus officer), 6–8
Colston Hall, Bristol, 13, 14–15
Columbia Lippincott Gazetteer of the World, The, 8
Columbia University, 235–6
Columbia Woman's Graduate Club, 236
Conditionally (EO; play), 179
Confessions of a Ghost Hunter (1928), 238
Coombs, Arthur, 114
Coram Street, Bloomsbury *see* Great Coram Street
Cornelius (actor), 151
Cornwall, EO in, 130–7, 138–41, 142, 265–6
Cory Coffin Circle, 202
Cosmopolitan Hotel, New York, 98
Covent Garden: Italian Ball (April 28, 1920), 193
Craddock, Samuel, 114
Craik, Mrs.: *John Halifax, Gentleman*, 226
Cranford Nursing Home, Northampton, 238–9
Cranton, E., 191
Crater Lake, Oregon, 70, 74
Cream, Dr. Thomas Neill, 111
Creed, Edward Austin: murder of, 217–18; vigil at murder site, 218–23
cremation, 54
cricket, 30–1, 47, 137–8, 191–2, 267
Crippen, Dr. Hawley Harvey, 152n, 210
Croker, B.M. ('Boss Croker'), 56, 119
crossing-sweepers, 15
Crowley, Aleister, 203–4
Crown Tavern, Drury Lane, 196
Crumbles, The (shingle beach), 211–16
Crystal Palace: haunted murder house investigation, 151–2
Cuba (Cunard liner), 5
Cummings, Vera, 86–8
Curzon, Lord, 167–8, 170

Dadd, Richard, 8
Daily Express, 198–9
Daily Graphic, 262
Daily Mail, 136, 230, 231–2, 257, 264–6
Dangerous Ghosts (1954), 166n, 262
Daventry Grammar School, 109
Davies, Marion, 232
Davies, W.H.: *The Truth* (poem), 172–3
Davis family (of Upper Leeson Street, Dublin), 42, 43
de Cosson, Baron, 8
De Cotton family, 10–11
de Paoli, Count, 60–1
Dead Riders, The (1952), 166n
Dean, Stella, 84–8
Deane-Tanner, William Cunningham (aka William Desmond Taylor):

murder of, 20
déjà vu experiences, 32, 58–9, 141–2
Dekon, Ernest, 53–4
Denham, Buckinghamshire, 13
Denver, 63–5, 84–8
Desmoulins, Camille, 161n
Devil's Bridge, Aberystwyth, 22
Dillon, Andrew, 113
Dinevah the Beautiful (1907), 124, 135
Dingwall, Dr. Eric, 119, 258–9
Dobbs, Hannah, 217
Dockerell, Professor (of Queen's Service Academy), 38
dogs, psychic sensitivity, 168
Dolin, Anton, 247
Donovan, Mary, 217
Doppelgängers, 100, 106
Doyle, Arthur Conan, 137, 138n, 147
Drake Hotel, Chicago, 233–4
dreamland, 33
Drury Lane Theatre, 108; Man in Grey ghost, 259–60
Dublin: artistic and cultural life, 40–1; Ely Place, 27, 36, 37–8, 44–5, 231, 232; Gaiety Theatre, 26–7; 'haunted' houses in, 36–7, 42–3, 44–5; Lower Merrion Street, 43, 48–9, 150–1; prostitution, 41; Queen's Service Academy, 38, 47; Wanderers Football Club, 41; Zoological Gardens, 15, 27
Dublin, EO in: childhood, 26–7, 36–7; student days, 37–8, 40–2, 47–8, 150–1; encounters strangling ghost, 42–4, 48–9; ghost hunting, 44–5; fleeting return visit, 232
Dudeney, Mrs. Henry, 136
Duff Gordon, Lucy, Lady, 231
Duke of York (public house), London, 180
Duke Street haunting, Glasgow, 51–2
Durdham Downs, 12, 14, 25, 28–30
Dutton, Miss (of Newquay), 24–5

Ealing: vigil at, 205–6
Earls Court Road, London: haunted house, 196
Edinburgh, 53–4
Edward, Prince of Wales (*later* King Edward VII): visits Bristol, 12
Egham, Surrey, 146
Elbe, S.S., 98–100
Elementals (spirits), 3, 11–12, 22, 73, 133–4, 149; defined and described by EO, 150–2
Ellis, Mrs. Havelock, 136
Ely Place, Dublin, 27, 36, 37–8, 44–5, 231, 232
Embankment, The, 106–8
Emerson, Alec, 112–13
Emin Pasha, 117
Epstein, Sir Jacob, 178
Epworth Rectory, Lincolnshire, 155–6
Eringle Truagh, County Monaghan, 49–50
Escaped from Justice (EO; unpublished novel), 112–15
Ethie Castle, 31–2
Euston Square Mystery (1879), 12, 217
Eva Dare theatre company, 121–4
Eveleigh Nash (publishers), 143, 146, 153, 177, 196
Everett, Mrs. (spirit medium), 198–9

Faculty of Arts (club), London, 173
fairies, 45–6
Family Ghosts and Ghostly Phenomena (1933), 226–8, 231–2, 238
Famous Curses (1929), 238
Fatal Kisses (1929), 238
Feilding, Everard, 167
Field, Jack, 211–12, 215
First World War, 183, 184, 188–90
1st Volunteer Battalion Gloucestershire Regiment, 34
Fischer, E.H., 138
Fitzroy (public house), London, 180
Folkestone, 183
Fontainebleau Forest: ghosts, 182–3
For Satan's Sake (1904), 115, 116, 134–5
Forbes, Archibald, 115
Ford, Charles, 33
Forsyth, Neil, 108

Index

Fortescue, W.B., 137
Foss, G.R., 121
Four Provinces of Ireland Club, Russell Square, 180, 243
Fowkes family (of Leicestershire), 10
Fox, Francis, 117, 134
Franklin Square haunting, New York, 57–8
Freak Club, Mayfair, 173–4, 175–6
'freak gatherings' (London parties), 193–6
French, Percy, 41
Frigard, Matilde, 182–3
Fuller, Leonard, 137

Gabbitas-Thring (scholastic agents), 108–9
Gaiety Theatre, Dublin, 26–7
Gannel, River, 27
Gartside, Fred, 121
Geddes, Sam, 179–80
George Inn, Bathampton, 114
Georgic (White Star liner), 232
Ghost Circle, 202
Ghost Dance of the Klamath Indians, 69
Ghostland (1925), 204, 228
Ghostly Phenomena (1910), 146, 150–2, 228
Ghosts: Stories of the Supernatural (ed. O'Donnell), 266
Ghosts Helpful and Harmful (1924), 201–2
Ghosts of London (1932), 230, 238
Ghosts With a Purpose (1951), 166n, 260
Gibbs, Snow, 249
Giffard, Sir Hardinge, 208
Gipsy Club, London, 177–8
Gipsy Hill, London, 145n
Gish, Lillian, 228–9
Giullgaut, Mr. (teacher at Queen's Service Academy), 38
Glasgow: Duke Street haunting, 51–2
Glen, The, Babbacombe Bay, 123–4
Glen Sannox, 55
Glyn, Elinor, 231, 233
Goatfell murder case (1889), 55

Godley, Mr. (headmaster at Henley House School), 111
Goimbault, Odette, 188
Gonne, Maude, 180–1
Grace, W.G., 31
Graham, Margot, 250
Grand Opera House, New York, 237
Graves, Percival, 173
Gray, Dora May, 216
Gray, William, 211–12, 215
Great Coram Street, Bloomsbury: EO lodges at, 123; murder of Harriet Buswell (1872), 216–17
Great Thames Mysteries (1930), 238
Great Western Railway line: lack of amenities, 122
Great Yarmouth *see* Yarmouth
Green Armitage, Mrs., 168, 170
Greening, Arthur, 134, 135
Grossmith, George, 178
Grosvenor Nursing Home, Clevedon, Bristol, 270
Grosvenor Railway Bridge, London, 192
Guilsborough, Northamptonshire, 125, 132, 135; Red House, 229, 230, 241
Gull, Ranger (Guy Thorne), 134
Gunness, Belle, 237n
Gwrach y Rhibyn (Hag of the Dribble), 23

Hacker, Matilda, 217
Hacon, Reverend Henry, 154
Hag of the Dribble, 23
Haggard, H. Rider, 231
Hal (swimming-bath attendant), 77–8
Ham Bone Club, Soho, 178
Hamilton, Charles: *The Oriental Zigzag*, 7
Hamnett, Nina, 180
Hampton Down, near Bath, 112–13, 114
Hanbury Street, Spitalfields, 209
Harding, Captain, 80
Harewood (country mansion), Hereford, 112
Harris, Sir Augustus, 108
Harrison, George, 5
Harrogate: haunted house, 164–6
Hart, Reverend Dean, 63

Index

Haunted Britain (1948), 119n, 166n, 249
Haunted Churches (1939), 244–5
Haunted Highways and Byways (1914), 173, 177
Haunted Houses of London (1909), 146, 196–7
Haunted People (1955), 262
Haunted Places in England (1919), 196, 228
Haunted Waters (1957), 263, 264–5
Hawkins, Mr. Justice, 217
Heath Cranton (publishers), 186, 191
Hengler's Circus, 14
Henley House School, Kensal Green, 110–11
Henry Neville Dramatic Studio, Oxford Street, 121
Hereford: Clyde School, 111–12
Hesketh-Prichard, Hesketh *see* Prichard, Hesketh
Hessel, Dr. Gottfried, 217
Hewson, Mrs. (EO's aunt), 226
Hickson, Edward, 83–4
Hilldrop Crescent, Holloway, 152n, 210
Hillside (house), Guilsborough, 125
Hinckley, Mrs., 235
Hind, Charles Lewis, 136
Hine, Reginald, 197, 199–200
Hoboken, New Jersey, 58–9
Hodge, Harry, 208
Hoffman, Georgina, 243
hogs, 68
Holborn: Red Lion Square haunting, 184; air raids, 184; creature in basement, 185
Holt, Hester, 84–8
Hornung, E.W., 137
Howth, Sam, 216
Hull, Miss Eleanor, 173
Hume, Fergus, 135–6
Huntley, Grace, 14
Hyde Park, 191, 253

Ideas (magazine), 138
Idler, The (magazine), 135
Ilfracombe, 16–17

Inskip, Tom, 19
International Hotel, San Francisco, 65–6, 80
Inveraray, 52
Irish Abroad, The (1915), 185–6, 228
Irish Club, Charing Cross Road, 179–80
Irish Literary Society, 173, 188
Isaacs, Lucy, 113–14

Jack the Ripper, 209–10
James, M.R., 2; *More Ghost Stories of an Antiquary*, 153
Jansen, Otto (and family), 93–6
Jeffery, Nora, 166n, 247, 249, 262, 266
Jennie Barlowe, Adventuress (1906), 135
Jepson, Edgar, 178
Jersey City, 237
Joad, C.E.M., 248 & n
John, Augustus, 178
Jones, Mr. (member of Freak Club), 173–5
Jones, Winnie, 62–3
J.W. Arrowsmith (publishers), 110

Kalowski (West Quay hotel-keeper), 98
Katebit mummy, 148–50
Kaye, Emily, 212–15
Keg, Mat, 70
Kegan Paul (publishers), 153
Kelly, Mary Jane, 210
Kensal Green: Henley House School, 110–11
Kerry, Mr. and Mrs. James, 113
Keyse, Emma, 123–4
Kitcat, S.A.P., 137
Klamath Indians, 69, 70
Knelligan, Dr. (of San Francisco), 75
Knowlton, Maud Briggs, 235
Kranz, Bill, 67

Lambeth, 102–3, 104–6, 209
Lambton, Arthur, 167
Lamorna Cove, Cornwall, 133–4
Lancaster Gate, Bayswater, 193–6
Landru, Henri Désiré, 182
Lane, Harriet, 12, 13n

Index

Lang, Andrew, 150
Latchmore, Thomas, 197–8, 199
Laurie, John Watson, 55
Lee, John, 124
Leeshome dame school, Clifton, 18–19
Lehman, Bert, 69–70
Leinster Terrace, Bayswater, 217–23
Leonard, Gladys Osborne, 148
Leslie, Christian, 166n
Lever, Hayley, 137
Levi, Jacob, 65–6
Liverpool: living phantasm, 163–4; Irish refugee deaths (1845–49), 186
Llandudno, 124
Loch Fynne, Argyll: death boat, 40
Logan, Alfred, 67
Lower Merrion Street, Dublin, 43, 48–9, 150–1
Luckock, Reverend T.G., 17
Ludlam, Harry, 266
Luke, Elsie Adeline, 112–14
Lyceum Club, London, 252

Machen, Arthur, 189n
Mackenzie, Lady Theresa Muir, 148, 231
MacPherson, Neil, 40
Macqueen-Pope, W., 259–60
Madison Square Garden Circus, 237
Mahon, Patrick, 212–16
Mahoney, Arthur, 243
Majestic (White Star liner), 56–7
man-hating feminist organisations, 203
Manchester, 163
Manchester Evening News, 203
Manchester Institute of Arts and Sciences, New Hampshire, 235
Market Street, San Francisco, 66, 75–6
Marquis of Granby (public house), London, 180
Marriott, Charles, 134, 193, 195
Marsdon, Edward, 75–6
Marshall Hall, Edward, 203
Masonic Female Orphanage of Ireland, Dublin, 41
Massowah (port), Abyssinia, 6–8
Matthews, Henry, QC, 30

Matthews, 'Maddy', 17, 29–30
Maunsell (EO's Dublin cousin), 37
Maybury, Miss (governess), 17
McKaye, James, 51–2
Meade, L.T., 231
Meerut, 201
Menace of Spiritualism, The (EO), 118, 166n, 228
Merstham railway tunnel, 215n
Mertens, Sidonia, 182
Methuen, Colonel, 34
Midnight Hearse and More Ghosts, The (ed. Ludlam), 266
Miller's Court, Spitalfields, 210
Milner, Fred, 137
Milward, Miss (sewing-maid), 13, 207–8
Minsden Chapel, Hertfordshire, 197–200
Money, Mary Sophia, 215n
Montagu, Ivor, 249
Montrose: farm, 31–2; haunted house, 38–9
Moody, Badger, 178
More Haunted Houses of London (1920), 196, 197, 228
Morrison, Steinie, 210
Morton, H.V., 198–9
Motley Club, 179
Mount Wise, Newquay, 24–5, 27
Mousley, Elizabeth Sarah M. (EO's step-sister): family background, 5; childhood skating, 12; EO's guardian, 18; sends money to EO in Chicago, 60; talent for music, 125; offers house to O'Donnells, 145; religion, 146; EO stays with during war, 247; death, 248–9
Mrs. E.M. Ward's Reminiscences (1911; edited EO), 153
Mrs. X. (medium at Red House), 229
Mugglestone Rocks, off Dalkey, 48
Mullins (Whitechapel costermonger), 209
Mullins, Mr. and Mrs. John, 46–7
mummies, Ancient Egyptian, 148–50, 178

Index

Munnings, Sir A.J., 178
Munro, Irene, 211–12
Munzinger, Werner, 7
Murder at Hide and Seek (1945), 166n
Murphy, Patrick, 99–100
Murray, Amy, 26
Myers, Frederic W.H., 119
Mystery of a Hansom Cab, The (Hume), 135–6

Nana Sahib, 201
Nash, Eveleigh *see* Eveleigh Nash
National Broadcasting Compay (NBC), 236–7
Nature Spirits *see* Elementals
Nelson, Kitty, 25–6
Neville, Henry, 121
Nevinson, C.R., 178
New York: Bowery, 98; Columbia University, 235–6; Franklin Square haunting, 57–8; Hoboken music-hall, 58–9; Radio City, 236–7; West Quay, 98; haunting, 92–6
New York, EO visits, 57–9, 92–3, 98, 232–3, 235–8
New York American Weekly, 241
Newcastle, Duke of, 166–7, 190
Newcastle Sunday Sun, 241
Newgate Prison: creepy incident, 230
Newquay, 24–5, 27
Niall of the Nine Hostages, 4, 265
Nichols, Mary Ann, 209
Norgrove, Joseph, 247
Norman, Dr. (friend of EO), 147
Norris, Lillian, 194
Northamptonshire ghosts and hauntings, 23–4, 27–8
Northcliffe, Lord, 191

Oasis Club, Dean Street, 180
Observer (newspaper), 153
Odette, Mary *see* Goimbault, Odette
O'Donnell, Ada (*née* Williams; EO's wife): EO meets, 109–10; background and qualities, 109–10; courtship with EO, 125, 132; wedding and honeymoon, 135; witnesses psychic projection, 139–40, 266; frightened by O'Donnell Banshee, 140; interests and virtues, 145–6; in Paris, 181; weird and uncanny experiences, 184, 205, 206; accompanies EO on U.S. speaking tour, 232, 235, 237; death, 238–9, 241
O'Donnell, Elizabeth Sarah (*née* Harrison; *then* Mousley; EO's mother), 5, 9, 10–11, 12, 13; death, 17; ghost of, 18
O'DONNELL, ELLIOTT:
Early life (1872-94): ancestry, 4; birth and family background, 4–5; death of father in Abyssinia, 5–8, 116; and family Banshee, 9–10, 17, 265; first psychic experience, 11; early childhood, 12–17; hears tales of ghosts and murderers, 12–13, 207–8; family holidays, 13, 16–17; death of mother, 17–18; becomes ward of Elizabeth Mousley, 18; schooling, 18–19; hanging game, 19; at Clifton College, 20–1, 30–1; school holidays, 22–8; supernatural experiences, 22–5, 27–8, 32, 38–40, 42–4, 45–7, 48–50, 150–1; first love and romantic infatuations, 25–6; in Dublin, 26–7, 36–7; scary incident on Durdham Downs, 28–30; ill-health, 31; recuperates in Montrose, 31–2; boarder at army crammer in Clifton, 33–5; joins Rifle Volunteers, 34; intrigued by birching machine, 34; at Queen's Service Academy, 38, 47; student life in Dublin, 40–2, 47–8; encounters strangling ghost, 42–4, 46–7, 48–9; decides to become professional ghost hunter, 43–4; abortive first investigations, 44–5; in County Wicklow, 45–7; fails Army medical examination, 47; returns to Clifton, 50; sojourns in Scotland, 51–5; investigates Glasgow haunted house, 51–2; the Rowlandson case,

52–4

In America (1894): sails to New York, 56–7; supernatural experiences in U.S., 57–9, 60–5, 68, 77–80, 82–4, 96–8; robbed en route to Chicago, 59–60; works as policeman during Chicago railroad strike, 60; continues journey westward, 61–5; ranch hand in Oregon, 66–8, 71; expeditions into backwoods and forests, 68–74; among Rogue River Indians, 73–4; in San Francisco, 65–6, 75–81; visits Sierra Nevadas, 82–4; at Denver, 63–5, 84–8; in New York, 57–9, 92–5, 98; narrowly escapes being shot, 98; returns to England, 98–100

In London and Cornwall (1894–1908): seeks lodgings in Waterloo, 101–3; employed as stockbroker's clerk, 103–4; infatuation with Alice, 104, 115; witness to stabbing, 104–6; visits Jack the Ripper murder sites, 209–10; supernatural experiences, 106–8, 110, 139–42, 151; job-hunting, 108–9; as schoolmaster, 109, 110–12, 116, 177; meets Ada Williams, 109–10; considers career as war correspondent, 115; as tutor in Hampstead, 116; meets H.M. Stanley, 116–17; relations with W.T. Stead, 117–18, 119, 134; relationship with Society for Psychical Research, 7, 118–19; Croker interview débâcle, 119; trains as actor, 121; on tour, 121–4, 151; at Yarmouth, 123, 216; trip to Babbacombe Bay, 123–4; family holidays in Bournemouth, 125; courtship with Ada, 125, 132; the Valencourt affair, 127–9; as tutor in St. Ives, 130–1; founds boarding school, 131; encounters Cornish ghosts and spirits, 131–4; marriage and honeymoon, 135; social circle and friendships in Cornwall, 135–7; plays for E.W. Hornung's XI, 137–8; psychic projection experiments, 139–40, 265–6; and family Banshee, 140–1; gives up teaching and returns to London, 143

In London (1908–1919): moves to Becondale Road, 145; at Authors' Club, 146–8; vigil at Roehampton haunted house, 148; investigates Katebit mummy, 148–50; vigil at Crystal Palace murder house, 151–2; Syderstone poltergeist case, 154–7; poltergeist activity at Becondale Road, 157–9; death of sister Helena, 159; non-psychic misadventures, 162–3; Liverpool phantasm case, 163–4; at haunted house in Harrogate, 164–6; further vigils, 166–70; at the Freak Club, 173–4, 175–6; the Brunswick Square haunting, 174–5; caged tiger stunt, 175; convenes gathering of clan O'Donnell, 180; pickpocketed, 180; visits Paris, 180–3; and outbreak of First World War, 183; lives in haunted house at Holborn, 184–5; employed as censor, 185; creature in basement story, 185; moves to Earl's Court, 185; bit part in West End production, 189; ferrets out spies, 189–90; experiences bombing raids, 190; enlists in United Arts Rifles, 191, 192

In London and Bristol (1920–65): attends Italian Ball at Covent Garden, 193; hosts 'Inferno' parties, 193–6; elected to Savage Club, 196; investigates Minsden Chapel haunting, 197–9; South Kensington séance, 200–1; gives talk on man-hating feminist groups, 203; with Aleister Crowley, 203–4; at haunted house near Ealing, 205–6; visits murder sites, 210–11; psychic stake-out on the Crumbles, 211–16; fascinated by Bloomsbury murders, 216–17; vigil at Bayswater murder house, 218–23; as radio broadcaster, 228, 236–7; buys Red House, 229; invites mediums to Guilsborough,

Index

229, 230; meets Bernard Shaw, 230–1; introduced to Rider Haggard and Yeats, 231; return visit to Dublin, 232; U.S. speaking tour, 232–8; holds meeting of clan O'Donnell, 237; death of Ada, 238–9, 241; sells Red House and moves to London, 241; investigates white slave trade, 241–2; tours of east London, 242–3; takes flat in Bayswater, 243; vigil at Bristol Cathedral, 244–5; part-time ARP warden, 245–7; stays with Elizabeth Mousley in Bristol, 247; and Harry Price, 248; sister Petronella's death, 248; and Elizabeth's death, 248–9; moves permanently to Bristol, 249; harrowing incident on train to York, 251; hunts ghosts in Bristol, 255–7; resumes friendship with Eric Dingwall, 258–9; briefly rejoins SPR, 258–9; St. Michael's Hill séance and cellar dig, 260–2; interviewed by Kenneth Allsop, 264–6; death, 270; as crown prince of ghost hunters, 1–2; as story-teller in full flow, 270–2

Characteristics and interests: afraid of the dark, 13, 42; afterlife compacts, 50, 270; animal welfare, 253; anti-hog prejudice, 68; appearance, 3, 161–2; belief in fairies, 45–6; boxing, 34, 267; as clubman, 173, 177–80, 196; dislike of Cornish folk, 138–9; cricket-playing, 47, 137–8, 191–2, 267; déjà vu experiences, 32, 58–9, 141–2; discretion in psychic matters, 146; dreams and dreaming, 32–3; drinking, 251–2; fishing, 40, 41–2, 47–8, 69; as lecturer and public speaker, 143, 203, 229, 232–8, 249–53, 262; as magnet for superphysical phenomena, 148, 205; pantomime-going, 14, 26–7; parachuting, 115–16; politics, 146; prankster, 20–2; religious and philosophic beliefs, 43–4, 70, 146, 267; snobbishness, 166; theatre history, 249, 259–60; *Who's Who* entry, 266–7

Health: childhood illnesses, 31; cholera, 63, 84; defective eyesight, 35; dental health, 89; influenza, 104; varicose veins, 47, 184

Literary life: early freelance writing, 77, 84; learns shorthand and typing, 104; writes for *Theatricals*, 108; approaches J.W. Arrowsmith publishers, 110; unpublished first novel (*Escape from Justice*), 112–15; advice from Guy Boothby, 116; career as journalist, 116–19, 125–7, 129, 134, 191; writings ignored by SPR, 118–19; works on second and third novels, 124; novels published, 134–5, 171; contributes to *The Idler* and *Weekly Dispatch*, 135; first collections of ghost stories published, 142–3; elected to Authors' Club, 146–8; responds to Morley Roberts, 148; edits Mrs. Ward's memoirs, 153; unfavourably compared with M.R. James, 153; series published in *Weekly Dispatch*, 161–2, 166; book dedications, 166n, 208, 249, 262; joins literary and art clubs, 173, 178–9, 196; forename misspelt, 228; avalanche of commissioned work, 241; ghost story anthologies, 266; *see also titles of individual books*

Views on: Ada, 145–6; animals in the hereafter, 171–2, 253; criminology, 92, 211; dangers of ghost hunting, 204; death and dying, 269–70; friendships old and new, 269; Elizabeth Mousley, 248–9; opium dens, 77; Petronella, 248; prostitution, 41, 103; psychic research and ghost hunting, 3–4, 187–8, 204–5; teaching, 143, 177, 192; transatlantic ghosts, 74

O'Donnell, Dr. Elliott (EO's grandfather), 5

O'Donnell, Helena (EO's sister): birth, 5; sees family Banshee, 17; orphaned,

Index

18; at Zoological Gardens in Dublin, 27; art studies and painting, 124; religion, 146; illness and death, 159
O'Donnell, Henry (EO's brother), 5, 27, 192, 269
O'Donnell, Reverend Henry (EO's father): background and marriage to Elizabeth, 4–5; mysterious death in Abyssinia, 5–8; Banshee warning, 9–10, 265; ghost of, 10–11, 116; will proved, 10
O'Donnell, Petronella (EO's sister): birth, 5; sees family Banshee, 9; writes account for SPR, 10n; orphaned, 18; chorus dancer, 27; writing career, 124–5; religion, 146; visits EO at Becondale Road, 159; death and burial, 248
O'Donnell Banshee, 9–10, 17, 140–1, 205, 225–8, 265
O'Donnell Clan, 180, 237
Ogden, Utah, 65
Old Bailey, 257–8
Oldbury House, St. Michael's Hill, Bristol, 257
Olsson, Julius, 137
Omaha, Nebraska, 62–3, 89
opium dens, 77
Oregon: Crater Lake, 70, 74; ranching, 66–8, 71; Red Indians, 69, 70, 73–4; Schuler killing, 71–2; Suicide Tree, 68
O'Rell, Max (Paul Blouët), 125
Owen, John, 12–13 & n
Oxendon Magna, Northamptonshire, 5
Oxford Hotel, Chicago, 60

parachuting, 115–16
Parker, Louis N.: *The Aristocrat*, 189
Parry, Mrs. Emma, 112
Parry, Henry, 112
Parry, Joseph, 112
Paul (village), Cornwall, 133–4
Payne, Melinda, 28–9
Peace, Charlie, 12
Pemberton, Max, 118
Penmaenmawr, 23

Perranzabuloe church, near Newquay, 244
Perrault, Charles, 187n
Perriam, Cliff, 261, 262
Perth, 52
phantasms of the living, 24–5, 139–40, 163–4, 252
Phantoms of the Night (1956), 166n, 262, 264–5
Phillips, Doug, 261, 262
Phillips, Stephen, 146n
Pitman & Sons (publishers), 153, 186
Pitman's School, Chancery Lane, 104
Plunket Greene, Harry, 173
Plymouth, 141–2, 151
Poe, Edgar Allan, 4, 234
Poland, Sir Harry, 208
Poole's Panorama, 13, 14–15
Porter, Henry, 208
pre-existence, 153–4
Price, Harry, 248
Price, Julius, 56
Prichard, Hesketh, 137
Prince's Theatre, Bristol, 14, 26
projection (psychic phenomenon), 33, 139–40, 164, 265–6
prostitution: in Dublin, 41; in Lambeth, 103, 105; white slave trade, 77, 241–2
Proudfoot, Mary Anne, 216

Queen's Service Academy, Dublin, 38, 47
Quiller Couch, A.T., 136–7

Race Street, Denver, 84–8
Radio City, New York, 236–7
Rambouillet forest, 182
Ramsey Mr. (fellow-lodger at York Road), 106
Ramsgate, 13
Red House, Guilsborough, 229, 230, 241
Red Hugh, 4
Red Indians, 69, 70, 73–4, 83
Red Lion Square, Holborn, 184–5
Redcliffe Square, London: vigil at, 167
Reynolds, Vivian, 189
Richards, Edward, 74, 98

Rider, William, 171; *see also* William Rider & Son
Ripley, Bill, 261, 262
Riverdale, Chicago, 59
Roberts, Morley, 148
robin redbreast, 172–3
Roche, David, 49
Roehampton: haunted house investigation, 148
Rogue River region, Oregon, 68–70, 71–4
Rogue River Indians, 73–4
Roker, Ern, 71
Roker, Gus, 71
Rorke's Drift, battle of, 13
Rose, Edwin, 55
Rossmore, Lord, 226–7
Rouillac (Denver journalist), 84, 87–8
Rouse, Helen, 189
Rowlandson, Major (suicide victim), 196n
Rowlandson, Robert and Maud, 52–4
Royal Irish Constabulary (R.I.C.), 38, 47
Rugby school, 250
Rushworth, Colonel, 53–4
Rushworth, Mrs., 53–4
Russell, Eric: on EO's literary style, 186–7
Russell Square, London, 180
Russia (Cunard liner), 5
Ryan, Kate, 14

Sacramento, California, 81–2
St. Bartholomew's church, Smithfield, 251
St. Ives: artistic cliques, 137, 139; cricket club, 138; EO opens boarding school, 131; ghosts and spirits, 131–4, 139–41, 142; inhospitality of townsfolk, 138–9
St. James' Theatre, London, 189
St. Louis haunting, 89–92
St. Michael's Hill, Bristol: haunted house, 260–2
St. Nicholas church, Bathampton, 114n
St. Peter's church, Windmill Street, 251

Samuel, Rachel, 217
San Francisco, 65–6; ghosts and hauntings, 75–6, 77–81; opium dens, 76–7
Sandhurst: Royal Military College, 35
Savage, Richard, 196
Savage Club, Adelphi Terrace, 196, 248
Schuler family (of Rogue River forest), 71–2
Scotsman, 170–1, 201
Scottish Ghost Stories (1912), 153
Screaming Skulls and Other Ghost Stories, The (ed. Ludlam), 266
Second World War, 245–7
Seppings, Thomas, 156
Shanahan, Miss, 200–1
Shaw, (George) Bernard, 230–1
Sherborne Villas, Clifton, 5, 9–11, 17–18, 45, 247
Shiners, The (black magic group), 259
Shirley House School, Blackheath, 112, 177
Sidmouth Hall temperance meeting, Brixton, 128–9
Sierra Nevadas: haunted gully, 82–4
Simpkins, Pete, 85, 87
Sinbad the Sailor (pantomime), 14, 26
slander of title, 45, 146
Smith, Mrs. (Northamptonshire cottager), 23–4
Smith, C. Aubrey, 138n, 148, 191
Smith, Myra, 200–1
Society for Psychical Research (SPR), 7, 10n, 118–19, 148, 197, 258–9, 264
Some Haunted Houses of England and Wales (1908), 143, 270–2
Sorcery Club, The (1912), 171
Southgate Street, Bristol: haunted house, 270–2
spirit photography, 197, 199
spirit-writing, 205–6
Spookerisms (1936), 238
SPR *see* Society for Psychical Research
spy mania, 189–90
Squando (Norwegian barque), 80–1
Stanger, Urban Napoleon, 238

Index

Stanley, H.M., 116–17
Stead, W.T., 117–18, 119, 134
Stephens, James, 181
Stewart, Reverend John, 154–6
Storrs, S. (principal at Shirley House School), 112
Strange Cults and Secret Societies of Modern London (1934), 238
Strange Disappearances (1927), 238
Strange Sea Mysteries (1926), 229n, 238
strangling ghost, 42–4, 46–7, 48–9
Stride, Elizabeth, 209–10
Stroud, Reverend Richard, 6
Studio Club, London, 178
Suicide Tree (Oregon), 68
Sunday Dispatch, 260–2
sunstroke, as euphemism for madness, 8
Sweeney, Mr. (drug store owner), 75–6
Swinton, Dr., 52
Syderstone Parsonage, near Fakenham: haunting at, 154–7

Tait, Mr. (Clifton College master), 82
Talmage, Algernon, 137
Taylor, William Desmond (William Cunningham Deane-Tanner): murder of, 20
Tempest, Marie, 171
Terry, Charles, 121
Thames, river: Embankment, 106–8
Thatcher, Heather, 178
The Meaning of Dreams (1911), 153
Theatre Royal, Drury Lane, 108; Man in Grey ghost, 259–60
theatrical profession: interest in psychism, 188, 245
Theatricals (journal), 108
Thomas, Herbert, 137
Thomas, Mrs. Julia, 12, 207–8
Thorne, Guy (Ranger Gull), 134
Titanic (liner), 231
Toledo, Ohio, 234
Townsend, Frank, 17, 56
transformation scenes, 153–4
tree ghosts and hauntings, 23, 68, 73–4, 263–4; *see also* vegetable phantasms

Trees of Ghostly Dread (1958), 263–4
Trial of Kate Webster (1925), 208
Troy, New York State, 233
Turner, Mr. (assistant master at Henley House School), 111
Turner, Charles and Eva, 91–2
Turner, Maisie, 91, 92
Twenty Years' Experiences as a Ghost Hunter (1916): published, 186; critical reception, 186–7; quoted, 187–9, 205–6; author's forename misspelt, 228
Twickenham, 207
Twining, Reverend Samuel, 177
Tyrone Street, Dublin, 41

Underwood, Peter, 270; *The Ghost Hunters*, 4n, 139–40
United Arts Rifles, 191, 192
United States of America, EO visits, 56–100, 232–8
Unknown Depths, The (1908), 124, 135
Upper Leeson Street haunting, Dublin, 42–3
Upton Snodsbury, near Worcester, 5

Vagrarians *see* Elementals
Valencourt, Benjamin Joshua, 127–9
Vandergooch, Ephraim B., 89–92
Vanity Fair (magazine), 153
vegetable phantasms, 153–4; *see also* tree ghosts and hauntings
Vereker, 'Cosie', 27
Victoria Rooms, Clifton, 12
Villiers, Frederick, 115
Vine Cottages, Richmond, 208
Vivian, Charlie, 26
Voice of the Commonwealth, The (journal), 136

Wainwright, Henry, 12, 13n
Wanderers Football Club, Dublin, 41
Wandering Jew, 65–6
war ghosts, 188–9
Ward, Edward Matthew, 153
Ward, Genevieve, 189

Index

Ward, Mrs. Henrietta, 153
Ward, Sir Leslie, 153
Warren, Mrs. (EO's aunt), 201
Washington, D.C., 235
water spirits, 263
Waterloo Bridge, 106
Waterloo Railway Station, 101
Waterloo Road, London, 127
Watts, PC, 217–18
Webb, Mrs. (St. Ives housekeeper), 132
Webster, Kate, 12, 207–8, 237
Weekly Dispatch, 135, 161–2, 166
Weekly Graphic, 153
Wehlen, Mrs. (of St. Louis), 91–2
Wellington Park, Clifton, 4
Wells, Bombardier Billy, 179
werewolves, 170–1
Werwolves (1912), 170–1
Wesley, John, 155–6
West Quay, New York, 98; haunting, 92–6
Weston (Sierra Nevadas guide), 82–4
Weston-super-Mare, 16, 33
Weymouth Swindling Gang, 7, 8
Whitaker, Frank, 248
white slave trade, 77, 241–2
Whitefriars Club, 173
Whiteladies Road, Bristol, 12
Whittington-Egan, Richard, 12n; speaks with EO, 243–4

Wicklow, County, 45–7
William Rider & Son (publishers), 153, 171, 201, 249, 260, 262
Williams, Ada *see* O'Donnell, Ada
Williams, Catherine, 125
Williams, Clara, 125
Williams, Henry, 125
Williams, Henry W. (EO's father-in-law), 109, 125 & n, 192
Windsor Inn, Ogden, 65
Wishart, George, 31
Wodehouse, P.G., 137–8
Wolverhampton Grammar School, 111
Women Bluebeards (1931), 238
Worcester, 123; haunted house, 13
World War I, 183, 184, 188–90
World War II, 245–7
Wyndham, Lewis, 198–9

Yarmouth, 123, 216
Yavorska, Lydia, 145n
Yeats, W.B., 231
York Road, Lambeth: café and lodgings, 102–3, 104–6, 209

Zoological Gardens, Dublin, 15, 27
Zulu War (1879), 13

www.ingramcontent.com/pod-product-compliance
Lightning Source LLC
Chambersburg PA
CBHW051035160426
43193CB00010B/949